Other Books in the
Reading the Bible Missiologically Series

Reading Hebrews Missiologically (2023)
Abeneazer G. Urga, Edward L. Smither, and Linda P. Saunders, Editors

Reading 1 Peter Missiologically (2024)
Abeneazer G. Urga, Jessica A. Udall, and Edward L. Smither, Editors

Reading Revelation Missiologically (forthcoming)
Abeneazer G. Urga, Edward L. Smither, and Michael P. Naylor, Editors

In *Reading James Missiologically,* a bricolage of essays uncovers the depth of missional theology in this short epistle. From the first part with its tightly argued exegetical work that utilizes both testaments coupled with historical precedencies in mission, through to the second part, that bypasses the binary approaches of social action and evangelistic proclamation to the final part with mission in various contexts, the collection of essays deepens and expands the character of true mission. This book charts the way to engaging mission and evangelism in our day that is at once biblical, credal, and global—from the whole church to the whole world following the spirit who calls the church from the future. *Reading James Missiologically* is biblically based and contains a socially conscious theology of missions *par excellence.*

Rev. Esther E. Acolatse, PhD
Professor of Pastoral Theology and World Christianity, and
Director of the DMin Program, Garrett-Evangelical Theological Seminary
Series Co-Editor, *African Christian Studies Series*

This groundbreaking volume places the epistle of James squarely at the center of missional theology. The contributors masterfully demonstrate how James's emphasis on holistic transformation speaks to our global context, while bringing fresh perspectives from Majority World voices. By bridging historical divides and integrating personal holiness with social justice, this work reflects the very heart of biblical mission. This is an essential reading for anyone seeking to understand how James's ancient wisdom can shape authentic mission in our time.

J. Ayodeji Adewuya, PhD
Professor of New Testament, Pentecostal Theological Seminary
Author, *An African Commentary on the Letter of James*

Reading James Missiologically is another volume in a series of books dedicated to giving missiological attention to the general epistles. I love Smither, Udall, and Urga's impulse to read Scripture closely, do careful biblical theological work, and to recognize the missional threads woven throughout while drawing out missiological applications in parts of Scripture not often mined for such gold. This volume looks at James in just such a way and it engages in some of the most important missiological questions of our day. Driven to the discussion of integral mission or proclamation priority by James's desire to hold faith and work together, various conclusions in this volume are unavoidably controversial. Thus, readers will doubtless walk away with different points of tension depending upon their position on the overall missiological discussion. However, the conversation is important, and the contribution of James cannot be ignored. This is a helpful compilation of essays that will no doubt provide reference material for missiological reflection in the future.

Matthew A. Bennett, PhD
Associate Professor of Missions and Theology, Cedarville University
Author, *Narratives in Conflict: Atonement in Hebrews and the Qur'an*

Do you think the often-neglected letter of James has little relevance for Christian mission today? Think again. A wide-ranging, international cast of stellar biblical scholars and missiologists demonstrates repeatedly how important James is for a holistic mission that in no way relegates either personal conversion or social action to a subordinate role. Studies focused on short passages combine with those that sweep through the whole letter to show how impoverished on this topic we would be without James in the canon. A must read!

Craig L. Blomberg, PhD
Distinguished Professor Emeritus of New Testament, Denver Seminary

Reading James Missiologically is a gift to the global church. Based on rigorous research and thoughtful engagement with ministry, these essays explore the intersection of James's letter with the missions movement. They discuss the message of James and how it informs the foundation, methods, and approaches to the expansion of the church. The editors have assembled an impressive team that features skilled scholars and ministry practitioners. The chapters are well-organized and display a thoughtful progression. The editors and authors are to be commended for their worthy contribution to the study of the epistle of James as well as the field of missiology.

Daniel K. Eng, PhD
Assistant Professor of New Testament Language & Literature, Western Seminary
Author, *Eschatological Approval*

This insightful collection of essays from a diverse group of missiologists more than delivers the promise in its title. It also moves us towards an understanding of James from various perspectives in global Christianity. That makes it doubly important for those of us who know that the future of our faith is for and from all peoples, not rooted permanently in the Western mindset.

Todd M. Johnson, PhD
Eva B. & Paul E. Toms Distinguished Professor of Mission and Global Christianity, Gordon-Conwell Theological Seminary

Reading James Missiologically

The Missionary Motive, Message, and Methods of James

Abeneazer G. Urga,
Jessica A. Udall,
Edward L. Smither

editors

visit us at missionbooks.org

Contents

Part 3: The Missionary Methods of James

Preface

While books on a New Testament theology of mission abound, most of them focus only on certain tried-and-true books and passages from the Gospels, Acts, and Pauline Epistles while often ignoring the contribution of the General Epistles. In *Reading Hebrews Missiologically* (2023) and *Reading 1 Peter Missiologically* (2024), we began to address this gap in missiological scholarship, and we seek to continue this approach in this study on the book of James.[1] As the previous volumes in this series have been structured, *Reading James Missiologically* consists of three parts: the missionary motive of James, the missionary message of James, and the missionary methods of James. The missionary motive is the reasons behind missionary efforts (the why), the missionary message refers to the content of what missionaries communicate (the what), and missionary methods are prescribed or described strategies for mission (the how).

Instead of putting forth a single definition of "mission" at the outset of the book, we have allowed each contributor to flesh out this complex concept in their own way as relates to their topic. Thus, we believe this book as a whole makes the idea of mission shine, highlighting its multifaceted aspects in unique and edifying ways. The contributors to this volume hail from a variety of cultures and backgrounds, all approaching the book of James from their unique vantage points with a common purpose: to explore the concept of mission through James's eyes.

Part 1—the missionary motive of James—begins with Allen Yeh's overview of the misreadings of James with the goal of proving "what is right by first proving what is wrong." In chapter 2, James A. Roh discusses the new birth as the vision of mission in James, with the "implanted word" as the beginning of a new missional relationship with the world based on the believer's new creation status. In chapter 3, Christopher Howles explores C. René Padilla's integral mission as it relates to James's missiology, particularly the relationship between proclamation and social action. In chapter 4, Benjamin A. Castenada argues that James understands missiological ideas in eschatological terms suggesting the promised restoration of Israel, and chapter 5 is Jeffrey S. Krohn's exploration of the relationship between

---

1 We want to acknowledge the excellent recent work of Graham Paul Dancy, "A Missional Reading of the Letter of James: Hearing the Voice of James in Mission" (PhD diss., University of Gloucestershire, 2021), as an exception to the "rule" of leaving out the General Epistles in missiological literature. Dancy's work was consulted by several of our contributors, and he makes a helpful contribution to fill the gap in missiological scholarship on the book of James. We want our multiauthor book to amplify his one voice by adding a chorus of varied perspectives to his own work in this area.

eschatology and mission in James with particular attention given to Majority World perspectives on the subject. In chapter 6, Nelson R. Morales Fredes demonstrates the important place of the poor in the mission of God and the necessity of their inclusion in the church's missional task. In chapter 7, Jessica Janvier digs into James's use of the story of Rahab and its corrective implications for mission.

Edward L. Smither begins part 2—the missionary message of James— by exploring James's view of ministry to the whole person and how some church fathers followed his example of holistic mission, considering some implications for the contemporary church. In chapter 9, Vuyani Stanley Sindo considers how James can help the church in South Africa to live missionally in a society characterized by extreme inequality. James E. Morrison seeks to unpack the phrase "doers of the word" with particular application to Bible translation in chapter 10, and Leita Ngoy explores the connection and integration of mission and prosperity in James and the modern day in chapter 11.

Part 3—the missionary methods of James—begins with John D. Harvey's exploration of mercy as mission in the ministry of Jesus and in the book of James, and in chapter 13, Joseph K. Pak examines James's unique messages to the rich and poor as they are invited to participate in the mission of God in the world. In chapter 14, Sarah Lunsford discusses how James advises those who want to move away from self-sufficient managerial mission and toward dependence on God alone. Thomas W. Seckler examines James 3:1–2 and its strong implications for those who are teaching and engaged in mission efforts today in chapter 15, and chapter 16 is Cindy M. Wu's examination of the parallels between the context in which James was written and the modern-day refugee crisis, demonstrating the relevance of James's teaching on the poor and vulnerable for those engaged in meaningful relationships with refugees. In chapter 16, Jeanne Wu explores a theology of perseverance through suffering as mission, and in chapter 17, Grant LeMarquand concludes the book by exploring the relationship between prayer and mission in James.

We hope that the contents of this book will encourage readers with the missiological purposes of God in James and inspire believers toward missional engagement with the world as "doers of the word, and not hearers only" (Jas 1:22 ESV).

Abeneazer G. Urga, Addis Ababa, Ethiopia\
Jessica A. Udall, Addis Ababa, Ethiopia\
Edward L. Smither, Columbia, South Carolina\
August 2024

Part 1

The Missionary Motive of James

Chapter 1

Holistic Mission

The Vision of Mission in James

Allen Yeh

Martin Luther infamously wanted to reject James from the Bible because he thought it reeked too much of works righteousness. Thus, James has been a point of contention between Protestants and Catholics for centuries, hearkening all the way back to the Reformation. This chapter will argue that—while Luther himself eventually came around and did not interpret James wrongly in the end—Protestants today still "swing the pendulum too far in the opposite direction" and misunderstand Luther's *sola fide* as cheap grace. James's holistic mission (as seen in 1:27) and his use of Abraham (not as oppositional but as the interpretive key) vitiates the notion that James somehow contradicts Paul. Original (eighteenth- and nineteenth-century) evangelicals like John Wesley and William Wilberforce, all the way up to modern (late twentieth- and early twenty-first-century) evangelicals like C. René Padilla, Samuel Escobar, and John Stott with the *Lausanne Covenant*, exhibit this holistic mission (also known as integral mission or *misión integral*). True Christianity always has at least two dimensions: social justice and personal morality, or love of neighbor and love of God. Unfortunately, the "Great Reversal" of early and mid-twentieth-century evangelicalism bifurcated the gospel. But James—with exegetical commentary from Catholic and Protestant theologians like Gustavo Gutiérrez and Elsa Támez—helps Christianity recover a holistic mission today. This chapter will also draw support from the book of Acts, namely the Jerusalem Council (chapter 15), which James himself adjudicated, as well as the holistic mission of the apostles and deacons (chapter 6).

James holds a unique place in the biblical canon for several reasons. First, it was written by the half-brother of our Lord Jesus. Given that Jesus never penned any still-extant document, the fact that one book of the Bible comes from a close genetic relative gives this book special consideration. Just to be clear, the special consideration has nothing to do with royal genealogies, apostolic succession, or anything along those lines. It simply is a matter of historical interest and makes James worthy of a second look because he cannot be discounted as a peripheral figure in the history of Christianity. Second, why would James even require a second look? In large part, this is due to the views of the father of the Protestant Reformation himself, Martin Luther. Luther, in his understandable zeal to advocate for the four *solas* (especially *sola fide* and *sola gratia*), nearly discarded James from the Bible. Of course, this would have gone against one of his other *solas*—*sola scriptura*—so thankfully Luther did not take it to that extreme. Third, because of Luther and others, James is often pitted unfairly against Paul, as if the two men's theologies are somehow contradictory (they are sometimes characterized unfairly as works vs. faith) instead of both inspired by the Holy Spirit. Fourth, given the sheer volume of Pauline biblical production, James stands seemingly alone in terms of authority. Not that quantity is equivalent to attestation, but there is a kind of *hapax legomenon* effect at work here. It is often easier to establish the meaning of a particular type of theology if one can "triangulate" (draw from three or more sources) rather than simply work from one "proof text." James seems to suffer from the lack of his own writings.

This chapter aims to undo many of these misreadings of James and in the process begins by "backing into" the truth. It will prove what is right by first proving what is wrong. This is actually how most cases of theology in history came about: A response to heresy helps to codify orthodoxy, as seen from the examples of the first four ecumenical councils (Nicaea, Constantinople, Ephesus, and Chalcedon) and their responses to heretics (Arius, Apollinaris, Nestorius, Macedonius, Pelagius, etc.), which gave rise to such doctrines as the Trinity, original sin, and the two natures of Christ. The second part of this chapter will explore how theology inevitably also comes from crossing cultures, hence "missions is the mother of theology."[1] So the function of this chapter is to use the twin engines of heterodoxy and missions to lead to proper theology. This is borne out by church history as well as Paul's missionary journeys.

James as the Brother of Jesus

Despite the fact that James was the son of Joseph and Mary, his sibling link to Jesus did not initially benefit him. According to Mark 6:3–6:

> Isn't this the carpenter? Isn't this Mary's son and the brother of James, Joseph, Judas and Simon? Aren't his sisters here with us?" And they took offense at him. Jesus said to them, "A prophet is not without honor except in his own town, among his relatives and in his own home." He could not do any miracles there, except lay his hands on a few sick people and heal them. He was amazed at their lack of faith.[2]

---

1 Kähler, *Schriften zur Christologie und Mission*, 190.
2 All Scripture quotations are from the NIV.

The suggestion here is that James was likely the eldest of the children of Joseph and Mary, given his order in the family list. Also, his proximity to Jesus—having grown up together—ironically lent to his disbelief because presumably he and his siblings saw Jesus as too "human." Thankfully this did not prove to be a lasting phenomenon. This trajectory is similar to that of Nicodemus, who initially could not accept Jesus's call to be "born again" (John 3:3–4) and thus could not comprehend the magnitude of the most famous verse in the entire Bible just a few paragraphs later (3:16), but he eventually became a faithful disciple and even helped Joseph of Arimathea procure a grave for the body of Jesus (19:38–42). James—despite his inauspicious beginnings—later became the bishop of the believers in Jerusalem and lent his leadership to the burgeoning early church.[3] His apparent conversion is recounted by Paul in 1 Corinthians 15:3–8:

> For what I received I passed on to you as of first importance: that Christ died for our sins according to the Scriptures, that he was buried, that he was raised on the third day according to the Scriptures, and that he appeared to Cephas, and then to the Twelve. After that, he appeared to more than five hundred of the brothers and sisters at the same time, most of whom are still living, though some have fallen asleep. Then he appeared to James, then to all the apostles, and last of all he appeared to me also, as to one abnormally born.

Though not the most important of the disciples, James the brother of Jesus did get his own mention. He is clearly to be distinguished from James the Greater (son of Zebedee, who was the earliest of the apostles to be martyred in Acts 12:2) and James the Less (son of Alphaeus), as both of them are included in the Twelve (1 Cor 15:5). James the brother of Jesus was granted an audience with the risen Lord in verse 7 and apparently followed him from that point forward.

Martin Luther

Martin Luther, the "father of the Protestant Reformation," was not able to judge James (a very Jewish book) on its own merit but saw it through the lens of Paul (interpreted as a champion of Hellenistic philosophy, the "pinnacle" of intellectual theology). He dismissed James as "an epistle of straw" because it had "nothing of the nature of the gospel about it." He wrote, "Away with James... . I almost feel like throwing Jimmy into the

---

3 Eusebius, *History of the Church*, 234.

stove… . It is flatly against St. Paul and all the rest of Scripture in ascribing justification to works."[4] Renowned Reformation scholar Timothy George expressed the perspective that Luther "found … a canon within the canon by which the whole text of Holy Writ was to be evaluated."[5] Luther thankfully did not throw James into the fire but instead placed it near the end of his Bible close to the apocryphal books, which he completely rejected. In other words, James was—to Luther—a lower status of canon.[6]

New Testament theologian N. T. Wright, drawing on the work of E. P. Sanders, offers a few helpful correctives to Luther. Even if one does not want to offer a full-throated defense of the New Perspective on Paul, it is important to understand that Wright has some solid rebuttals against the traditional Protestant view. First, Wright views Paul as more Hebrew than Greek, in contradistinction to Luther. This helps to align Paul and James much more closely to each other rather than in opposition.[7] It also smooths the continuity between Old and New Testaments.[8] Second, Wright challenges Luther's work as being based on eisegesis (the opposite of exegesis), where someone reads into a text the meaning they want to assign it instead of drawing out the original authorial intent from the text. Luther's theological battles against the Roman Catholic Church were so momentous that it is understandable why that would inform his every interpretation, but it is also unfair to simply "map" sixteenth-century theological battles onto the first century. Luther's contention that the sixteenth-century Protestants and Catholics represented the first-century Pharisees and Christians, respectively, is dubious. It is an overly simplistic read of the first-century context to say that history was simply repeating itself.[9]

Wright says of Luther, Calvin, and the Reformers: "The greatest honor we can pay the Reformers is not to treat them as infallible—they would be horrified at that—but to do as they did."[10] In other words, ostensibly the Reformers would want us to derive theology from Scripture and not from would-be "saints" in the history of the church, even themselves.

---

4   George, *Theology of the Reformers*, 84.

5   George, 84.

6   George, 84.

7   Wright, *What Saint Paul Really Said*, 12–13.

8   This is similar to my argument in the companion volume to this book that Hebrews is most authentically viewed through an Old Testament/Jewish lens. See Yeh, "Christ Outside the Gate," 37–52.

9   Wright, *Justification*, 112.

10 Wright, 22–23.

James vs. Paul

The apparent difficulty with reconciling James with Paul is actually the advantage. When comparing texts such as Romans 4:1–5 with James 2:14–26, one cannot simply argue away the apparent "contradictions" between the two passages as simply referring to different things, especially since they both specifically cite Abraham and thus prove how much both authors' Jewishness causes them to delve deep into the Old Testament.

Compare Romans 4:1–3:

What then shall we say that Abraham, our forefather according to the flesh, discovered in this matter? If, in fact, Abraham was justified by works, he had something to boast about—but not before God. What does Scripture say? "Abraham believed God, and it was credited to him as righteousness."

with James 2:20–24:

You foolish person, do you want evidence that faith without deeds is useless? Was not our father Abraham considered righteous for what he did when he offered his son Isaac on the altar? You see that his faith and his actions were working together, and his faith was made complete by what he did. And the scripture was fulfilled that says, "Abraham believed God, and it was credited to him as righteousness," and he was called God's friend. You see that a person is considered righteous by what they do and not by faith alone.

Although these two passages, when compared side-by-side, seem to directly conflict with each other, it turns out that Abraham is the interpretive key and not the problem.

The Romans 4 passage refers to earlier Abraham's faith journey. The Abrahamic covenant, as initiated in Genesis 12, explores how Abraham—by faith—followed God from Ur of the Chaldeans to the promised land and thus was the recipient of the Lord's promise to be the father of many nations with the concomitant responsibility to be a blessing to them. This is one of the first explicit calls to mission in the Bible, and the foundation of the Jewish impetus to be "a light to the Gentiles" (Isa 42:6; 49:6; cf. Luke 2:29–32). Scholars estimate Abraham was around seventy-five years old at this time.

The James 2 passage refers to an older Abraham as seen from the explicit reference to the "sacrifice" of Isaac (Gen 22). Given that Isaac was born when Abraham was one hundred years old, and according to Josephus,

Isaac was twenty-five years old when God called Abraham to sacrifice him, that would have put Abraham at 125 years old—fifty years after the events of Romans 4. This passage is also missional in that it is grounded in an injunction to help the poor (Jas 2:1–17), which will be expounded upon later in this chapter.

In other words, justification is by faith at the beginning of one's walk with God (not by works righteousness), but it is by works later in life. If the word "works" causes some Protestants to recoil, perhaps the word "fruit" may be more helpful. Salvation does not just involve justification (past—"you have been saved") but also sanctification (present—"you are being saved") and glorification (future—"you will be saved"). Paul is talking about justification, and James is referring to sanctification and glorification. The two authors are not contradicting each other but rather complementing each other.

This is further proved by Paul's explicit statement that works (or fruit) is needed after faith in Ephesians 2:8–10:

> For it is by grace you have been saved, through faith—and this is not from yourselves, it is the gift of God—not by works, so that no one can boast. For we are God's handiwork, created in Christ Jesus to do good works, which God prepared in advance for us to do.

James likewise is confident that it is not our own efforts—but rather God's—that initiates our faith journey:

> Every good and perfect gift is from above, coming down from the Father of the heavenly lights, who does not change like shifting shadows. He chose to give us birth through the word of truth, that we might be a kind of firstfruits of all he created. (1:17–18)

Paul is combating works righteousness as the key to salvation, and James is combating nominalism. One cannot save oneself, but also resting on one's laurels without attendance to obedience leads to no guarantee of salvation (Matt 7:21; 21:19).

The Venerable Bede, the "father of English history," helpfully reconciles the two authors:

> Although the apostle Paul preached that we are justified by faith without works, those who understand by this that it does not matter whether they live evil lives or do wicked and terrible things, as long as they believe in Christ, because salvation is through faith, have made a great mistake. James here expounds how Paul's words ought to be understood. This

is why he uses the example of Abraham, whom Paul also used as an example of faith, to show that the patriarch also performed good works in the light of his faith. It is therefore wrong to interpret Paul in such a way as to suggest that it did not matter whether Abraham put his faith into practice or not. What Paul meant was that no one obtains the gift of justification on the basis of merits derived from works performed beforehand, because the gift of justification comes only from faith.[11]

C. S. Lewis similarly supports the reconciliation between Paul and James:

[To have faith in Christ] means, of course, trying to do all that He says. There would be no sense in saying you trusted a person if you would not take his advice. Thus if you have really handed yourself over to Him, it must follow that you are trying to obey Him. But trying in a new way, a less worried way. Not doing these things in order to be saved, but because He has begun to save you already. Not hoping to get to Heaven as a reward for your actions, but inevitably wanting to act in a certain way because a first faint gleam of Heaven is already inside you.[12]

James's "Lack" of Attestation

James has a significant presence in the Bible beyond his singular epistle. Given that he was the adjudicator of the Jerusalem Council in Acts 15, he plays a prominent role in setting precedent for future development of theology. In fact, at the Jerusalem Council—which can be seen as the first ecumenical council in history, preceding even Nicaea, Constantinople, Ephesus, and Chalcedon— he directly interacts with Paul. This proves to be one of the most important moments in church history and helps reconcile the two authors.

The Jerusalem Council bridges Paul's first and second missionary journeys. This gives credence to the idea that "missions is the mother of theology." Paul crossed many cultural boundaries in his first missionary journey, raising many questions about how to integrate gentiles into the faith. This led to a theological crisis where the Judaizers confused their culture with their theology, in that they wanted to require gentiles to be circumcised. Confusing culture with theology has been a problem with missionaries throughout history, which is why it is necessary to establish new theologies to deal with new intercultural issues.

Although Paul is known for the penning of many epistles (in quantity he wrote nearly half of the books of the New Testament—thirteen out of

---

11 Bray, *James, 1–2 Peter*, 31.

12 Lewis, *Mere Christianity*, 130–31.

twenty-seven), in this particular instance it is actually James who—along with the apostles and elders—wrote another epistle. This was actually the earliest epistle in the entire Bible, and it may be dubbed the "epistle to the Antiochenes" in Acts 15:23–29:

With them they sent the following letter:

The apostles and elders, your brothers,

To the Gentile believers in Antioch, Syria and Cilicia:

Greetings.

We have heard that some went out from us without our authorization and disturbed you, troubling your minds by what they said. So we all agreed to choose some men and send them to you with our dear friends Barnabas and Paul—men who have risked their lives for the name of our Lord Jesus Christ. Therefore we are sending Judas and Silas to confirm by word of mouth what we are writing. It seemed good to the Holy Spirit and to us not to burden you with anything beyond the following requirements: You are to abstain from food sacrificed to idols, from blood, from the meat of strangled animals and from sexual immorality. You will do well to avoid these things.

Farewell.

James sided with Peter and Paul in the ultimate decision, not requiring gentiles to be circumcised to enter the faith, which is what the Judaizers had wanted. While not lengthy, this epistle establishes a few salient points moving forward with missional theology: (1) There is a distinction to be made between culture and theology. (2) There is a distinction to be made between nonessential and essential points of theology. (3) Ecumenical councils are required to establish new theologies (and to define heresies), as a majority consensus is needed in a "priesthood of all believers." This is why "missions is the mother of theology" but indeed also "heresy is the mother of theology." The former implies that crossing cultural boundaries requires Christians to articulate new theologies to address new contexts, and the latter implies that heterodox beliefs—when articulated or exhibited— require an equal and opposite reaction of codification of orthodox beliefs.

Mission in James

Now that we have established what mission *is not* in James (it is not equating Christianity with Greek culture, nor it is not just getting people to accept faith bereft of fruit), let us explore what mission *is* and how he envisions it. The three parts to this will include (1) James 1:27 as *the* banner verse of holistic mission in the New Testament; (2) holistic mission in the twentieth century, as supported by early British evangelicals, more contemporary Latin American *evangélicos*, and the *Lausanne Covenant*; and (3) an expansion of holistic mission as it applies to the twenty-first century.

James's Holistic Mission

James's main thesis in his first two chapters is that mission is holistic. It is not simply verbal confession and heartfelt belief; it is also followed by physical action and ministry. Unlike Paul who emphasizes the former (faith), James emphasizes the latter (fruit), although both men can rightly be said to affirm both sides. This holistic balance of James is captured most eloquently in 1:27: "Religion that God our Father accepts as pure and faultless is this: to look after orphans and widows in their distress and to keep oneself from being polluted by the world." This acts like a banner verse—if not *the* banner verse—for holistic mission in the New Testament.[13]

James 1:27 is reminiscent of what Jesus said to the Pharisees in Matthew 23:23, "Woe to you, teachers of the law and Pharisees, you hypocrites! You give a tenth of your spices—mint, dill and cumin. But you have neglected the more important matters of the law—justice, mercy and faithfulness. You should have practiced the latter, without neglecting the former." Just two chapters later, Jesus also gave a lesson (often mistaken for a parable) about the sheep and goats with the perhaps surprising statement that "whatever you did for one of the least of these brothers and sisters of mine, you did for me" (25:40). In other words, there is a profound link between loving one's neighbor and loving God, even to the point where Jesus practically equates them. Indeed, Jesus's holistic ministry cause is taken up by his brother James.

However, James not only strives for balance, but he also gives an order of operations. In the following chapter, he makes strikingly clear:

---

13 In the Old Testament, something like Micah 6:8—"And what does the LORD require of you? To act justly and to love mercy and to walk humbly with your God"—might serve similarly; or Psalm 24:3–4, "Who may ascend the mountain of the LORD? Who may stand in his holy place? The one who has clean hands and a pure heart." See Blomberg and Kamell, *James*, 94.

> Suppose a brother or a sister is without clothes and daily food. If one of you says to them, "Go in peace; keep warm and well fed," but does nothing about their physical needs, what good is it? In the same way, faith by itself, if it is not accompanied by action, is dead. (Jas 2:15–17)

This is an important point as social justice must precede evangelism. This is not an order of primacy but an order of operations; it's not an "order of estimation" but an "order of execution." Seventeenth-century Puritan pastor Richard Baxter wrote in a 1682 treatise that in the Lord's Prayer, "We pray for our daily bread before pardon and spiritual blessings, not as if it were better, but that nature is supposed before grace, and we cannot be Christians if we are not men."[14] This reflects the idea later expounded by Abraham Maslow in his famous hierarchy that physiological needs must come before other needs, such as safety, relationships, self-esteem, and self-actualization. Baxter continues:

> God has so placed the soul in the body that good or evil shall make its entrance by the bodily senses to the soul. God himself conveys many of his blessings this way, and this way he inflicts his corrections. … Do as much good as you are able to men's bodies in order to the greater good of souls. If nature be not supported, men are not capable of other good.[15]

James surely would have been familiar with the Acts 6 separation of duties between the twelve apostles and the seven deacons. The apostles realized that, as the church multiplied, they could not keep up with all the ministerial duties, so they chose to devote themselves to prayer and the ministry of the word like preaching and evangelism, while they chose deacons (from among the seventy-two disciples) who would devote themselves to physical social justice ministries, such as collecting the money and feeding the poor. There should not be any implication that the deacons were not somehow inferior to the apostles, as the first Christian to be martyred was Stephen the deacon in Acts 7 (even before James the Greater in Acts 12), whose death led to the eventual conversion of the apostle Paul. The first missionary to have a more global impact was Philip the deacon in Acts 8, who witnessed to the Ethiopian eunuch, which led to Christianity entering Africa for the first time, whereas the apostles were called to remain ministering to the Jews (Gal 2:9).

---

14 Baxter, *How to Do Good*, 303.

15 Baxter, 303.

Holistic Mission in the Twentieth Century

In the early twentieth century, the Fundamentalist-Modernist Controversy in the United States led to a bifurcation of Christianity. With the advent of new teachings from Europe such as Darwinian evolution and German higher biblical criticism, American Christians were forced to reckon with these new ideas. (In many ways, this is not unlike what we are seeing now with Christians trying to decide what they think about ideas such as critical race theory or the New Perspective on Paul.) Some—called fundamentalists—chose to wholesale reject these ideas. Others—called modernists—embraced them. However, this dichotomization led to American Christians having to decide between evangelism versus social justice, faith versus science, biblical literalism (a hermeneutic resulting from a premillennial dispensationalism) versus creation care, etc. This loss, especially of social justice by the fundamentalists, was known as the "Great Reversal."[16] It reversed what early (eighteenth- and nineteenth-century) evangelicals did regarding championing social justice. For example, Charles Finney invented the concept of the "altar call" to recruit people for the abolitionist movement. William Wilberforce, the British MP who led the fight in Parliament to abolish the slave trade in England, had as his mantra "God Almighty has set before me two great objects, the suppression of the slave trade and the reformation of manners [morals]." This was practically a modern-day restatement of James 1:27.

By the mid-twentieth century, some fundamentalist Christians grew frustrated with the divisions and opted for a more moderate, civil, middle ground. These "neo-evangelicals" (or simply "evangelicals") tried to integrate their faith with science and reunite evangelism with social justice. Chief among them were the American evangelist Billy Graham and the British pastor John Stott. They started the Lausanne Movement in 1974 and crafted the *Lausanne Covenant* with Stott as its chief architect.[17] This *magna carta* document on evangelical beliefs reforged evangelism and social justice under the idea of holistic mission.[18]

However, the history of the *Lausanne Covenant* is not as well known. Stott did not come up with his ideas ex nihilo. Latin American *evangélicos*, embodied in the form of the *Fraternidad Teológica Latinoamericana* (FTL, or Latin American Theological Fraternity, now Fellowship), never went

---

16 Moberg, *Great Reversal*, 28.

17 Billy Graham and John Stott somewhat disagreed, in that Graham still prioritized evangelism over social justice, but he deferred to Stott in the writing of *The Lausanne Covenant*.

18 Lausanne Movement, *Lausanne Covenant*, esp. paragraph 5.

through a fundamentalist-modernist split (nor did Latin America ever go through a Protestant Reformation, as the Iberians colonized the New World in 1492—twenty-five years before Luther ever nailed his *Ninety-Five Theses* on the church door at Wittenberg). The lack of these two divisive North Atlantic movements actually served Latin American Christians well, in the sense that they never had to decide between either/or or both/and. They have always practiced holistic mission as a matter of course.

So, while the British and the Americans were debating these issues, the Latino *evangélicos* saw things differently. For example, Orlando Costas from Puerto Rico wrote:

> The church of Jesus Christ has been inflicted in our day by a diabolic polarization in its missional program. Christians, missionary organizations and movements, church and ecumenical bodies, have been spending endless energies arguing among themselves about whether their missional programs should include teaching and preaching the gospel or engaging in the sociopolitical liberation of the weak and oppressed, or both; whether the gospel should be in word or in deed only, or in word *and* deed. This is as useless a debate as it is a senseless and satanic waste of time, energies and resources. The true test of mission is not whether we proclaim, make disciples or engage in social, economic and political liberation, but whether we are capable of integrating all three in a comprehensive, dynamic *and consistent* witness. We need to pray that the Lord will liberate us not only *from* this stagnant situation, but that he may liberate us *for* wholeness and integrity in mission.[19]

Stott's ear was bent toward the Latin American *evangélicos* like René Padilla from Ecuador and Samuel Escobar from Peru, and their input helped to shape the *Lausanne Covenant* into its final form.[20] Padilla, in particular, has become known as the champion of *misión integral*.[21] The FTL also helped to expand this movement internationally into INFEMIT (initially the International Fellowship of Mission Theologians from the Two Thirds World, now the International Fellowship of Mission as Transformation) in 1980, where Asians, Africans, and others joined in the global movement toward holistic mission.

---

19 Costas, *Integrity of Mission*, 75, emphasis original.
20 Padilla, *Mission between the Times*, 6.
21 Padilla, *Misión Integral*.

Catholic Latin American theologians concurred on the nature of *misión integral*. Gustavo Gutiérrez of Peru, the father of Latin American liberation theology, wrote:

> Was not Christ's first preaching to "proclaim the liberation of the oppressed?" The content of the message itself, the process of liberation in Latin America, and the demands for participation on the part of the people, all determine "the priority of a conscienticizing evangelization. This evangelization will free, humanize, and better man ... and will be nourished by the recovery of a living faith committed to human society."[22]

It seems that the Latino *evangélicos* would not disagree on this point. North Atlantic theologians may get nervous at this apparent "consensus" between Latino liberation theologians and *evangélicos*, but perhaps this betrays the dichotomist theology of the Global North.

Elsa Támez of Mexico is another liberation theologian (Presbyterian-turned-Methodist, not Catholic) who specifically addresses holistic mission through the lens of James. She asserts, "For us there is no doubt that oppression is one of the principal motives that compelled the author to write the letter." For Támez, a feminist theologian, her antennae would be naturally attuned to the plight of poor women, so she would resonate deeply with James 2:15, which mentions that both gender and class afflict them. The oppression of the poor by the wealthy is of particular note in James (e.g., 2:6; 4:13–17; 5:1–6). And yet, Támez sees the telos of all of this as hope and redemption. James 2:5 promises, "Has not God chosen those who are poor in the eyes of the world to be rich in faith and to inherit the kingdom he promised those who love him?" But this is not a "pie in the sky" kind of hope, it is one grounded in praxis (a hallmark of liberation theologians): "For James, it seems, Christians are recognized not by their being but by their doing; by their fruits they are known."[23] She sees the praxis as reflective of the Sinaitic law and the Old Testament prophets (Jas 5:10), smoothing the continuity between the testaments as Wright has also attempted to do. She also sees almost the entirety of Jesus's Sermon on the Mount contained in James. Ultimately, lest one dismiss her as being only about praxis rather than being holistic, she finds the hope in God through prayer (Jas 4:3; 5:4): "We should dialogue with God in situations of oppression and violence, pain and

---

22 Gutiérrez, *Theology of Liberation*, 69.

23 Támez, *Scandalous Message*, 42.

abandonment. Moments of prayer strengthen the spirit and inspire us to the practice of liberation. This prayer gives us confidence that God is present and accompanies these practices."[24] The wealthy oppressing the poor are universal, timeless themes that are easily transferable from the first century to the modern day.

Holistic Mission in the Twenty-First Century

Two themes have emerged from this chapter: mission as envisioned in James is holistic, and there is an order of operations to evangelism and social justice.

John Stott, six years after the first Lausanne Congress in 1974, expanded his thinking on holistic mission and diverged ever more from Billy Graham, who veered more toward an evangelism-only model. Stott wrote in the Lausanne Occasional Paper 21, "Evangelism and Social Responsibility: An Evangelical Commitment":

> social activity not only follows evangelism as its consequence and aim, and precedes it as its bridge, but also accompanies it as its *partner.* They are like the two blades of a pair of scissors or the two wings of a bird. This partnership is clearly seen in the public ministry of Jesus, who not only preached the gospel but fed the hungry and healed the sick. In his ministry, *kerygma* (proclamation) and *diakonia* (service) went hand in hand. His words explained his works, and his works dramatized his words. Both were expressions of his compassion for people, and both should be of ours. Both also issue from the lordship of Jesus, for he sends us out into the world both to preach and to serve. If we proclaim the Good News of God's love, we must manifest his love in caring for the needy. Indeed, so close is this link between proclaiming and serving, that they actually overlap. This is not to say that they should be identified with each other, for evangelism is not social responsibility, nor is social responsibility evangelism. Yet, each involves the other.[25]

The analogy of wings and scissors has become a famous analogy.

However, twenty-first-century mission has identified yet a third component, as Christianity rises in the Majority World and declines in the wealthy West. No longer is the old paradigm of mission "from the West to the rest" applicable, but it is also no longer "the wealthy evangelizing the poor." As the poor are now the majority of Christians, they are now often the ones doing the evangelism, a concept known as "reverse mission." But with the

---

24 Támez, 58.

25 Lausanne Movement, "Evangelism and Social Responsibility."

rise of Gen Z and Gen Alpha, mental health epidemics have revealed a third dimension to the gospel: social honor (not to be confused with social justice). Social justice is working on the bottom two levels of Maslow's hierarchy (physiological, safety), while social honor is working on the next two levels (relationships, self-esteem). American anthropologist Eugene Nida was one of the first to identify this, as he saw that sin led to three debilitating effects: guilt, fear, and shame.[26] The gospel addresses each of these, creating three binary pairs: the solution to guilt is innocence, to fear is power, and to shame is honor. The innocence/guilt binary is often stressed by Western evangelicals, namely Jesus's imputed righteousness and substitutionary atonement through justification by faith. The power/fear binary is one often at work in the Global South, with liberation theologies stressing social justice and the awareness of spiritual realities like power encounter, stemming from the rise of Pentecostalism. The honor/shame binary is the contribution of the East, which in many ways is the most primal of the three, as Judaism and Christianity are Semitic (Eastern) religions. When Adam and Eve first sinned, their initial reaction was actually shame, not guilt. Their reaction pre-fall was: "Adam and his wife were both naked, and they felt no shame." (Gen 2:25). And post-fall it was: "I heard you in the garden, and I was afraid because I was naked; so I hid [due to shame]" (3:10).

More recently, Jayson Georges has popularized this more holistic understanding of mission with his book *The 3D Gospel*. Of the four Gospels, the one that most stresses the honor/shame dimension is John, the apostle closest to Jesus. Jesus's first miracle in John 2, turning water into wine at the wedding feast at Cana, was all about saving the wedding couple from shame and instead bestowing honor on them. As such, one can think about the gospel as about saving souls (evangelism), saving bodies (social justice), and saving face (social honor).

George G. Hunter III, following Lesslie Newbigin's idea that perhaps the toughest mission field today is the post-Christian West, wrote a well-received book called *The Celtic Way of Evangelism*, contrasting the Roman model of evangelism with the Celtic model. The former is presentation, then decision, and finally assimilation; the latter is fellowship, then ministry and conversation, and finally belief/invitation to commitment.[27] Both are Western models, but one appeals more to older generations, while the

---

26 Nida, *Customs and Cultures*, 150.

27 Hunter, *Celtic Way of Evangelism*, 42–43.

other works better with younger generations. Some have phrased this as: the Roman model is believing → behaving → belonging, while the Celtic model (and what we see in the Bible) is belonging → believing → behaving. Another way to say it is: the Roman model is facts → faith → feeling, while the Celtic model (and what we see in the Bible) is feeling → faith → facts. It is not *who* I am, it is *whose* I am, and then how I act will flow out of that belief (fruit).

James Choung's book *True Story* helpfully provides a paradigm of how to reach the generations, at least in the West.[28] He posits that the "gateway" questions for each generation are as follows: Boomers want to know, "What is true?" Gen X ask, "What is real?" For Millennials, the pertinent question is, "What is good?" And for Gen Z, they want to know, "What is beautiful?" This is why apologetics, which is what Boomer theologians teach in seminaries, does not work with Gen Z, who are more captivated by the beauty of Jesus portrayed, for example, in the TV show *The Chosen*. For Gen Z, hospitality needs to be emphasized more, Christianity has to be more "caught" than "taught," and evangelism is more about helping people to belong so that they can believe.

Do we see honor, belonging, relationships, and beauty in James though? Indeed it is there, if we will only have eyes to see and ears to hear (e.g., 1:9–10, 12, 27; 2:24; 3:17–18; 4:4, 8–10; 5:13–16, 19–20). Perhaps it is time for a new Reformation, one in which the gospel is rethought yet again in order to return to its biblical roots. This Reformation not only brings the gospel from two dimensions into a fuller three-dimensional rendering; it also reaches across time and space: time because it will speak to different generations and space because it will span countries and continents. While James is not the only book of the Bible to showcase the fullness of the 3D gospel, it is surely one of the most obvious places to start, and one of the most succinct (often scholars see James as exhibiting a Proverbs-like genre). May this timeless wisdom— penned by Jesus's half-brother no less—be one that helps to transform our mission into one that is truly holistic and speaks to the twenty-first century and beyond.

---

28 James Choung, quoted in Kim, "Shining Light in Turbulent Times."

Bibliography

Baxter, Richard. *How to Do Good to Many: The Public Good Is the Christian's Life*. Grand Rapids: Christian's Library, 2018.

Blomberg, Craig L., and Mariam J. Kamell. *James*. Zondervan Exegetical Commentary on the New Testament 16. Grand Rapids: Zondervan, 2008.

Bray, Gerald, ed. *James, 1–2 Peter, 1–3 John, Jude*. Ancient Christian Commentary on Scripture NT 11. Downers Grove, IL: IVP Academic, 2000.

Costas, Orlando E. *The Integrity of Mission: The Inner Life and Outreach of the Church*. San Francisco: Harper & Row, 1979.

Eusebius. *The History of the Church*. London: Penguin, 1965.

George, Timothy. *Theology of the Reformers*. Nashville: Broadman & Holman, 1988.

Georges, Jayson. *The 3D Gospel: Ministry in Guilt, Shame, and Fear Cultures*. N.p.: Timē Press, 2017.

Gutiérrez, Gustavo, *A Theology of Liberation: History, Politics, and Salvation*. 15th-anniversary ed. Maryknoll, NY: Orbis Books, 1988.

Hunter, George G., III. *The Celtic Way of Evangelism: How Christianity Can Reach the West ... AGAIN*. 10th-anniversary ed. Nashville: Abingdon, 2010.

Kähler, Martin. *Schriften zur Christologie und Mission*. Munich: Kaiser, 1971.

Kim, Walter. "A Shining Light in Turbulent Times." *CCCU Magazine* (Spring 2022). Accessed June 7, 2024. https://www.cccu.org/magazine/a-shining-light-in-turbulent-times/.

Lausanne Movement. *The Lausanne Covenant*. Accessed January 3, 2024. https://lausanne.org/content/covenant/lausanne-covenant.

Lausanne Movement, "Evangelism and Social Responsibility: An Evangelical Commitment." Lausanne Occasional Paper 21. Accessed January 3, 2024. https://lausanne.org/occasional-paper/lop-21.

Lewis, C. S. *Mere Christianity*. 1943. Reprint. New York: Simon & Schuster, 1996.

Moberg, David O. *The Great Reversal: Reconciling Evangelism and Social Concern*. New York: Lippincott, 1972.

Nida, Eugene A. *Customs and Cultures: Anthropology for Christian Missions*. New York: Harper & Row, 1954.

Padilla, C. René. *Misión Integral: Ensayos sobre el Reino de Dios y la Iglesia*. Miami: Kairos, 2012.

Padilla, C. René. *Mission between the Times: Essays on the Kingdom*. 2nd ed. Carlisle: Langham, 2010.

Támez, Elsa. *The Scandalous Message of James: Faith without Works Is Dead.* New York: Crossroad, 1990.

Wright, N. T. *Justification: God's Plan & Paul's Vision.* Downers Grove, IL: IVP Academic, 2009.

Wright, N. T. *What Saint Paul Really Said: Was Paul of Tarsus the Real Founder of Christianity?* Grand Rapids: Eerdmans, 1997.

Yeh, Allen. "Christ Outside the Gate: How Hebrews 13 and Galilee Locate Mission for Jesus and Relocate Mission for Us." In *Reading Hebrews Missiologically: The Missionary Motive, Message, and Methods of Hebrews,* edited by Abeneazer G. Urga, Edward L. Smither, and Linda P. Saunders, 37–52. Littleton, CO: William Carey Publishing, 2023.

Chapter 2

The New Birth and the Vision of God's Mission in James

James A. Roh

Scholars have long observed echoes of Matthew's Gospel in the epistle of James, especially with respect to the Sermon on the Mount.[1] Although we see many parallels between the two, echoes of Matthew's Great Commission (28:18–20) are lacking in James. The topic of mission is quite veiled in James in this regard. Aside from the implications of James's call to care for the widow, orphan, and poor, the theme of mission emerges most explicitly in his treatment of salvation. James considers his hearers as "a kind of firstfruits of his creatures" (1:18), which implies that their presence signals the beginning of God's eschatological renewal of creation.[2] James's soteriology, thus, serves as a proper entry point for our discussion on reading the epistle missiologically.

James's treatment of salvation is distinct from that of other New Testament authors and developed along a different line of thinking. Rather than centering on Christ's atoning death, James concentrates on God's choice in salvation, beginning with his initiative in the new birth and extending to final eschatological judgment. Mariam J. Kamell argues, "The epistle of James concerns itself with the relationship between the conduct of believers and their salvation."[3] In so doing, James raises the dangers of false professions of faith and the necessity of perseverance and obedience in view of God's eschatological judgment. James 1:16–21 comprises the heart of James's soteriology and contains several important missiological implications. The "implanted word" (1:21) is crucial to James's understanding of salvation, which he describes with the imagery of "birthing" new believers by the "word of truth" (1:18). This chapter will argue that the "implanted word" signals the conception of a new creation and marks the believer's fundamental change in status in relation to the world. Accordingly, James's soteriology suggests that Christian mission must be grounded in a robust view of conversion.

---

1 See, for example, Bauckham, *James*.

2 All Scripture quotations are my own translation unless otherwise noted.

3 Kamell, "Soteriology of James," 3.

The New Birth and the "Word of Truth"

James's discussion on the nature of salvation in 1:16–21 is found in the introductory prologue of the epistle (1:2–27) within a series of binary choices that lead to either sin and death, on the one hand, or salvation and eschatological approval, on the other (1:12–25).[4] Ursula Ulrike Kaiser considers this section to be the theological foundation of the entire epistle.[5] Following the statement in 1:12 ("Blessed is the man who remains steadfast under trial"), James argues that God is not the source of temptation (1:13) but rather the giver of all good gifts (1:17).[6] While sin and death are "conceived" (τίκτω) and "brought forth" (ἀποκυέω) by one's own desire, James's hearers are "brought forth" (ἀποκυέω) according to God's will and by "the word of truth" (λόγῳ ἀληθείας, 1:18). The birth metaphor frames James's contrast between one's own desire and God's will: desire (under temptation) gives birth to sin and, ultimately, death, whereas God gives birth to James's hearers through his word.[7]

There is some debate as to what exactly is being birthed in relation to the "word of truth": (1) the creation of humanity through God's creative word (Gen 1:26); (2) the election of Israel as God's people through the law; or (3) the conversion or regeneration of believers through the word of the gospel?[8] In support of the creation view, James describes those who are birthed as "his creatures" (τῶν αὐτοῦ κτισμάτων, 1:18), which suggests a broad reference to humanity in general rather than Christians more narrowly.[9] From a different perspective, the second view argues that the epistle is addressed to the "twelve tribes" (1:1), who meet in synagogues (2:2), receive the "word of

---

4 Eng, *Eschatological Approval*, 116.

5 Kaiser, "Receive the Innate Word," 472.

6 See Eng, *Eschatological Approval*, who concludes that eschatological approval is the epistle's unifying theme and that 1:12 serves as the thesis statement that presents both the main idea of the prologue and the cohesive thread that runs throughout the body.

7 The verb ἀποκυέω only occurs in the New Testament in these two instances. For the view that God takes on the feminine role, see Martin, *James*, 39; and Baker, "Who's Your Daddy?," 195–207. However, ἀποκυέω is not restricted to the female identity, and its use in James may resemble γεννάω. See BDAG, s.v. ἀποκυέω; and Hans Conzelmann, "φῶς κτλ," in *Theological Dictionary of the New Testament*, 9:310–58 (365n390).

8 Allison, *James*, 280; Laws, *Commentary on the Epistle of James*, 73.

9 In the preceding verse, James refers to God as "the Father of lights" (τοῦ πατρὸς τῶν φώτων, 1:17), an expression generally understood in reference to God as Creator of the heavenly lights (cf. Ps 136:7 [135:7 LXX]). The exact expression, however, is not found in the Old Testament. Psalm 135:7 LXX reads, "to him who made great lights alone" (τῷ ποιήσαντι φῶτα μεγάλα μόνῳ).

truth" as the Torah (as in Ps 119), and are designated as "firstfruits" (as in Jer 2:3 LXX).[10] In further support, Dale C. Allison Jr. points out the birthing imagery in Deuteronomy 32:18: "You were unmindful of the Rock that bore you; you forgot the God who gave you birth." Despite these arguments, most commentators support the third view that James 1:18 refers to the birthing of Christians.[11] They make several arguments from corresponding key terms and imagery: ἀπαρχή ("firstfruits") is typically used in a soteriological sense throughout the New Testament to depict believers (Rom 8:23; 1 Cor 15:20, 23; 16:15; 2 Thess 2:13; Rev 14:4);[12] λόγος ἀληθείας occurs several times in reference to the word of the gospel (Eph 1:13; Col 1:5; 2 Tim 2:15), and birthing imagery is related to Christian conversion (John 1:13; 3:1–10; Tit 3:5; 1 Pet 1:23; 1 John 2:29).[13] If we examine James 1 more closely, several arguments in support of the conversion view emerge from the flow of James's argument.

First, James's birthing imagery presents a vivid contrast between eschatological life and death. Daniel K. Eng draws attention to the binary choice that James offers his hearers "to choose the better of two ways that will lead to a favourable final result."[14] The notion of eschatological death is addressed in 1:13–15, which likely alludes to the fall of Adam and Eve in Genesis 3 with spiritual death as the final outcome of the lifecycle of sin.[15] Conversely, the birthing imagery in 1:16–18 serves as the antithesis of sin's lifecycle with the final result of eschatological life, depicted by the language of "firstfruits."

Second, in response to the creation view, Esther Yue L. Ng discusses several notable parallels between James 1:17–18 and Psalm 136 (Ps 135 LXX): e.g., "good gift" (Jas 1:17a) and [the Lord] is "good" (Ps 135:1 LXX); "Father of lights" (Jas 1:17a) and [God who made] "great lights" (Ps 135:7 LXX); "no variation or changing shadow" (Jas 1:17b) and "his love endures forever" (*passim*); "firstfruits" (Jas 1:18a) and "firstborn" (Ps 135:10 LXX); and "his

---

10 Allison, *James*, 282–83. The precise term in Jeremiah 2:3 LXX is αρχή (not ἀπαρχή as in Jas 1:18).

11 See, e.g., Dibelius, *James*, 90; Moo, *Letter of James*, 79–80; McKnight, *Letter of James*, 128–80; Varner, *James*, 98; Blomberg and Kamell, *James*, 75; Cheung and Spurgeon, *James*, 32–33; Davids, *Epistle of James*, 90; and Martin, *James*, 40–41.

12 Moisés Silva, "απαρχη," in *New International Dictionary of New Testament Theology and Exegesis*, 1:347.

13 See Konradt, *Christliche Existenz*, 44–47.

14 Eng, *Eschatological Approval*, 127.

15 Eng, 127; Ellis, *Hermeneutics of Divine Testing*, 185–98.

creatures" (Jas 1:18a) and "every creature" (Ps 135:25 LXX).[16] Based on these parallels, she suggests that James 1:17–18 evokes a creation-redemption sequence found in later Jewish benedictions established on the precedent of Psalm 136.[17] This general sequence offered thanksgiving to God as Creator of the luminaries, followed by thanksgiving for God's election of Israel and redemption out of Egypt. She contends that James likely had Psalm 136 in mind as he wrote 1:17–18, and if so, "there is all the reason to see   1:18a as referring to the redemption of God's people and 18b as hinting at the hope of the eschatological renewal of all creation."[18] The latter point leads to our next argument.

Third, James's use of ἀπαρχή suggests that he views his audience as the sign of a new created order, which is birthed on the basis of God's redemptive work in Christ.[19] James qualifies the term with τινα ("a sort of"), which clarifies the figurative sense: his audience is *like* a firstfruit.[20] In other words, they are like "a temporary down-payment to be followed by the remaining members of the species."[21] This reading of ἀπαρχή also suggests that James's birthing imagery does not refer to individual Christians in a general sense but to the messianic community in particular. Luke L. Cheung comments, "Just as the firstfruits were the prelude to the full harvest, so the renewed messianic people of God are the prelude to the new creation of the whole universe, the representative beginning of the redemption of all creation (Rom 8:21; 2 Cor 5:17; Gal 6:15; Eph 4:24)."[22] Understood in this way, James's birthing imagery coheres with the address to "the twelve tribes" (1:1) and the mention of the "synagogue" (2:2) in line with Allison's earlier arguments.

Finally, James's birthing imagery implies the presence of a new nature in contrast with 1:13–15.[23] James's hearers are no longer trapped in the cycle of sin due to a fallen nature; instead, they have been re-created by the "word of truth." Just as desire under temptation produces a destructive progression

---

16 Ng, "Father-God Language," 43–47.

17 Ng, 45–46, who cites Verseput, "James 1:17 and the Jewish Morning Prayers," 177–91.

18 Ng, "Father-God Language," 48.

19 Kamell Kovalishyn, "Salvation in James," 133.

20 Blomberg and Kamell, *James*, 75.

21 Dibelius, *James*, 106.

22 Cheung and Spurgeon, *James*, 32–33. See also Varner, *James*, 98; Kamell Kovalishyn, "Salvation in James," 133; McKnight, *Letter of James*, 131, who similarly concludes: "James is referring here to the messianic community as a harbinger of a universal ecclesial community—perhaps even the kingdom of God."

23 Kamell, "Soteriology of James," 137.

from sin to death, so the "word of truth" births believers, who constitute the messianic community, with the goal of salvation.[24] The expression "save your souls" (1:21) clearly has a future orientation, referring to eschatological salvation (cf. 2:14; 4:12; 5:20). In this progression from regeneration to final salvation, we see the instrumental operation of the word, in which the "word of truth" (1:18) is also the "implanted word" (ἔμφυτος λόγος, 1:21). Matthias Konradt argues that the word (1:18, 21–23), according to James, governs Christian existence and preserves the vital connection between the renewed present and the eschatological future contained in the birthing imagery.[25] In this way, James, as Konradt argues, is centered on the word. Thus, James presents God's salvation from creation to new creation and from regeneration to final salvation.

At the same time, there is some ambiguity as to the precise referent of the "word" throughout the broader context of James 1–2. Immediately following James's mention of the "implanted word," he exhorts his audience to be "doers of the word" (1:22–23). In verse 25, he expands on this thought by relating the "word" to the "perfect law" and the "law of liberty" (νόμον τέλειον τὸν τῆς ἐλευθερίας). In a Judaic context these occurrences would typically be understood as a reference to the Torah.[26] If we understand the "word of truth" (1:18) as the word of the gospel (cf. Eph 1:13; Col 1:5), how do we understand the "implanted word" in relation to the "law"?

The "Implanted Word," the "Law" of James, and the "Word" in Matthew

At first glance, λόγος and νόμος are used almost interchangeably. Most notably, they are both objects of hearing and doing (1:22–25). Kamell delineates five discrete interpretations of the "word" in James: (1) the gospel, which may include Jesus's teaching and the required response; (2) a Christianized view of "innate reason"; (3) wisdom; (4) a modified view of the Mosaic law; and (5) Jeremiah's promise of a new covenant.[27] Concurrently, she outlines the wide range of readings of νόμος: (1) the Mosaic law with emphasis on the moral aspects; (2) the Torah as interpreted through Jesus's teachings (especially in the Sermon on the Mount); (3) the Sermon on the Mount in replacement of the Torah; (4) the ethical aspects of the Mosaic

---

24 Kaiser, "Receive the Innate Word," 467–68.

25 Konradt, *Christliche Existenz*, 287–88.

26 Adam, *James*, 25.

27 Kamell, "Incarnating Jeremiah's Promised New Covenant," 19–20.

law (excluding the demands for ritual and purity); (5) the law of love and mercy according to Leviticus 19:18 (reissued in the New Testament); and (6) fulfillment of the new covenant promise in Jeremiah.[28]

Kamell rightly insists that λόγος and νόμος are mutually interpreting.[29] In chapter 1, James maintains a general focus on λόγος with a limited number of modifiers: the "word of truth" and the "implanted word." In chapter 2, James consistently uses νόμος as the object of study and obedience with a variety of modifiers: the "perfect law of freedom," the "royal law"; the "law of freedom"; and the "whole law" to which believers are to obey. This shift between λόγος to νόμος in chapters 1 and 2 is rather seamless to the casual reader. If we follow the flow of James's argument carefully, the distinct phrase "the implanted word" (τόν ἔμφυτον λόγον) serves as the crucial link between "word" and "law." We will focus on this phrase as we explore how James relates the two concepts.

In 1:21, the referent of λόγος and the sense of ἔμφυτος (*hapax legomenon*) are both disputed. Though λόγος may refer to the "word of truth" (λόγῳ ἀληθείας) in 1:18, the sense is also dependent on the interpretation of ἔμφυτος.[30] The latter term is rare in Jewish and Christian literature. It can be translated as "innate" or "inborn"[31] but is more typically rendered as "implanted" (NRSV, NASB, NIV, ESV, CSB). The former sense occurs only once in Wisdom of Solomon 12:10, "their wickedness inborn (ἔμφυτος ἡ κακία αὐτῶν)," which connotes a person's natural capacity, in this case, for wickedness. Some scholars favor this reading with the sense of λόγος as "reason" as in the Stoic usage (λόγος σπερματικός).[32] As Douglas J. Moo argues, however, this reading does not cohere with the soteriological significance James attaches to λόγος ("which is able to save your souls").[33] Additionally, the Stoic interpretation assumes an optimistic anthropology, which seems to run counter to James's presentation of sinful desire (1:14–15) as expressed in the "restless evil" of the tongue (3:1–12). Accordingly, James instructs his audience to look beyond one's natural capacities to God's wisdom and word.[34]

---

28 Kamell, 20–22.

29 See Kamell, 19–28. She cautions: "However one understands the 'word of truth' which James further describes as the 'implanted word able to save your souls', this 'word' cannot be separated from James' description of the law—as is so often done" (19).

30 Adam, *James*, 25.

31 Lidell-Scott-Jones, s.v. "ἔμφυτος."

32 See, e.g., Jackson-McCabe, *Logos and Law*, 29–133.

33 Moo, *Letter of James*, 87.

34 Whitlark, "Ἔμφυτος Λόγος," 151.

Jason A. Whitlark situates James's use of ἔμφυτος λόγος within a broader motif of divine enablement. He states, "The problem according to James is that humans lack the resources to master their desires and suffer joyfully in the face of trials."[35] James's audience needs God's wisdom to navigate trials and the "implanted word" to overcome sinful desire and receive eschatological salvation. He examines the usage in the Epistle of Barnabas (1:2: ἔμφυτον τῆς δωρεᾶς πνεθματικῆς χάριν; 9:9: τὴν ἔμφυτον δωρεὰν διαθήκης) and concludes that ἔμφυτος is "an appropriate term to describe God's salvific enabling activity within the believer."[36] In particular, the use of the term is shaped by new covenant thinking (cf. Jer 31:33).[37] Several scholars, thus, contend that Jeremiah 31 is the essential background of ἔμφυτος λόγον.[38] As such, ἔμφυτος λόγον is properly understood as God's promise of a new covenant. The "word" serves as the active agent in James's birthing imagery: the "word" is the law of the new covenant now internalized; the "word of truth" is the essential content of the new covenant; and the "law" refers to the moral requirements (the "royal law" as a summary of the whole law; cf. Lev 19:12–18) of God's messianic people reconstituted in Christ (cf. Matt 5:43–48; 19:19; Mark 12:28; Luke 10:25–28).[39]

Another layer of background to James 1:21 is Jesus's parable of the sower and the four soils in Matthew 13:1–9. In James 1, the expression "doers of the word" (v. 22) echoes Jesus's teaching in Matthew 7:24–27: "Everyone who hears these words of mine and does them will be like a wise man who built his house on the rock." Kamell Kovalishyn suggests, "One can hear echoes of Jesus's parable of the four soils (Matt 13) in Jas 1:21–25."[40] Davies and Allison maintain that the point of the parable of the sower is that "people should hear and do the word Jesus speaks (cf. Mt. 7.24–27)."[41] James may have picked up on the connection between these two passages in Matthew. Beyond the obvious planting imagery, if the seed is not received in good soil, it lacks the potential to bear fruit due to "tribulation" and the "deceitfulness of riches" (Matt 13:21–22)—critical themes accentuated throughout James (1:2–3, 9–10; 2:5–6; 5:1–5).

---

35 Whitlark, 149.

36 Whitlark, 160.

37 Whitlark, 155–62.

38 Moo, *Letter of James*, 32; Bauckham, *James*, 141, 146; Kamell, "Incarnating," 26–27.

39 Kamell, "Incarnating," 24, 26.

40 Kamell Kovalishyn, "Salvation in James," 135n17.

41 Davies and Allison, *Matthew 8–18*, 375–76.

In summary, James views salvation as the beginning of a new created order, which succeeds where Israel failed, through the messianic community (the church). The messianic community, moreover, is now reconstituted by the lordship of Christ and birthed by the "word of truth," the promise of a new covenant fulfilled in Christ. Finally, this word is implanted in believers to free them from the cycle of sin and death so that they might obey the royal law, persevere under various trials, and obtain the reward of eschatological approval. Considering the letter as a whole, James's soteriology emphasizes God's initiative in salvation through the agent of the word and his role as eschatological judge.

Missiological Implications of James's Soteriology: New Covenant and New Creation

James's soteriology has much to contribute to current conceptions of salvation in many contemporary contexts, but it is neglected in most missiological discussions. As argued above, the crux of James's soteriology revolves around God's initiative in the new birth through the word implanted in believers as part of the new creation. A similar emphasis is found in 1 Peter 1:3–9 and 22–25. I would like to touch upon two emphases in James with particular missiological implications: the new covenant and new creation.

Picking up on the work of Daniel J. Treier, K. K. Yeo observes that the cosmic dimensions of salvation are the chief lacunae in Western dogmatic soteriologies.[42] Salvation, according to Yeo, is "not simply forgiveness, but also regeneration."[43] He further argues that Western readings of Scripture are abstract and often turned inward, thus focusing too exclusively on individualized implications of salvation. Likewise, Treier inquires whether there are lines of biblical teaching that widen the scope of salvation without minimizing its personal aspects.[44] He argues,

> Such incomplete soteriologies focus too exclusively on the personal blessings of participation in the new covenant. Hence I conclude by suggesting that "new creation," with which the Old Testament prophets surround the new covenant, might fill up what is lacking in the soteriologies surveyed here—without divorcing sociopolitical and cosmic concerns from the new covenant's personal elements.[45]

---

42 Yeo, "Introduction to Part Four," 354.

43 Yeo, 354.

44 Treier, "New Covenant and New Creation," 377.

45 Treier, 362.

Treier's concern finds striking resonance with James's presentation of salvation. James offers a cosmic vision of salvation that stresses the social responsibilities of the believer. Western conceptions of salvation are sometimes construed as an individual's decision in response to hearing the gospel. James's emphasis, however, lies in God's initiative from creation to new creation, beginning with the new birth. He grounds the believer's hope for eschatological approval in his or her participation in the new covenant, which includes both privileges and responsibilities. James's soteriology, thus, fills some of the gaps in Western soteriologies in at least two ways.

First, James's emphasis on the new covenant integrates divine initiative and human transformation. The "implanted word" speaks of both divine grace in the new birth ("every good and every perfect gift") and the resulting sanctification of God's people ("put away all filthiness and rampant wickedness"). In this way, new covenant hope is anchored "in loving divine initiative rather than human self-help—whether individual or communal or revolutionary or systemic."[46] Believers are not individuals who have made a transactional decision regarding their religious identity; rather, they are participants in the new covenant community who have received God's word implanted in them (i.e., written on their hearts). In framing salvation around the new covenant, James raises the dangers of false professions of faith.[47] If the actions of those who profess faith in Christ demonstrate an ongoing "friendship with the world" (4:4), "it raises the question of whether they have indeed received God's gift of the 'word of truth' or have let it lie fallow amid 'every filthiness and rampant evil' (1:21)."[48] Ralph P. Martin argues that the "implanted word" recalls "the baptismal response when the message was heard and acted on (e.g., Rom 10:9–10)."[49] However, Jeremiah 31:27–34 is typically quoted in the New Testament in the context of the Lord's Supper (Matt 26:28; Luke 22:20; 1 Cor 11:25). Although a sacramental reading of the "implanted word" is not likely suggested by the text, James's emphasis on the new covenant corresponds with the church's role in affirming the faith of believers through the practices of baptism and the Lord's Supper. Viewing salvation as incorporation into the messianic community reframes the incomplete notion of conversion as an exclusive individualistic experience.

---

46 Treier, 378.

47 Crowe, *Message of the General Epistles*, 158–59.

48 Kamell Kovalishyn, "Salvation in James," 134.

49 Martin, *James*, 49.

This demonstrates the intricate link between soteriology and communality.[50] As members of the new covenant community, believers are distinguished from the world as they receive the word and participate in the sacraments.

Second, James's reference to the new creation orients believers with an eschatological outlook rooted in present reality. Some conceptions of salvation fall into the trap of dualism between the material and the spiritual. For example, Treier comments that traditional Western accounts "narrowly construe salvation's future, overemphasizing personal destiny in disembodied, individualistic, and unearthly ways."[51] In contrast, salvation in African Traditional Religions is largely viewed as physical wholeness.[52] By connecting salvation with the new creation, James directs believers toward the ultimate hope that God will renew all of creation. At the same time, he readily acknowledges the present reality of temptation, sin, and death, which requires obedience and perseverance. One of the primary sources of temptation and sin, according to James, is material wealth (5:1–6). He identifies the fundamental issue between eschatological life and death as an internal matter: desire overcome by temptation and sin or reborn through the "implanted word." James resists, on the one hand, an unhealthy dualism that frames salvation as an escape from the body, community, and cosmos, and on the other hand, an over-realization of eschatological hope that clings to notions of prosperity in the present.[53] James's presentation of salvation is not framed in terms of wholeness, but it is certainly holistic.[54]

James situates his hearers in the broader redemptive mission of God from creation to new creation. His presentation of salvation does not concentrate on a point of decision in conversion but rather on God's initiative and enablement in view of final judgment. As a result, James provides the church with a vision of how the community of believers expresses its missional identity. The community does so by demonstrating God's wisdom, especially under trials, caring for one's neighbors, and exhibiting godly speech. The maturity or perfection of James's audience indicates "a deeply missional purpose for the letter."[55] They are the "firstfruits" in the story of

---

50 Kyama Mugambi, "Jesus Is My Personal Savior," 61.

51 Daniel Treier, "New Covenant and New Creation," 375.

52 Mavulu, "Balanced Approach to Understanding," 208–21; cf. Mbiti, *Bible and Theology*; Mugabe, "Salvation from African Perspective," 31–42.

53 Treier, "New Covenant and New Creation," 374.

54 Kovalishyn, "Salvation in James," 143.

55 Dancy, "Missional Reading," 338.

salvation from creation to new creation. They are to participate in this story by responding with patience and endurance. Although there are no explicit commands to proclaim the gospel, the community of believers retains an attractional quality in its missional identity.

In addition, James contributes to our understanding of the church's mission by articulating "the necessity of a gospel-empowered life from beginning to end for the realization of eschatological salvation."[56] The call to salvation includes the call to maturity through wisdom and perseverance. The proclamation of the word of the gospel also includes a word of divine enablement; the word is both proclaimed and heard as well as received and implanted. James's hearers are not passive recipients of the word, but instead, they must appropriate its power to overcome temptation and obtain salvation in the age to come.[57] As Graham Paul Dancy points out, this concern is so fundamental throughout James's letter that "the church's mission should likewise prioritise this and not settle for an anaemic concept of salvation as only pertaining to the eschatological judgment."[58] James helps us to see more clearly that post-conversion faith, as demonstrated by works, is integral in the church's missional identity.

Conclusion

James presents the story of salvation beginning with God's gracious initiative in the new birth, continuing through his word implanted in believers, and culminating in his role as eschatological judge. This chapter has argued that James's soteriology serves as a proper entry point for reading the epistle missiologically and suggests that Christian mission must be grounded in a view of conversion that accounts for the believer's initial reception of the word and ongoing transformation through the internalization of the word. In this way, James raises the dangers of false professions of faith and demonstrates the necessity of obedience and perseverance.

---

56 Whitlark, "Ἔμφυτος Λόγος," 164.
57 Dancy, "Missional Reading," 342.
58 Dancy, 342.

Bibliography

Adam, A. K. M. *James: A Handbook on the Greek Text*. Baylor Handbook on the Greek New Testament. Waco, TX: Baylor University Press, 2013.

Allison, Dale C., Jr. *James: A Critical and Exegetical Commentary*. International Critical Commentary. London: T&T Clark, 2013.

Andria, Solomon. "James." In *Africa Bible Commentary: A One-Volume Commentary Written by 70 African Scholars*, edited by Tokunboh Adeyemo, 1535–42. Grand Rapids: Zondervan, 2006.

Bachmann, E. Theodore, ed. *Luther's Works: Word and Sacrament I*. Volume 35. Philadelphia: Fortress, 1960.

Baker, William R. "Who's Your Daddy? Gendered Birth Images in the Soteriology of the Epistle of James (1:14–15, 18, 21)." *Evangelical Quarterly* 79, no. 3 (2007): 195–207.

Bauckham, Richard. *James: Wisdom of James, Disciple of Jesus the Sage*. New Testament Readings. New York: Routledge, 1999.

Blomberg, Craig L., and Mariam J. Kamell. *James*. Zondervan Exegetical Commentary on the New Testament 16. Grand Rapids: Zondervan, 2008.

Bruno, Chris. *Paul vs. James: What We've Been Missing in the Faith and Works Debate*. Chicago: Moody, 2019.

Cheung, Luke L. *The Genre, Composition, and Hermeneutics of the Epistle of James*. Eugene, OR: Wipf & Stock, 2006.

Cheung, Luke L., and Andrew B. Spurgeon. *James: A Pastoral and Contextual Commentary*. Asia Bible Commentary. Carlisle: Langham, 2018.

Crowe, Brandon D. *The Message of the General Epistles in the History of Redemption: Wisdom from James, Peter, John, and Jude*. Phillipsburg: P&R, 2015.

Dancy, Graham Paul. "A Missional Reading of the Letter of James: Hearing the Voice of James in Mission." PhD diss., University of Gloucestershire, 2021.

Danker, Frederick W., Walter Bauer, William F. Arndt, and F. Wilbur Gingrich. *A Greek-English Lexicon of the New Testament and Other Early Christian Literature*. 3rd ed. Chicago: University of Chicago Press, 2000.

Davids, Peter H. *The Epistle of James: A Commentary on the Greek Text*. New International Greek New Testament Commentary. Grand Rapids: Eerdmans, 1982.

Davids, Peter H. "The Meaning of Ἀπείραστος Revisited." In *New Testament Greek and Exegesis: Essays in Honor of Gerald F. Hawthorne*, edited by Amy M. Donaldson and Timothy B. Sailors, 225–40. Grand Rapids: Eerdmans, 2003.

Davies, W. D., and Dale C. Allison Jr. *Matthew 8–18: Volume 2*. International Critical Commentary. London: T&T Clark, 1991.

Deppe, Dean B. *The Sayings of Jesus in the Epistle of James*. Chelsea: Bookcrafters, 1989.

Dibelius, Martin. *James: A Commentary on the Epistle of James*. Revised by Heinrich Greeven. Translated by Michael A. Williams. Edited by Helmut Koester. 11th ed. Hermeneia. Philadelphia: Fortress, 1976.

Dunn, James D. G. *Beginning from Jerusalem*. Christianity in the Making 2. Grand Rapids: Eerdmans, 2009.

Ellis, Nicholas. *The Hermeneutics of Divine Testing: Cosmic Trials and Biblical Interpretation in the Epistle of James and Other Jewish Literature*. Wissenschaftliche Untersuchungen zum Neuen Testament 2/396. Tübingen: Mohr Siebeck, 2015.

Eng, Daniel K. *Eschatological Approval: The Structure and Unifying Motif of James*. New Testament Monographs 45. Sheffield: Sheffield Phoenix, 2022.

Eng, Daniel K. "The Letter of James." In *An Asian Introduction to the New Testament*, edited by Johnson Thomaskutty, 449–66. Minneapolis: Fortress, 2022.

Friedrich, Gerhard, ed. *Theological Dictionary of the New Testament*. Vol. 9, trans. and ed. Geoffrey W. Bromiley. Grand Rapids: Eerdmans, 1974.

Green, Gene L., Stephen T. Pardue, and K. K. Yeo, eds. *Majority World Theology: Christian Doctrine in Global Context*. Downers Grove, IL: IVP Academic, 2020.

Jackson-McCabe, Matt A. *Logos and Law in the Letter of James: The Law of Nature, the Law of Moses, and the Law of Freedom*. Supplements to Novum Testamentum 100. Leiden: Brill, 2001.

James, Arthur. "James." In *South Asia Bible Commentary*, edited by Brian Wintle, 1732–40. Grand Rapids: Zondervan, 2015.

Kaiser, Ursula Ulrike. "'Receive the Innate Word That Is Able to Save You' (Jas 1:21b): Soteriology in the Epistle of James." In *Sōtēria: Salvation in Early Christianity and Antiquity; Festschrift in Honour of Cilliers Breytenbach on the Occasion of His 65th Birthday*, edited by David du Toit, Christine Gerber, and Christiane Zimmermann, 460–75. Supplements to Novum Testamentum 175. Leiden: Brill, 2019.

Kamell, Mariam J. "God Gave Us Birth." In *Christian Reflection: The Letter of James*, edited by Robert B. Kruschwitz, 11–19. Waco, TX: Baylor University Press, 2011.

Kamell, Mariam J. "Irrevocable Nature of Salvation: Evidence from the Epistle of James." *Testamentum Imperium* 2 (2009): 1–28.

Kamell, Mariam J. "James 1:27 and the Church's Call to Mission and Morals." *Crux* 46, no. 4 (2010): 15–22.

Kamell, Mariam J. "Soteriology of James in Light of Earlier Jewish Wisdom Literature and the Gospel of Matthew." PhD diss., University of St Andrews, 2010.

Kamell Kovalishyn, Mariam. "Endurance unto Salvation: The Witness of First Peter and James." *Word and World* 35, no. 3 (2015): 231–40.

Kamell Kovalishyn, Mariam. "Salvation in James: Saved by Gift to Become Merciful." In *Reading the Epistle of James: A Resource for Students*, edited by Eric F. Mason and Darian R. Lockett, 129–44. Atlanta: Society of Biblical Literature, 2019.

Konradt, Matthias. *Christliche Existenz nach dem Jakobusbrief: Eine Studie zu seiner soteriologischen und ethischen Konzpetion.* Studien zur Umwelt des Neuen Testaments 22. Göttingen: Vandenhoeck & Ruprecht, 1998.

Laato, Timo. "Justification according to James: A Comparison with Paul." *Trinity Journal* 18, no. 1 (1997): 43–84.

Laws, Sophie. *A Commentary on the Epistle of James*. Harper New Testament Commentary. San Francisco: Harper & Row, 1980.

Martin, Ralph P. *James*. Word Biblical Commentary 48. Waco, TX: Word, 1988.

McKnight, Scot. *The Letter of James*. New International Commentary on the New Testament. Grand Rapids: Eerdmans, 2011.

Moo, Douglas J. *The Letter of James*. Pillar New Testament Commentary. Grand Rapids: Eerdmans, 2000.

Mugabe, Henry J. "Salvation from African Perspective." *Indian Journal of Theology* 36 (1994): 31–42.

Mußner, Franz. *Der Jakobusbrief.* 4th ed. Herders theologischer Kommentar zum Neuen Testament 13. Freiberg: Herder, 1981.

Ng, Esther Yue L. "Father-God Language and Old Testament Allusions in James." *Tyndale Bulletin* 54, no. 2 (2003): 43–47.

Reed, Rodney L., and David K. Ngaruiya, eds. *Salvation in African Christianity*. Africa Society of Evangelical Theological Series. Carlisle: Langham, 2023.

Silva, Moisés, ed. *New International Dictionary of New Testament Theology and Exegesis*. 2nd ed. 5 vols. Grand Rapids: Zondervan, 2014.

Treier, Daniel J. "The New Covenant and New Creation: Western Soteriologies and the Fullness of the Gospel." In *Majority World Theology: Christian Doctrine in Global Context*, edited by Gene L. Green, Stephen T. Pardue, and K. K. Yeo, 362–77. Downers Grove, IL: IVP Academic, 2020.

Varner, William. *James: A Commentary on the Greek Text*. Lexington: Fontes, 2017.

Verseput, Donald J. "James 1:17 and the Jewish Morning Prayers." *Novum Testamentum* 39, no. 2 (1997): 177–91.

Whitlark, Jason A. "Ἔμφυτος Λόγος: A New Covenant Motif in the Letter of James." *Horizons in Biblical Theology* 32 (2010): 144–65.

Chapter 3

What Has Quito to Do with Jerusalem?

C. René Padilla's Integral Missiology in the Context of James 2:1-17

Christopher Howles

The relative priority of gospel proclamation and social responsibility in the missionary task was a central theme throughout twentieth-century missiological discourse, and even today it continues to produce intra-evangelical debate and division. Entering into such a contentious conversation carries the risk of generating more acrimonious heat than illuminating light, but doing so with curiosity, generosity, and humility is normally a constructive endeavor. In that spirit, this chapter seeks to explore Quito-born Ecuadorian missiologist C. René Padilla's concept of integral mission through the lens of a missional interpretation of James of Jerusalem in order to contribute a fresh perspective to the discourse.

The "Great Reversal" in Twentieth-Century Evangelicalism

In his 2021 work *Evangelicals and Social Action* Ian J. Shaw demonstrates the rich evangelical tradition of integrating social action and evangelistic gospel proclamation.[1] This missional approach went relatively unchallenged until the early and middle decades of the twentieth century, when divergent methodologies arose. Many evangelicals perceived these to be unbiblical social gospel movements, believing they compromised the promise of kingdom life by divorcing economic, technological, and moral progress from the redemptive and restorative work of Christ. Filipino American missiologist Al Tizon describes these social missiologies as "ultraliberal definitions of mission" that prioritized social justice to the detriment of evangelization.[2]

Evangelicals responded by retreating into a "missionary myopia,"[3] constructing narrower frameworks in deliberate contradistinction to

---

1 Shaw, *Evangelicals and Social Action*.

2 Tizon, "Evangelism and Social Responsibility," 171.

3 Tizon, 171.

the social visions emanating from ecumenical and liberal circles, a move commonly referred to as the "Great Reversal."[4] As Jerry M. Ireland explains,

> Fundamentalism responded to the human-centered social agenda of liberal theology by mostly withdrawing from cultural engagement and social action. Rather than developing a more biblically balanced response to social issues, fundamentalism instead tended to truncate the gospel's temporal relevance in favor of an exclusive focus on eternal matters.[5]

Although not all evangelicals abandoned social concerns during this period, it is widely acknowledged that "efforts to change social, political, or economic structures were viewed with considerable suspicion as a compromise to the social gospel."[6]

As the twentieth century unfolded some evangelicals expressed concerns that this reversal had swung the missiological pendulum too far and thus lost the broader biblical emphasis on the social dimensions of God's purposes for the church in the world. A prominent example was US theologian Carl F. H. Henry, whose 1947 publication *The Uneasy Conscience of Modern Fundamentalism* challenged evangelicals to reconsider the social implications of their faith. Tizon credits Henry's work for "reawakening … the evangelical social conscience in America and beyond."[7] Henry's efforts to reverse the Great Reversal are well known, but the crucial roles of Majority World evangelicals in pushing the pendulum toward a more balanced perspective are often overlooked.[8]

---

4 Tizon (*Transformation after Lausanne*, 22–23) defines the Great Reversal as "the move of evangelicals from spearheading social reform in the eighteenth and nineteenth centuries to retreating almost totally from mainstream society by the late 1920s." Goheen (*Introducing Christian Mission Today*, 229) identifies two crucial contributory factors. The first was their shift from an optimistic postmillennialism to a pessimistic premillennialism that induced an eschatocentric neglect of present "worldly" concerns. The second factor was a hamartiological reorientation of the concept of sin by narrowing its focus solely to individualistic dimensions and neglecting societal implications. This reorientation resulted in social concern being confined to personal acts of compassion rather than engaging with broader issues of social justice.

5 Ireland, "Carl F. H. Henry's Regenerational Model," 51.

6 Ott, Strauss, and Tennent, *Encountering Theology of Mission*, 138. Kirkpatrick (*Gospel for the Poor*, 7), correctly observes that the "Great Reversal" narrative is a monochrome simplification of a broader and more complex narrative, pointing out that "many African American Christian leaders continued to maintain a robust understanding of social action in Christian mission right through the twentieth century."

7 Tizon, "Precursors and Tensions," 64.

8 Kirkpatrick (*Gospel for the Poor*, 143–44) suggests that the story of Latin American influence in global evangelicalism is "obscured" due to the "appropriation" of their ideas by Western evangelicals.

Emerging Majority World Influence in Global Evangelicalism

In 1966, evangelicals from one hundred countries convened in Berlin for the World Congress on Evangelism, a gathering organized by the Billy Graham Evangelistic Association. A primary objective was to reiterate commitment to the ultimate primacy of gospel proclamation in the missionary task, and social action was widely viewed as characteristic of a liberal and ineffective gospel. As such, the congress reinforced the predominance of Western Christians as gatekeepers and guides within the global evangelical community.

However, this was poised to be challenged from an unexpected direction: increasingly determined and independent leaders from the rapidly growing churches of Africa, Asia, and Latin America. British missiologist Timothy Chester notes that during 1966–1974,

> Third World theology and practice were coming of age and asserting their independence from First World theology. Third World theology was finding First World models inadequate to deal with the reality of its own missionary experience... . First World Christians began to be confronted with the fact that their theological presuppositions might to some degree be culturally determined and that their received understanding of theology might be inadequate for the issues facing their Third World brothers and sisters.[9]

Many Western evangelical leaders encountered missiologists from Majority World contexts characterized by extreme poverty and injustice and heard their concerns about the Western reluctance to embrace social responsibility. Notably, Latin American missiologists played a prominent role in this, with figures such as Ecuadorian C. René Padilla, Peruvian Samuel Escobar, and Puerto Rican Orlando Costas emerging as influential voices. Tizon describes these leaders as "radical evangelicals who called for an uncompromising socio-political commitment to biblical compassion and justice as integral to the gospel," and their influence was rapidly growing.[10] For example, British Anglican evangelical John Stott articulated a progressively more sympathetic, integrated approach to the role of social action in mission between 1966 and 1974, a change influenced by his ministry travels across Latin America and his developing friendship with Padilla.[11]

---

9   Chester, *Awakening to a World of Need*, 34.

10   Tizon, "Precursors and Tensions," 65.

11   Kirkpatrick, *Gospel for the Poor*, 145–50.

By the time of the Lausanne Congress on World Evangelization in 1974, organizers had made meticulous efforts to ensure that participants represented the diversity of global evangelicalism.[12] Half of all participants hailed from Africa, Asia, and Latin America, and Escobar played a crucial role in shaping the movement's foundational documents. Additionally, several Majority World participants delivered addresses during the congress, which made indelible impacts on the global evangelical community, including Padilla himself whose speech is described by the Lausanne Movement as "the speech that shook the world."[13]

Padilla's Impact at the 1974 Lausanne Congress

C. René Padilla (1932–2021) was born in Quito, Ecuador, and raised in Colombia. He underwent theological studies at Wheaton College (US) and pursued doctoral research in New Testament studies at the University of Manchester (UK) before ministering across Latin America with the International Fellowship of Evangelical Students, where he encountered some of the Marxist-inspired liberation theologies prevalent in the region during the 1950s and 1960s. This missiological backdrop led Padilla to the main stage at Lausanne, where he spoke about two incomplete gospels: one where salvation "is reduced to the future salvation of the soul and the present world is nothing more than a preparatory stage for life in the hereafter," and the other where salvation "fits within the limits of the present age, in terms of social, economic, and political liberation... . There is little or no place for forgiveness from guilt and sin."[14] His alternative approach to these polarized extremes merits quoting at length:

> I refuse, therefore, to drive a wedge between a primary task, namely the proclamation of the Gospel, and a secondary (at best) or even optional (at worst) task of the church. In order to be obedient to its Lord the church should never do anything that is not essential; therefore, nothing that the church does in obedience to its Lord is unessential. Why? Because love to God is inseparable from love to men; because faith without works is dead; because hope includes the restoration of all things to the Kingdom of God. I am not confusing

---

12 Stanley, "Lausanne 1974," 540.

13 Lausanne Movement, "Late René Padilla," Kirkpatrick (*Gospel for the Poor*, 352) notes that "the most incisive contributions at Lausanne came from leaders from the Global South, from men such as Padilla rather than Western Evangelical leaders such as Stott and Graham."

14 Padilla, "Evangelism and the World."

the two kingdoms. I do not expect the ultimate salvation of man or society through good works or political action. I am merely asking that we take seriously the relevance of the Gospel to the totality of man's life in the world.[15]

It is noteworthy that approximately 10 percent of the *Lausanne Covenant* clearly reflects Padilla's call to integrate social responsibility into the missionary task.[16] For example, Article 5 on "Christian Social Responsibility" affirms that "evangelism and socio-political involvement are both part of our Christian duty ... faith without works is dead!" This underscores the profound impact of Padilla and his contemporaries in reshaping global evangelical discourse and catalyzing an expansion of the definition of mission to include new language and priorities concerning social responsibility, something further legitimized by John Stott's public support of Padilla's emphases.[17] As British missiological educator Christopher Sugden aptly describes, "The blue touchpaper for evangelical involvement in social responsibility was lit at the Lausanne Congress in 1974 by ... René Padilla and Samuel Escobar."[18] This flame, ignited five decades ago, continues to burn today.

The Influence of Padilla on Contemporary Global Missiology

Tizon observes that following the Lausanne Congress in 1974, "the status of social concern enjoyed a new level of validation that it had not experienced since the days before the fundamentalist-modernist debacle,"[19] and "the *Lausanne Covenant*—particularly Article 5—provided new impetus for evangelicals to engage in social ministries."[20] A decade later, Padilla asserted

---

15 Padilla, "Evangelism and the World."

16 The full *Lausanne Covenant* can be accessed from https://lausanne.org/content/covenant/lausanne-covenant#cov. Birdsall, executive chairman of the Lausanne Movement from 2004 to 2013, has stated that the covenant is "perhaps the greatest document in the church since the reformation" ("Unpacking 50 Years"). Interestingly, the Lausanne Movement website quotes David Ruiz's (World Evangelical Alliance Mission Commission) estimation that "85% of mission organizations in Latin America use *The Lausanne Covenant* as their statement of faith."

17 Kirkpatrick (*Gospel for the Poor*, 145) describes how "Stott's public conversion to social Christianity in the 1970s was a crucial moment of legitimacy for *misión integral*, as it signaled to a broad constituency—including large swaths of conservative evangelicalism—that social Christianity was not the boogeyman of the past."

18 Sugden, "Evangelicals and Wholistic Evangelism," 30.

19 Tizon, "Precursors and Tensions," 68.

20 Tizon, "Evangelism and Social Responsibility," 173.

that the *Lausanne Covenant* represented a missiological stance "against a mutilated gospel and a narrow view of the Christian mission,"[21] and he rejoiced that "social involvement had finally been granted full citizenship in evangelical missiology, mainly under the influence of people from the Two-Thirds World."[22] Padilla considered this development to be "a paradigmatic shift in the concept of mission"[23] and "an awakening of the evangelical social conscience."[24]

Such conclusions, however, might be considered exaggerated or even triumphalist. The missiological shifts initiated, consolidated, and codified at Lausanne continue to generate debate and division today.[25] Donald A. McGavran described social action as a focus of mission as a "lion" that "threatens to devour mission by deflecting attention away from discipling the whole of humanity" and so must be "recognized as the enemy [in order for] missiology do the work to which God has so clearly called it."[26] Today some prominent evangelical works argue that the *Lausanne Covenant* effectively sacralized momentary sociopolitical forces and thus failed to prioritize the central missional themes of Scripture.[27]

Following Lausanne, Padilla and other Latin American missiologists sought to deepen the discourse on Christian social responsibility through the concept of *misión integral* (integral mission).[28] This approach moves away from an "either/or" dichotomy toward a "both/and" integration of

---

21 Padilla, *Mission between the Times*, xvi.

22 Padilla, "Evangelism and Social Responsibility," 29.

23 Padilla, "Holistic Mission."

24 Padilla, *Mission between the Times*, 2. Others have echoed similar sentiments. In 2011, theologian and social activist Sider ("Evangelizing the World," 48) noted that "combining evangelism and social action is now part of our spiritual DNA [as evangelicals]." Additionally, in 2014, Tizon ("Evangelism and Social Responsibility," 170) observed that "the very fact that younger evangelicals view the evangelism vs. social concern issue as a curious debate of a less enlightened time attests to the maturing of an evangelical social vision. The Lausanne Movement has been catalytic in this shift."

25 Stanley ("Lausanne 1974," 550) notes that "Lausanne did not settle the arguments over identity and missiological emphasis which were emerging in world Evangelicalism. Rather it brought them into the open and raised them to a new level of intensity."

26 McGavran, "Missiology Faces the Lion," 335, 340. Wagner ("Lausanne Twelve Months Later") described social action as a "torpedo" that "divert[ed] the [Lausanne] Congress from its proper goal of promoting world evangelization."

27 See, for example, DeYoung and Gilbert, *What Is the Mission of the Church?*

28 Padilla consistently uses "integral mission" in his English writings, and for consistency, this expression will be retained throughout this chapter. In missiological literature, "integral" is frequently used interchangeably with holistic, wholistic, or transformational. When quoted authors use such language, it is preserved with the understanding that no conceptual differentiation is intended between those terms and integral mission.

evangelism and social action. Integral mission emphasizes integration over the earlier language of "partnership." The concept of integral mission was prominent in the *Cape Town Commitment* at the Third Lausanne Congress in 2010, which deliberately avoided language of "primacy" or "priority" in the missionary task.[29] As Christopher R. Little notes, "Those who advance evangelism as the priority in the mission of the church are now in the clear minority among self-described evangelicals."[30]

Before evaluating Padilla's concept of "integral mission" in light of James's epistle, it is necessary to explore how Padilla defined and expounded on the concept.

Two Characteristics of Padilla's Integral Mission

Padilla's integral mission approach is broadly distinguishable by two features, both derived from the term itself. First, it is missiologically *integrative*, and second, it is integratively *missiological*.

Missiologically Integrative

Padilla's development of integral missiology after 1974 sought to advance the intra-evangelical discourse beyond the "two-mandate" approach characteristic of the original *Lausanne Covenant*'s missiological outlook whereby two distinct obligations are delineated and held in balance. South African missiologist David J. Bosch summarized these as first "the commission to announce the good news of salvation through Jesus Christ" and second "responsible participation in human society, including working for human well-being and justice."[31] Such dualistic language likely represented the only viable means of crafting a statement that could gain assent at that time from a broad spectrum of global evangelicals and thereby foster partnership in mission between Christians from diverse cultural and sociopolitical settings. However, as much as this marked missiological progress for Padilla compared to what preceded it, in subsequent years he explicitly criticized the *Lausanne Covenant*'s "failure to point to the inextricable relation between evangelism and social responsibility."[32]

The fundamental problem was that, as Bosch explained,

The moment one regards mission as consisting of two separate components one has, in principle, conceded that each of the two has

---

29 The *Cape Town Commitment* can be found at https://lausanne.org/content/ctc/ctcommitment.

30 Little, "Case for Prioritism," 140.

31 Bosch, *Transforming Mission*, 403.

32 Padilla, *Mission between the Times*, 6.

> a life of its own … if one suggests that one component is primary and the other secondary, one implies that the one is essential, the other optional.[33]

Padilla feared that such dichotomized or "de-integrated" terminology would inevitably lead to a gradual minimization of Christian social responsibility and a return to the fundamentalist stance of earlier in the century. His post-1974 promotion of integral mission is thus grounded in the *"inseparability* of love and justice, of the material and the spiritual, of faith and works, of the personal and the social, of evangelization and socio-political responsibility."[34] This emphasis on the synthetical inseparability, or integration, of seemingly disparate or contrasting concepts is pivotal to the integral mission approach.

Integral mission has its roots in the Majority World, particularly in Latin America. Highlighting these origins is not merely a peripheral addition or an elevation of anthropological or praxeological concerns over theological ones. Rather, it contributes to a better understanding and definition of the concept. Analogous to a fish responding to the question "How's the water?" with "What's water?," Majority World missiologists have commonly observed that their Western counterparts may be so deeply immersed in an inherently fragmented Greek-inherited and Enlightenment-oriented dualism that they struggle to discern its presence and impact on their scholarly endeavors. In essence, the separation and subsequent ranking of evangelism and social action so prevalent in modern missiological discourse reflects a fundamentally Western secular-sacred dichotomy between body and soul—a characteristic that Bosch argues is "contrary to the gospel."[35] Integral mission seeks to realign and reunite such dualisms into a creative tension from a non-Western, non-Enlightenment, integrated perspective, benefiting the entire church and advancing God's mission through it. This serves as a tangible illustration of multiperspectival, multicultural missiologizing, enriching all through the interaction and integration of diverse viewpoints from different cultures.

Integratively Missiological

For Padilla, the integration of faith and works, encompassing word and deed, or proclamation and justice, constitutes an inherently missiological endeavor. He asserts,

> The Christian life in all its dimensions, on both the individual and the community levels, is the primary witness to the universal

---

33 Bosch, *Transforming Mission*, 405.

34 Padilla, *Mission between the Times*, 18, emphasis added.

35 Bosch, *Transforming Mission*, 417.

lordship of Jesus Christ and the transforming power of the Holy Spirit. Mission is much more than words; it involves the quality of life—it is demonstrated in the life that recovers God's original purpose for the relationship of the human person with his Creator, with his neighbor, and with all of creation.[36]

According to Padilla, mission transcends mere words; it encompasses a life restored to God's original purpose. His emphasis on the inseparability of faith and works, in contrast to the dual-mandate approach of "balance" or "priority," avoids viewing the relationship between evangelism and social responsibility as a delicate balancing act. He does not adopt a zero-sum mentality, where strengthening one aspect is assumed to come at the expense of the other. In Padilla's perspective, focusing on social responsibility does not imply neglecting verbal gospel proclamation. Instead, he underscores the missiocentricity of integral mission in the conviction that it represents the clearest application of how God calls the church to bear witness.

This conviction was prominently articulated in his Lausanne Congress speech:

> The future of the church does not depend on our ability to persuade people to give intellectual assent to a truncated Gospel, but on our faithfulness to the full Gospel of our Lord Jesus Christ and God's faithfulness to his Word.[37]

Padilla was committed to Lausanne's vision to see the world come to Jesus in full repentance and obedience. However, he underscored that repentance and comprehensive godly living were foundational prerequisites for world evangelization. He expressed deep concern that certain Western missiological approaches were falling prey to a "culture Christianity," risking ungodly compromises on the ethical demands of the gospel in pursuit of church growth and rapid multiplication. Thus, Padilla argues,

> It is far better to emphasize the wholeness of mission—mission as including justification by faith and doing justice, faith and works, word and action; mission as addressing spiritual needs and physical and material needs, the personal and the social, the private and the public.[38]

Notably, Padilla's understanding of the "wholeness" of mission extended beyond transcultural missionary-sending paradigms from the West to the

---

36 Padilla, "What Is Integral Mission?"

37 Padilla, "Evangelism and the World."

38 Padilla, *Mission between the Times*, 12.

Majority World. He ardently supported polyvocal, polycentric mission, aiming to decenter wealth, power, and lineality that is so prevalent in the modern missionary movement. For Padilla, integral missiology leads to the inevitable conclusion that "all churches send and all churches receive. In other words, all churches have something to teach and something to learn from other churches."[39]

Our discussion now shifts to James's epistle to explore its implications for an "integral mission" approach to social involvement in the missionary task.

Toward a Missional Interpretation of James

The epistle of James has faced skepticism among certain biblical scholars, primarily due to perceived inconsistencies with a Pauline soteriology of justification by faith and its lack of explicit mention of Christ's death and resurrection and the work of the Holy Spirit.[40] However, in the twenty-first century, such scholarly suspicion is giving way to substantial theological reflections that rightly acknowledge James as both a formidable theologian and a cogent rhetorician who deploys a powerful arsenal of "persuasive artistry."[41]

Despite this scholarly renewal, missional reflections on James remain noticeably absent. A literature review conducted by Graham Paul Dancy in 2021 highlighted that "mission remains a neglected field in Jacobean scholarship."[42] This neglect of James as a substantive dialogue partner in mission does not reflect a lack of authorial intent on James's part but rather a failure to apply missional hermeneutics to the letter. In short, the missional negligence has been ours, not his.

If mission is understood solely as cross-cultural evangelism or centrifugal gospel proclamation, then James has little value as a missional text, concerned as it is with the internal life of Christian communities. However, recognizing

---

39 Padilla, "Our Mission in the World," 27.

40 Martin Luther and Martin Dibelius—two German theologians—have become particularly influential detractors of the letter: Martin Luther with his 1522 description of James as "a right strawy epistle," and Dibelius with his complaint that the letter "has no theology." Dibelius, *James*, 21.

41 Green, "Reading James Missionally," 211.

42 Dancy, "Missional Reading," 19. Dancy identified only five chapter-length missional readings of James in the English language as of 2020–2021, with some of those approaching the topic only tangentially. Since then, Köstenberger included a three-page chapter on James in the second edition of *Salvation to the Ends of the Earth* and Zimbabwean biblical scholar Batanayi Manyika presented on "Cruciform Mission: Reading James 2:1–13 Against the Grain of Privilege" at the 2023 African Biblical Studies Consultation during the annual Evangelical Theological Society meeting.

that God had a missional purpose in inspiring and preserving the epistle opens up fruitful observations regarding James's subtle yet significant contributions to a robust evangelical missiology. Viewing James not as a collection of disconnected and atomistic proverbial aphorisms but rather as a hortatory attempt at "world-building" with the purpose of "remolding the thought and behavior of its addressees to conform with a particular understanding of God's truth" means that the letter's missional perspectives shine brightly.[43]

This hermeneutical approach aligns with Padilla's articulation of integral mission. In an evangelical context that rarely employs James missiologically, the frequency of Padilla's explicit and implicit references to the epistle is striking. Observant readers may have noted Padilla's reference to "faith without works is dead" (Jas 2:17) in his Lausanne speech quoted previously, a phrase later included in Article 5 of the *Lausanne Covenant*. In his Lausanne Occasional Paper on holistic mission, Padilla again cites James 2:17 and its surrounding context as a crucial biblical foundation.[44] The question must be asked then, To what extent can James 2 support the weight of integral missiology?

Missiological Contributions of James 2

The following section will assess the validity of Padilla's derivation of integral mission principles from James 2. In conjunction with the earlier examination of the two characteristics of integral mission, this section will explore both integrative and missiological dimensions.

Missiologically Integrative (2:14–17)

Discussions about apparent incongruities between Jacobean and Pauline theologies of works in relation to faith in God's economy of salvation are extensive and lie well beyond the boundaries of this chapter. It is worth simply noting that James was likely familiar with, and in agreement with, the Pauline doctrine of justification through faith. However, he was responding in this epistle to an antinomian caricature of Paul's teachings circulating within his Judean diaspora audience.

James's response centers on 2:14–17, a passage that opens with two rhetorical questions expecting a negative response: "What good is it, my brothers and sisters, if someone claims to have faith but has no deeds?

---

43 Dancy, "Missional Reading," 12.
44 Padilla, "Holistic Mission."

Can such faith save them?"[45] This is followed by a distressing hypothetical illustration of supposed faith resulting in the neglect of a needy person within the Christian fellowship: "Suppose a brother or a sister is without clothes and daily food. If one of you says to them, 'Go in peace; keep warm and well fed,' but does nothing about their physical needs, what good is it?" (vv. 15–16). The subunit concludes with a challenging summative statement: "In the same way, faith by itself, if it is not accompanied by action, is dead" (v. 17).

James demonstrates that faith and works should not, indeed cannot, be detached within the Christian life. Attempting to do so is evidence of a fallacious faith, which even jeopardizes the salvation of that individual. As Peter H. Davids explains: "A 'faith' which is purely doctrinal and does not result in pious action (i.e., charity) is a dead sham, totally useless for salvation. True faith reveals itself in pious deeds of love."[46]

While James's rhetoric may appear to focus only on internal ethical matters within the Christian fellowship, the missiological implications become evident when considering the broader setting. James, like all New Testament epistles, is written from and for a minority faith community living amid religiously unsympathetic or hostile neighbors and authorities. Theological ethics in such a context will inevitably be missionally oriented. Riffing off of the famous dictum of Cyprian of Carthage that outside the church there is no salvation (*extra ecclesiam nulla salus*), it might even be argued, in reference to the New Testament, that outside of mission there is no theology (*extra missiologiam nulla theologia*).[47] James's appeal for piety is not a call for his audience to leave the world as much as it is a call for them to embody God's character in the world as countercultural participants in God's mission: "an ethic of holy non-conformity."[48] Disembodied faith devoid of praxis is not missionally effective. Thus, James "invites reflection on what it means for the church to be a missionary outpost in a world whose patterns and conventions are out of step with God's mission."[49]

Hence, Padilla's reliance on 2:14–17 in expounding integral mission is justifiable, as this passage underscores the necessity of integrating orthodoxy and orthopraxy in Christian living for obedient engagement in God's

---

45 All Scripture quotations are from the NIV.
46 Davids, *Epistle of James*, 119.
47 Phan, "Teaching Missiology," 15. See also, Bosch, *Transforming Mission*, 496.
48 John C. Elliott, quoted in Dancy, "Missional Reading," 293.
49 Green, "Reading James Missionally," 195.

mission. As Dancy explains, "If a faith that fails to look after the needs of others is defective, dead even, then mission that does not encompass this practical care is also defective."[50] Integral mission is characterized by this integration of faith and works in the task of mission. While there is no direct equivalence between Padilla's response to the evangelical Great Reversal and the faith-filled but ultimately uncharitable actors whom James critiques in his parable of 2:15–16, both can be viewed as missiologically unbalanced and unsound. Indeed, one might reasonably speculate that James would be unlikely to sympathize with the oscillation between evangelism and social action polarities outlined earlier in this chapter.

Padilla's integrative approach aligns with James's commitment to, comfort with, and confidence in the congruency between faith and works held in a missiologically robust creative tension. It is not a coincidence that integral mission primarily emerged from Latin American and not North American or European soil. Just as Ghanaian theologian Kwame Bediako reckoned non-Enlightenment influenced African theologizing to be aligned with pre-Christendom early church theologizing, so Padilla's integrated Latin American approach appears to be more consistent with James's than some Western enlightenment-oriented dualistic missiological approaches. As Australian theologian Charles Ringma explains,

> Much of the discussion on holistic mission reflects the problems of Western philosophy, the separation of the sacred and secular since the Enlightenment, the structuration of life and institutions in the modern world, and the dualism that runs through much of historical Christianity. As such, this is more a problem of the Western world than of the Third World.[51]

In short, Padilla's integral mission approach is both founded on and consistent with the missiologically integrative nature of James's thought in 2:14–17.

Integratively Missiological (2:1–13)

This chapter highlighted Padilla's conviction that integral mission is the most theologically appropriate application of how God calls the church to missional engagement in the world. He understood it to be the best representation of the "wholeness" inherent in God's comprehensive mission purposes, making it the most dependable foundation for the pursuit of world evangelization—a goal to which Padilla was deeply committed. Integral

---

50 Dancy, "Missional Reading," 247.

51 Ringma, "Holistic Ministry and Mission," 433.

mission inherently decenters power and privilege, asserting that God's plans and purposes have always been oriented toward a polyvocal and polycentric vision of intercultural mission. Padilla identified this in James's writing, particularly 2:1–13. While wealth and poverty, specifically the relational dynamics between the poor and the rich, are prominent themes in James, they have rarely been explored with a missional hermeneutic.

James 2:1–13 constitutes a subunit, commencing with a foundational premise ("My brothers and sisters, believers in our glorious Lord Jesus Christ must not show favoritism") followed by a vivid parable illustrating the incompatibility of Christocentric faith and partiality (vv. 2–4). James's illustration of two men entering a gathering and being subjected to such markedly disparate treatment (the one wearing a gold ring and fine clothes receives a good seat while the poor man in filthy clothes is commanded to sit on the floor by my feet) invites his hearers to consider the un-Christlike nature of practicing favoritism. Through his ensuing discussion of the issues raised by the parable (vv. 5–13) James echoes his half-brother Jesus in condemning the abusive and exploitative tendencies of the rich in light of the call for Christ's disciples to "love your neighbor as yourself" (v. 8). South African biblical scholar Stephan Joubert has demonstrated that the broader cultural context encouraged and even required asymmetrical relationships of power and partiality as integral components of the social fabric.[52] However, James redirects his missional community of Jesus's disciples away from this by urging them instead toward the profoundly countercultural practice of unconditionally loving and serving others. He calls the missional community of God to embody, before a watching world, the impartiality—or, more precisely, anti-partiality—exemplified by Jesus himself. As Dancy rightly observes, this would be an especially compelling missional initiative toward those actively marginalized and disenfranchised by the prevailing Greco-Roman norms of society.[53] Consequently, James effectively "draws on the biblical narrative of God's concern for the poor and vulnerable in concord with the social concerns of holistic mission."[54]

Crucially, James's description of the election of the poor in 2:5 within the context of anti-partiality in 2:1–4 effectively illustrates the fundamentally integrative nature of his missiology. By employing language that echoes God's prior election of the Israelites, James aligns with New Testament

---

52 Joubert, "*Homo Reciprocus* No More," 392–97.
53 Dancy, "Missional Reading," 233.
54 Dancy, 215.

traditions of the church being God's elect people, chosen and called into God's own missional purposes. James's distinctive contribution is to identify the poor as coequal participants in God's own missional purposes even from their position of societal marginalization and disempowerment, instead of them being merely recipients of a top-down movement. As Dancy expresses it, "God dignifies the poor by choosing them to participate in his mission."[55] This is a counterculturally radical initiative with significant missiological implications.

The modern mission movement of the nineteenth and twentieth centuries was primarily constructed and dominated by wealthy Western agents. Mission was assumed to flow unidirectionally from "the West to the rest" and has commonly been undertaken using the power, proceeds, and privileges of European and American colonial and postcolonial structures and systems.

James's denunciation of partiality regarding behavioral differentiation toward rich and poor, and his integration of the poor into the chosen people and purposes of God, provide a robust basis for Padilla's vision of integral mission as a decentered, polycentric, and polyvocal movement. As Latin American theologian Paulo Suess rightly observes:

> Jesus' project is for those who are poor, depressed, captive, blind, hungry, hated, foreign-looking, ill and excluded. They are both the addressees and promoters of this project.... . When those who are poor are not just at the receiving end of the gospel but commissioned as its bearers, then this church will be able to claim that it has taken the *missio Dei* to heart and is truly a missionary church.[56]

As such, Padilla's integratively missiological vision finds robust support in James 2.

Conclusion

Some missional readings of the New Testament focus predominantly on the Gospels and Acts before seeking imperatival references to the "Great Commission" in Paul's epistles and concluding with the multicultural eschatological vision of Revelation 7:9–10. While such approaches have value, their lack of substantive engagement with the General Epistles, notably James, fails to capture the full wealth of New Testament missiological

---

55 Dancy, 237.

56 Suess, "*Missio Dei* and the Project of Jesus," 557–58.

thought. This chapter seeks to address this gap and contribute to a more comprehensive understanding of New Testament missiological perspectives by reflecting on James 2:1–17 in light of the integral mission framework propounded by Padilla.

Integral missiology as a conceptual framework is both integratively missiological and missiologically integrative. It advocates for the inseparability of verbal proclamation and social deeds of justice and mercy, particularly emphasizing good works in the context of serving the needs of the marginalized. Padilla posits that this convergence of word and deed represents the most theologically precise articulation of God's mission in the world. This chapter has demonstrated that many of the primary concerns and characteristics of Padilla's concept of integral mission emanate from and depend upon key Jacobean motifs in 2:1–17. Reading that passage through a missional hermeneutic can shift the broader missiological discourse toward the richly integrated missiology of James. As Dancy observes,

> What James does bring to the table is an oft-neglected NT voice to what is sometimes seen (and therefore often marginalised) as an OT concern, or as a concern in the gospels that can be spiritualised away. James resists such a reading and lends force to an understanding of mission as holistic.[57]

Bibliography

Birdsall, Doug. "Unpacking 50 Years: The Legacy of the Lausanne Movement with Doug Birdsall and Ramez Atallah." Lausanne Movement Podcast, 2023. https://lausanne.org/podcast/unpacking-50-years-the-legacy-of-the-lausanne-movement-with-doug-birdsall-and-ramez-atallah.

Bosch, David J. *Transforming Mission: Paradigm Shifts in Theology of Mission.* American Society of Missiology Series 16. Maryknoll, NY: Orbis Books, 1991.

Chester, Timothy. *Awakening to a World of Need: The Recovery of Evangelical Social Concern.* Leicester: Inter-Varsity Press, 1993.

Dancy, Graham Paul. "A Missional Reading of The Letter of James: Hearing the Voice of James in Mission." PhD diss., University of Gloucestershire, 2021.

Davids, Peter H. *The Epistle of James: A Commentary on the Greek Text.* New International Greek Testament Commentary. Grand Rapids: Eerdmans, 1982.

---

57   Dancy, "Missional Reading," 248.

DeYoung, Kevin, and Greg Gilbert. *What Is the Mission of the Church? Making Sense of Social Justice, Shalom, and the Great Commission.* Wheaton: Crossway, 2011.

Dibelius, Martin. *James: A Commentary on the Epistle of James.* Revised by Heinrich Greeven. Translated by Michael A. Williams. Edited by Helmut Koester. 11th ed. Hermeneia. Philadelphia: Fortress, 1976.

Goheen, Michael W. *Introducing Christian Mission Today: Scripture, History and Issues.* Downers Grove, IL: IVP Academic, 2014.

Green, Joel B. "Reading James Missionally." In *Reading the Bible Missionally*, edited by Michael W. Goheen, 194–212. Grand Rapids: Eerdmans, 2016.

Ireland, Jerry M. "Carl F. H. Henry's Regenerational Model of Evangelism and Social Concern and the Promise of an Evangelical Consensus." In *Controversies in Mission: Theology, People, and Practice of Mission in the 21st-Century*, edited by Rochelle Cathcart Scheuermann and Edward L. Smither, 51–73. Evangelical Missiological Society Series 24. Pasadena, CA: William Carey Library, 2015.

Joubert, Stephan. "*Homo Reciprocus* No More: The 'Missional' Nature of Faith in James." In *Sensitivity towards Outsiders: Exploring the Dynamic Relationship between Mission and Ethics in the New Testament and Early Christianity*, edited by Jacobus Kok, Tobias Nicklas, Dieter T. Roth, and Christopher M. Hays, 382–400. Wissenschaftliche Untersuchungen zum Neuen Testament 2/364. Tübingen: Mohr Siebeck, 2014.

Kirkpatrick, David C. *A Gospel for the Poor: Global Social Christianity and the Latin American Evangelical Left.* Philadelphia: University of Pennsylvania Press, 2019.

Köstenberger, Andreas J., and T. Desmond Alexander. *Salvation to the Ends of the Earth: A Biblical Theology of Mission.* 2nd ed. New Studies in Biblical Theology 53. Leicester: Apollos, 2020.

Lausanne Movement. "The Late René Padilla and the Speech That Shook the World." April 28, 2021, https://lausanne.org/best-of-lausanne/the-late-rene-padilla-and-the-speech-that-shook-the-world.

Little, Christopher R. "The Case for Prioritism: Part 1." *Great Commission Research Journal* 7, no. 2 (2016): 139–62.

McGavran, Donald A. "Missiology Faces the Lion." *Missiology* 17, no. 3 (1989): 335–41.

Ott, Craig, Stephen J. Strauss, and Timothy C. Tennent. *Encountering Theology of Mission: Biblical Foundations, Historical Developments, and Contemporary Issues.* Encountering Mission. Grand Rapids: Baker Academic, 2010.

Padilla, C. René. "Evangelism and Social Responsibility: From Wheaton '66 to Wheaton '83." *Transformation* 2, no. 3 (1985): 27–33.

Padilla, C. René. "Evangelism and the World." Lausanne Movement. July 25, 1974. https://lausanne.org/content/evangelism-and-the-world.

Padilla, C. René. "Holistic Mission." Lausanne Occasional Paper: Pattaya, Thailand: Lausanne Committee for World Evangelization, 2004. https://lausanne.org/content/holistic-mission-lop-33.

Padilla, C. René. *Mission between the Times: Essays on the Kingdom.* 2nd ed. Carlisle: Langham Monographs, 2010.

Padilla, C. René. "Our Mission in the World: Integral Mission." In *Live Justly: Global Edition*, edited by Jason Fileta, 26–28. Portland: Micah Challenge, 2017.

Phan, Peter C. "Teaching Missiology in and for World Christianity: Content and Method." In *Teaching Christian Mission in an Age of World Christianity*, edited by Association of Professors of Mission, 11–24. Wilmore, KY: First Fruits, 2016.

Ringma, Charles. "Holistic Ministry and Mission: A Call for Reconceptualization." *Missiology* 32, no. 4 (2004): 431–48.

Shaw, Ian J. *Evangelicals and Social Action: From John Wesley to John Stott.* London: Inter-Varsity Press, 2021.

Sider, Ron. "Evangelizing the World: Reflections on Lausanne III." *Prism*, 2011.

Stanley, Brian. "'Lausanne 1974': The Challenge from the Majority World to Northern-Hemisphere Evangelicalism." *Journal of Ecclesiastical History* 64, no. 3 (2013): 533–51.

Suess, Paulo. "*Missio Dei* and the Project of Jesus: The Poor and the 'Other' as Mediators of the Kingdom of God and Protagonists of the Churches." *International Review of Mission* 92, no. 367 (2003): 550–59.

Sugden, Christopher. "Evangelicals and Wholistic Evangelism." In *Proclaiming Christ in Christ's Way: Studies in Integral Evangelism; Essays Presented to Walter Arnold on the Occasion of His 60th Birthday*, edited by Vinay Samuel and Albrecht Hauser, 29–51. Eugene, OR: Wipf & Stock, 2007.

Tizon, Al. "Evangelism and Social Responsibility: The Making of a Transformational Vision." In *The Lausanne Movement: A Range of Perspectives*, edited by Margunn Serigstad Dahle, Lars Dahle, and Knud Jørgensen, 170–81. Regnum Edinburgh Centenary Series 22. Oxford: Regnum, 2014.

Tizon, Al. "Precursors and Tensions in Holistic Mission: An Historical Overview." In *Holistic Mission: God's Plan for God's People*, edited by Wonsuk Ma and Brian Woolnough, 61–75. Regnum Edinburgh 2010 Series. Oxford: Regnum, 2010.

Tizon, Al. *Transformation after Lausanne: Radical Evangelical Mission in Global-Local Perspective.* Regnum Studies in Mission. Oxford: Regnum, 2008.

Wagner, C. Peter. "Lausanne Twelve Months Later." *Christianity Today* 19, no. 20 (July 4, 1975): 7–9.

Chapter 4

Restoring the Kingdom to Israel

Promise and Eschatology in the Epistle of James

Benjamin E. Castaneda

James has often been overlooked by missiological treatments of the New Testament.[1] If it receives any comment at all, the letter is characterized as having little to contribute, being narrowly preoccupied with the internal affairs of the recipient congregation(s). This stereotype is seemingly confirmed by (or stems from?) the letter's so-called "Jewish" character, with its mention of the synagogue (2:2), its positive view of "works" (2:14–26), its rare references to Jesus (1:1; 2:1), and especially its address to "the twelve tribes in the Dispersion" (1:1).[2] Further complicating James's missiological potential is that there is no reference to "the nations" (τὰ ἔθνη) nor any direct allusion to the archetypal mission text, the blessing of Abram in Genesis 12:1–3. Traditional readings of James have not helped in this regard, as the letter has often been approached as a collection of disconnected wisdom sayings or paraenetic discourse.[3]

I would suggest that the oversight of James by missiologists is due not to a paucity of relevant terminology or motifs but to misconceived notions of how the New Testament authors *ought* to construe their missionary vision. As Joel B. Green aptly notes,

> From [the] traditional viewpoint, the pressing question is whether James urges his audience to engage in mission. In reality, this way of putting things does not take us very far, since it assumes that we know already what mission entails, even before we begin our reading of the letter.[4]

---

1 E.g., James is referred to only five times in Wright, *Mission of God*, in each instance drawing solely upon its ethical injunctions. Similarly, Köstenberger does not appear to know what to do with James in his book (coauthored with Alexander) *Salvation to the Ends*. Köstenberger summarizes James's teaching in one and a half pages but finds little to say other than that it exemplifies a "form of Jewish Christianity" (68). Schnabel likewise offers minimal engagement with James in his massive work *Early Christian Mission*. For a thorough overview of the relevant secondary literature, see Dancy, "Missional Reading," 20–47.

2 Unless otherwise noted, all Scripture quotations are from the NRSV.

3 This approach goes back at least to Martin Dibelius, who contended that James was essentially composed of disconnected sayings and lacked a coherent theology. He categorized James as belonging to the genre of paraenesis: "By paraenesis we mean a text which strings together admonitions of general ethical content." *James*, 3.

4 Green, "Reading James Missionally," 195.

A similar critique is leveled by Amos Yong, who queries, "How might we be able to discern afresh missional strategies from adhering to these documents on their own terms … rather than attempting to import our own modern constructions and categories of assessment?"[5]

Closer attention needs to be paid to the texture of James, observing how the letter positions itself within the broader scriptural witness. This is perhaps an area where biblical studies can contribute to the missiological conversation. There has been a proliferation of research in recent years on Jewish restoration eschatology,[6] which can be defined simply as "the theological conviction that Israel has fallen under the curses of YHWH's covenant and awaits a time of glorious redemption and restoration."[7] A fruitful line of inquiry in current scholarship on James is to approach the epistle as a document that taps into these same hopes for restoration.[8]

Gleaning from this research, I will argue in this chapter that James construes "mission" in terms of the promised eschatological restoration of Israel, communicated via a constellation of lexical clues and motifs drawn from the Jewish Scriptures.[9] In particular, I will (1) trace the biblical roots of the language of the "twelve tribes" who are "in the Dispersion" (1:1), (2) argue that the recipients of the letter are portrayed as the "first fruits" (1:18) of the promise of the new covenant, and (3) suggest that restoration

---

5 Yong, *Mission after Pentecost*, 229.

6 Restoration eschatology shares much in common with the traditional biblical-theological approach of many missiologists. For example, Wright identifies the Old Testament promises of Israel's restoration as foundational for the incorporation of the nations into the blessings of Abraham (*Mission of God*, 454–500). Goheen also notes, "When Israel fails to carry out its vocation faithfully and is exiled from the land, God does not abandon his intention to use Israel to bring blessing to the nations. Rather, through the prophets he promises to gather and renew Israel to fulfill their calling (e.g., Ezek 36:16–27)." "History and Introduction," 17.

7 Staples, *Idea of Israel*, 94, emphasis suppressed. Restoration eschatology is often linked with specific, recurring motifs in the biblical text. Aune and Stewart identify these motifs as "the restoration of sovereignty over the land of Palestine, the restoration of the kingship, i.e., the reestablishment of theocratic monarchy in the ideal form of the Davidic messiahship, the regathering of the twelve tribes of Israel, and the final restoration of the city of Jerusalem and the Temple." "From the Idealized Past," 150. For a few discussions of restoration eschatology in a vast and variegated field, see Sanders, *Jesus and Judaism*, 77–119; Wright, *New Testament and the People of God*, 280–338; Scott, *Restoration: Old Testament*; Staples, *Idea of Israel*; and Nyende, *Restoration of God's Dwelling*, 117–50.

8 E.g., Penner, *Epistle of James*; Jackson-McCabe, "Messiah Jesus," 701–30; Marcus, "Twelve Tribes in the Diaspora," 433–47; Bauckham, "Messianic Jewish Identity," 101–20.

9 See the exceptional discussion in the unpublished PhD dissertation of Dancy, "Missional Reading," 77–111.

eschatology clarifies the odd concluding exhortation to bring back the sinner from wandering (5:19–20).

Regathering the Twelve Tribes

James is addressed "to the twelve tribes in the Dispersion" (ταῖς δώδεκα φυλαῖς ταῖς ἐν τῇ διασπορᾷ, 1:1). Most recent commentators treat "twelve tribes" as essentially synonymous with "Jews" or "Judeans."[10] Despite the frequency of this interpretive move in the secondary literature, the identification is problematic.[11] "Twelve tribes" in the Jewish Scriptures and Second Temple literature always refers to the descendants of Jacob corporately and functions as shorthand for the entire nation of Israel (e.g., Exod 24:4; Josh 4:5; 1 Kgs 18:31; Ezek 47:13; Sir 44:23; T. Benj. 9.2). There is never a case where "twelve tribes" is used as an equivalent expression for the ethnonym "Jew" or "Jewish."[12]

A more plausible explanation for the terminology is its symbolic and theological freight. For those familiar with the biblical story, the language of "James" (Ἰάκωβος, lit. Jacob) writing a letter to the "twelve tribes" in the "Dispersion" evokes a network of scriptural images.[13] From the Joseph narrative (esp. Gen 49) to the burial of Joseph's bones in Canaan (Josh 24:32), "twelve tribes" serves as an oft-repeated moniker for idealized Israel as the nation collectively experienced oppression in Egypt, exodus out of bondage, and inheritance in the land of promise. Darian Lockett remarks, "Within the biblical narrative 'twelve tribes' usually refers to the constitution of the

---

10 Erasmus, *Paraphrases*, 136; Calvin, *Commentaries on the Catholic Epistles*, 278; Mayor, *James*, cx–cxviii, 29–30; Davids, *Epistle of James*, 64; Martin, *James*, 9; Johnson, *Letter of James*, 170–71; McKnight, *Letter of James*, 67–68; Bauckham, "Messianic Jewish Identity," 101–20. In his magisterial commentary, Allison offers a variation of this view, reviving a suggestion going back to Bede that the recipients are a mix of Christian and non-Christian Jews meeting in synagogues in the diaspora. See Allison, *James*, 32–50; and Bede, *Seven Catholic Epistles*, 7–8. This error, though to a lesser extent, is also made in Dancy, "Missional Reading," 8.

11 This point was made twenty years ago by Jackson-McCabe, "Messiah Jesus," 713n47.

12 I suspect some of the terminological slippage in James 1:1 is due to a (correct) identification of "twelve tribes" with "Israelite," which is then wrongly equated with "Jew/Judean." I am influenced here by the philological paradigm proposed by Staples. Staples contends that conflating "Israel" and "Jew/Judean" obscures how these terms were used in the literature of Second Temple Judaism. He demonstrates that "Israel" designates the overall set, while "Jew/Judean" describes only a subset: "Rather than being synonymous, the evidence from Josephus suggests the relationship between these terms is *partitive*, with Jews a subset of the larger category of Israel." *Idea of Israel*, 25–83, here 52–53, emphasis original.

13 For a helpful survey of some of these scriptural associations, see Niebuhr, "Israel's Scriptures in James," 506–8.

Israelite people who descended from 'Jacob and the twelve patriarchs' and the nation of Israel as a whole especially with respect to their covenantal relationship to God."[14] Accordingly, "twelve" is repeatedly used to symbolize the nation in its ideal totality: an altar of twelve stones is built on Sinai (Exod 24:4), twelve precious stones are mounted on the high priest's breastpiece (Exod 28:20), twelve loaves of the presence are kept in the tabernacle (Lev 24:2), and twelve stones of remembrance are taken from the Jordan riverbed to be a memorial of God's faithfulness to his people and promises (Josh 4:4–9). Within this biblical logic, the near-loss of even one of the twelve tribes (e.g., Benjamin in Judg 21:1–6, 15–17) constitutes a national tragedy that threatens the integrity of God's purposes and demands rectification.

In James 1:1, the modifier "in the Dispersion" (often referred to as "diaspora") would remind the recipients of James of the tragic outcome for the twelve-tribe nation. It did not remain united under a Davidic king but, as a consequence of Solomon's covenant infidelity (1 Kgs 11:1–13), was divided into northern (Israel) and southern (Judah) kingdoms. The prophet Ahijah graphically portrayed the tearing apart of the twelve tribes by tearing his cloak into twelve pieces and giving ten to Jeroboam (1 Kgs 11:29–39). Yet the memory of the twelve tribes endured. In his confrontation with the prophets of Baal on Mount Carmel, Elijah built an altar of "twelve stones, according to the number of the tribes of the sons of Jacob, to whom the word of the LORD came, saying, 'Israel shall be your name'" (1 Kgs 18:31). However, hopes for restoration were never realized. Israel and Judah slid into greater wickedness and were subjected to the curses of the covenant (Deut 28:15–68) until they were ultimately cast out of the land and "scattered" among the nations (Lev 26:33; Deut 4:27; 28:64; Ps 43:12 LXX; Jer 15:7; Bar 2:4, 13; 3:8; Ezek 12:15; 20:23; 36:19; cf. Philo, *Conf.* 196).[15] In 722 BCE the northern ten tribes were taken into exile by the Assyrians, with the two southern tribes finally carried into captivity to Babylon in 586 BCE.

While the Jewish Scriptures narrate the scattering of Israel and Judah among the nations, they also prophesy that God would act in the eschatological future to bring back all his wayward people, regathering both Judah and Israel (often termed "Ephraim" or "Joseph" in prophetic discourse). Isaiah

---

14 Lockett, *Purity and Worldview*, 71.

15 The climactic covenant curse is to be "scattered" (from the verb זרה, translated in the Old Greek by διασπείρω; cf. the cognate noun διασπορά). As van Unnik observes, "Die Zerstreuung unter den Völkern ist die letzte Strafe für den Ungehorsam; sie ist ein großes Unglück, das der Vernichtung fast gleich kommt." *Das Selbstverständnis der jüdischen Diaspora*, esp. 89–107, here 106.

11:12–13 predicts that God will "assemble the outcasts of Israel, and gather the dispersed of Judah," and Ephraim and Judah would be at peace with one another. In those days "the house of Judah shall join the house of Israel" and return to the promised land out of their places of exile (Jer 3:18; cf. 31:8–14). Using the image of two sticks joined into one, Ezekiel prophesied a coming reunification of the houses of Israel and Judah under one Davidic monarch (Ezek 37:15–28), with the result that the "twelve tribes of Israel" would again inherit the land of promise (Ezek 47:13).

Though some of the exiles of Judah did return under Cyrus, a sense of exile along with an expectation of future restoration persisted among at least a portion of them (Ezra 9:7–9; Neh 9:36).[16] Thus, Zechariah 10:6–12, written after the return of the Judean exiles, still anticipates the salvation of "the house of Joseph." The book of Tobit characterizes itself as the story of one of the exiles of the northern tribes (1:1–2) who awaits the time when God "will gather" (συνάξει) all the children of Israel from the nations where they have been scattered (13:5). The Psalms of Solomon likewise expect a Davidic messianic figure who "will gather" (συνάξει) the "tribes" (φυλάς) of God's holy people (17.26–28).

Jesus himself invoked this same expectation with his selection of twelve disciples, whom he announced would sit on twelve thrones in the new creation and judge the twelve tribes of Israel (Matt 19:28; Luke 22:30). The Shepherd of Hermas appeals to similar imagery, describing the twelve apostles being sent and preaching to the twelve tribes, who are dispersed throughout the whole world (Herm. Sim. 9.17.1; cf. Barn. 8.3). Acts 26:7 contains a fascinating distinction between the singular twelve-tribe entity (τὸ δωδεκάφυλον) and members of a subset (Ἰουδαίων) of that larger entity. Paul's point (as recorded by Luke) is that the "twelve tribes" still await the fulfillment of God's promise to the patriarchs. While its meaning is debated, Revelation 7:4–8 depicts twelve thousand saints from each of the twelve tribes sealed by the Spirit of God, and in Revelation 21:12 the gates of the new Jerusalem are engraved with the names of the twelve tribes, thus symbolizing that the totality of Israel at last dwells secure in the presence of God.

In summary, E. P. Sanders contends that "the expectation of the reassembly of Israel was so widespread, and the memory of the twelve tribes remained so acute, that *'twelve' would necessarily mean 'restoration.'*"[17] Luke L. Cheung and Andrew B. Spurgeon therefore rightly conclude that

---

16 See Piotrowski, "Concept of Exile," 214–47.

17 Sanders, *Jesus and Judaism*, 98, emphasis original.

"when James addressed those he was writing to as 'the twelve tribes' and referred to himself as 'a servant of God … and *Christ*' [Messiah], he was evoking familiar imagery of God actively restoring his people to their former glory."[18] The recipients of the letter are thus identified with (and as) the recipients of God's promises of eschatological restoration. As those who follow Jesus the Messiah (1:1; 2:1), they have become members of the reconstituted twelve tribes of Israel.

Receiving the New Covenant

If the scriptural drama of exile and restoration provides a hermeneutical lens for reading James, how might that affect our interpretation? In this section, I will examine James 1:18 as a useful test case: "In fulfillment of his own purpose he gave us birth by the word of truth [ἀπεκύησεν ἡμᾶς λόγῳ ἀληθείας], so that we would become a kind of first fruits [ἀπαρχήν] of his creatures."

This verse has long been considered a key to unlocking the message of the epistle; as a result, every feature of it has been hotly contested. Debate especially surrounds the referent of the "word of truth" (λόγος ἀληθείας).[19] Most argue that it denotes the gospel—the redemptive message about Jesus or perhaps the message preached by Jesus himself.[20] Others read it as alluding back to the creative word by which God formed human beings (cf. Gen 1:26) or to a rational principle imbued in human beings at creation.[21] Yet others see the word of truth as referring to the giving of the law of Moses to Israel at Mount Sinai (cf. Ps 119:43), thereby "birthing" them as a nation (Deut 32:18).[22]

The verses that follow are critical for understanding what is going on in 1:18. The letter refers to λόγος three more times in the context. Verse 21 enjoins the recipients to "welcome with meekness the implanted word [τὸν ἔμφυτον λόγον] that has the power to save your souls." This is immediately followed in verse 22 with the admonition to "be doers of the

---

18 Cheung and Spurgeon, *James*, 13, emphasis original.

19 For comparison, the phrase λόγος ἀληθείας occurs in 2 Cor 6:7; Eph 1:13; Col 1:5–6; 2 Tim 2:15. See also 1 Pet 1:23–25 as a close parallel.

20 Bede, *Seven Catholic Epistles*, 16–17; Erasmus, *Paraphrases*, 142; Calvin, *Catholic Epistles*, 292; Mayor, *James*, 63; Dibelius, *James*, 103–4; Davids, *Epistle of James*, 89; Martin, *James*, 39–40; Blomberg and Kamell, *James*, 75; McKnight, *Letter of James*, 132.

21 Spitta, *Der Brief des Jakobus*, 44–47; Elliott-Bins, "James I.18," 148–61, esp. 151–52; Jackson-McCabe, *Logos and Law*, 233–38.

22 Allison, *James*, 282–85. Israel is called "first fruits" in Jer 2:3; Philo, *Spec.* 4.180; 1 Clem. 29.3. See also Kloppenborg, "Diaspora Discourse," 246–48; and Schlatter, *Der Brief des Jakobus*, 138.

word [ποιηταὶ λόγου], and not merely hearers who deceive themselves." The hearer of the word (ἀκροατὴς λόγου) is described in verse 23 via an analogy to the person who looks at their reflection in a mirror, then goes away and forgets what they look like. The logic is clear up to this point. However, verse 25 strikingly switches the terminology, going on to describe the blessedness of the person who is not merely a forgetful "hearer" (ἀκροατής) but a "doer" (ποιητής) of the "law" (νόμος). By using the same descriptors (hearer and doer) alongside both λόγος and νόμος, the text appears to be treating "word" and "law" as interchangeable.

I believe the word/law conception here refers to the Mosaic Torah. The combination of "blessed" (μακάριος) and "law" (νόμος) in James 1:25 is similar to Psalm 1:1–2 and 118:1 LXX. Both psalms begin by affirming the blessedness of the person who keeps the Torah. Additionally, the word used in James 1:24–25 for "forgetting" (ἐπιλανθάνομαι) is often used in contexts that describe covenantal infidelity to God and the Torah.[23] Moreover, "word" and "law" are treated as synonyms in James much like in Psalm 118 LXX, which uses an abundance of alternative expressions (including λόγος and νόμος) to refer to the Torah. Psalm 118 LXX also uses ἐπιλανθάνομαι in verses 16, 30, 61, 83, 93, 109, 139, 141, 153, and 176 to describe failing to keep the law. The psalmist thus depicts himself not as a forgetful hearer but as a faithful doer of the Torah, the same point made in James 1:18–25.

James is describing what it looks like to be a true member of the twelve tribes. Torah observance is now possible because the word/law has been implanted within them (1:21), giving birth to them as the first fruits of God's creatures (1:18). In line with a position articulated by Mariam J. Kamell, I would maintain that this is best understood as an expression of restoration eschatology and specifically alludes to the internalized law of the new covenant.[24]

In Jeremiah 31:31–34, God promises to the house of Judah and the house of Israel that in the latter days he will make with them a new covenant. The key difference between this covenant and the one made at Sinai is that "I will put my law within them, and I will write it on their hearts" (v. 33). Jeremiah's prophecy evokes Deuteronomy 30:6, where God promises to

---

23 See the usage of ἐπιλανθάνομαι in Deut 6:7; 8:11, 14, 19; 9:7; 25:19; 26:13; 32:18; Judg 3:7; 1 Sam 12:9; 2 Kgs 17:38; Pss 9:18 LXX; 43:18, 21 LXX; 49:22 LXX; 1 Macc 1:49; 2 Macc 2:2; Philo, *Somn.* 1.246; *Decal.* 62; Josephus, *Ant.* 2.327; *J.W.* 6.107; *Life* 14. In early Christian literature, see also Herm. Sim. 6.2.2; 6.4.2.

24 Kamell, "Incarnating Jeremiah's Promised New Covenant," 19–28.

"circumcise your heart and the heart of your descendants, so that you will love the LORD your God with all your heart and with all your soul, in order that you may live." Covenant infidelity led to their scattering, exile, and death, but at the restoration the Torah inscribed on stone tablets will become the "implanted word" (ἔμφυτος λόγος) written on their hearts, signifying divine enablement and wholehearted devotion.[25] Similar terminology is found in Barnabas 9.9, which refers to the "covenant" (διαθήκη) as "the implanted gift" (τὴν ἔμφυτον δωρεάν). This likely echoes the restoration promise of the new covenant with an internalized law and possibly displays an awareness of James 1:21.

I would suggest that this reading of James 1 is supported by noting the presence of additional lexical and conceptual links with Jeremiah 31. First, both the Masoretic Text and Septuagint texts of Jer 31:33 (38:33 LXX) use the language of gift (δώσω νόμους μου / נתתי את־תורתי) to characterize the divine act of putting the law in the inmost being of God's covenant people. In a similar manner, James 1:18 characterizes the "word of truth" as the preeminent example of the "perfect gift" (δώρημα τέλειον) that comes down from above (1:17). This is supported by noting that the language of "perfect gift" exhibits a catchword association with "perfect law" (νόμον τέλειον) in 1:25.[26]

Second, James 1:17 affirms that every perfect gift descends from the Creator of the heavenly lights, with whom there is no variation or shadow of turning. This well-known description of God echoes Jeremiah 31:35–36, which depicts God as the unchanging Creator of the heavenly lights. He "gives the sun for light by day and the fixed order of the moon and the stars for light by night…. 'If this fixed order were ever to cease from my presence,' says the LORD, 'then also the offspring of Israel would cease to be a nation before me forever.'" Just as the sun, moon, and stars never cease to rise and set and will never shift course, so God will certainly keep his promise to bring about the restoration of his covenant people.

Third, the gift of the law/word in James 1:18 serves to give birth to God's people as the "first fruits" (ἀπαρχήν) of his "creatures" (κτισμάτων).

---

25 Whitlark, "Ἔμφυτος Λόγος," 162–64. Regarding wholehearted devotion, see the related restoration promise of Ezekiel 11:19–20: "I will give them one heart, and put a new spirit within them; I will remove the heart of stone from their flesh and give them a heart of flesh, so that they may follow my statutes and keep my ordinances and obey them." This forms a strong contrast with the distinctively Jamesian figure of the "double-minded" (δίψυχος) person (Jas 1:8; 4:8). See Kamell, "Incarnating Jeremiah's Promised New Covenant," 25.

26 On the presence of catchwords in James 1, see Eng, "Role of Semitic Catchwords," 245–67.

The imagery of creation and harvest evokes Jeremiah 38:22 LXX, where God declares that he has "created salvation" (ἔκτισεν … σωτηρίαν) for Israel that they may be a "new planting" (καταφύτευσιν καινήν).[27] In other words, Israel in exile is comparable to a once-fruitful field that is now hardened and barren. At the restoration, however, this field—which Jeremiah 38:27–28 LXX identifies as the house of Israel and Judah—will be sown with seed. In this context, the seed sown probably represents the internalized Torah. The result is that God's people will spring up as "the first part [ἀρχή] of the harvest" (Jer 2:3).

The outcome of this analysis is that the new covenant of Jeremiah 31 serves a programmatic role in James. The recipients of the letter—identified as the twelve tribes in the Dispersion—are the first fruits of God's eschatological harvest. God has kept his promises, the turn of the ages has come, and he is at work to change hearts from hardened unbelief to wholehearted devotion.

Returning Sinners from Wandering

In this last section, I will suggest that the restoration of Israel offers a fruitful context for understanding the curious final exhortation of the epistle:

> My brothers and sisters, if anyone among you wanders from the truth and is brought back by another, you should know that whoever brings back a sinner from wandering will save the sinner's soul from death and will cover a multitude of sins. (Jas 5:19–20)

At first glance, this appears to be simply an *intra muros* exhortation, with little benefit to outsiders. The opening address "my brothers and sisters" (ἀδελφοί μου) and the qualifier "among you" (ἐν ὑμῖν) seem to limit its application to those within the community. However, such a perspective devalues legitimate inferences for the mission of the epistolary audience.

As Dancy points out, the application of this passage "must involve the effort of someone from the community to seek out those who have wandered to persuade them to return."[28] He goes on to note that this is precisely the sort of action enjoined by Jesus in the parable of the lost sheep (Matt 18:12–14; Luke 15:3–7).[29] In an intriguing lexical connection, the Matthean version of the parable describes the lost sheep as "the one who wandered"

---

27 My translation.

28 Dancy, "Missional Reading," 106.

29 Dancy, 106.

(τὸ πλανώμενον). Similarly, James 5:19–20 depicts the errant person as "wandering" (πλανηθῇ) from the truth, with the mission of the community to bring them back "from their wandering way" (ἐκ πλάνης ὁδοῦ αὐτοῦ). While the Lukan parallel does not refer to the lost sheep using the verb πλανάω or a cognate, it describes the errant person in the punchline of the parable this way: "There will be more joy in heaven over one sinner [ἁμαρτωλῷ] who repents than over ninety-nine righteous persons who need no repentance" (Luke 15:7). James 5:20 likewise affirms that "whoever brings back a sinner [ἁμαρτωλόν] from wandering" will save that person's soul from death. Regardless of what one makes of the lexical connections, the duty demanded of the recipients is crucial for the eschatological welfare of the wanderer and imitates the compassionate heart of Jesus, who welcomed sinners and ate with them (Luke 15:2).

In another fascinating connection with Jesus's ministry, Mark 6:12–13 reports that Jesus's disciples were sent out two by two, proclaiming the need for repentance, casting out demons, and healing the sick by anointing them with oil. James 5:14–16 provides the only other occasion in the New Testament where the sick are anointed with oil and healed. The anointing of the sick in Mark 6:13 thus parallels the activities of James 5:14–16, while the preaching of repentance in Mark 6:12 parallels James 5:19–20. This perhaps provides a more concrete picture of the actions envisioned in James 5.[30] Turning back sinners from their wandering requires going into the towns and villages and neighborhoods of one's own people, proclaiming a message of repentance and faith in God's appointed Messiah. Even more poignantly, in the Matthean parallel to Mark 6, Jesus explicitly identifies those to whom he sends his disciples as "the lost sheep of the house of Israel" (Matt 10:6).

Once again, restoration eschatology stands behind this description. These synoptic passages and James 5:19–20 cast comparable visions of restoring the lost due to a shared reliance on Ezekiel 34. In graphic terms, God accuses the false shepherds of Israel of neglecting and abusing and slaughtering the sheep entrusted to their care (34:3). He further observes, "You have not strengthened the weak [τὸ ἠσθενηκός], you have not healed the sick … you have not brought back the strayed [τὸ πλανώμενον οὐκ ἐπεστρέψατε], you have not sought the lost [τὸ ἀπολωλὸς οὐκ ἐζητήσατε]" (34:4). The result is that the sheep "were scattered" (διεσπάρη) over the face of the whole earth

---

30 The missing verses in the middle—James 5:17–18—concern Elijah, who makes an appearance in Mark 6:15 as well.

(34:6). It is precisely in this situation, while his sheep are lost and scattered, that God acts to save his people: "I will seek the lost [ἀπολωλός], and I will bring back the strayed [τὸ πλανώμενον ἐπιστρέψω]" (34:16).

The lexical and thematic connections to Matthew 10:6 and James 5 are self-evident. Jesus sends his disciples in Matthew 10:6 to "the lost sheep [τὰ πρόβατα τὰ ἀπολωλότα] of the house of Israel." Additionally, Dale C. Allison Jr. points out that James 5:13–20, like Ezekiel 34:4 and 16, combines the themes of healing the sick (ἀσθενεῖ; 5:14) and bringing back the wanderer (ὁ ἐπιστρέψας ... ἐκ πλάνης ὁδοῦ; 5:20).[31]

Within this larger scriptural context, James 5:19–20 does not necessarily envision only seeking out wanderers who were once part of the messianic community but then left. If Ezekiel 34 stands behind this injunction, with Mark 6 and Matthew 10 depicting analogous situations, then James 5:19–20 envisions turning back wanderers who were never part of the community in the first place and seeking them out wherever they might be. Ezekiel 34 sets out a program of eschatological restoration for the lost sheep of Israel, a program in which Jesus—the Davidic shepherd of Ezekiel 34:23—involves his disciples and in which James involves its recipients as well.

Conclusion

The biblical matrix of restoration eschatology provides a coherent and creative framework for reading James. As followers of Jesus the Messiah, the recipients are instructed to view themselves as the seed of the eschatologically renewed Israel. They are identified as the twelve tribes in the dispersion, yet they have had the Mosaic Torah inscribed on their hearts in fulfillment of the promise of the new covenant. The result is that they ought now to be actively engaged in bringing back the lost and wandering sheep of the house of Israel.

Bibliography

Allison, Dale C., Jr. *The Epistle of James*. International Critical Commentary. London: Bloomsbury T&T Clark, 2013.

Aune, David, and Eric Stewart. "From the Idealized Past to the Imaginary Future: Eschatological Restoration in Jewish Apocalyptic Literature." In *Restoration: Old Testament, Jewish, and Christian Perspectives*, edited by James M. Scott, 147–77. Journal for the Study of Judaism Supplement 72. Leiden: Brill, 2001.

---

31 Allison, *James*, 780–81.

Bauckham, Richard J. "Messianic Jewish Identity in James." In *Muted Voices of the New Testament: Readings in the Catholic Epistles and Hebrews*, edited by Katherine M. Hockey, Madison N. Pierce, and Francis Watson, 101–20. Library of New Testament Studies 587. London: Bloomsbury T&T Clark, 2017.

Bede. *Commentary on the Seven Catholic Epistles*. Translated by David Hurst. Cistercian Studies Series 82. Kalamazoo: Cistercian, 1985.

Blomberg, Craig L., and Mariam J. Kamell. *James*. Zondervan Exegetical Commentary on the New Testament 16. Grand Rapids: Zondervan Academic, 2009.

Calvin, John. *Commentaries on the Catholic Epistles*. Translated and edited by John Owen. 1855. Repr., Grand Rapids: Baker, 1993.

Cheung, Luke L., and Andrew B. Spurgeon. *James: A Pastoral and Contextual Commentary*. Asia Biblical Commentary. Carlisle: Langham, 2018.

Dancy, Graham Paul. "A Missional Reading of the Letter of James: Hearing the Voice of James in Mission." PhD diss., University of Gloucestershire, 2021.

Davids, Peter H. *The Epistle of James*. New International Greek Testament Commentary. Grand Rapids: Eerdmans, 1982.

Dibelius, Martin. *James: A Commentary on the Epistle of James*. Revised by Heinrich Greeven. Translated by Michael A. Williams. Edited by Helmut Koester. 11th ed. Hermeneia. Philadelphia: Fortress, 1976.

Elliott-Bins, L. E. "James I.18: Creation or Redemption?" *New Testament Studies* 3, no. 2 (1957): 148–61.

Eng, Daniel K. "The Role of Semitic Catchwords in Interpreting the Epistle of James." *Tyndale Bulletin* 70, no. 2 (2019): 245–67.

Erasmus. *Paraphrases on the Epistles to Timothy, Titus and Philemon, the Epistles of Peter and Jude, the Epistles of James, the Epistles of John, and the Epistle to Hebrews*. Translated by John J. Bateman. Vol. 44 of Collected Works of Erasmus. Edited by Robert D. Sider. Toronto: University of Toronto Press, 1993.

Goheen, Michael W. "A History and Introduction to a Missional Reading of the Bible." In *Reading the Bible Missionally*, edited by Michael W. Goheen, 3–27. Grand Rapids: Eerdmans, 2016.

Green, Joel B. "Reading James Missionally." In *Reading the Bible Missionally*, edited by Michael W. Goheen, 194–212. Grand Rapids: Eerdmans, 2016.

Jackson-McCabe, Matt A. *Logos and Law in the Letter of James: The Law of Nature, the Law of Moses, and the Law of Freedom*. Supplements to Novum Testamentum 100. Leiden: Brill, 2001.

Jackson-McCabe, Matt. "The Messiah Jesus in the Mythic World of James." *Journal of Biblical Literature* 122, no. 4 (2003): 701–30.

Johnson, Luke Timothy. *The Letter of James: A New Translation with Introduction and Commentary*. Anchor Bible 37A. New Haven: Yale University Press, 1995.

Kamell, Mariam J. "Incarnating Jeremiah's Promised New Covenant in the 'Law' of James." *Evangelical Quarterly* 83, no. 1 (2011): 19–28.

Kloppenborg, John S. "Diaspora Discourse: The Construction of *Ethos* in James." *New Testament Studies* 53, no. 2 (2007): 242–70.

Köstenberger, Andreas J., and T. Desmond Alexander. *Salvation to the Ends of the Earth: A Biblical Theology of Mission*. 2nd ed. New Studies in Biblical Theology 53. London: Apollos, 2020.

Lockett, Darian. *Purity and Worldview in the Epistle of James*. Library of New Testament Studies 366. London: T&T Clark, 2008.

Marcus, Joel. "'The Twelve Tribes in the Diaspora' (James 1.1)." *New Testament Studies* 60, no. 4 (2014): 433–47.

Martin, Ralph P. *James*. Word Biblical Commentary 48. Waco, TX: Word, 1988.

Mayor, Joseph B. *The Epistle of St. James*. London: Macmillan, 1892.

McKnight, Scot. *The Letter of James*. New International Commentary on the New Testament. Grand Rapids: Eerdmans, 2011.

Niebuhr, Karl-Wilhelm. "Israel's Scriptures in James." In *Israel's Scriptures in Early Christian Writings: The Use of the Old Testament in the New*, edited by Matthias Henze and David Lincicum, 500–22. Grand Rapids: Eerdmans, 2023.

Nyende, Peter. *The Restoration of God's Dwelling and Kingdom: A Biblical Theology*. Carlisle: Langham, 2023.

Penner, Todd C. *The Epistle of James and Eschatology: Re-reading an Ancient Christian Letter*. Journal for the Study of the New Testament Supplement 121. Sheffield: Sheffield Academic, 1996.

Piotrowski, Nicholas G. "The Concept of Exile in Late Second Temple Judaism: A Review of Recent Scholarship." *Currents in Biblical Research* 15, no. 2 (2017): 214–47.

Sanders, E. P. *Jesus and Judaism*. Philadelphia: Fortress, 1985.

Schlatter, Adolf. *Der Brief des Jakobus*. Stuttgart: Calwer, 1956.

Schnabel, Eckhard J. *Early Christian Mission*. 2 vols. Leicester: Apollos, 2004.

Scott, James M., ed. *Restoration: Old Testament, Jewish, and Christian Perspectives*. Journal for the Study of Judaism Supplement 72. Leiden: Brill, 2001.

Spitta, Friedrich. *Der Brief des Jakobus; Studien zum Hirten des Hermas*. Vol. 2 of *Zur Geschichte und Litteratur des Urchristentums*. Göttingen: Vandenhoeck & Ruprecht, 1896.

Staples, Jason. *The Idea of Israel in Second Temple Judaism: A New Theory of People, Exile, and Israelite Identity*. Cambridge: Cambridge University Press, 2021.

van Unnik, Willem Cornelis. *Das Selbstverständnis der jüdischen Diaspora in der hellenistisch-römischen Zeit*. Edited by Pieter W. van der Horst. Arbeiten zur Geschichte des antiken Judentums und des Urchristentums 17. Leiden: Brill, 1993.

Whitlark, Jason A. "ἜΜφυτος Λόγος: A New Covenant Motif in the Letter of James." *Horizons in Biblical Theology* 32 (2010): 144–65.

Wright, Christopher J. H. *The Mission of God: Unlocking the Bible's Grand Narrative*. Nottingham: Inter-Varsity, 2006.

Wright, N. T. *The New Testament and the People of God*. Christian Origins and the Question of God 1. Minneapolis: Fortress, 1992.

Yong, Amos. *Mission after Pentecost: The Witness of the Spirit from Genesis to Revelation*. Grand Rapids: Baker Academic, 2019.

Chapter 5

Eschatology and Mission in James

Jeffrey S. Krohn

James urges his readers to be "slow to speak" (1:19). However, he is *quick* to speak out against injustice and to call his readers to live out their faith. He warns of eschatological realities—specifically the coming Judge—as well as the perils of societal inequalities. He repeatedly and forcibly compels his readers to remember the plight of the poor and marginalized. His unrelenting words illustrate the urgency of the situation. In James, eschatology and mission are seen in the following way: In light of the coming Judge, who will right all wrongs, we are to proclaim the gospel, live out our faith, and passionately labor and toil on behalf of the poor and marginalized. In addition to examining this confluence of eschatology and mission, I will discuss various perspectives on mission by Majority World authors. In today's context of globalization and interconnectedness, we need to hear from varying voices to gain a better understanding of mission in the twenty-first century.

Exhortation

To accomplish his purposes, James employs specific rhetorical strategies. He continually challenges his readers to stop and think and ponder. In the second verse of the book, he causes his readers to "reflect on their own bitter experience."[1] The verb "consider" in 1:2 is not only the first imperative of the book, it is also the first of many calls to think and reflect.[2] With these commands, James encourages his readers to gain a proper perspective, specifically "an eschatological perspective."[3] In 3:1–10, he stirs them toward reflection with more than ten stunning descriptions of the tongue, summoning them to realize the potentially inflammatory nature of spoken words.[4] He asks in 3:13: "Who is wise and understanding among you?" Other piercing questions include the following: "Have you not discriminated?" (2:4); "What causes fights and quarrels among you?" (4:1); "Don't you know?" (4:4); "Do you think?" (4:5); "But you—who are you to judge your neighbor?"

---

1 Támez, *Scandalous Message*, 30–31.

2 "Consider it pure joy, my brothers and sisters, whenever you face trials of many kinds, because you know that the testing of your faith produces perseverance. Let perseverance finish its work" (Jas 1:2–4a). Unless otherwise noted, all Scripture quotations are from the NIV.

3 Davids, *Epistle of James*, 67.

4 E.g., the tongue is "a fire" (3:6); "a world of evil" (3:6); "set on fire by hell" (3:6); "a restless evil" (3:8) and "full of deadly poison" (3:8).

(4:12); "What is your life?" (4:14). Similar questions are found in 2:5 and 14. While James obviously has several objectives in his letter, one is to cause his readers to reflect on their manner of living, especially related to financial and eschatological matters.

James often speaks directly to his readers. He calls them "brothers and sisters" (cf. 1:2, 16, 19; 2:1, 5, 14; 3:1, 10, 12; 4:11; 5:7, 9, 10, 12, 19).[5] We can appreciate his pastoral heart and personal affection in this frequent and caring address.[6] Yet he also uses harsh and surprising titles: "you foolish person" (2:20); "you adulterous people" (4:4); "you sinners" (4:8), and "you double-minded" (4:8).[7] Such stern language would cause reaction and reflection in the minds of his readers. Other direct speech includes the familiar "look" (ἰδού), also translated as "behold!" (3:4, 5; 5:4, 7, 9, 11). A serious consideration of his words would be warranted, especially since judgment was coming (5:7). Other similar examples include "take note" (1:19; "know this" in ESV); "listen" (2:5); "Now listen" (4:13; 5:1; "come now" in ESV); and "but now" (4:16, author's translation). James regularly orients his readers toward certain attitudes and actions by speaking directly to them through these commands. His letter contains fifty-four imperatives (out of 108 verses).[8] He gives specific guidance on what they should or should not say: e.g., in 2:3: "[do not] say" (to a rich man); "[do not] say" (to a poor man) (cf. 1:13; 2:16, 18; 3:9, 10; 4:11, 13, 15; 5:9, 12). Surprisingly, he even tells them to "speak" (2:12)![9] Thus, James uses strong words in various rhetorical strategies to force his readers to stop and think, as well as to confront those perpetuating societal inequalities.[10] By doing this, he is giving us a model for mission.

---

5   According to McKnight, when the personal pronoun "my" is used, as in 1:2 (ἀδελφοί μου), the term "brothers" indicates the entire community, thus, "my brothers and sisters." *Letter of James*, 70n9.

6   Pérez Millos, *Comentario exegético*, 318.

7   Another potential title is found in 5:1: "you rich people." However, there is debate whether those addressed in 5:1–6 can be considered Christians. For the view that this passage does not address believers, see Blomberg and Kamell, *James*, 31, 214–20. Others discuss the opposing view, e.g., Pérez Millos, *Comentario exegético*, 269.

8   Baker, *Personal Speech-Ethics*, 6.

9   "Speak and act as those who are going to be judged" (Jas 2:12).

10   One author implies that the "polemical rhetoric" of James "undermines" his own message, for if he "actually practised what he preached in Jas 3.1–12, a passage concerning how a believer should handle his or her tongue, he could hardly be so bold as to call people adulteresses (4.4)." Coker, "Nativism," 47. This pessimistic view, however, does not adequately account for the urgency of the situation or the prophetic trajectory that James demonstrates.

Eschatology

The strong words of James are present, in part, because of the eschatological urgency of the coming Judge. Eschatological *judgment* is referenced with the indifferent actions of the rich (1:10–11; 5:1–6); the unmerciful (2:12–13); the teacher (potentially) (3:1); those who grumble against each other (5:9); and those who "swear" and are unable to answer "yes" or "no" (5:12). Indeed, "the Judge is standing at the door" (5:9; cf. 4:12). "The threat of judgment is pervasive in the letter."[11] Similar eschatological exhortations include a faith that cannot save (2:14) and life as a mist that vanishes (4:14). The former exhortation is given to correct potential misunderstandings regarding the gospel (and this has eschatological implications), while the latter would cause readers to consider the brevity of life and the nonnegotiable certainty of their impending death. James, then, because of an eschatological urgency, writes solemn and penetrating admonitions.

Further eschatological echoes are present in the letter. Those who persevere will receive the crown of life (1:12); the "poor" will inherit the kingdom (2:5); and those with faith *and* works will be rewarded with righteousness/eschatological salvation (2:24). Readers are called to be patient in view of the Lord's coming (5:7–8) and commanded to "know" that turning sinners from their ways will save them (5:20).

What is meant by the term "eschatology"? Although many will posit that it refers to the return of Jesus or topics such as death, heaven and hell, in this chapter I will assume that it indicates a firm belief that God will accomplish a "new world of justice, healing and hope."[12] In other words, eschatology is the doctrine that centers on the biblical reality of God bringing history forward to complete his purposes. In fact, "God is utterly committed to set the world right in the end."[13] A result of such a view is that "eschatology must serve as the dominant interpretive lens through which Christian teaching must be refracted."[14] Given that God is moving history toward the completion of his goals, all that we do (including Christian teaching, theological education, and proclaiming the gospel) should be lived in consideration of this reality. Throughout his book, James relates eschatological realities to the lives of his readers and urges them toward certain actions.

---

11 Davids, *Theology of James*, 84.

12 Wright, *Surprised by Hope*, 134.

13 Wright, 191.

14 Pardue, "Eschatology," 594.

Mission and Proclamation

When we combine the rhetorical strategies of James, along with his eschatological foci, several missiological implications become apparent, especially in relation to proclamation. This, again, is a model that James is demonstrating. These implications at times have an economic thrust. The readers of James were to continue the prophetic trajectory found in Scripture by speaking "in the name of the Lord" (5:10) against injustice (5:1–6). James thunders "against the oppressive rich of his day," and his words "point ultimately to the Final Judgment."[15] James is speaking on behalf of the poor and the marginalized. The readers of James were also to teach others of sound doctrine regarding salvation (2:14–26) and to avoid erroneous teaching (3:1–2). Although James does not specifically explain the gospel or even mention the death and resurrection of Jesus, an implication is present in light of these two passages (2:14–26; 3:1–2): his readers were to proclaim the gospel. They were also to avoid cursing others (3:9) and slandering their fellow brothers and sisters (4:11). While many observers have highlighted the importance of the tongue/speaking for James, his eschatological warnings give poignancy to this concept of proclamation.[16] Given the exhortations of James, we can conclude that mission includes proclamation. In light of the coming Judge, who will right all wrongs, we are to proclaim the gospel and passionately labor and toil on behalf of the poor and the marginalized.

Tension in Mission

Exhortation and proclamation do not comprise the totality of James's missiological impulses. He strongly advocates faith in action. However, at times, there is a tension in the church that is "torn between emphasizing evangelism and social action."[17] Many assert that proclamation of the gospel needs to be supplemented by social action, given "the pressing needs confronting the church in the here and now."[18] Verbal explanation of the gospel is crucial, but so is "standing against oppression and advocating for the marginalized and voiceless [since that] is at the heart of the message of the good news."[19] For Jon Sobrino, speaking from the context of Latin America, the mission of

---

15 Maynard-Reid, *Poverty and Wealth*, 97.

16 E.g., Pérez Millos, *Comentario exegético*, 163–92; Andria, "James," 1539; Blomberg and Kamell, *James*, 150–66.

17 Jusu, *Africa Study Bible*, 1841.

18 Pardue, "Eschatology," 597; cf. Moore-Keish, *James*, 176; Jusu, *Africa Study Bible*, 1852. Of course, the biblical picture of salvation "shows more concern with the redemption of the whole of creation than with only the salvation of individuals." Kim, "Preface," v.

19 AlKhouri, "Critical Analysis," 181.

the church is to be like "Jesus' own mission," which involved "good news to the poor, evangelism and prophetic denunciation."[20] Christopher J. H. Wright reminds us that the early church (of which James was a part, see Acts 1:14; 12:17; 15:13; 21:18), was a "radically prophetic community" that not only sought "economic equality" but also wedded evangelism with the call to "do good" and "be models of practical love in a world full of hatred."[21]

For James, there is no dichotomy—no "verbal proclamation of the gospel versus social action." He advocates for "genuine faith … demonstrated in action."[22] He is like the Old Testament prophets and Jesus, and he exhibits "no tension between (and indeed weds closely together) orthodoxy and orthopraxy—correct belief and correct behavior."[23] Yosef K. AlKhouri, a Palestinian Christian Arab, admonishes us to have "a theology that is faithful to both orthodoxy and orthopraxy."[24] Mission in James, in light of the eschatological urgency of the coming Judge, involves proclamation of the gospel combined with faith in action. This is not optional for James. We noted James's many strong words, as well as his frequent commands and calls to reflection. James is forthright, resolute, and single-minded: the Judge is coming—we have work to do!

The Poor: Mission as Proclamation and Action

James spoke on behalf of the poor. His strong words throughout his letter are given, in part, because of the incredibly challenging context of the poor and marginalized community. This is a clear and unmistakable emphasis— one that must be met with both proclamation and faith in action. James's preoccupation with the poor is "high on the agenda,"[25] with "poverty and wealth" as an "important theme."[26] The context of his readers involved poverty, suffering, and oppression.[27] The frequency with which James returns

---

20 Sobrino, "La centralidad del 'Reino de Dios,'" 277; quoted in Morales Fredes, "Kingdom of God," 653.

21 Wright, *Mission of God*, 311.

22 Jusu, *Africa Study Bible*, 1841.

23 Blomberg and Kamell, *James*, 35.

24 AlKhouri, "Critical Analysis," 180.

25 Maynard-Reid, *Poverty and Wealth*, 38; We have already mentioned that the "poor" will inherit the kingdom (Jas 2:5).

26 Morales, *Poor and Rich*, 1. Some have supposed that the "poor" in James is a spiritual concept (a "pious poor": this idea is attributed to Martin Dibelius). However, this has "been relegated to a secondary plane" since "socioeconomic" realities are so prevalent in the book. Morales, *Poor and Rich*, 14.

27 Támez, *Scandalous Message*, 7.

to the issue of the rich and poor alerts us to the fact that "socioeconomic disparities were causing problems for his congregations."[28]

Specifically, in the well-known verse 1:27, the visiting of widows and orphans "includes both encouraging conversation and tending to physical needs."[29] In 2:1–4, James mentions the sin of verbal insults, especially to "the poor man" in 2:3, alongside making distinctions (judging others) based only on external circumstances rather than who they really are.[30] This issue of partiality is elaborated in 2:6 ("you have dishonored the poor") as well as 2:12, which involves "the level of conversation and of action."[31] This is emphasized by the phrase "Speak *and* act."[32] Even the famous passage of 2:14–26, which normally engenders furious debate about salvation and justification, demonstrates that "economic need" drives the theology contained in the passage.[33] The pericope is introduced with someone "without clothes and daily food" (2:15).

In 4:12, we again note the piercing question "But … who are you?" This is given in the context of judging others. This judging is often manifested by murmuring and despising others.[34] Although the poor are not mentioned in chapter 4, it is highly likely that slander and judgment against the poor were common occurrences in the first century, as they are today. James 5:1–6 uses "harsh and intense language" about the misery coming upon the rich.[35] James fires off a series of blunt verbal outbursts and proclamations: "weep and wail" (5:1); "Your wealth has rotted" (5:2); "Your gold and silver are corroded. Their corrosion will testify against you and eat your flesh" (5:3); "You have fattened yourselves in the day of slaughter" (5:5). He uses this shocking language in the hope that the poor will receive their wages (5:4). Arthur James points out that the hoarded wealth of the rich "will serve as evidence of their lack of concern for the poor *in the last days*."[36] For Támez, this is "the strongest part of the letter. Just as the rich person, in the case of the landowner, had no mercy on the peasant, neither will James have mercy on the rich; he vents all his just fury."[37]

---

28 Blomberg and Kamell, *James*, 30.

29 Baker, *Personal Speech-Ethics*, 102.

30 Carro, "Santiago," 217–18.

31 Baker, *Personal Speech-Ethics*, 102.

32 "Speak and act as those who are going to be judged by the law that gives freedom" (Jas 2:12).

33 Blomberg and Kamell, *James*, 30.

34 Pérez Millos, *Comentario exegético*, 257.

35 Maynard-Reid, *Poverty and Wealth*, 98.

36 James, "James," 1737, emphasis original. We also mentioned earlier the indifferent actions of the rich (Jas 1:10–11).

37 Támez, *Scandalous Message*, 39.

James speaks passionately on behalf of the poor and the marginalized. He consistently provokes his readers toward reflection. He insists that they not forget the poor and the oppressed. He speaks repeatedly of economic matters. Since we live today in "a world of injustice and inequality," we must acknowledge that economics is "a central category of theology."[38] How we view money cannot be separated from our faith and doctrine. Indeed, because of "the significance of economics," especially in light of globalization, we need "fresh thinking" on how to fulfill mission in today's world.[39] We should consider a "new reading of the Bible based on the perspective of the oppressed."[40] We cannot do everything, but we must do something.[41] As Wright reminds us (speaking of the example of debt remission for poorer countries), "every time we put it off one more day, several hundred children die."[42] The plight of the poor and marginalized is a somber reality. We must not only proclaim the gospel but must combine this message with faith in action. The situation is urgent: "The Judge is standing at the door!" (5:9).

Colonialism and Mission

The current context of the world related to missions is complex and overwhelming in scope. However, for the past two hundred years, in general, a "prevalent reality" is that missions has been "owned and controlled dominantly, if not exclusively, by western churches."[43] Thankfully, there have been many positive results. For example,

> Areas where Protestant missionaries had a significant presence in the past are on average more economically developed today, with comparatively better health, lower infant mortality, lower corruption, greater literacy, higher educational attainment (especially for women), and more robust membership in nongovernmental associations.[44]

A specific example occurred in China. Although the Chinese invented a type of printing press hundreds of years before Gutenberg in AD 1440, the printed

---

38　Carroll R., "Challenge," 207.

39　Carroll R., 200.

40　Barreto, "Protestant Liberation," 206. See Morales Fredes, "Kingdom of God," 649–61, for a helpful combination of the topics of eschatology, the kingdom of God, proclaiming the gospel, and bringing help to those in need.

41　There is truth to Paul's admonition to "to lead a quiet life," and "to mind your own business" (1 Thess 4:11). However, this cannot be at the expense of the poor and marginalized.

42　Wright, *Surprised by Hope*, 229.

43　Kim, "Preface," vii.

44　Robert Woodberry quoted in Dilley, "World the Missionaries Made," 39.

page was considered to be only for the elites in China. However, missionaries arrived in the 1800s and printed thousands of religious books, "making those available to the masses, and teaching women and other marginalized groups how to read."[45] Many more positive stories could be told.

Nonetheless, there is another side. One writer comments that "in most Global South contexts, the growth and expansion of Christianity was largely due to effective Indigenous agency independent of Western influences."[46] More negatively, Andrew M. Mbuvi writes of some African theologians exposing "missionaries' complacency, duplicity, and collusion with the racially and economically motivated European colonizing of Africa."[47] For some, mission was synonymous with colonialism, which stemmed from "a common European expansionist culture that felt itself superior."[48] Less than one hundred years ago the situation was stark: "Eighty-four percent of the world's land mass was under colonial rule as late as the 1930s."[49] For one Christian Filipino author, his country has been among the "most liberated" in the world, with a long history of colonization and then "liberation": first Spain, then the US, then Japan, and finally the US again.[50] In other areas of the South Pacific Ocean, "economic and political powers [were] gained through colonial and imperial history."[51]

Similarly, Christians in Palestine speak of "injustice, occupation, humiliation, insecurity, and displacement."[52] Palestinian theologians lament that their context "continues to be one of occupation and oppression."[53] In parts of Asia, there exist situations of "extreme socioeconomic disparity."[54] This is despite "factors such as globalization, technological advances, and market-oriented reform."[55] Given the military dictatorships in Latin America

---

45 Dilley, "World the Missionaries Made," 41.

46 Tahaafe-Williams, "Oceania Reflective Essay," 777; cf. McLellan, *Messengers of Ethiopia*.

47 Mbuvi, "Christology and *Cultus*," 203.

48 Raheb and Lamport, "Interpretative Challenge," 25.

49 Ramachandra, "Globalization," 215.

50 Fernandez, "Filipino Theology," 319–20.

51 Tahaafe-Williams, "Oceania Reflective Essay," 779.

52 Lodberg, "Palestinian Contextual Theology," 401.

53 Ateek, *Palestinian Christian Cry*, xiii. For a response, see AlKhouri: "As with many liberation theologians, Ateek prioritizes the context more than the Scripture." "Critical Analysis," 179.

54 Cheung and Spurgeon, *James*, 1.

55 Cheung and Spurgeon, 1.

in previous decades, a present concern still centers on the "ubiquitous poverty and systematic injustice," along with "oppressive systems."[56] Although these issues in the Majority World are not all the direct result of mission work, many Majority World authors are sounding the alarm concerning the severe realities of their contexts.

Because of the tragic mixture of missions and colonialism by some, we are now more cognizant of cultural influences on our biblical interpretations and our missiological undertakings. As one Majority World author reminds us: "One's social and cultural milieu and experience affect one's interpretive strategies and theology."[57] It is not possible to "engage with the gospel independent of culture. Our interaction with the gospel relies on human language, worldview, and cultural context."[58] As a reminder of James's rhetorical strategy and emphasis on the tongue, it is undeniable that we "are utterly dependent on human language to speak about the gospel."[59] An author from Botswana writes that biblical interpretation "cannot be separated from politics, economics, and cultural identity, of the past and present."[60] Any discussion on mission in the twenty-first century must acknowledge cultural realities of both the sending ethnicity and the receiving ethnicity.

When discussing the complex and challenging task of engaging in mission in the modern day, we need to ponder and reflect on past missiological endeavors. We should then contemplate the situation of the worldwide church. One observer uses eschatology to paint a pessimistic view of the church today: "If the Lord is coming to take his Bride, we have to do something about this Bride of his. Her state is deplorable. She is dismembered, divided, prostituted, filled with sin, confused, sterile, passive, and defeated to say the least. It is indeed a horrible picture."[61] Not all believers will agree with such a negative stance, nor with how we reached this point, nor whether it relates to colonialism and mission. Nonetheless, we need to listen to those from the Majority World and allow them to lead the missiological undertakings in their own contexts and cultures. The rest of this chapter will offer brief comments on this possibility.

---

56 Morales Fredes, "Kingdom of God," 649.

57 Ho, "From Judeophilia to Ta-Tung," 682.

58 Shenk, "Foreword," 9.

59 Shenk, 9.

60 Dube, "Introduction," 4.

61 Deiros, "Eschatology and Mission," 19–20.

Way Forward: Missions Today by the Majority World

We are witnessing a significant demographic change. In less than thirty years, nearly 75 percent of all Christians will live in Africa, Asia, and Latin America, "and a sizable share of the remainder will have roots in one or more of those continents."[62] Around the same time, in 2050, "only about one-fifth of the world's 3.2 billion Christians will be non-Hispanic whites."[63] Thus, "the phrase 'a white Christian' may sound like a curious oxymoron, as mildly surprising as 'a Swedish Buddhist.'"[64] This "seismic shift" is illustrated by the fact that in 1910 over 80 percent of Christians were living in Europe or North America.[65] Therefore, much of the mission work in the coming decades will be carried out by those from the Majority World. This has numerous advantages, for many Majority World missionaries have already lived missional lives, having "been birthed in suffering and sacrifice. They understand that doing missions involves a high cost."[66] For example, "few missionaries from the West have had the experience of starting new churches while in prison, yet missionaries from Ethiopia to India have had these experiences."[67]

There will be a continued role for the West, however. One Majority World author recognizes the "extensive influence" that the West has had on the worldwide church, "with its wealth, resources, publications, theological institutions, faith-influenced state policies, and grassroots mission activities."[68] The United States sends the most missionaries worldwide and is "still a major player on the world religious stage."[69] Nonetheless, given the reality of globalization, we need to dialogue with Christians worldwide regarding the mission of the church and strive for "global inter-connectedness and interdependence."[70] For example, Ethiopian author Alemayehu Mekonnen calls for Christian leaders (in Africa) to have a "global perspective."[71] All Christians need this perspective. Now is the time to consider the central role that Majority World missionaries will take in the coming decades regarding the mission of the church. Any discussion on mission needs to include this reality.

---

62 Jenkins, *Next Christendom*, xi.

63 Jenkins, 3.

64 Jenkins, 3.

65 Raheb and Lamport, "Interpretative Challenge," 23–24.

66 Plueddemann, "Theological Implications," 258.

67 Plueddemann, 258.

68 Yang, "Afterword," 957; quoted in Tahaafe-Williams, "Oceania Reflective Essay," 779.

69 Tahaafe-Williams, "Oceania Reflective Essay," 779.

70 Stinton, "Koinonia (Fellowship)," 59. This idea of striving for global interconnectedness is taken from the Association of Theological Schools.

71 Mekonnen, "Christian Leadership," 98.

Way Forward: Listening

James admonishes us to be "quick to listen" (1:19). However, many in the West have found it challenging "to shed the false sense of confidence they receive from their cultures and to really listen to their Christian brothers and sisters from less powerful places."[72] At the present moment, "it is the American church that needs most to listen to the theological critique coming to it from the church worldwide."[73] For instance, African cultural ideas can "inform the thought of worldwide Christianity."[74] This is true of any God-created culture and ethnicity.[75] The worldwide church "has an amazing diversity. God willed it that way."[76] Related to our topic in this chapter, Africans can help Westerners conceive of "eschatology not as some far-distant phenomenon but as an aspect of the doctrine of the providence of God in the here and now."[77] We need to consider others in their specific cultural contexts. One specific example describes the process of a Hindu coming to Christ. For Hindus, their concept of "dharma," or duty, is cultural as well as religious.

> It takes time for a Hindu to be completely committed to Christ. It is a process, because it involves living and fulfilling one's dharma to the family, community and sociocultural domain. Culture and religion and social duties are often integrated in Hinduism… . Drastic rejection of all things Indian or Hindu encourages extraction from culture and society, thus eliminating any future impact for Christ.[78]

Thus, it is necessary to listen to those in India for an appropriate missiological strategy for their culture. Also, Westerners can learn to look at Scripture through the perspective of others. Elsa Támez, representing Latin America, reads James "with the eyes of an 'oppressed and believing' people."[79] Considering the history of missions and colonialism, along with the emerging missions of the Majority World, it is imperative for us in the West to listen to our brothers and sisters around the world.

---

72 Meneses, "Bearing Witness," 245–46.

73 Meneses, 246.

74 Kombo, "Past," 626.

75 See Bryan, *Cultural Identity*, for the view that cultural and ethnic identity is a specific purpose of God himself.

76 Deiros, "Eschatology and Mission," 20.

77 Kombo, "Past," 620.

78 Bhattacharya, "Exploring Hindu 'Insider Movements,'" 98.

79 Támez, *Scandalous Message*, 11.

Way Forward: Militant Patience

James states: "Be patient, then, brothers and sisters, until the Lord's coming" (5:7). We have already seen how this pericope contains strong and brutal words against the rich. Yet, with this eschatological reference to the Lord's coming, how were James's readers to be patient, especially "in the face of the injustices that [he] has so sharply condemned"?[80] Is James implying that his readers just "sit back and wait for the Lord to appear and fix everything"?[81] No, James is calling for a "militant patience, that is, a very active and heroic patience, one that watches for the propitious moment."[82] This is also described as a "valiant perseverance."[83] As Martha Moore-Keish reminds us, this is a "tricky balance, since the call to be patient amid suffering has sometimes led to tolerance of evil injustice and oppression, particularly in African American and other minority communities. It can sound like a call simply to accept whatever suffering comes, without protest or resistance."[84] However, this interpretation would misunderstand the content of James's words. He is calling for active patience—or faith in action.[85] We have repeatedly seen James's call to live out the Christian faith. Yet, there is still a limit to what James's readers could do: "God alone is the giver of all good gifts (1:17). God alone is the source of wisdom (1:5). God alone is the judge and lawgiver (4:12)."[86]

Way Forward: Speaking Prophetically

Listening to others in the Majority World will challenge us to speak boldly against injustice and exploitation. Just as James fearlessly confronts the rich in 5:1–6, and brazenly labels his readers as "adulterous people" (4:4) and "double-minded" (4:8), so also today's believers should speak prophetically. For one Majority World author from Oceania, this includes anger. For her, "anger is a theologically under-explored and undervalued concept" because of "the culture of niceness in the church [that] is so pervasive that often it gets in the way of doing what is right or in keeping and maintaining a high level of accountability."[87] In the midst of discrimination and injustice in her

---

80 Moore-Keish, *James*, 176.

81 Moore-Keish, 176.

82 Támez, *Scandalous Message*, 43.

83 Támez, 44.

84 Moore-Keish, *James*, 177.

85 Moore-Keish, 177.

86 Moore-Keish, 177.

87 Tahaafe-Williams, "Oceania Reflective Essay," 784.

context, she admits that the "prophets of the Hebrew Bible always speak in prophetic anger—sometimes their words are quite harsh that I often feel my anger pales in comparison."[88] She does caution, however, that with "a theology of anger," we need to "be aware of our own biases, social locations, privileges, and complicities."[89] Finally, N. T. Wright reminds us that there are many things in this world that are evil and need to be condemned. We cannot tolerate the diabolical chaos we see in many parts of the world. Far from colluding with wickedness, we must stand for justice and prophetically denounce that which is evil.[90] By doing this, we will be following in the footsteps of James.

Conclusion

We have seen the rhetorical strategy of exhortation used by James to cause his readers to reflect. Mission today requires much reflection and dialogue, as well as an imitation of the prophetic model that James demonstrates throughout his book. We noted several eschatological echoes in James, along with its resultant urgency. Concerning the tension of "evangelism versus social action," we concluded that James would not support such a dichotomy but would passionately promote both. He would speak the loudest, perhaps, in the defense of the poor and marginalized. Again, we simply cannot forget the poor. We need to see that "biblical eschatology should push Christians to greater engagement with this-worldly realities in light of God's desire to renew all things."[91] Mission in the twenty-first century will, by and large, be carried out by Majority World Christians. Granted that there have been mistakes and short-sightedness in missions in the past, listening will need to be an increasingly important element within missiology. At the same time, a declaration of the gospel, a prophetic denunciation of evil and injustice, as well as a militant patience and faith in action will be essential. In light of the coming of the Judge who will right all wrongs, we are to unite with the entire worldwide church, proclaim the gospel, live out our faith, and passionately labor and toil on behalf of the poor and marginalized.

---

88 Tahaafe-Williams, 785. See, for example, Jer 16:1–4.
89 Tahaafe-Williams, 787.
90 See Wright, *Surprised by Hope*, 191.
91 Pardue, "Eschatology," 596.

Bibliography

AlKhouri, Yousef K. "A Critical Analysis of Naim Ateek's Palestinian Liberation Theology." In *Majority World Theologies: Theologizing from Africa, Asia, Latin America, and the Ends of the Earth*, edited by Allen Yeh and Tite Tiénou, 173–83. Evangelical Missiological Society Series 26. Littleton, CO: William Carey Publishing, 2018.

Andria, Solomon. "James." In *Africa Bible Commentary: A One-Volume Commentary Written by 70 African Scholars*, edited by Tokunboh Adeyemo, 1535–42. Grand Rapids: Zondervan, 2006.

Ateek, Naim Stifan. *A Palestinian Christian Cry for Reconciliation*. Maryknoll, NY: Orbis Books, 2008.

Baker, William R. *Personal Speech-Ethics in the Epistle of James*. Tübingen: Mohr Siebeck, 1994.

Barreto, Raimundo C., Jr. "Protestant Liberation Theologies." In *Emerging Theologies from the Global South*, edited by Mitri Raheb and Mark A. Lamport, 203–23. Eugene, OR: Cascade, 2023.

Bhattacharya, Natun. "Exploring Hindu 'Insider Movements': Syncretism or Authentic Contextualization? A Theological and Missiological Appraisal with a Fresh Approach." In *Majority World Theologies: Theologizing from Africa, Asia, Latin America, and the Ends of the Earth*, edited by Allen Yeh and Tite Tiénou, 89–100. Evangelical Missiological Society Series 26. Littleton, CO: William Carey Publishing, 2018.

Blomberg, Craig L., and Mariam J. Kamell. *James*. Zondervan Exegetical Commentary on the New Testament 16. Grand Rapids: Zondervan, 2008.

Bryan, Steven M. *Cultural Identity and the Purposes of God: A Biblical Theology of Ethnicity, Nationality, and Race*. Wheaton: Crossway, 2022.

Carro, Daniel. "Santiago." In *Hebreos, Santiago, 1 y 2 Pedro, Judas*, edited by Juan Carlos Cevallos, 175–302. Vol. 23 of *Comentario Bíblico Mundo Hispano*. El Paso: Editorial Mundo Hispano, 2006.

Carroll R., M. Daniel. "The Challenge of Economic Globalization for Theology: From Latin America to a Hermeneutics of Responsibility." In *Globalizing Theology: Belief and Practice in an Era of World Christianity*, edited by Craig Ott and Harold A. Netland, 199–212. Grand Rapids: Baker Academic, 2006.

Cheung, Luke L., and Andrew B. Spurgeon. *James: A Pastoral and Contextual Commentary*. Asia Bible Commentary. Cumbria: Langham, 2018.

Coker, K. Jason. "Nativism in James 2.14–26: A Post-Colonial Reading." In *Reading James with New Eyes: Methodological Reassessments of the Letter of James*, edited by Robert L. Webb and John S. Kloppenborg, 27–48. London: T&T Clark, 2007.

Davids, Peter H. *The Epistle of James: A Commentary on the Greek Text*. New International Greek Testament Commentary. Grand Rapids: Eerdmans, 1982.

Davids, Peter H. *A Theology of James, Peter, and Jude: Living in Light of the Coming King*. Biblical Theology of the New Testament. Grand Rapids: Zondervan, 2014.

Deiros, Pablo A. "Eschatology and Mission: A Latin American Perspective." *Mission Frontiers* 37, no. 6 (2015): 18–21.

Dilley, Andrea Palpant. "The World the Missionaries Made." *Christianity Today* 58, no. 1 (Jan/Feb 2014): 35–41.

Dube, Musa W. "Introduction." In *Postcolonial Perspectives in African Biblical Interpretations*, edited by Musa W. Dube, Andrew M. Mbuvi, and Dora R. Mbuwayesango, 1–10. Atlanta: Society of Biblical Literature, 2012.

Fernandez, Eleazar S. "Filipino Theology." In *Emerging Theologies from the Global South*, edited by Mitri Raheb and Mark A. Lamport, 316–35. Eugene, OR: Cascade, 2023.

Ho, Shirley S. "From Judeophilia to Ta-Tung in Taiwanese Eschatology." In *Majority World Theology: Christian Doctrine in Global Context*, edited by Gene L. Green, Stephen T. Pardue, and K. K. Yeo, 677–90. Downers Grove, IL: IVP Academic, 2020.

James, Arthur. "James." In *South Asia Bible Commentary: A One-Volume Commentary on the Whole Bible*, edited by Brian Wintle, 1732–38. Rajasthan: Open Door Publications, 2015.

Jenkins, Philip. *The Next Christendom: The Coming of Global Christianity*. 3rd ed. Oxford: Oxford University Press, 2011.

Jusu, John, ed. *Africa Study Bible*. N.p.: Oasis International, 2016.

Kim, Caleb Chul-Soo. "Preface." In *African Missiology: Contributions of Contemporary Thought*, edited by Stephen Mutuku Sesi, Henry Mutua, Alemayehu Mekonnen, Steven Rasmussen, Mark Shaw, Josephine Mutuku Sesi, and Caleb Chul-Soo Kim, v–xi. Nairobi: Uzima, 2009.

Kombo, James Henry Owino. "The Past, the Present, and the Future of African Christianity: An Eschatological Vision for African Christianity." In *Majority World Theology: Christian Doctrine in Global Context*, edited by Gene L. Green, Stephen T. Pardue, and K. K. Yeo, 615–26. Downers Grove, IL: IVP Academic, 2020.

Lodberg, Peter. "Palestinian Contextual Theology." In *Emerging Theologies from the Global South*, edited by Mitri Raheb and Mark A. Lamport, 401–21. Eugene, OR: Cascade, 2023.

Maynard-Reid, Pedrito U. *Poverty and Wealth in James*. Maryknoll, NY: Orbis Books, 2004.

Mbuvi, Andrew M. "Christology and *Cultus* in 1 Peter: An African (Kenyan) Appraisal." In *Majority World Theology: Christian Doctrine in Global Context*, edited by Gene L. Green, Stephen T. Pardue, and K. K. Yeo, 200–12. Downers Grove, IL: IVP Academic, 2020.

McKnight, Scot. *The Letter of James*. New International Commentary on the New Testament. Grand Rapids: Eerdmans, 2011.

McLellan, Dick. *Messengers of Ethiopia*. UK: Lost Coin Books, 2013.

Mekonnen, Alemayehu. "Christian Leadership in Africa: Effectively Challenging Cultural Contexts." In *African Missiology: Contributions of Contemporary Thought*, edited by Stephen Mutuku Sesi, Henry Mutua, Alemayehu Mekonnen, Steven Rasmussen, Mark Shaw, Josephine Mutuku Sesi, and Caleb Chul-Soo Kim, 74–103. Nairobi: Uzima, 2009.

Meneses, Eloise Hiebert. "Bearing Witness in Rome with Theology from the Whole Church: Globalization, Theology, and Nationalism." In *Globalizing Theology: Belief and Practice in an Era of World Christianity*, edited by Craig Ott and Harold A. Netland, 231–49. Grand Rapids: Baker Academic, 2006.

Moore-Keish, Martha. *James*. Belief: A Theological Commentary on the Bible, edited by Amy Plantinga Pauw and William C. Placher. Louisville: Westminster John Knox, 2019.

Morales Fredes, Nelson R. "The Kingdom of God: Latin American Biblical Reflections on Eschatology." In *Majority World Theology: Christian Doctrine in Global Context*, edited by Gene L. Green, Stephen T. Pardue, and K. K. Yeo, 649–61. Downers Grove, IL: IVP Academic, 2020.

Morales, Nelson R. *Poor and Rich in James: A Relevance Theory Approach to James's Use of the Old Testament*. Bulletin for Biblical Research Supplement 20. University Park, PA: Eisenbrauns, 2018.

Pardue, Stephen T. "Eschatology in the Majority World." In *Majority World Theology: Christian Doctrine in Global Context*, edited by Gene L. Green, Stephen T. Pardue, and K. K. Yeo, 593–98. Downers Grove, IL: IVP Academic, 2020.

Pérez Millos, Samuel. *Comentario exegético al texto griego del Nuevo Testamento: Santiago*. Barcelona: CLIE, 2011.

Plueddemann, James E. "Theological Implications of Globalizing Missions." In *Globalizing Theology: Belief and Practice in an Era of World Christianity*, edited by Craig Ott and Harold A. Netland, 250–66. Grand Rapids: Baker Academic, 2006.

Raheb, Mitri. *Decolonizing Palestine: The Land, The People, The Bible*. Maryknoll, NY: Orbis Books, 2023.

Raheb, Mitri, and Mark A. Lamport. "The Interpretative Challenge for Grace and Peace in the Global South: A Hermeneutical Perspective." In *Emerging Theologies from the Global South*, edited by Mitri Raheb and Mark A. Lamport, 22–40. Eugene, OR: Cascade, 2023.

Ramachandra, Vinoth. "Globalization, Nationalism, and Religious Resurgence." In *Globalizing Theology: Belief and Practice in an Era of World Christianity*, edited by Craig Ott and Harold A. Netland, 213–30. Grand Rapids: Baker Academic, 2006.

Shenk, Wilbert R. "Foreword." In *Globalizing Theology: Belief and Practice in an Era of World Christianity*, edited by Craig Ott and Harold A. Netland, 9–11. Grand Rapids: Baker Academic, 2006.

Sobrino, Jon. "La centralidad del 'Reino de Dios' en la Teología de la Liberación." *Revista Latinoamericana de Teología* 3, no. 9 (1986): 247–81.

Stinton, Diane. "Koinonia (Fellowship) around the Mwaki (Fireplace): Reflections on Twenty-First Century Global Theological Education." In *Majority World Theologies: Theologizing from Africa, Asia, Latin America, and the Ends of the Earth*, edited by Allen Yeh and Tite Tiénou, 58–74. Evangelical Missiological Society Series 26. Littleton, CO: William Carey Publishing, 2018.

Tahaafe-Williams, Katalina. "Oceania Reflective Essay: Theology of Prophetic Anger." In *Emerging Theologies from the Global South*, edited by Mitri Raheb and Mark A. Lamport, 776–90. Eugene, OR: Cascade, 2023.

Támez, Elsa. *The Scandalous Message of James: Faith without Works Is Dead*. Rev. ed. New York: Crossroad, 2002.

Wright, Christopher J. H. *The Mission of God: Unlocking the Bible's Grand Narrative*. Downers Grove, IL: InterVarsity Press, 2006.

Wright, Tom. *Surprised by Hope*. London: SPCK, 2007.

Yang, Fenggang. "Afterword." In *Encyclopedia of Christianity in the Global South*, edited by Mark A. Lamport, 957–58. Lanham, MD: Rowman & Littlefield, 2018.

Chapter 6

The Poor at the Heart of the Mission

A Call to the Church to Align with God's Mission

Nelson R. Morales Fredes

> God's mission can become the church's mission only if the
> church obeys the King and follows him in his mission.[1]
> —Vladimir Ubeivolc

What is God's mission? The answer to this question has been the subject of a long-running discussion.[2] There is still no complete agreement. Some authors argue that the concept of *missio Dei* is unnecessary and dangerous because it tends to blur the mission of the church. For example, Keith Ferdinando views the mission of God as a redemptive mission; thus, the mission of the church is to make disciples of Christ. After analyzing the development of the concept of *missio Dei*, he concludes: "There is a tendency for mission in the disciple-making sense to be eclipsed, even swallowed up, by other concerns, and that tendency is enhanced if it is seen as simply one 'missional' responsibility among many others."[3] Other authors tend to equate *missio Dei* with the proclamation of the gospel and with making disciples, the classic way of seeing the church's mission.[4] Still others tend to reduce *missio Dei* to social action.[5]

---

1 Ubeivolc, *Rethinking Missio Dei*, 193.

2 I highly recommend the summary of the development of the concept and its tensions in Tsvirinko, *Context and Contextuality*, 13–48.

3 Ferdinando, "Mission: A Problem," 59.

4 For example, David Ruiz—an important Latin American missiologist—even though he uses the idea of "missional church," quotes the *Cape Town Commitment*, and mentions integral mission, his main focus continues to be evangelization and making disciples. *El diseño misional de Dios*. Something similar happens with the work of Myanmar missiologist Peter Nyunt. He points out, "It [mission] is spelled out as the participation of the church in the *missio Dei* to communicate his work in reconciling sinful humankind to himself." Even though he recognizes the concept, Nyunt reduces *missio Dei* to reconciliation and the church's mission to evangelism. *Missions amidst Pagodas*, 1.

5 The so-called social gospel was criticized for placing most of its focus on achieving social justice. See the occasional paper on "Evangelism and Social Responsibility: An Evangelical Commitment," https://lausanne.org/occasional-paper/lop-21, accessed on July 8, 2024.

Nevertheless, there is a significant consensus around the concept of *missio Dei* that may help us better understand what is happening in James. Missiologists agree that the concept of *missio Dei* depicts the acting of God on the redemption of his creation, human beings included. This chapter contends that in order to be faithful to God, the mission of the church must be completely aligned with the *missio Dei*. In that vein, this chapter demonstrates that, in James's epistle, the poor have a prominent place in the *missio Dei*. God's heart is explicitly revealed. He has chosen the poor to be rich in faith and heirs of his kingdom (Jas 2:5). Therefore, the church is called to include the poor in her mission.[6]

Missio Dei and *Missio Ecclesiae*

W. Rodman MacIlvaine III points out that even though the concept of mission of God seems to have been used as early as 1839, Karl Barth coined the phrase *actio Dei* in 1932, and in 1933 Karl Hartenstein transformed the phrase into *missio Dei* to describe that "from eternity past the triune God has been on a mission."[7] However, as MacIlvaine explains, it is in the work of Georg Vicedom in the International Missionary Council in Willingen, Germany, 1952, that the concept crystallizes.[8] In the words of Vyacheslav Tsvirinko, "The classical doctrine of [the] Trinity means God the Father sending the Son, and God the Father and the Son sending the Spirit. The idea of *missio Dei* includes one more sending action: Father, Son, and Holy Spirit are sending the church into the world."[9] According to this definition, *missio Dei* and *missio ecclesiae* are intimately related. The mission is a work of God, not of the church. Nevertheless, the church becomes "a vehicle for implementing God's mission in this world."[10]

The debate during the rest of the twentieth century revolved around the content of the *missio Dei* and its implications for the church and her mission

---

6 Joubert has a slightly different take on mission and the missional church. He focuses more on the concept of faith in James. However, he arrives at similar conclusions to those I express here. "*Homo Reciprocus* No More," 382–400. Similarly, Brazilian missiologist Paulo Suess explores the topic of the poor in the *missio Dei* but focuses on the Gospels. "*Missio Dei* and the Project of Jesus," 550–59.

7 MacIlvaine, "What Is the Missional Church," 96.

8 MacIlvaine, 96.

9 Tsvirinko, *Context and Contextuality*, 18.

10 Tsvirinko, 17.

in the world.[11] Nevertheless, a consensus is growing on the importance of the concept of *missio Dei*, particularly among those related to the Lausanne Movement. Several definitions have been proposed.[12] Among them, Christopher J. H. Wright's *The Mission of God* has become an important reference. He understands *missio Dei* as "to restore creation to its full original purpose of bringing all glory to God himself and thereby all creation to enjoy the fullness of blessings that he desires for it."[13] This is a robust biblical-theological definition of *missio Dei* that includes not only humanity but also the whole creation. From this definition, a *missio ecclesiae* could be derived. Wright adds, "Fundamentally, our mission … means our committed participation as God's people, at God's invitation and command, in God's own mission within the history of God's world for the redemption of God's creation."[14] This mission implies the manifestation of God's compassion. As Sharron George highlights, "Mission is the incarnation of the profound and tender mercy, justice, and compassion of God for humanity in human history."[15]

The church, as God's people, is sent by him into the world to be part of God's mission. Thus, she has to be aligned with God's mission in order to fulfill her mission. Again, I mention the pertinent words of Sharron George. She says:

> Mission emerges from God's entrails and affects ours; from the inner being of a God who feels, loves, suffers, weeps. We do mission because we experience God's passion for the world and share the passion. We feel the pain, the needs and the injustices of humanity and respond in love.[16]

The Lausanne Movement presents a good summary of the mission of the church in its *Cape Town Commitment*:

> We commit ourselves to the integral and dynamic exercise of all dimensions of mission to which God calls his Church.

---

11 Tsvirinko presents an updated summary of the debate and concerns about *missio Dei* (22–28). Other approaches to the relationship between *missio Dei* and *missio ecclesiae* take this debate into account and propose a *missio ecclesiae* with a more secular focus. See Baik, "Critical Analysis," 329–40; and Youn, "*Missio Dei Trinitatis*," 225–39.

12 For a good summary of the concept of *missio Dei* and the church's mission among evangelical theologians, see Ubeivolc, *Rethinking Missio Dei*, 113–39.

13 Wright, *Mission of God*, 188.

14 Wright, 22–23.

15 George, "Constructing Latin American Missiology," 56.

16 George, 57.

> God commands us to make known to all nations the truth of God's revelation and the gospel of God's saving grace through Jesus Christ, calling all people to repentance, faith, baptism and obedient discipleship.
>
> God commands us to reflect his own character through compassionate care for the needy, and to demonstrate the values and the power of the kingdom of God in striving for justice and peace and in caring for God's creation.[17]

This declaration excellently describes what has been a permanent concern for Latin American churches. It conforms with the concept of *misión integral* (holistic mission). Recently, Guatemalan theologian and missiologist Israel Ortiz defined holistic mission in a manner that reflects the concept well and helps to advance the argument of this chapter. He says that holistic mission

> is the proclamation of the gospel of the kingdom of God through words and the demonstration of the gospel through good deeds, in favor of the integral transformation of the being and doing of all people in all the spheres of human life and in the context of society in general.[18]

As the *Cape Town Commitment* points out, the church's mission should include compassionate care for the needy. However, either care is absent or done paternalistically. For that reason, Samuel Escobar believes that when working in a holistic mission, "by applying biblical principles of reciprocity, solidarity and mutuality, poor Christians will be empowered to become agents of their own liberation and not passive recipients of a handout."[19]

Samuel Escobar and Eduardo Delás, reflecting on James, say: "The church is sent on a mission from the commitment on a way already walked by Jesus, which is to be walked in a communal way, through the power of the risen Jesus who sent the Spirit, through a living faith which is accredited by works."[20] But how can we be sure that our local church has the correct focus? Is our mission as a particular church aligned with God's mission? The next section studies the situation in James and gleans several principles to help us examine our practice and determine to what extent our mission is aligned with God's mission regarding the poor.

---

17 Birdsall and Brown, *Cape Town Commitment*, 47.

18 Israel Ortiz, email message to author, October 21, 2023, my translation. Ortiz, director of the Ezra Center (Centro Esdras), is a renowned Guatemalan thinker of *misión integral*.

19 Escobar, *New Global Mission*, 148.

20 Escobar and Delás, *Santiago*, 7, my translation.

The Poor in the *Missio Dei* as Presented in James

A key statement in James is 2:5, "Listen to me, dear brothers and sisters. Hasn't God chosen the poor in this world to be rich in faith? Aren't they the ones who will inherit the Kingdom he promised to those who love him?"[21] The apostle makes it clear that God has made a decision regarding the poor. The expression of our faith in Jesus should be consistent with God's decision. God has chosen the poor from the perspective of the world to be rich in the sphere of faith and heirs of the kingdom he promised to those who love him. In order to better appreciate the theological impact of these words and how the church should align her mission with God's, the theme is presented throughout the letter.

Before proceeding to an analysis of the texts, a rhetorical note is necessary. In the letter, from a socioeconomic perspective, three types of readers are perceived. There is a group of addressees who are poor. James mentions a humble brother (1:9), a brother or sister under the subsistence line (2:15), and impoverished laborers in the fields of the unjust rich (5:4). Also, there are a few merchants (4:13) and some rich individuals (1:10–11). The main group is neither poor nor rich. They are looking for patronage, discriminating against the poor, and being insensitive toward the needs of the poor. They are called to visit the widows and orphans and have a consistent faith (1:27–2:17). Each group experiences the letter in different ways. The poor are offered consolation and hope. The rich are called to repentance. The rest of the community is exhorted to align themselves with God's will. This literary characteristic of the letter helps modern readers approach it, paying attention to its rhetorical impact and the variety of illocutionary effects on the readers.[22]

The Reversal of Fortunes (1:9–11)

Of the five mentions of the poor in James, the first is in the introduction. In 1:9–11, James contrasts two perspectives of life now in light of the future. In the midst of suffering, trials, and a need for wisdom (1:2–8), James introduces a socioeconomic contrast. Both the poor and rich are challenged to think about their future and live in light of it. The lowly brother should boast in his exaltation. God will come and bring the great reversal of vindication

---

21 Unless otherwise noted, all Scripture quotations are from the NLT.

22 For more details on these rhetorical effects on the primary audience and an analysis of each passage addressed in this chapter, see Morales, *Poor and Rich*, 74–226.

of the oppressed and the punishment of the impious (5:7–11).[23] God will give the poor the honor that the world has denied them. In light of that promise, they should face their circumstances with hope. At the same time, the rich should change their attitudes toward wealth and their treatment of others, taking into account the judgment that they are beginning to experience (1:10–11).[24] The rest of the congregation should take note of these words. As Sharon H. Ringe remarks, "At the end of the day, wealth is a false repository of trust."[25] Later in the letter, it is apparent that the community has lost its focus. Instead of caring for the poor and honoring them, they are looking for patronage from the rich and discriminating against the poor.

In 1:9–11, it is clear that the culmination of salvation history reveals that the *missio Dei* includes the exaltation of the poor. The believing poor have a hope that permits them to face trials.[26] The community should align itself with that value in its treatment of the poor and be a place where poor Christians can find refuge.

True Religion (1:27)
A second insight into the poor's importance in the *missio Dei* appears in 1:27. In 1:26–27, James expresses what includes holistic worship of God. In order to be genuine worshipers, people should have control of their speech; otherwise, they deceive themselves (v. 26). Furthermore, pure and undefiled worship of God the Father includes visiting orphans and widows in their afflictions (v. 27). As I mentioned elsewhere, "God is the protector of the widows and orphans (Deut 10:17–18; 24:19–21; Pss 68:5; 94:3–7; 146:9; Prov 15:25). So his people must follow his example (Exod 22:21; Deut 16:14; 24:17–21; 26:12–13; 27:19)."[27]

23　For a well-documented summary of the reversal motif in James 1:9–11, see Krüger, "El vuelco irritante y definitivo," 45–77.

24　For a relevant discussion on the ironic language of James 1:10–11 and the condemnation of the rich, see Allison, *James*, 203–13. Douglas Moo insists that this rich person is a believer and he should remember that "in your humble status as a person who identifies with one who was 'despised and rejected' by the world." *Letter of James*, 91. However, he does not take into account that humiliation, in particular in this text, implies punishment. The humiliation is something done by God, not by the rich himself. Also, sadly, the cases of rich Christians acting unjustly, in the way James criticizes in his letter, are more frequent than one would think.

25　Ringe, "Letter of James," 373.

26　Kirk J. Franklin says: "Since the triune God is the perfect embodiment of hope, and the originator and source of mission, he calls and enables his people to be a community of the witness of his hope." *Toward Global Missional Leadership*, 43. Clearly, we are called to bring hope to those without hope, the needy in particular.

27　Morales, *Poor and Rich*, 106–7.

There is an implied connection between James 1:9 and 27. In the Old Testament, God is frequently presented as the redeemer of the poor. He will finally exalt them into a position of honor. The church is called to bring them some of that comfort now by visiting them amid the vulnerability in which they currently live.[28] As Robert W. Wall says, "The community's practices of caring for the poor and powerless anticipate the inevitable reversal of their fortunes in the coming Jubilee."[29] In that sense, James calls for worship that takes the welfare of the poor seriously. In order to obey God, the church should align her mission with God's mission of caring for the needy.[30]

At this point in the letter, James has described the place that the poor have in God's heart and the implications for the mission of the church. In 1:9, the eschatological goal paves the way for the poor to have hope and guides the church in the role that the poor should have in her mission. In 1:27, it is clear that the poor are important to God. In order to be pleasing to God, our worship and, as an implication, our mission as a church should include visiting the vulnerable in their afflictions. The next three occurrences of the poor in James show three risks in the church implementing her mission due to a lack of clarity about the *missio Dei*.

True Faith Concretely Expressed (2:1–6, 14–17)
The third and fourth mentions of the poor reveal a loss of alignment with God's mission due to problems inside the community. The third reference is in the context of discrimination against them (2:1–6). Through a hypothetical situation, James unmasks a deep problem in the community (vv. 1–4). He denounces two incongruencies of their faith in Jesus, expressed by their conduct. They are discriminating against the poor and looking for patronage from the rich.[31] With that treatment toward the poor, they have become judges with evil thoughts (v. 4) and have dishonored the poor (v. 6). James highlights the problem by presenting the place the poor have in the *missio Dei*. Through a rhetorical question requiring a positive answer, he appeals to Jesus's teachings to reinforce his argument: "Listen, my dear brothers and sisters, has not God chosen the poor in the eye of the world to be rich in faith

---

28　The idea of "visiting" is not just helping the widows and orphans. It implies presence, emotional involvement, care for, and sincere interest in their situation.

29　Wall, *Community of the Wise*, 101.

30　For an insightful exposition of the church's responsibility for the needy, see Kamell, "James 1:27 and the Church's Call," 15–22; and Krüger, "Una definición muy peculiar de religión según Santiago 1:27," 79–91.

31　The insightful work of Vyhmeister sheds light on this issue of patronage behind the attitude described by James. "Rich Man in James 2," 265–83.

and inheritors of the kingdom, which he promised to those who love him?" (v. 5; cf. Luke 6:20).[32] Thus, "instead of aligning with Jesus's perspective, with their attitude of discrimination against the poor, they dishonor the poor and disobey Jesus. Instead of honoring those whom God honors, they are looking for patrons in the wrong place."[33]

When the apostle Paul began his ministry to the gentiles, James and two other pillars asked him to remember the poor (Gal 2:9). Now, James is doing the same to this community. God's mission, as Wright phrases it, "is to restore creation to its full original purpose of bringing all glory to God himself and thereby to enable all creation to enjoy the fullness of blessing that he desires for it."[34] This mission impacts the mission of the people of God. It continues from the Old Testament to the New Testament. For that reason, Wright argues, "There is no hint at all [in the New Testament] that the ubiquitous message of the Old Testament about social and economic justice, about personal and political integrity, about practical compassion for the needy are in any sense provisional or dispensable."[35] James makes this concern for the poor clear. God has chosen the poor to be part of his kingdom and his blessings. For that reason, the mission of the people of God should be aligned with God's mission. James criticizes them for doing the opposite of God's mission. Their communal meeting is worthless because of their attitudes toward the poor. In order to align her mission with God's, the church should examine her treatment of the poor inside and outside her community and make the due corrections. The church should give dignity to the needy.

The fourth mention of the poor is in the context of the community's insensitivity to those in need (2:14–17). James emphasizes that a true faith in Jesus is a faith that works. He insists that a faith without works is dead in itself (v. 17). As an example, he describes a poor brother or sister in deep need, but the community lacks sensitivity.[36] This blindness is expressed by them saying "go in peace, be warm and be filled" but not providing the things needed for the body (v. 16, NASB). The precarious situation is so patent that

---

32 My own translation.

33 Morales, *Poor and Rich*, 148.

34 Wright, *Mission of God*, 188.

35 Wright, 305.

36 Luke Cheung observes that these women could be widows or abandoned women. He also emphasizes: "As believers in Christ, we are to obey the royal law and provide the necessities of life to those who need them. Our faith should drive us to action without demanding anything in return, not even gratitude." Cheung and Spurgeon, *James*, 55.

no word is needed. However, the community does not see the situation.[37] This lack of sensitivity is a symptom of a weak faith, an immature faith, or, in other words, a loss of alignment between the mission of that church and the mission of God. The church should provide mechanisms of protection and care for the needy.

Abuse and Lack of Sensitivity Condemned (5:1–6)
The final mention of the poor is the open condemnation of the unjust rich who are abusing the poor (5:1–6). Unlike 2:1–6 and 14–17, here the problem seems to occur outside the Christian community, but it has an impact on it.[38] James pronounces a severe prophetic judgment. The scene includes witnesses against the rich and God as the judge who dictates the sentence. The witnesses against the rich include the wages of the laborers who worked in the fields of the rich (5:4a), which the rich have held back—"by fraud" the ESV infers. The cries of the harvesters have reached the ears of the Lord of hosts (5:4b). In this case, the withholding of salaries provokes this poverty, or at least aggravates it. The rich are condemned because of this abuse and lack of sensitivity toward their workers, as well as the indulgent use and accumulation of their wealth.

The recipients of the letter would hear this with different ears. The poor would hear this pronouncement with hope and consolation.[39] God has heard their cries, and James's words translate their impotence in the face of such an abuse into a message of God's holy vindication. The rich would hear these words with fear of what God was about to do to these wicked rich, preventing them from following the same evil practices. The rest of the congregation would hear this proclamation as a warning against their wrong attitudes.

37　The expression Τί τὸ ὄφελος (2:14, 16) has the sense of "What difference does it make?" Johnson, *Letter of James*, 237. There is no sense in saying that one has faith if there is no concrete evidence of that faith in the daily life of the church.

38　There is a substantial consensus among studies on James that these landowners in 5:1–6 are unbelievers. If this is the case, the described situation occurs outside the church, but it has a direct impact on her because some of her poor members are suffering the retention of their salaries. Sadly, as Byron states, "This systemic crisis of inequitable wages is also a point of contention for many African Americans and other ethnic minorities who still live in impoverished conditions in both urban and rural settings. This passage is a warning and a summons to all who participate in the personal and systemic economic crisis that is plaguing the world today." "James," 469. This situation includes Christian business owners.

39　Martin says that "the speech is intended to serve as an encouragement to his Christian brethren (1:1–2) who have suffered at the hands of the rich (5:6)." *James*, 173. However, the poor are not the only members of the community who hear the letter read out loud. The other two groups of believers would hear these words in a different manner.

Even though the Christian laborers are present here, the rest of the church is not mentioned in the paragraph. However, in light of chapter 2, it could be inferred that the rest of the church seems to keep a complicit silence. James exhorts them instead to be steadfast until the coming of the Lord, like the farmer, and not grumble against one another (5:7, 9). One could speculate that part of the problem in this community is that it has been looking for patronage with this type of wicked rich person. In so doing, they have turned a blind eye to the situation of some of their members. Instead of adopting this attitude, they should, at the very least, visit them and provide food and clothing.

These Examples as Indicators of the Alignment between *Missio Dei* and *Missio Ecclesiae*

It has been argued that, for the church to fulfill her mission, she must align herself with God's mission. Additionally, the examples from James show that the poor are an important part of God's mission. Thus, the church is called to examine her attitudes and commitments toward the needy to align with God's mission. To that end, this section presents five questions that arise from this study, which the church should consider to see how aligned her mission is with God's regarding the poor.

First, to what extent does the church recognize the eschatological status of the Christian poor? James 1:9 and 2:5 explicitly reveal that God has shown his love for those in need. He brings them honor now and in the future. For that reason, the church is called to give them the honor God has given them. In that way, the church aligns her mission with God's mission. This honor could be expressed through projects that give them dignity—spaces of full inclusion in the congregation that give them a real perception of being part of it and not just invited for the occasion.

Second, does the church recognize that complete worship of God includes visiting the needy in their affliction? Today the church could encourage spaces for caring for the needy, promote the creation of employment or entrepreneurship among them, or drive educational initiatives that enable the orphans or at-risk kids to be better positioned to face life.

Third, to what extent does the church eradicate attitudes of discrimination against the poor among believers? The manifestation of discrimination could be subtle, and so it is hard to detect and eradicate. Having social activities in churches is no indication of the absence of discrimination.[40] These activities could be done paternalistically so that those who are supposed to be helped still feel denigrated. For that reason, it is important to monitor our attitudes and take concrete actions to help build a nondiscriminatory community.

Fourth, is the church sensitive to the needs of the poor, and does it provide for them? In the Global South, poverty rates are high. It is common to see people asking for money at every streetlight. Thus, the community of believers can easily become insensitive to that reality due to overexposure to the patent poverty and abuse by people who deceive to get money or support from churches, Christian organizations, or individuals. However, the church should be aware or recognize that a mature faith is expressed in that sensitivity, in particular for those in need within the community. Institutions like Feed the Hungry or Compassion are good examples of this type of wise work.

Fifth, is the church aware of any circumstances of abuse that could affect those in need? The strength of a community could be a protective shield for those who suffer injustice. A ministry such as the International Justice Mission is a good example of how this is possible. Also, foster care houses are a more recent way that churches in the Global South are caring for children who are being abused. Sometimes, good advice can help workers move from one precarious place to another with better conditions. The church must be attentive to the situation of the community.

Conclusion

The *missio Dei* is still in effect. God is working to restore creation, including the holistic salvation of human beings. He has invited his church to participate in his mission. This chapter demonstrates that in order to fulfill the *missio ecclesiae*, it is necessary for the church to be aligned with God's mission. In this mission, the poor have an important place. God has chosen the poor to be heirs of his kingdom. Thus, the church has to include them in her mission.

This study in James provides some insight into the matter. Five indicators emerge from the analysis, showing us that since God has given the poor dignity, the church should do the same. Discrimination against the poor

---

40 Commenting on the involvement of the wealthy within Black American churches, Byron says: "The *plousioi* within African American communities often acknowledge their responsibility to support or reach out to the *penêtoi* and *ptöchoi*, but usually this is done through charitable 'politically correct' contributions to organizations that assist the 'poor' instead of through genuine relationship-building with those of different classes. The letter of James may offer some insights into how such relationship-building might take place— without a trace of partiality or hypocrisy." "James," 465–66.

and a lack of sensitivity to their needs misalign the church with the *missio Dei*. The church should be attentive to any circumstances in which the poor are being abused and support them. The *Cape Town Commitment* is a good reminder for the church to include in her mission not just the proclamation of the gospel but also care for the needy. As Emilio A. Núñez states, "God desires the salvation of the whole of humanity and the whole of the human being."[41] Surely, God's desire includes the entire being of the one who is poor. James shows us some concrete examples of how to include the poor in the church's mission. Without a doubt, just as the poor have a prominent place in the mission of God, so do they in the mission of his church.

Bibliography

Allison, Dale C., Jr. *A Critical and Exegetical Commentary on the Epistle of James*. International Critical Commentary. New York: Bloomsbury, 2013.

Baik, Chung-Hyun. "A Critical Analysis of the Concept of *Missio Dei*: Suggestions for a Trinitarian Understanding." *Neue Zeitschrift für systematische Theologie und Religionsphilosophie* 63, no. 3 (2021): 329–40.

Birdsall, S. Douglas, and Lindsay Brown. *The Cape Town Commitment: A Confession of Faith and a Call to Action*. Orlando: Lausanne Movement, 2010.

Byron, Gay L. "James." In *True to Our Native Land: An African American New Testament Commentary*, edited by Brian K. Blount, Cain Hope Felder, Clarice J. Martin, and Emerson B. Powery, 461–75. Minneapolis: Fortress, 2007.

Cheung, Luke L., and Andrew B. Spurgeon. *James: A Pastoral and Contextual Commentary*. Asia Bible Commentary. Carlisle: Langham, 2018.

Escobar, Samuel. *The New Global Mission: The Gospel from Everywhere to Everyone*. Christian Doctrine in Global Perspective. Downers Grove, IL: InterVarsity Press, 2003.

Escobar, Samuel, and Eduardo Delás. *Santiago: La fe viva que impulsa a la misión*. Bogotá: Ediciones Puma, 2012.

Ferdinando, Keith. "Mission: A Problem of Definition." *Themelios* 33, no. 1 (2008): 46–59.

Franklin, Kirk J. *Toward Global Missional Leadership: A Journey through Leadership Paradigm Shift in the Mission of God*. Regnum Practitioner Series. Oxford: Regnum, 2017.

---

41 Núñez, *Hacia una misionología evangélica latinoamericana*, 270.

George, Sharron. "Constructing Latin American Missiology: How the Holistic Perspective Overcomes Traditional Stereotypes." In *The Reshaping of Mission in Latin America*, edited by Miguel Alvarez, 45–71. Regnum Edinburgh Centenary Series 30. Oxford: Regnum, 2015.

Johnson, Luke Timothy. *The Letter of James: A New Translation with Introduction and Commentary*. Anchor Bible 37A. New Haven: Yale University Press, 1995.

Joubert, Stephan. "*Homo Reciprocus* No More: The 'Missional' Nature of Faith in James." In *Sensitivity towards Outsiders: Exploring the Dynamic Relationship between Mission and Ethics in the New Testament and Early Christianity*, edited by Jacobus Kok, Tobias Nicklas, Dieter T. Roth, and Christopher M. Hays, 382–400. Wissenschaftliche Untersuchungen zum Neuen Testament 2/364. Tübingen: Mohr Siebeck, 2014.

Kamell, Mariam J. "James 1:27 and the Church's Call to Mission and Morals." *Crux* 46, no. 4 (2010): 15–22.

Krüger, René. "El vuelco irritante y definitivo: Santiago 1:9–11 y el anuncio de la inversión total de la situación." *Cuadernos de teología* 23 (2004): 45–77.

Krüger, René. "Una definición muy peculiar de religión según Santiago 1:27." *Cuadernos de teología* 22 (2003): 79–91.

MacIlvaine, W. Rodman, III. "What Is the Missional Church Movement?" *Biblioteca Sacra* 167, no. 665 (2010): 89–106.

Martin, Ralph P. *James*. Word Biblical Commentary 48. Waco, TX: Word, 1988.

Moo, Douglas J. *The Letter of James*. Pillar New Testament Commentary. 2nd ed. Grand Rapids: Eerdmans, 2021.

Morales, Nelson R. *Poor and Rich in James: A Relevance Theory Approach to James's Use of the Old Testament*. Bulletin for Biblical Research Supplement 20. University Park, PA: Eisenbrauns, 2018.

Núñez, Emilio A. *Hacia una misionología evangélica latinoamericana*. Santa Fe, Argentina: Comibam, 1997.

Nyunt, Peter Thein. *Missions amidst Pagodas: Contextual Communication of the Gospel in the Burmese Buddhist Context*. Carlisle: Langham Monographs, 2014.

Ringe, Sharon H. "The Letter of James." In *A Postcolonial Commentary on the New Testament Writings*, edited by Fernando F. Segovia and R. S. Sugirtharajah, 369–79. The Bible and Postcolonialism 13. London: T&T Clark, 2007.

Ruiz, David D. *El diseño misional de Dios: Decifrando los cinco elementos fundamentales de la iglesia*. Puebla: ELA, 2021.

Suess, Paulo. "*Missio Dei* and the Project of Jesus: The Poor and the 'Other' as Mediators of the Kingdom of God and Protagonists of the Churches." *International Review of Mission* 92, no. 367 (2003): 550–59.

Tsvirinko, Vyacheslav. *Context and Contextuality: Towards an Authentic Mission Perspective for the Churches of the Pacific Coast Slavic Baptist Association.* Carlisle: Langham Monographs, 2018.

Ubeivolc, Vladimir. *Rethinking Missio Dei among Evangelical Churches in an Eastern European Orthodox Context.* Carlisle: Langham Monographs, 2016.

Vyhmeister, Nancy J. "The Rich Man in James 2: Does Ancient Patronage Illumine the Text?" *Andrews University Seminary Studies* 33 (1995): 265–83.

Wall, Robert W. *Community of the Wise: The Letter of James.* The New Testament in Context. Valley Forge, PA: Trinity Press International, 1997.

Wright, Christopher J. H. *The Mission of God: Unlocking the Bible's Grand Narrative.* Downers Grove, IL: IVP Academic, 2006.

Youn, Chul Ho. "*Missio Dei Trinitatis* and *Missio Ecclesiae*: A Public Theological Perspective." *International Review of Mission* 107, no. 1 (2018): 225–39.

Chapter 7

Rahab in James

A Corrective Missiological Paradigm

Jessica Janvier

James has garnered significant attention within Protestantism for its perceived controversy regarding the correlation between faith and works, particularly the relationship between Paul's and James's theology of *saving* faith. However, more attention needs to be given to the epistle's teleological understanding of Christian faith and its missiological imperatives. This chapter seeks to put James's teleology and missiology in conversation. In doing so, I will focus on the epistle's use of Rahab, a convert who embodied the goal of mission. Viewing the epistle and Rahab from a missiological perspective may provide a corrective paradigm for understanding the mandate of mission and faithful methodology.

James and the *Missio Dei*

James is a text that has elicited many questions, starting with its opening line, and its canonicity has been questioned throughout its reception history. Its controversial and argumentative aspects have helped to distract from its obvious missiological usefulness. Its opening verse—"James, a servant of God and of the Lord Jesus Christ, To the twelve tribes in the Dispersion: Greetings"—has led scholars to question the identity of the author and the audience that is being addressed.[1] The traditional approach has argued that the epistle was written by James the half-brother of Jesus and the audience being addressed were Jewish Christians. Scholars moving away from the long-held tradition have conjectured that the author is a different James, or someone associated with James, and therefore James is a work of pseudepigraphy. Other scholars have argued that the audience is a mixed Christian community with the "dispersion" language symbolizing the Christian community as the new or enlarged Israel with gentiles incorporated into it. Other significant questions have circulated about the epistle's argument, with Martin Dibelius contending that the text "lacks continuity of thought."[2]

---

1 All Scripture quotations are from the NRSV.

2 Dibelius, *James*, 2.

Most scholars have not aligned themselves with Dibelius's extreme opinion and see the text's connectedness by comparing it with Jewish wisdom literature. In the history of the church, the epistle was among the more slowly accepted New Testament writings. Early ecclesial historian Eusebius grouped it with writings that were "disputed, yet familiar to most," which meant some early Christian communities initially rejected it.[3] It was compiled with Jude, 2 Peter, and 2 and 3 John—all of which over time became accepted, authoritative texts. However, in the period of the Reformation, the legitimacy of James was once again questioned by Martin Luther, who initially considered axing the epistle from holy writ because he believed the author "mangles the Scriptures and thus contradicts Paul and all of Scripture."[4] For Luther, James had no "evangelical way about it" because he understood it to nullify *justification by faith alone*, the central doctrine of the Reformation. Despite Luther's early protestations, the epistle retained its scriptural status within Lutheranism and Protestantism overall. While the epistle has had its share of controversy and evoked a myriad of questions from scholars, most can agree on the author's spotlight on the concepts of "completion" or "perfection."

The author draws attention to the notion of being "complete" or "perfect" seven times, using τέλειος (1:4, 17, 25; 3:2), τελέω (2:8), τελειόω (2:22), τέλος (5:11). These words carry the connotation of bringing something to its intended purpose or drawing something to completion or fulfillment. These words serve the author's purpose for writing: to cultivate a countercultural community that lives with contradistinctive values (4:1–10); resists partiality toward the rich and honors the poor (2:1–7; 5:1–7); centers loving one's neighbor as oneself (2:8–13); honors the Lord, each other, and their neighbors in their speech (3:1–12; 4:11–12; 5:12); expresses an embodied wisdom shown in gentleness toward all (3:13–18); lives patiently in suffering, in light of the nearness of the Lord's parousia (5:7–12); and seeks to restore those who have strayed (5:19–20). The author of James purposed the letter to be instructive in "shap[ing] a community as an alternative to the world around him."[5] As Richard Bauckham noted, "It communicates to the Diaspora the teaching of the revered head of the mother church in Jerusalem on how Messianic Jews should live."[6] William F. Brosend II pointed out the societal strain that

---

3 Eusebius, *History of the Church*, 134.

4 Lane, "Luther's Criticism of James," 111.

5 McKnight, *Letter of James*, 40.

6 Bauckham, *James*, 20.

surrounded the epistle's community, which would have made it difficult to live by the prescribed values:

> The letter of James was written at a time and in a place of considerable social and political tumult and of considerable socioeconomic stratification.… In Jerusalem and Judea, Samaria and Galilee the general climate was exacerbated by political and religious conflict between ruling parties and classes, and a fairly long list of very distinguished appointments by Rome… . By contemporary standards there was an extreme concentration of wealth among the ruling elite (2%–3% of the population), a small class of retainers, a small merchant class, and the vast majority of the population surviving as peasants, peasant artisans, and slaves. Within Judea, Samaria, and Galilee the latter grouping may have accounted for 85% or more of the population, with most of the arable land controlled by only a few.[7]

Resisting anger, violence, and the temptation to favor the rich in the hope of attracting beneficial patrons would have been no easy task, especially in an environment leading toward the Jewish wars. The author's teaching, as many scholars have acknowledged, was founded on the teachings of Jesus, especially the Sermon on the Mount.[8] It provides insight into not only how a community persisting under the lordship of Christ should live but also the teleological purpose of Christian faith, which is *faith* and *faithfulness* (πίστις carries both meanings). This faith is brought to completion, not only through orthodoxy but through orthopraxy as well, so that believers are found justified in the present and in the eschatological judgment, as the epistle anticipates the coming of Jesus.[9] As John Chrysostom so aptly expressed,

---

7   Brosend, *James and Jude*, 31; quoted in Witherington, *Letters and Homilies*, 402–3.

8   For example, see Bauckham, *James*, 152; Parker, "Introductory Formulae," 20–39; and Batten, "Jesus Tradition and the Letter of James," 347–74.

9   The lexical range and gloss of πίστις is no secret, as virtually all Greek lexicons will show its meaning to carry faith in the sense of trust or belief and its use to express the idea of faithfulness. For example, see Danker, *Concise Greek-English Lexicon*, 284–85. Bauckham has noted that "James' argument slips unobtrusively between these two meanings of 'faith.'" *James*, 122. What has become somewhat controversial in Protestant circles is the idea of faithfulness in relation to soteriology. Will works play any part in the final judgment of Christians, that is, in our eschatological justification? While this is an affirmative moot point in Roman Catholic and Orthodox Christian circles, there are still tense discussions among Protestants. Piper is representative of those who answer negatively. He has argued, "I believe it is *actually* true, not just hypothetically true, that God 'will render to each one according to his works … to those who by patience in well-doing seek for glory and honor and immortality, he will give eternal life.' (Rom.2:6–7). I take the phrase 'according to' (κατὰ) in a sense different from 'based on.' I think the best way to bring together the various threads of Paul's teaching on justification by faith apart from works is to treat the necessity of obedience not as any part of the bases of our

> Faith without works is dead, and works without faith are dead as well. For if we have sound doctrine but fail in living the doctrine it is of no use to us. Likewise if we take pains with life but are careless about doctrine, that will not be any good to us either. It is therefore necessary to shore up the spiritual edifice in both directions.[10]

Communities are set apart by Jesus's present lordship over his people in the present as they look forward to his lordship being revealed to all upon his return.

The countercultural community James is trying to nurture is endangered by a misunderstanding of the relationship between faith and works, and Abraham is called to the front of the congregation as an adjudicating witness, alongside Rahab. The author says in 2:24, "You see that a person is justified by works and not by faith alone." Scholars are divided as to whether the author is directly responding to the apostle Paul, a misinterpretation of the Pauline articulation of the gospel, or an error within his context without reference to Paul.[11] James 2:24 is often contrasted with Romans 3:28, in which Paul proclaims, "For we hold that a person is justified by faith apart from works prescribed by the law." Sharyn Dowd helpfully pointed out, "James is using Paul's vocabulary, but not his dictionary."[12] Whereas Paul was addressing a primarily gentile audience about entering into a right relationship with God without taking on the outward cultural distinctiveness of Judaism, such as

---

justification, but strictly as the evidence and confirmation of our faith in Christ whose blood and righteousness is the sole basis of our justification." *Future of Justification*, 110. Representative of the blooming counterargument, Matthew Bates is a concise voice. Bates notes Piper's weak linguistic argument and his admission of weakness. He continues, "The conclusion is that *good works form part of the basis of judgment for final salvation* in Romans 2:5–8. This is reinforced subsequently when Paul says, 'For it is not the hearers of the law who are righteous before God, but *the doers* of the law who will be *justified*' (Rom. 2:13). The most straightforward interpretation of this verse is to accept that *the actual doing or performance of the law forms part of the basis for justification*. This is because justification is not a mere declaration of innocence but involves a change in the person's very being (liberation from bondage to sin's power)." *Gospel Allegiance*, 190, 192. The strength of the argument is with Bates from a historical theology standpoint. Detractors will point to being unconvinced by those influenced by the "New Perspective on Paul." However, Matthew Thomas has shown that the most relevant view from the "New Perspective" as it relates to Christian soteriology (which is a reinterpretation of "works of the law" in its correlation to salvation) is quite old, as it was held by many of the earliest Christian theologians. See Thomas, *Paul's "Works of the Law."*

10　John Chrysostom, *The Fathers of the Church*, 37.

11　A sample of the discussions concerning the diversity of outlook among scholars can be seen in McKnight, *Letter of James*, 245–57; Bauckham, *James*, 120–40; and Moo, *James*, 114–17.

12　Dowd, "Faith That Works," 202.

circumcision or varying food laws (works of the law), James was speaking to a Jewish-Christian community that was already in relationship with God. He taught that authentic faith must be lived out in works consistent with externalized actions of faithfulness toward the Lord and neighbor.

Considering Abraham's prominence in Second Temple Judaism as the father of faith, it is not surprising that the author calls on him as a model of saving faith, or faith "brought to completion" by reaching its *telos*. What is more interesting is the author's paralleling of Rahab and Abraham to illustrate his point. As Abraham served as the model of the kind of faith that would inherit the blessings of the world to come in the Judaism of this era, Rahab served as the convert par excellence who became an heir of God's promises, illustrating the *telos* of conversion and for Christians, the *telos* of the *missio Dei*.

Rahab in Jewish Tradition and Early Christianity

Unlike the epistle of James, Rahab's presence within the Judeo-Christian tradition has not been at risk of elimination, as she appears in the Torah, which is venerated as a collection of foundational writings for Jews and Christians alike. However, the introduction of Rahab as a prostitute in the book of Joshua has caused her and those associated with her to be viewed with ethical and theological ambiguity. Scot McKnight succinctly lays out the controversies surrounding her: "Among the problems include why the spies took up space at a prostitute's home (Josh 2:1, 4), her prostitution being mentioned without repentance, her lying (2:5–6), how she knew of the God of Israel (2:9–11), and the complicity of the spies in deceit."[13] Despite the troublesome introduction, the tradition built around Rahab in the Second Temple period and in early Christianity helped to exalt her status. Josephus, in his *Antiquities*, removed the stigma of her being a prostitute by referring to her instead as an "innkeeper."[14]

Modern feminist voices from the Majority World have also elevated Rahab by removing the stigma surrounding the ethics of prostitution altogether and presenting her as a selfless heroine who wisely used her position to rescue her family. Representative of this position, Ira Mangililo, utilizing autobiographical criticism to speak in the voice of Rahab, asserted, "I was able to understand that the brothel business was another type of labor that could bring home

---

13 McKnight, *Letter of James*, 256n132.
14 Hanson, "Rahab the Harlot," 55.

money—and that there was nothing wrong with that."[15]

Others adding to the tradition around her from the ancient world did not see the need to eliminate the Torah's initial designation of her as a prostitute, but they did elaborate on what it meant for her to be incorporated into Israel. The Talmudic Tractate Megillah presented her as the wife of Joshua and an ancestor of some of Israel's later prophets.[16] Thus, it is unsurprising that early Christian tradition, as seen through 1 Clement, characterized her as a prophet and one whose actions foreshadowed the work of Christ.

> And they also gave her a sign, that she should hang a scarlet thread out of her house, thereby intimating beforehand that through the blood of the Lord there would be redemption for all who believe and put their hope in God. You perceive, beloved, that not only faith but also prophecy is found in that woman.[17]

With the complex reception history and various interpretations surrounding Rahab, her status within tradition gave her an elevated standing during the period that produced James. Thus, it is unsurprising that the author uses her as a model. What remains somewhat of a mystery is what version of the book of Joshua the author pulls from in order to insert her into the epistle. James was composed before the solidification of the canon. Accordingly, Joshua existed in various forms, as evidenced by the differences among its versions in the Septuagint, the Masoretic Text, and the Qumran scrolls. The Septuagint and Masoretic Text both feature Rahab but with some variations in the structure of the narrative sections in which she appears. Nevertheless, James's point of utilizing Rahab as found in Joshua stands untarnished, as she was a person who not only believed in the greatness of YHWH (Josh 2:8–11) but also acted in faithfulness in accordance with that belief in refusing to hand over the spies from Israel and hiding them (2:2–7). Ultimately she was saved by the cord placed on her window (2:17–21; 6:17, 25). Bauckham suggests that an interpretive scriptural tradition of the time may have even bolstered James's understanding of Rahab as a person whose "faith was brought to completion" by her faithful works. Bauckham relays,

---

15 Mangililo, "Rahab and Indonesian Christian Women," 60–61.
16 Hanson, "Rahab the Harlot," 56.
17 Hanson, 55–56.

Evidently there was a tradition of interpretation which took the "sign of faith" which Rahab requests to be her scarlet cord. It was understood as a sign attesting her faith in the God of Israel, which she had expressed in verse 11… . Hence Rahab could be said to have been saved by her faith. She was perhaps the only Old Testament figure other than Abraham of whom this could be said on the basis of the Old Testament test itself. So, if one were going to make a case for faith as a sufficient alternative to works, the kind of case that James is refuting, Rahab would be the obvious choice, after Abraham, for arguing such a case. She therefore serves James's purpose in that he can show that, important as was her faith, it was not by faith alone that she was justified, since her faith, like Abraham's, was completed by works, in her case her assistance to the spies.[18]

What is important from a missiological perspective is not only how the epistle uses Rahab to showcase what it means to have complete faith in YHWH but also her function within the Second Temple period as an example of a convert par excellence. This conforms with the epistle's overarching purpose of cultivating a community that practices a *complete* faith. The missiology implicit in the narratives and tradition surrounding Rahab suggests that she is a picture of not only the *telos* of faith but the *telos* of conversion and, by inference, mission. Her example of saving faith within the author's teleological outlook challenges dominant perspectives on the purpose of mission and missiological methodology.

The Disconnect between Teleology and Methodology

What is the goal and mandate of mission? This question is answered differently by varying camps within Christianity. Observing the variation present among missiologists, A. Scott Moreau said,

For many within ecumenical churches the goal is the promotion of justice and freedom in human societies and institutions. Recently evangelical mission agencies have been promoting the planting of a church movement among every people group as the goal. Others promote holistic approaches which see church planting as only part of the picture of enabling people to live humanely in their social settings.[19]

To Moreau's observation can be added mission strategies that focused on confession and sacramentalism, which can be seen in all three branches

---

18 Bauckham, *James*, 125.
19 Moreau, "Missiology," 783.

of the church as it entered into the early modern period (1500–1800).[20] If James's teleology is used to inform our missiology, then the aim shifts toward creating countercultural Christian communities that embody—in their presence, outlook, and expressed values—life under the lordship of Christ. Additionally, if Rahab is used as the teleological paradigm for conversion, then transformed lives that embody "faith … brought to completion by … works" (Jas 2:22) become the goal and mandate of mission.

This does not exclude ecumenical mission approaches that see the flourishing of justice and freedom throughout varying societies as important; neither does it exclude evangelical mission approaches that set church planting as a goal; nor does it overlook mission strategies that see right confession along with the sacramental life of the church as vital to the birth of new life within the fellowship of believers. The epistle's teleology sets these goals in service to create countercultural communities rather than make them a means to an end.[21] Mission methodology that does not centralize the counterculturalism that James sees as crucial to producing Rahab-like believers and converts with complete faith, remain incomplete in mission or in lockstep with methodologies that will bring disdain to the receiving culture's view of mission and missionaries, even as some come to salvation. Such strategies have caused many converts to deconstruct their faith in order to find a truly complete faith that differed significantly from that of their missionaries in terms of values reflective of Christ's kingdom. A short episodic historical overview of such mission strategies in the early modern to modern period will demonstrate this point.

Confessionalism and Sacramentalism
Mohammed Ali Ben Said, perhaps better known by his Christian name Nicholas Said, was an African Muslim "born in Kouka, the capital of the Kingdom of Bornou, in Soudan: a few years after the invasion of the Wadays, or about the year 1836."[22] His birth was in present-day Nigeria. He tells his captivating life story in his autobiographical work, *The Autobiography of*

---

20 I am using the era designations from Smither, *Christian Mission*, 75–101.

21 For the sake of clarity, this position does invalidate mission strategies that incorporate universalism. I agree with Moreau when he says, "If the nature of mission is to celebrate Jesus as only one of the many possible ways to God, then the method will be dialogue in which the goal is to simply learn how to celebrate differences, and evangelism will either be redefined or discarded altogether." Moreau seeks a missiology that will maintain the uniqueness of Jesus Christ within the realm of soteriology. "Missiology," 783.

22 Said, *Autobiography of Nicholas Said*, 9.

Nicholas Said: A Native of Bornou, Eastern Soudan, Central Africa. Said's work has been of interest to historians of early Muslim migration into the United States and historians of African American Christianity alike. In his autobiography, Said tells the story of his capture into slavery, but unlike many African Americans who were forced into the transatlantic slave trade, he was forced into the trans-Saharan slave trade. His movement as a slave took him on many journeys through different parts of Africa, the Middle East, and Eastern Europe.

During his stay in Russia, he encountered Orthodox Christianity. It was there that he converted from being a practicing Muslim to entering the Eastern Orthodox Church through the efforts of Prince Nicholas Troubetzkoÿ. Matriculating to the United States in the antebellum period, he became the first known Black Orthodox Christian in America. However, his conversion seemed less than transformative or particularly meaningful. On the day of his conversion, he recounted,

> Whenever he went to prayers, he [Prince Nicholas] made me stand before him, *bon gré, mal gré*, and imitate every action of his, such as kneeling, bowing, making the sign of the cross, etc., and I used to enjoy myself hugely, cutting capers and going through all sorts of pantomimic performances when he thought I was acting in a very devotional manner. One day, as I was indulging extensively in my favorite amusement, the Prince happened to turn, and caught me in my most striking attitude, whereupon he gave me a *striking* reminder of what was decent and respectful on such solemn occasions, by administering to my ears a good boxing and depriving me of my dinner. Finally, my prejudices gave way, however, and I consented to embrace the Greek faith, the State religion of Russia. I was baptized in Riga on the 12th of November, 1855, leaving my Mohammedan name of *Mohammed Ali Ben Said* at the font, and bearing therefrom the Christian name of Nicholas. This performance ended, I thought the job was complete, but the next day the *papa*, or priest who had me baptized, sent for me, and on getting where he was, I found myself in a beautiful chapel, handsomely paved with marble of different colors. He caused me to kneel before an immense *tableau* of the Saviour for hours, asking pardons for my past sins. As the marble was harder than my knees, I was in perfect agony during the greater portion of the time, and became so enraged with the *papa*, that I fear I committed more sins during that space of time than I had done in days before. In fact, I am not sure but that a few ungainly Mohammedan asperities of language bubbled up to my lips.

> But I managed to get through without any overt act of rebellion. When I
> had become a confirmed Christian, the Prince presented me with a solid
> gold cross, and a chain of the same metal to suspend it around my neck
> by, in the prevailing Russian fashion.[23]

Said's master, Nicholas Troubetzkoÿ, and the Russian state church of that day viewed the goal of mission as right confession and sacramental participation in the life of the church, but this failed to produce transformed people with complete faith like that of Rahab. The risk of this mission strategy is the production of people with dead orthodoxy, which James makes clear is not salvific.

As Western Europeans were moving into what they would call the "New World" in the seventeenth century, this approach was initially utilized by England's Society for the Propagation of the Gospel in Foreign Parts. This strategy yielded little results among Native Americans and enslaved Africans. Additionally, ministers who tried to gain access to enslaved people were blocked by nominal English Christians who believed conversion would equal emancipation. This points to the negative quality of Christianity that the English state church was generating among lay people at that time. A desire for a more robust and heartfelt Christianity would spread with the advent of evangelicalism.

Evangelical and Ecumenical Missiology

Evangelicalism's appearance in the United States during the mid-1700s created a fervent change in the practice of Protestant Christian faith. It inspired many evangelicals to partake in cross-cultural mission endeavors. As Edward L. Smither noted in his history of global mission, the former Virginian slave George Liele became America's first cross-cultural missionary, traveling to Jamaica in 1783 to plant churches and minister to the enslaved.[24] In Jamaica he began his missionary enterprise inside a colonized land that intertwined Christianity with ideas of racial superiority in order to maintain slavery and the racial hierarchy.[25]

What is painful about this period is that the Protestant boom in the mission field coincided with the rise of European colonialism. Smither explained: "Amid Western colonial expansion and evangelical renewal movements, Protestant mission came into its own and became a significant global movement in the nineteenth century."[26] While some missionaries who

---

23 Said, 144–46, emphases original.

24 Smither, *Christian Mission*, xiii.

25 For an overview of Liele's life and contribution to mission, see Saunders, "Laying an Historical Foundation," 60–63.

26 Smither, *Christian Mission*, 103.

meant well entered the mission field at this time, many nonetheless entered with a colonial mindset and in league with colonial powers, which were accompanied by ideas of racial superiority.[27] Perhaps the conflation was impossible to avoid, as Palestinian postcolonial scholar Edward Said stated: "Modern imperialism was so global and all-encompassing that virtually nothing escaped it."[28] This created a situation in which Christianity was associated with imperialism and oppression in much of the Majority World.

In this situation, Majority World Christian theologians, preachers, and missionary practitioners responded in mainly two ways, which can be seen through the pastoral and evangelistic ministry of Nicholas Bhengu and biblical scholar Musa W. Dube. Both lived through the experience of being Black Africans exposed to Christianity in colonized Southern Africa. Bhengu came to faith in an evangelical milieu and operated within the theological paradigms of the Assemblies of God even after he split from them. As a fruitful evangelist, he led many to Christ with an evangelical presentation of the gospel. However, Bhengu went further in his gospel presentation than what he received from his White missionaries and included a message that addressed the ills that imperialism had sown. Anthony O. Balcomb noted, "Although the core of his message was salvation through repentance from sin and faith in Christ his understanding of salvation included the restoration of self-confidence and dignity for African people in the face of apartheid."[29] Bhengu, like many Majority World Christians who are committed to the evangelical tradition, pushed back against the intertwining of colonialism, racial oppression, and Christianity by creating countercultural Christian communities that intentionally signified a difference between their practice of the faith from that of those missionaries who were shaped by colonialism. Dube explained the negative stigma Christians had to endure from their wider milieu seeking liberation. She recounted,

> Debating societies passed one motion after another and constantly summoned us to the debating floors. We were called upon to explain the ethics of our religion: to justify its practice, its practitioners, and its institutions. Debating societies demanded to know why the biblical

---

27 I do not intend to categorize all missionaries negatively but to draw out the problematic aspects of mission in the early modern and modern era. Also, I am not implicating White missionaries alone in coming to the Majority World with attitudes of supremacy. For example, some Black American missionaries who went to Africa under the auspices of the American Colonization Society also carried a sense of Western cultural superiority as they approached mission endeavors.

28 Said, *Culture and Imperialism*, 68.

29 Balcomb, "Evangelicalism in Africa," 122.

text and its Western readers were instruments of imperialism, and how we, as Africans justify our faith in a religion that has betrayed us—a religion of the enemy, so to speak.[30]

Dube, in line with an ecumenical approach to mission, takes a critical approach to Scripture that embraces forms of universalism, which allows her to confront readings of Scripture brought by evangelical missionaries who sought to embrace imperialism while simultaneously uplifting biblicism. She argues, "Such a stance refuses to be confined to texts that are often both patriarchal and imperialistic canons of those in power."[31]

The evangelical method of mission in the modern era revealed its weakness in creating countercultural Christian communities through its practitioners. Even models such as Henry Venn's and Rufus Anderson's "three-self" formula, which advocated for self-propagating, self-governing, and self-supporting churches, suffered, as many of the missionaries were not people formed by a counterculture shaped by the values and ethics produced by living under the lordship of Christ.[32] They came with a faith that James would see as *faith made incomplete by lack of works*, especially that of loving one's neighbor as one's self. On the one hand, Rahab-like Christians did emerge despite the entanglement between colonialism and Christianity, but on the other hand, this faith produced non-Rahab-like Christians who doubted altogether the classical notions of mission.

Conclusion

The epistle of James and its use of Rahab the prostitute-turned-convert par excellence has much to say to contemporary missiological thought. It grates against a dead orthodoxy, which shows up in mission methodology that prioritizes confessionalism and sacramentalism. The epistle beckons this type of missiology to listen to the experiences represented through the voice of Nicholas Said. James shows the error of a missiology that sees the goal of mission as church planting, because mission is not completed by sending and church planting alone. Thus the epistle urges this type of missiology to heed the voices reflected in the experiences of Musa W. Dube and to examine the theological consequences it helps to create: a generation of Christians who doubt the morality of mission and the authority of Scripture because of a biblicism brought by missionaries that upheld Scripture yet degraded

---

30 Dube, "Toward a Post-Colonial Feminist Interpretation," 2.

31 Dube, 214. Dube is describing the approach to Scripture that African Independent Church (AIC) women embrace, which she makes her own as well.

32 Moreau, "Missiology," 781.

the peoples they targeted. The goal and mandate of mission must coincide with the teleological purpose of the Christian faith, which the epistle and the rebukes of Nicholas Bhengu make clear.

James calls for spiritual formation that is nurtured by Christian communities that are willing to live counterculturally, displaying values shaped by living under Christ's lordship. This begins with aspiring missionaries so that when they go out into the mission field they are prepared to cultivate communities that can produce Rahab-like converts who embody the *telos* of the *missio Dei*—a complete faith.

Bibliography

Balcomb, Anthony O. "Evangelicalism in Africa: What It Is and What It Does." *Missionalia* 44, no. 2 (2016): 117–28.

Bates, Matthew W. *Gospel Allegiance: What Faith in Jesus Misses for Salvation in Christ.* Grand Rapids: Brazos, 2019.

Batten, Alicia J. "The Jesus Tradition and the Letter of James." *Review and Expositor* 108, no. 3 (2011): 347–474.

Bauckham, Richard. *James: Wisdom of James, Disciple of Jesus the Sage.* New York: Routledge, 1999.

Brosend, William F., II. *James and Jude.* New Cambridge Bible Commentary. New York: Cambridge University Press, 2024.

Chrysostom, John. *The Fathers of the Church: St John Chrysostom Homilies on Genesis 1–17.* Translated by Robert C. Hill. Washington, DC: The Catholic University of America Press, 1986.

Danker, Frederick William. *The Concise Greek-English Lexicon of the New Testament.* 3rd ed. Chicago: University of Chicago Press, 2009.

Dibelius, Martin. *James: A Commentary on the Epistle of James.* Revised by Heinrich Greeven. Translated by Michael A. Williams. Edited by Helmut Koester. 11th ed. Philadelphia: Fortress, 1976.

Dowd, Sharyn. "Faith That Works: James 2:14–26." *Review and Expositor* 1997 (2000): 195–205.

Dube, Musa W. "Toward a Post-Colonial Feminist Interpretation of the Bible." PhD diss., Vanderbilt University, 1997.

Eusebius. *The History of the Church from Christ to Constantine.* Translated by G. A. Williamson. New York: Penguin, 1965.

Hanson, A. T. "Rahab the Harlot in Early Christian Tradition." *Journal for the Study of the New Testament* 1 (1978): 53–60.

Lane, Jason D. "Luther's Criticism of James as Key to His Biblical Hermeneutic." In *Auslegung und Hermeneutik der Bibel in der Reformationszeit*, edited by Christine Christ-von Wedel and Sven Grosse, 111–24. Berlin: de Gruyter, 2017.

Mangilio, Ira D. "When Rahab and Indonesian Christian Women Meet in the Third Space." *Journal of Feminist Studies in Religion* 31, no. 1 (2015): 45–64.

McKnight, Scot. *The Letter of James.* New International Commentary on the New Testament. Grand Rapids: Eerdmans, 2011.

Moo, Douglas. *James.* Tyndale New Testament Commentaries 16. Grand Rapids: Eerdmans, 1985.

Moreau, A. Scott. "Missiology." In *Evangelical Dictionary of Theology*, edited by Walter A. Elwell, 780–83. 2nd ed. Grand Rapids: Baker Academic, 2007.

Parker, Thomas J. "Introductory Formulae and Jesus's Teaching in James." *Evangelical Quarterly* 93, no. 1 (2022): 20–39.

Piper, John. *The Future of Justification.* Wheaton: Crossway, 2007.

Said, Edward. *Culture and Imperialism.* New York: Alfred Knopf, 1993.

Said, Nicholas. *The Autobiography of Nicholas Said: A Native of Bornou, Eastern Soudan, Central Africa.* Memphis: Shortwell, 1873.

Saunders, Linda P. "Laying an Historical Foundation to Examine the African-American Church's Relationship to 21st Century Global Missions to Create a Contextualized Missions Training Model for Future Generations of African-American Missionaries." PhD diss., Columbia International University, Columbia, 2020.

Smither, Edward L. *Christian Mission: A Concise Global History.* Bellingham, WA: Lexham, 2019.

Thomas, Matthew J. *Paul's "Works of the Law" in the Perspective of Second Century Reception.* Tübingen: Mohr Siebeck, 2018.

Witherington, Ben, III. *Letters and Homilies for Jewish Christians: A Socio-Rhetorical Commentary on Hebrews, James and Jude.* Downers Grove, IL: IVP Academic, 2007.

Part 2

The Missionary Message of James

Chapter 8

Holistic Mission in James and the Early Church

Edward L. Smither

In a letter to one of his pagan priests in AD 363, the Roman Emperor Julian "the Apostate" (331–363) complained that the "impious Galileans [his name for Christians] supported not only their own poor but ours as well."[1] In his first-century epistle, James declared that "faith without deeds is dead" (2:26) and that "pure and faultless" religion included "look[ing] after orphans and widows in their distress" (1:27).[2] The early church within the Roman Empire seemed to heed James's admonitions and value holistic Christian mission. In addition to proclaiming the good news of Jesus, the church declared their faith through their good works.

In this chapter, I first explore James's teaching for ministering to the whole person. Second, I discuss how a representative group of church fathers emulated James's teaching on holistic mission in their contexts. Finally, I offer some brief reflections on how the contemporary global church might read James and consider the historic practice of the church as they pursue mission in word and deed today.

Holistic Mission in James

The consensus of evangelical commentators affirms that the letter was written by James, the Lord's half-brother and pastor of the Jerusalem church.[3] In writing to "the twelve tribes scattered among the nations" (1:1), James's audience appears to be Jewish Christians dispersed both geographically and among the gentiles. One possible explanation for this dispersion is that, following the stoning of Stephen, these believers fled to Phoenicia, Cyprus, and Syrian Antioch (Acts 8:1; 11:19).[4]

---

1 Julian, *Letter to Arsacius* in Chinnock, *Few Notes on Julian*, 75–78.

2 Witherington calls it a homily, while Moo affirms that it was a letter as does Simon Kistemaker. See further Witherington, *Letters and Homilies*, 401; Moo, *Letter of James*, 7–11; and Kistemaker, *James*, 3–5. All Scripture quotations are from the NIV.

3 See, e.g., Jobes, *Letters to the Church*, 148–58; Witherington, *Letters and Homilies*, 401; Moo, *Letter of James*, 11–26; Vlachos, *James*, 3–5; and Kistemaker, *James*, 7–9.

4 See Jobes, *Letters to the Church*, 163–65; also Moo, *Letter of James*, 26–30; Green, "Reading James Missionally," 205–6; and Kistemaker, *James*, 6–7.

"Faith that works" seems to be the strongest theme in the letter.[5] James asserts, "Do not merely listen to the word, and so deceive yourselves. Do what it says" (1:22). Elsewhere he declares that "faith without deeds is dead" (2:26). Drawing on the Ten Commandments, Old Testament wisdom literature, and Jesus's Sermon on the Mount, James exhorts his readers to live the Christian life in a practical godly manner.[6] While faith-filled deeds should characterize how believers ought to treat one another, these principles also apply to how the church should relate missionally to the broader nonbelieving community.

Godly Speech

The first way that James exhorts his readers to witness unto Christ is through their speech. As image bearers of a God who speaks, human beings also communicate through words. Our words and the way in which we deliver them are a testimony to our faith. Karen H. Jobes writes: "Spiritually mature people exhibit godly speech that is consistent with who they are becoming in Christ."[7]

James repeatedly urges his readers to show restraint in their speech to avoid sinning. He calls them to be "quick to listen, slow to speak and slow to become angry" (1:19). Recalling Solomon's wisdom—"Sin is not ended by multiplying words, but the prudent hold their tongues" (Prov 10:19)—James teaches that words can be sinful, especially if they are spoken out of anger.[8] He adds that those who are "religious … keep a tight rein on their tongues" (1:26). Later, using a variety of metaphors, he emphasizes how destructive one's words can be and how difficult it is to "tame the tongue" (3:8). Through these negative descriptions, Douglas J. Moo writes that James is teaching that "Christ followers should not use the tongue in a destructive way."[9] In the following chapter, James affirms this by exhorting the church, "Do not slander one another" (4:11). As sinful speech has already been linked to anger, slander is connected to the sins of pride and jealousy.[10]

When James talks about godly speech, he is not directly talking about proclaiming the gospel. However, when the people of God control

---

5   See further Jobes, *Letters to the Church*, 221; also Kistemaker, *James*, 15–16.

6   See further Jobes, *Letters to the Church*, 161–62, 174–75; also Moo, *Letter of James*, 1.

7   Jobes, *Letters to the Church*, 172.

8   See further Moo, *Letter of James*, 108–11; also Kistemaker, *James*, 57.

9   Moo, *Letter of James*, 181.

10 See further Moo, *Letter of James*, 249.

their tongues and bless one another, they testify to the reality of God in their midst—a witness to an onlooking nonbelieving community. When evangelists proclaim Christ with gentleness, humility, and respect (1 Pet 3:15–16), their manner of speech brings credibility to their gospel message.

Caring for the Most Vulnerable

James asserts that one of the fruits of spiritual wisdom is being "full of mercy" (3:17). Writing these words, James surely remembers the teachings of Christ in the Sermon on the Mount, "Be merciful, just as your Father is merciful" (Luke 6:36).[11] A key aspect of mission in James is caring for and showing mercy to the most vulnerable and poor in society.

Orphans and widows. Regarding true Christian faith and mission, James declares, "Religion that God our Father accepts as pure and faultless is this: to look after orphans and widows in their distress" (1:27). While James is surely talking about real orphans and widows, he is also speaking concretely about those who are most at risk and vulnerable within a given community.[12]

By "looking after" or "visiting" (*episkeptomai*) widows and orphans, James's readers are called to imitate the heart and ways of a missionary God. In the Old Testament, God is described as a "father to the fatherless, a defender of widows" (Ps 68:5), one who "watches over the foreigner and sustains the fatherless and the widow" (Ps 146:9), and one "defends the cause of the fatherless and the widow, and loves the foreigner … giving them food and clothing" (Deut 10:18). They are admonished to continue in Israel's righteous call to "not take advantage of the widow or the fatherless" (Exod 22:22), to collect tithes "so that the Levites … the foreigners, the fatherless and the widows who live in your towns may come and eat and be satisfied" (Deut 14:28–29), and to "take up the cause of the fatherless; plead the cause of the widow" (Isa 1:17). If James's readers are indeed Jewish Christians from Jerusalem dispersed after the stoning of Stephen, then they had already developed the habit of caring for the needs of the Hellenistic and Hebrew widows in Jerusalem (Acts 6:1–6).[13]

The poor. James also taught that mission involved showing mercy to the poor. While some Old Testament passages (e.g., Isa 61) and the Sermon on the Mount (Luke 6:20) speak of the pious poor, James seems to understand

---

11 See further Jobes, *Letters to the Church*, 189–90, 193.

12 See further Vlachos, *James*, 64.

13 See further Moo, *Letter of James*, 249; Kistemaker, *James*, 65; and Vlachos, *James*, 64.

"poor" (*ptōchos*) primarily in a material and economic sense.[14] He describes the poor as those with clothes that are "filthy" and "old" (2:2) and who are "poor in the eyes of the world" (2:5).[15] However, since they are vulnerable and without hope, they are more likely to cry out to God for help and become "rich in faith" (2:5).[16] According to Jobes, at the time of James's writing in the middle of the first century, at least 90 percent of the inhabitants of the Roman Empire lived in economic poverty.[17]

In responding to the needs of the poor, James echoes the Old Testament writers who often spoke of God's heart for the poor. Job writes that God "saves the needy from the sword in their mouth; he saves them from the clutches of the powerful. So the poor have hope, and injustice shuts its mouth" (Job 5:15–16). The psalmist adds, "He will deliver the needy who cry out, the afflicted who have no one to help. He will take pity on the weak and the needy and save the needy from death" (Ps 72:12–13).[18]

For James, the question of relating to the poor emerges from his audience's house church meetings.[19] He writes:

> My brothers and sisters, believers in our glorious Lord Jesus Christ must not show favoritism. Suppose a man comes into your meeting wearing a gold ring and fine clothes, and a poor man in filthy old clothes also comes in. If you show special attention to the man wearing fine clothes and say, "Here's a good seat for you," but say to the poor man, "You stand there" or "Sit on the floor by my feet," have you not discriminated among yourselves and become judges with evil thoughts? Listen, my dear brothers and sisters: Has not God chosen those who are poor in the eyes of the world to be rich in faith and to inherit the kingdom he promised those who love him? But you have dishonored the poor. (2:1–6)

While it is possible that James is talking about rich and poor believers, this scenario seems to more closely reflect how the house churches welcomed visitors—particularly nonbelievers—into their gatherings. In their outreach and hospitality, were they guilty of following the ways of the world and giving priority to the rich and well dressed? Or would they imitate God and

---

14   See further Kistemaker, *James*, 77.

15   See further Moo, *Letter of James*, 137–38; also Vlachos, *James*, 69.

16   See further Jobes, *Letters to the Church*, 226; also Moo, *Letter of James*, 45–46, 136–37.

17   Jobes, *Letters to the Church*, 228.

18   See Deut 10:17–18; Job 31:16–23; Amos 2:6–7; see further Moo, *Letter of James*, 45; and Jobes, *Letters to the Church*, 226–27.

19   See further Kistemaker, *James*, 73.

offer shelter and care to the poor?[20] James exhorts them that attending to the needs of the poor is the same as keeping the "royal law found in Scripture" and "lov[ing] your neighbor as yourself" (2:8).

In addition to caring for the downcast, Christian mission for James meant dealing with the poor in a righteous and just manner. James appears to condemn wealthy landowners who are exploiting their poor workers.[21] He accuses them of

- Hoarding—"You have hoarded wealth in the last days" (5:3);
- Exploitation—"You failed to pay the workers" (5:4);
- Extravagance—"You have lived … in luxury and self-indulgence" (5:5); and
- Oppression—"You have condemned and murdered the innocent" (5:6).

In this litany of charges against wealthy oppressors, James restates admonitions from the Law and Prophets. For example, in Deuteronomy, the Israelites are commanded:

> Do not take advantage of a hired worker who is poor and needy, whether that worker is a fellow Israelite or a foreigner residing in one of your towns. Pay them their wages each day before sunset, because they are poor and are counting on it. Otherwise they may cry to the LORD against you, and you will be guilty of sin. (24:14–15)[22]

James's instructions certainly apply to how wealthy Christians ought to treat fellow believers in their employ. However, given that his admonitions follow closely God's commands to Israel for welcoming and loving the stranger (foreigners, widows, orphans, and the poor), James's teaching seems to apply as the church crosses boundaries and engages nonbelievers in a missional way.[23]

Holistic Mission in the Early Church

James's letter was circulated, read, and preached in the early church (AD 100–400).[24] Though some church fathers did not quote James directly, we can observe James's mission principles—particularly care for society's most vulnerable and poor—at work in their ministries. To support this, I briefly

---

20 See further Kistemaker, 73; Vlachos, *James*, 69; and Moo, *Letter of James*, 129, 140.

21 See further Kistemaker, *James*, 159–61; Vlachos, *James*, 158; and Moo, *Letter of James*, 140.

22 See also Lev 19:13; Jer 22:13; and Mal 3:5.

23 See further Jobes, *Letters to the Church*, 169.

24 See further Moo, *Letter of James*, 2–5.

explore the ministries of three church fathers from different parts of the ancient church: Cyprian of Carthage (195–258) from Latin-speaking North Africa, Basil of Caesarea (329–379) from Greek-speaking Asia Minor, and Ephraem of Syria (ca. 306–373) from Syriac-speaking Edessa.

Cyprian of Carthage

Cyprian was born into a prominent pagan family in Carthage. He was educated in classical and religious literature, and he probably initially worked as a teacher of rhetoric. He became a Christian and was baptized in 246. Only two years after his conversion, Cyprian was set apart as the bishop of Carthage. Though a minister ordinarily would first be ordained to a lower order of ministry (reader, deacon, or priest), Cyprian apparently possessed significant leadership skills, which prompted his early consecration as bishop.

During Cyprian's tenure as bishop of Carthage (248–258), the North African church endured years of suffering at the hands of the Roman emperors Decius (249–250) and Valerian (257–258). Aiming to revive paganism and suppress Christian worship, the emperors essentially ordered them to deny their faith by paying homage or making sacrifices to the Roman deities and emperors. During the persecution under Decius, Cyprian chose to go into hiding. Though he strove to lead the church from a distance, his decision to flee drew mixed reactions from his clergy. During Valerian's persecution, Cyprian refused to make sacrifices and was banished for a year before being executed.[25]

Martyrdom. As we evaluate Cyprian's ministry, particularly to those outside of the church, I would first characterize it as a mission of martyrdom. Cyprian presented a winsome gospel witness amid his own "trials of many kinds" (Jas 1:2), which included pressure for being a Christian and bishop, as well as exile and death.

Cyprian inherited the leadership of a North African church that had already experienced much discrimination and persecution.[26] While the New Testament word "martyr" (*martys*) simply meant a "witness," by the second century it came to mean those who witnessed unto Christ through their death.[27] When on trial, North African Christians gave a clear verbal witness of their faith in Christ. For example, Speratus, one of the twelve Scillitan martyrs put to death in Carthage in 180, testified to the Roman authorities: "I do not recognize the empire of this world. Rather, I serve that God whom no man has seen, nor can see, with these eyes." When the

---

25 See further Decret, *Early Christianity in North Africa*, 69–81.

26 See further Smither, *Christian Martyrdom*, 17–20.

27 See further Smither, xiv.

others were interrogated, one by one they confessed, "I am a Christian."[28] During her famous trial in 203, Perpetua, who was martyred alongside her servant Felicitas, responded to the governor of Carthage's questions about her Christian faith by simply stating, "Yes, I am."[29]

On the day of his execution, Cyprian joined this chorus of Christian martyrs by declaring: "I am a Christian and a bishop. I recognize no other gods but the one true God who made heaven and earth, and the sea, and all that is in them."[30] Through his verbal testimony during his trial and execution, Cyprian presented a powerful witness for Christ to the people of Carthage. Given his stature as the leader of the Christian community in the city, this witness was only magnified.

Almsgiving. Well before the North African church had any official status in the eyes of the Roman government, the church at Carthage was well established and supported by the financial offerings of believers. In addition to Cyprian, nearly forty full-time clergy labored to serve the church in the city. Under Cyprian's leadership, the church financially supported widows, the sick, and the poor. During times of crisis, particularly the Decian and Valerian persecutions, in which poor believers were thrown into jail, Cyprian provided for their needs. At other times, he paid ransoms to free Christians taken captive along the African roads.

Cyprian's thoughts on financial giving were founded on the spiritual discipline of almsgiving (giving offerings to the poor). Similar to the practice of corporate prayer, almsgiving reminded believers that they were more than mere individuals; instead, they were part of the body of Christ, the church. Like fasting, the almsgiver sacrificed something material in view of the hope of eternal life. When a believer fasted, they were to take the money saved on food and give it to the poor.[31]

Most of Cyprian's almsgiving went to care for the needs of poor, imprisoned, or refugeed Christians. However, as bishop of the church at Carthage, he also used church and personal funds to care for the material needs of the nonbelieving poor as well. Through his life and ministry, he demonstrated James's admonition to care for orphans, widows, and the poor.

---

28 *Acts of the Scillitan Martyrs* in Mursurillo, *Acts of the Christian Martyrs*, vol. 2.

29 *Passion of Perpetua and Felicitas*, 3, 5–6, in Mursurillo, *Acts of the Christian Martyrs*, vol. 2.

30 *Acts of Cyprian*, 1, 3, in Mursurillo, *Acts of the Christian Martyrs*, vol. 2.

31 See further Burns and Jensen, *Christianity in Roman Africa*, 570–75.

Basil of Caesarea[32]

Basil was born into a wealthy Christian family that practiced household asceticism. After studying philosophy and rhetoric in Cappadocia, Constantinople, and Athens, he returned to Cappadocia, was baptized, and then pursued a monastic calling with his friend Gregory of Nazianzus. While continuing to live as a monk, Basil was ordained to the ministry and eventually became bishop of Caesarea in 370. Because Caesarea was located on a significant Roman road, the city became an intercultural crossroads as diverse peoples from Asia Minor, Armenia, Syria, Persia, and the northern Gothic regions regularly spent time and interacted in Caesarea.[33]

In addition to his regular ministry as a bishop (preaching, administering the sacraments, teaching, writing, and overseeing other bishops), Basil devoted a great deal of time ministering to the poor in Asia Minor. In 368, a famine ravaged Caesarea. Gregory of Nazianzus wrote: "There was a famine, the most severe one ever recorded. The city was in distress and there was no source of assistance."[34] As the famine raged on for four years, other social problems developed such as hoarding food, theft, and riots, leading many to die of starvation. Basil grouped the poor in his community into two categories: (1) those who were born poor and had never escaped it (*penēs*); and (2) those who once had plenty and were even wealthy but had fallen into poverty (*ptōchos*). The latter group was the most common in Caesarea, with desperate families even abandoning their children on the doorstep of the church.[35]

Preaching. As Basil led the church during this humanitarian crisis, he seemed to prioritize ministering to their spiritual needs through the ministries of preaching and evangelism. Gregory of Nazianzus commented:

> [Basil] provided the nourishment of the Word and that more perfect good work and distribution being from heaven and on high; if the bread of angels is the Word, whereby souls hungry for God are fed and given to drink, and seek after nourishment that neither diminishes nor fails but remains forever; thus [i.e., by his sermons] this supplier of grain and abundant riches [he who was] the poorest and most needy [person] I have known, provided, not for a famine of bread or a thirst for water,

---

32 This section is adapted from my chapter on Basil in Smither, *Missionary Monks*, 27–41.

33 See further Rousseau, *Basil*, 4–5, 9–11, 68–69, 84–85, 133–34; Sterk, *Renouncing the World*, 36, 43, 74–76; and Holman, *Hungry Are Dying*, 69–70.

34 Gregory of Nazianzus, *Oration* 43.34, cited in Holman, *Hungry Are Dying*, 65.

35 See further Holman, *Hungry Are Dying*, 6, 78–80; also Holman, "Hungry Body," 339.

but a longing for the truly life-giving and nourishing Word, which effects growth to spiritual maturity in those nourished well on it.[36]

Following in the way of James (5:1–6), Basil preached against various groups of people and their ungodly response to the famine.[37] First, he rebuked moneylenders for exploiting the poor by loaning money at exorbitant interest rates. He preached repeatedly that "[the righteous man] does not lend out his money at interest" and urged these lenders to provide interest-free loans.[38] In the same sermons, he also rebuked merchants for price gouging.

Second, Basil condemned those who hoarded food supplies during the famine. Rebuking the rich for being spiritually poor in their greed, he urged them to imitate the patriarch Joseph, who was motivated by love and supplied grain to Egypt and the surrounding nations during seven years of famine.[39]

Third, Basil chastised the wealthy in general for their failure to be generous to the poor. Reminding them that they were stewards of their possession and not owners, Basil called the wealthy to love their poor neighbors as themselves. He effectively challenged them to demonstrate their faith through their good works (Jas 2:18, 26), imitating the faith of the Good Samaritan (Luke 10:25–37).[40]

Fourth, Basil preached to the poor, urging them to repay their debts, refrain from borrowing more, and be content with their simplicity. He rebuked those who had abandoned their own children and even sold them into slavery. Finally, he challenged the poor to recognize that they were not so desperate that they could not be generous themselves.[41]

Care for the poor. In addition to his preaching ministry, Basil was actively involved in aiding the poor in Caesarea. Leveraging his position as bishop, he appealed to the Roman government to provide tax relief for the poor and to contribute to his projects for the poor. He also urged the wealthy to leave a portion of their estate to ministries helping the poor.[42]

---

36 Gregory of Nazianzus, *Oration* 43.36, cited in Holman, *Hungry Are Dying*, 65.

37 In Basil's sermon corpus, these are Sermons 6–9 and two sermons from Psalm 14. See further Holman, "Hungry Body," 338; also Daley, "Building a New City," 438.

38 Cited in Holman, *Hungry Are Dying*, 114.

39 See further Holman, *Hungry Are Dying*, 103; also Holman, "Hungry Body," 349.

40 See further Daley, "Building a New City," 444–45; Holman, *Hungry Are Dying*, 105, 109, 112; and Rousseau, *Basil*, 178–79.

41 See further Holman, *Hungry Are Dying*, 81, 114.

42 See further Sterk, *Renouncing the World*, 66–70; Rousseau, *Basil*, 140–43, 159, 170–71; and Holman, *Hungry Are Dying*, 18, 75, 98.

Modeling his preaching to the wealthy Cappadocians, Basil liquidated some of his inherited family assets to purchase grain and distribute it to the poor. Inspired by the Joseph narratives from Genesis, Basil preached, "I shall open my barns. I shall be like Joseph in proclaiming the love of my fellow man."[43]

The most concrete expression of Basil's ministry to the poor in Caesarea was the *basileas* ("new city"), a compound built at the edge of the city in the early 370s. Constructed on Basil's family land or perhaps on land donated by the emperor, the *basileas* was a hub for several ministries to the poor and sick. First, the complex included a home for the poor. Some of the residents were probably abandoned children. Second, there was a hospital—arguably the first of its kind in the world. Some of the patients suffered from leprosy. Third, the *basileas* served as a center for job skills training for the poor and unemployed. Fourth, the complex included the storehouses of food supplies administered by Basil. Finally, since Caesarea was located on a crossroads between Asia Minor, Syria, Armenia, and the Gothic regions, the *basileas* also included a hospitality house for travelers. Basil insisted that his disciples be able to show hospitality to minister to other believers and also to witness to non-Christians.[44]

For Basil, the *basileas* ministry was the clearest expression of what it meant to be a monk-bishop ministering in a city. His monastic vision was shaped by voluntary poverty inspired by John the Baptist (if one has two coats, give the other away), Jesus (sell all you have and give it to the poor), and the early Christians in Acts (selling their goods and sharing everything in common). He believed that authentic community should undergird the monastery and the church. In this way, his life resonates with James's admonition to welcome the rich and the poor into church gatherings (2:1–8). As the people of God building a "new city," their mission ought to include deliberate care for the poor and the sick, especially during times of crisis.[45]

Ephraem of Syria

Originally from Persia, where Christians were persecuted well into the fourth century (after Constantine had given peace to the church in the Roman Empire), Ephraem migrated to Edessa where he was set apart as a deacon in the church. Edessa, a Syriac-speaking city and intercultural crossroads

---

43 Basil, *Sermon* 6.2, cited in Holman, *Hungry Are Dying*, 128.

44 See further Sterk, *Renouncing the World*, 69; Holman, *Hungry Are Dying*, 74, 80; Rousseau, *Basil*, 133, 142; and Patitsas, "St. Basil's Philanthropic Program," 269.

45 See further Daley, "Building a New City," 439.

between the Roman Empire and the East, became part of the Roman Empire in the third century.

Ephraem is remembered as the most important theologian of the fourth-century Syriac church. Unlike his Latin- and Greek-speaking counterparts, Ephraem's theological approach was unique because he articulated Christian thought in the form of hymns and poetry. This approach was strategic for connecting with the oral peoples in Syria who had a love for poetry and song. Ephraem's theology also proved to be foundational for the Church of the East, a Syrio-Persian church that flourished along the Silk Road between Persia, Central Asia, and China from the fourth to eighth centuries. A missionary church, the Church of the East was the only Christian community that thrived in the Eastern world after the rise of Islam.[46]

Ephraem's cross-cultural ministry can be described as mission in deed and word. In response to a plague and famine that hit Edessa in the AD 360s, Ephraem spent the last decade of his life ministering to those affected. He organized food drives for the hungry, founded a hospital for the sick, and collected money to care for the sick and poor. The church historian Sozomen (ca. 400–450) noted that after Ephraem received the necessary donations, he "had about three hundred beds fitted up in the public porches and here he tended those that were ill and suffering from the effects of the famine."[47] Since Edessa was a multicultural city, Sozomen noted that the poor in Ephraem's care included "foreigners or natives of the surrounding country."[48]

In addition to caring tangibly for the hungry, sick, and poor, Ephraem proclaimed the gospel through singing hymns that were rich in gospel and biblical themes. On one hand, Ephraem made the gospel message clear through an accepted and beloved poetic form. On the other hand, the beautiful form of his songs and poetry comforted the sick and dying. Amid his courageous care for the sick and poor, Ephraem contracted the plague and died in 373.[49]

Reflections for Today

James and these selected church fathers believed that Christian mission should include both word (gospel proclamation) and deed (caring for the vulnerable and the poor). While James does not address proclamation

---

46 See further Baum and Winkler, *Church of the East.*

47 Sozomen, *History of the Church* 3.16, cited in Holman, *Hungry Are Dying*, 60.

48 Sozomen, *History of the Church* 3.16, cited in Holman, *Hungry Are Dying*, 60.

49 See further Smither, *Mission in the Early Church*, 133.

directly, his admonition to practice godly speech applies to the gentle and humble manner in which Christians ought to speak about their faith. The church fathers surveyed also cared about verbally proclaiming the gospel—Cyprian during his trial and martyrdom, Basil through his preaching ministry, and Ephraem through his ministry of song and poetry. These fathers would not have recognized deed ministry alone.

James and these church fathers show us that Christian mission must address the real physical needs of the poor and vulnerable in society. Reminding his readers of God's great heart for the poor in the Old Testament Scriptures and through the earthly ministry of Jesus, James raises the plight of the vulnerable and poor in three of the letter's five chapters. To love God and to follow Jesus means that God's people care for widows, orphans, and the poor.

For Cyprian, Basil, and Ephraem, caring for the vulnerable and poor was a built-in, understood value in their church ministries. As missional church leaders, each was engaged with the issues and challenges facing their communities. In Basil's and Ephraem's contexts, they were responding to significant humanitarian crises ravaging their cities. Though Basil collaborated with the Roman government to care for the poor, he clearly took the lead and from all appearances, he recruited their help. During Basil's and Ephraem's ministries, the emperor Julian uttered his famous words about Christians caring for "their poor but ours as well." Though their energies could have been occupied by the challenges and needs within the church, Cyprian, Basil, and Ephraem were engaged in their communities, preaching the gospel and relieving human suffering.

What might the global church today learn from James and these church fathers about mission in word and deed? First, the early church shows us the vital integration of gospel proclamation and caring for human needs. Only in the last two centuries has the church in the West drawn a clear distinction between evangelism and social action in Christian mission. Many churches in the Western world (e.g., affluent suburban congregations in the United States) have reduced mission to evangelism because they have not been forced to deal with poverty in their communities.

The Majority World church today seems to have a more intuitive grasp on holistic mission. I learned this firsthand while serving in a poor African country ruled by a dictator. As I encountered poor and needy people daily, I went to my ministry partner (a local pastor) and asked if we ought to add a line item in our ministry budget for benevolence. Rather confused by my question, he responded, "Well … yes." I realized that this pastor already helped the poor and needy regularly with jobs, medicine, small loans, and other help. Most of this came out of his own pocket. It never occurred to him that the ministry needed to establish a special fund. It was not a ministry strategy; it was just what believers do.

Second, the church and parachurch compassion ministries can take the lead in responding to global crises. While it is often good and appropriate to collaborate with governmental and nongovernmental agencies, church and ministries should not be hampered in their initiatives. Several years ago, following a natural disaster in the central United States, government agencies were divided over the best course of action, which delayed their response. Meanwhile, a Baptist relief organization quickly deployed its teams to the disaster location and got to work while the government agencies were still debating their response.

While governments are sometimes the agents of persecution against Christians, at other times government organizations are grateful for the leadership of Christian ministries. One Christian relief group was doing courageous work among refugees in a country in the Middle East. A new leader for the United Nations High Commissioner on Refugees (UNHCR) arrived in the country and summoned the leader of the relief organization. Fearing the worst from the UNHCR official, the Christian leader took the meeting and was surprised when the official praised their work and asked, "How can we help you?"

Like James, Cyprian, Basil, and Ephraem, the global church today must be engaged with the needs facing our communities. We must pray for and tangibly care for the poor, the homeless, refugees, widows, and orphans— those who are not flourishing as image bearers of the Living God. We must preach the gospel in our words and demonstrate the reality of the gospel through our deeds.

———————————

Bibliography

Baum, Wilhelm, and Dietmar W. Winkler. *The Church of the East: A Concise History.* Central Asian Studies. London: Routledge, 2000.

Burns, J. Patout, Jr., and Robin M. Jensen. *Christianity in Roman Africa: The Development of Its Practices and Beliefs.* Grand Rapids: Eerdmans, 2014.

Chinnock, Edward J. *A Few Notes on Julian and a Translation of His Public Letters.* London: David Nutt, 1901.

Daley, Brian E. "Building a New City: The Cappadocian Fathers and the Rhetoric of Philanthropy." *Journal of Early Christian Studies* 7, no. 3 (1999): 431–61.

Decret, François. *Early Christianity in North Africa*. Translated by Edward L. Smither. Eugene, OR: Cascade, 1999.

Green, Joel B. "Reading James Missionally." In *Reading the Bible Missionally*, edited by Michael W. Goheen, 242–62. Grand Rapids: Eerdmans, 2016.

Holman, Susan R. *The Hungry Are Dying: Beggars and Bishops in Roman Cappadocia*. New York: Oxford University Press, 2001.

Holman, Susan R. "The Hungry Body: Famine, Poverty, and Identity in Basil's Hom. 8." *Journal of Early Christian Studies* 7, no. 3 (1999): 337–63.

Jobes, Karen H. *Letters to the Church: A Survey of Hebrews and the General Epistles*. Grand Rapids: Zondervan, 2011.

Kistemaker, Simon J. *James and I–III John*. Grand Rapids: Baker, 1986.

Moo, Douglas J. *The Letter of James*. Pillar New Testament Commentary. 2nd ed. Grand Rapids: Eerdmans, 2021.

Mursurillo, Herbert. *Acts of the Christian Martyrs*. Vol. 2. Oxford: Oxford University Press, 1999.

Patitsas, Timothy. "St. Basil's Philanthropic Program and Modern Microlending Strategies for Economic Self-Actualization." In *Wealth and Poverty in Early Church and Society*, edited by Susan R. Holman, 267–86. Grand Rapids: Baker Academic, 2008.

Rousseau, Philip. *Basil of Caesarea*. Berkeley: University of California Press, 1998.

Smither, Edward L. *Christian Martyrdom: A Brief History with Reflections for Today*. Eugene, OR: Cascade, 2020.

Smither, Edward L. *Mission in the Early Church: Themes and Reflections*. Eugene, OR: Cascade, 2014.

Smither, Edward L. *Missionary Monks: An Introduction to the History and Theology of Missionary Monasticism*. Eugene, OR: Cascade, 2016.

Sterk, Andrea. *Renouncing the World Yet Leading the Church: The Monk-Bishop in Late Antiquity*. Cambridge: Harvard University Press, 2004.

Vlachos, Chris A. *James*. Exegetical Guide to the Greek New Testament. Nashville: B&H Academic, 2013.

Witherington, Ben, III. *Letters and Homilies for Jewish Christians: A Socio-Rhetorical Commentary on Hebrews, James and Jude*. Downers Grove, IL: IVP Academic, 2007.

Chapter 9

Riches and Poverty in James

Exploring Christian Identity within a Covenantal Framework

Vuyani Stanley Sindo

Grounding James in the Reality of South Africa

Since the time of the debate between Marcion (AD 85–160) and Irenaeus (130–ca. 200), scholars have continued to pit James against Paul. During the Reformation, it became common for scholars to assume that Paul and James contradicted each other, especially concerning the debate of faith and works. Part of the problem with pitting James against Paul is that James's teachings on faith and works are often taken out of their immediate context, and a foreign context (i.e., Paul's) is imposed on it, which is not James's primary concern as he writes his letter. This eisegesis of James has caused the church to miss the missiological imperatives of James. The focus on this debate has unfortunately robbed the church in South Africa of understanding her missional mandate. This is compounded by the general lack of missiological studies on James. This has led to churches in South Africa being marked by division, favoritism for the rich, and indifference and intolerance toward poor believers.

Discrimination against the poor in favor of the rich is still common in the Majority World, which a missiological reading of James would challenge. This chapter, looking at James's teachings regarding the poor versus the wealthy, will argue that any Christian community that is indifferent to the poor is at odds with its missional identity.

Acts 4:32–35 describes a Christian community whose life was characterized by unity, sharing, and the display of its in-Christ identity:

> Now the full number of those who believed were of one heart and soul, and no one said that any of the things that belonged to him was his own, but they had everything in common… . There was not a needy person among them, for as many as were owners of lands or houses sold them and brought the proceeds of what was sold and laid it at the apostles' feet, and it was distributed to each as any had need. (ESV)[1]

---

1 Unless otherwise noted, all Scripture quotations are from the NIV.

In this community, the church displayed and fulfilled the identity of the people of God that Deuteronomy 15:4–11 anticipated in the Sabbatical year. The people were not hardening their hearts to the needs of the poor. The early church acted with unity and mutuality; resembling how Aristotle saw friendship as akin to love and mutuality: "'Friends have one soul between them,' 'Friends' goods are common property,' 'Amity is equality.'"[2]

This depiction of the church in Acts 4:32–35 is far from the picture that we see in the church in South Africa, something that this chapter hopes to explore through the missiological reading of James 2. South Africa is a country of extremes. On the one hand, according to Henley and Partners' 2023 report on Africa's wealth, South Africa is the wealthiest country in Africa "in terms of resident high-net-worth individuals."[3] On the other hand, the World Bank declared South Africa the most unequal country in the world for three consecutive years, from 2020 to 2022. The World Bank report highlights the various contributing factors to why extreme inequalities persist in South Africa.[4] In the 2020 assessment conducted by the United Nations Human Development Report, South Africa was positioned at 114th among the 189 countries evaluated. This ranking was determined based on diverse indicators encompassing average life expectancy, educational outcomes, and income inequality.[5] The irony of these statistics is that 80 percent of the population of South Africa claim to be Christian.[6] Yet, even with such a high number of Christians, the country is marked by the worst inequalities in the world.

Despite so many South Africans claiming to be Christians, the wealthy in South Africa continue to flaunt their wealth in the midst of a country plagued with poverty, and the church is no exception. The city that I currently reside in, Cape Town, secured the accolade of "Best Worldwide City" in the 2023 Telegraph Travel Awards for the eighth consecutive year, but the poor in this city do not get to enjoy its beauty as they are constantly victimized and pushed out of sight. Scholars such as Louise Edwards argue that cities like Cape Town, through their bylaws, continue to discriminate against and criminalize the poor purely on the basis of being poor.[7]

---

2 Aristotle, *Eth. nic.* 9.8.

3 Henley and Partners, "Africa Wealth Report 2023," 20.

4 International Bank for Reconstruction and the World Bank, "Overcoming Poverty and Inequality in South Africa."

5 United Nations Development Programme, "Human Development Report 2020."

6 South African Embassy in The Netherlands, "Religions."

7 Edwards, "Framing the Challenge," 1–5.

With 80 percent of the population claiming to be Christians, one would assume that South Africa would be a place where Christian values of human dignity and equality would be celebrated, particularly because religious freedom and practices are enshrined in the South African constitution. The South African constitution guarantees freedom of belief, which encompasses the right to establish, join, and sustain religious associations. It also permits religious practices in state or state-supported institutions, given that they are voluntary and conducted impartially.[8] Discrimination on the grounds of religion is unlawful in South Africa, and one can be taken to the Equality Court if one discriminates against another on the grounds of religion. Thus, South Africa ought to be a country where Christians flourish and display their identity boldly for all to see. But this is not the case.

The church is no exception either; within the church in South Africa are increasing cases of inequality and disunity. In South Africa, thanks to the legacy of apartheid, we still have the so-called White churches, which are predominantly White and rich, and the so-called Black churches, which are primarily attended by Black people, who are poor in comparison. While you will often find a few Black people attending White churches, these people are often not in leadership positions and thus give little to no input regarding the churches' direction. Similarly, Kelebogile T. Resane has also observed that when Black people move into so-called White spaces in South Africa, this tends to cause White flight from both the cities and the churches, which used to be predominantly White. He observes that when Black people move into areas and churches that used to be reserved for White people during apartheid, "instead of [White people] changing their worship style to accommodate the demographics of the area, the white people opt to exit the community or sell the church building for another purpose."[9]

Resane observes a number of factors that give rise to White flight. He writes that White flight is often based on the unfounded belief that mixed-race and Black individuals are more prone to crime. This misguided notion suggests that an increased presence of Black residents leads to rising crime rates, decreased property values, and overall neighborhood decline.[10] Resane also notes that some White people are fearful of multiculturalism and view it as a threat to "white identity and self-determination."[11] This is, in part, due

---

8   For more on how the South African constitution protects and promotes religious freedom and practices, see U.S. Department of State, "2022 Report on International Religious Freedom."

9   Resane, "Demographic Change," 3.

10 Resane, 3.

11 Resane uses the term "cultural convergence" (2), while I prefer the term multiculturalism.

to the fact that, according to Resane, some White people in South Africa still view Black people as "subhumans" and a "species of the lower class."[12] Thus, even in the church, poverty and racism contribute to divisions in the church. This has led to a number of previously White churches closing down or being converted for different uses than worship or being leased to other independent churches that are exclusively Black to be used for Black people.[13]

Thus, in South Africa, there is not much unity in the church. To use the words of Acts 4:32, there is not "one heart and soul" among the believers here. It is worth noting that not only the White church is indifferent to or discriminates against the poor, who are mostly perceived as Black, but within the Black church itself, there is discrimination against the poor as well, in part due to prosperity gospel teachings.[14] The prosperity gospel uses the laws of causality—if one sacrifices financially to the man/woman of God, one will receive material blessings and prosper both physically and spiritually.[15] This sacrificial giving is often presented as the seed. This often leaves poorer Christians blaming themselves for their lack of material prosperity, while the wealthier Christians tend to flaunt their wealth as the fruit of their faith, as if their wealth is a sure sign that God has blessed them because they are faithful.

These societal problems in South Africa, especially in the church, have called into question its missiological outlook. Believers in South Africa, and other parts of the world facing similar trends, need the book of James to rediscover afresh the missiological purpose of being the people of God, particularly amid inequalities and racial division.

Using the insights of scholars such as Christopher J. H. Wright, Dean Flemming, and Graham Paul Dancy, this chapter seeks to explore how James relates to the *missio Dei*.[16] It explores James's unique contribution to the identity formation of the people of God who are set apart; crucially, it investigates how James can help the church in South Africa to live out the missional mandate in a context marked by such inequality. This chapter will place James within the overall biblical narrative concerning wealth and poverty, with the caveat that this will be exploratory, not exhaustive.

---

12 Resane, 2.

13 For more on this, see Resane, "Demographic Change."

14 For a detailed description of the prosperity gospel see Sanou, "Prosperity Gospel," 18–46; Nwaomah, "Overview of the Prosperity Gospel," 3–17; and Akabike, Ngwoke, and Chukwuma, "Critical Analysis of Tithe."

15 This teaching has elements of truth even though it has been manipulated to favor the so-called man/woman of God. McKnight, "Poverty, Riches," 162.

16 Dancy, "Missional Reading."

James and Inequalities

James can help the church in South Africa with its missional purpose since it was written to people who are similar to us. Peter H. Davids writes that James has a lot to say about "wealth and its use."[17] He notes that "47 verses out of 105," roughly 45 percent of the epistle, is dedicated to economic themes.[18]

James describes his audience as the twelve tribes in the diaspora (1:1).[19] The NASB renders this as "To the twelve tribes who are dispersed abroad." Douglas J. Moo notes that "dispersed" signifies that the community "was forced to live outside their home country," which helps us to reconstruct the characteristics of the audience of James, that is, they experienced poverty and oppression.[20] Similarly, Craig L. Blomberg argues that James was written to Christ-followers at the eastern end of the Mediterranean basin, who were mostly composed of poor people "experiencing some significant discrimination, including the mistreatment."[21] Poignantly, Blomberg observes the correlation between James's audience and the church in our day when he writes that there are:

> parallels between today's affluent Christians' behaviour and what is described in James 5:5–6—living on the earth in luxury and self-indulgence while condemning the righteous who do not oppose them— make us too uncomfortable to spend much time dwelling on it, so we domesticate James and/or return to our favourite biblical writer, Paul, from whom we think all real theological and ethical blessings flow![22]

Scholarship has extensively examined the social conditions of James's audience and how he seeks to encourage them to be faithful in the midst of trials of various kinds (1:2), which in part seem to have been caused by the socioeconomic disparities of their milieu.[23]

In addition, the understanding of James's central structure and theme has progressed since the time of Martin Dibelius, who argued that there was no

---

17 Davids, "Test of Wealth," 355.

18 Davids, 355.

19 There is a debate among scholars regarding the identity of the community that James was writing to. See DeSilva, *Introduction to the New Testament*, 724; and Moo, *Letter of James*, 23.

20 Moo, *Letter of James*, 24.

21 Blomberg, "Perfect Law of Liberty," 173–74.

22 Blomberg, 174.

23 See Blomberg and Kamell, *James*, 29.

overarching structure to James.[24] Recently, Blomberg observed that James is a "purposeful theologian with an overarching structure in mind."[25] Scholars such as Blomberg, Davids, and Mariam J. Kamell have observed three main themes throughout James.[26] These are tests and trials, wisdom, and wealth versus poverty.[27] Blomberg, upon analyzing the structure of James using chiastic structure, concludes that wealth versus poverty is the central and climactic topic of the epistle.[28] These findings are also evident in the work of Davids.[29] This chapter will limit its investigation to the theme of wealth and poverty, primarily concentrating on James 1–2.

The Structure of James, with a Focus on Wealth and Poverty

There is a lack of consensus among scholars concerning the structure of James, even though they argue there is a coherent discourse in the epistle.[30] Broadly speaking, the following structure has been observed: the prescript (1:1), the introduction or "the double opening statement" (1:2–27),[31] the main body (2:1–5:6), and the conclusion (5:7–20).[32] Our interest in the structure of James is, however, on the missional dimension of the text, particularly in its relationship to the subject of wealth and poverty. This is not to deny that there are other themes present in the epistle.

Davids notes that James has a lot to say about the theme of wealth and how one uses wealth.[33] In 1:9–11, James contrasts the position of the poor believers and wealthy believers. Dancy notes that this is a "powerful

---

24 Dibelius, *James*, 2, argues that *"the entire document* [James] *lacks continuity in thought"* (emphasis original).

25 Blomberg, *From Pentecost to Patmos*, 391.

26 Davids, *Epistle of James*, 22–28; Blomberg, *From Pentecost to Patmos*, 391–92; Blomberg and Kamell, *James*, 23–27.

27 DeSilva, *Introduction to the New Testament*, 730–33, argues that James addresses "a wide array of specific trials and temptations faced by believers, in which the genuineness of their faith can be demonstrated or belied," many of which involve the issues of wealth and poverty.

28 Blomberg, "Perfect Law," 173.

29 Davids, "Test of Wealth," 355; Moo, *James*, 24, however, cautions against looking at James only through the lens of a socioeconomic perspective.

30 See Porter, "Cohesion in James," 45–68; and Dancy, "Missional Reading," 14–15.

31 Moo, *Letter of James*, 44.

32 Moo, 44; see also Dancy, "Missional Reading," 15.

33 Davids, "Test of Wealth," 355. I am not arguing that James is only concerned about the issue of the wealthy versus the poor but that this is one of its main topics.

reversal theme that taps into the overarching mission of God."[34] In 1:27, he underscores the "importance of caring for the orphans and widows, two of the four cardinal categories of the poor in Hebrew scripture."[35]

James's ethical framework centers on the proper treatment of the poor/destitute and includes cautionary messages about the dangers of greed. In 2:1–13, James argues against favoritism toward the rich and discrimination of the poor.[36] In 2:14–26, he argues that taking care of the poor is faith that pleases God, "without which faith is dead."[37] In 4:2–3, he points to the futility of coveting as it does not change anyone's social status, especially when one does not pray. In 4:13–17, he condemns self-reliant merchants who do not include God in their planning. James 5:1–6 "condemns the rich who oppress laborers who work for them."[38] In 5:7–11, he encourages patience on the side of those oppressed by the rich and reminds them that God's judgment is at hand.[39]

Davids asks a pertinent question that we ought to reckon with: Why is James "devoting such a large portion of his work to the issue of wealth"?[40] He suggests that it is because James is following the Jesus tradition.[41] Richard Bauckham holds a similar view: "The discussion [about James within the wisdom tradition] has established beyond question that James knew a tradition of the sayings of Jesus, in oral or written form, and that a few passages of James are certainly related to specific sayings of Jesus known to us from the Synoptic Gospels."[42] As we have already seen in the prescript, James describes himself as a slave of God and of the Lord Jesus Christ. Scholars such as Bauckham, Kamell, and Dan G. McCartney argue that James, by using this description of himself as a slave of God and Jesus, centers his story within the story of God and Jesus. McCartney writes: "No matter how this verse is read [Jas 1:1], James is setting forth a high Christology, identifying Jesus not just as Christ (Messiah) but also as Lord, mentioned in the same breath with God.[43]

34　Dancy, "Missional Reading," 17.

35　Davids, "Test of Wealth," 355.

36　Davids, 355.

37　Davids, 355.

38　Davids, 355.

39　Davids, 355. A similar structure to this can also be found in the work of Blomberg, *From Pentecost*, 391, even though he uses a chiastic structure to analyze James under the three broader themes of trials, wisdom, and riches/poverty.

40　Davids, "Test of Wealth," 356.

41　Davids, 356.

42　Bauckham, *James*, 82.

43　McCartney, *James*, 78.

Bauckham observes that James's teachings have "special authority because it is the wisdom of a sage whose own teacher was Jesus."[44] Kamell notes, "James's prescript serves to pave the way for a christological reading in the text, even while serving as a call to proper humility, since the author of the text claims only low status for himself."[45]

While looking at James through the Jesus tradition will yield valuable insight for our missiological reading of James, it also misses a broader missiological component of James. We need to read James in light of God's mission and our role in that story. Jesus's tradition will be part of it, but there is more to it as well. In the words of Scot McKnight, we need to read James as part of the Bible story.[46]

James 1:9-11, 17: A Missiological Outlook within the Story of God

We now turn to the main section of this chapter, the book of James itself. We first need to clarify three key issues that scholars often disagree about, all concentrated in verses 9–10. The first two deal with the translation of the Greek words ἀδελφός and ταπεινός in verse 9, while the third concerns the identity of the rich in verse 10.

Ἀδελφός: Brother or Believer?

James 1:9–11 begins with a contrast between the positions of poor and wealthy believers, with the poor seemingly good and the rich bad.[47] Interestingly, James uses ἀδελφός and not believers, as suggested by the NRSV and the NIV.[48] While there might be grounds to translate ἀδελφός as "believer" instead of "brother," as suggested by McKnight—who argues the notion of the believer is inherent to James's use of the term—it is important not to lose sight of James's emphasis in the process.[49] Translating ἀδελφός as "believer" minimizes the impact of James's teachings and is dangerous for the church in South Africa as it leaves wealthy Christians still seeing the poor as simply "others" outside their community. James, by using the sibling language of ἀδελφός, emphasizes that the poor and the rich are part of the

---

44 Bauckham, *James*, 85; cf. Kamell, "Soteriology of James," 130.

45 Kamell, "Soteriology of James," 130.

46 McKnight, "Poverty, Riches," 161–74.

47 McKnight, 168.

48 See James 1:2, 16, 19; 2:1, 5, 14; 3:1, 10, 12; 4:11; 5:7, 9, 12, 19, where James also uses brother.

49 McKnight, "Poverty, Riches," 168.

family. Thus, I prefer to translate the term as "brother" in order to underscore the impact of James's teachings on the church in South Africa.

Ὁ Ταπεινός: Economically Poor or Spiritually Poor?

The second issue in verse 9 is the identity of the poor, or what we mean by the term ταπεινός. James 1:9–11 contrasts the terms ὁ ταπεινός and ὁ πλούσιος, but who these people are and how we translate these terms have been a subject of debate.

Scholars such as Kamell, who read James within the Jesus tradition, are quick to try to link ὁ ταπεινός with the spiritual poverty of Matthew 5:2.[50] While Kamell admits that ὁ ταπεινός "does contain the idea of physical poverty," she is quick to add that the term is more theological and that it "conveys the Hebraic idea of the 'righteous poor.'"[51] Citing Matthew 5:2 to support her case, she adds that "this passage introduces what will be important particularly in chapters 4 and 5 regarding a person's salvation: the necessity of a humble heart before God without dependence upon worldly goods or status."[52] At this point, Kamell moves the discussion of James 1:9–11 away from what might be perceived as the ethical concerns of James to soteriology. While soteriology might be in view in James 4–5, it is important to analyze James 1 in its immediate context.

In chapters 1 and 2, James contrasts ὁ ταπεινός and ὁ πλούσιος. The context of the epistle makes it clear that the rich are the oppressors (2:1–13; 5:1–6), while the poor are the oppressed.[53] While James 4:6 might have spiritual poverty in view, chapters 1 and 2 make it clear that it is the economically poor and socially marginalized in view. This view also resonates with another Jesus tradition, particularly Luke. McKnight notes that James draws from the "Jewish *anawim* tradition" of the righteous poor (Luke 1:48, 52–53), but the person is still socially destitute.[54] Thus, ὁ ταπεινός refers to the socioeconomically destitute and oppressed, i.e., the physically poor. Moo warns us, especially those in the West who enjoy comfortable lifestyles, that in our quest to distance James from the extreme "liberation" perspective, we must be careful not to trivialize James's message to the poor

---

50 Kamell, "Soteriology of James," 134.

51 Kamell, 134.

52 Kamell, 134.

53 McKnight, "Poverty, Riches," 168.

54 McKnight, 168. See also Davids, "Test of Wealth," 357, who argues that "James reflects a sharp prophetic denunciation of the rich that is only found in the Lucan tradition within the New Testament."

and his warnings to the rich. Similarly, the poor need to be careful not to radicalize James's teachings about poverty and wealth.[55]

James 1 encourages poor believers who are experiencing oppression and rejection (James 2) to consider it pure joy to face their trials (1:2–3) because of their relationship with God. Kamell notes that James 1:9–11 corresponds with the verses found throughout the wisdom literature that encourage the oppressed that "God will bring about justice on their oppressors" (cf. Prov 18:12; Sir 11; and 4Q418 126 II, 6–8).[56] Reading the Old Testament, one soon discovers that the poor have a special place in God's heart. Franz Mussner writes that James appeals to the Old Testament and Jewish tradition in his treatment of the poor. He writes: "There is hardly a single element of the OT-late Jewish tradition about poverty and piety that is not also encountered in the letter of James."[57] Moo notes that James appeals to three elements of the Jewish tradition to ground his argument, which is important for our missiological reading.[58]

First, God has a special concern for the poor, especially those who are part of his covenantal people. In Psalm 68:5, David describes God as "a father to the fatherless, a defender of widows." Meanwhile, in Deuteronomy 10:14–17, God is described as the one true God who is above all gods and lords. He is the one who owns everything; he is mighty and awesome; and he shows no partiality. In the midst of this description of God's grandeur and awesome power, Deuteronomy 10:18 says: "He defends the cause of the fatherless and the widow, and loves the foreigner residing among you, giving them food and clothing."[59]

Second, Moo notes that within the Old Testament tradition, God's people were expected to "imitate God by showing a similar concern for the poor and the disadvantaged."[60] This comes up clearly in Deuteronomy 10:19: "And you are to love those who are foreigners, for you yourselves were foreigners in Egypt." The Old Testament prophets denounced the Israelites for not keeping this law, such as in Amos 2:6–7.[61] Thus James demonstrates a continuity with this missiological purpose of God for his people when he

---

55 Moo, *Letter of James*, 36.

56 Kamell, "Soteriology of James," 133.

57 Mussner, *Der Jakobusbrief*, 249, quoted in Moo, *Letter of James*, 35. Similar arguments are found in Davids, *Epistle of James*, 42.

58 Moo, *Letter of James*, 35.

59 Cf. Moo, 35.

60 Moo, 35.

61 Moo, 35.

writes in James 1:27, "Religion that God our Father accepts as pure and faultless is this: to look after orphans and widows in their distress and to keep oneself from being polluted by the world." God cares for the poor, and he expects his people to likewise care for them.

Third, in the Old Testament tradition, particularly the Psalms (i.e., 10; 37:8–17; 72:2, 4; see also Isa 29:19), there is "an association of the 'poor' (*'ani*) with the righteous."[62] A few things need to be pointed out at this juncture. First, these are poor people within Israel whose relationship with the covenantal God is assumed. This comes up clearly in the Jesus tradition, as reported in Matthew 5:3 and Luke 6:20. The poor who are blessed "are both economically marginalized and those who trust in God as their only hope."[63] Second, because of their relationship with God, in the face of oppression by the wealthy and powerful, "they call out to God for deliverance."[64] Conversely, God promises to hear, help, and deliver the poor from the wicked oppressors through judging the oppressor.[65] James 1:9 uses the imperative of καυχάομαι to urge the poor brother (whom the context makes it clear is a believer) to glory or take pride ἐν τῷ ὕψει αὐτοῦ ("in their high position"). In 1 Corinthians 1:31, ἐν is used with καυχάομαι to introduce the object of boasting. Thus, James says the poor are to boast about their high position in God. But the preposition ἐν can also have a causal use and denote that the poor brother is to boast because of his high position or exaltation since ὕψος can mean both.[66]

Blomberg and Kamell suggest that James speaks so positively about the poor brother here because the poor brother trusts in God alone. They note that "most of us turn to God only when we have exhausted every other option," but the poor brother's only option is God.[67] James says he should boast about his high status because there is promised "spiritual, eschatological compensation for abject poverty among God's people in this world."[68] James's exhortation to take pride echoes the trajectory of the Old Testament story when God, through the prophet Jeremiah, exhorted his people, saying:

---

62 Moo, 35.

63 Blomberg and Kamell, *James*, 63.

64 Moo, *Letter of James*, 35.

65 Moo, 35.

66 Vlachos, *James*, 33. I use the term brother to mean both brother or sister since ἀδελφός can be gender inclusive.

67 Blomberg and Kamell, *James*, 63.

68 Blomberg and Kamell, 63.

> Let not the wise boast of their wisdom or the strong boast of their
> strength or the rich boast of their riches, but let the one who boasts
> boast about this: that they have the understanding to know me, that
> I am the LORD, who exercises kindness, justice and righteousness
> on earth, for in these I delight," declares the LORD. (Jer 9:23–24)

While his audience faces terrible treatment and oppression by the rich, James
wants them to lift their eyes and boast about who they are in God. James 2:5
states it beautifully: God has "chosen those who are poor in the eyes of the
world to be rich in faith and to inherit the kingdom he promised those who
love him."

Ὁ Πλούσιος: Is He a Brother/Believer or Just an Oppressor?

In 1:10, James turns his attention to the rich with a contrast introduced by
the soft adversative conjunction δέ.[69] In this verse, James speaks negatively
toward the rich. He uses imagery from Isaiah 40:6b–8, and possibly Psalm
103:15–16, about the possible fate of the rich: those who trust in their wealth
are just like grass that disappears in a moment of dry wind; so is their fate.[70]

There is, however, a debate about the identity of the rich person
(πλούσιος) of James 1:10. The question is whether this person should be
seen as a believer or nonbeliever, especially in light of the denunciation of
the unbelieving rich in James 2:6. Davids suggests that the rich person is
not a Christian and he does this by appealing to the finding of Dibelius who
argued that in the Jewish thought "the rich are often contrasted with the poor
remnant of Israel."[71] I, however, concur with the scholars who take the rich
of verse 10 to be believers. Grammatically, scholars such as Chris Vlachos
have observed that the adjective πλούσιος is in the substantive "position
with no explicit noun that the adj. [adjective] qualifies; it seems natural to
supply ἀδελφός from verse 9."[72]

Moreover, within the Old Testament, there was another tradition that saw
wealth as an outflow of God's blessing to those who are obedient, something
that Davids himself alludes to.[73] The case in point is the story of Abraham.
Thus, I take James in this section to speak to poor and wealthy brothers who
are part of the Jesus movement. He wants both of them to have minds that are

---

69 Vlachos, *James*, 33.

70 Kamell, "Soteriology of James," 133. See also Moo, *Letter of James*, 67.

71 Davids, *Epistle of James*, 77.

72 Vlachos, *James*, 33.

73 Davids, *Epistle of James*, 45.

missiologically shaped by the story of God and his dealings with his people. More than anything, in verses 9–10, James speaks of "the great reversal."[74] It is tempting for the rich to trust in and worship their wealth like the rich fool of Jesus's parable in Luke 12:13–21, but James warns them about the transitory nature of this life. Blomberg notes that the humble circumstance in which the rich brother is to glory is the awareness that he, "like everyone else … will die and face judgment."[75] Psalm 49:16–19 reflects the heart of James's message here:

> Do not be overawed when others grow rich, when the splendor of their houses increases; for they will take nothing with them when they die, their splendor will not descend with them. Though while they live they count themselves blessed—and people praise you when you prosper—they will join those who have gone before them, who will never again see the light of life.

James commands the rich brothers to boast about their humiliating circumstances, not their riches. Life is transitory, and they cannot take their riches with them. James 1:11 says, "For the sun rises with scorching heat and withers the plant; its blossom falls and its beauty is destroyed. In the same way, the rich will fade away even while they go about their business." James's point has been captured well by Moo: "Christians must always evaluate themselves by spiritual and not material standards."[76] This is something that the church in South Africa appears to have a lot to learn about its missional mandate. The church in South Africa seems to fall in the category that James rebukes in James 2:1–7—showing favoritism to the rich and disdain for the poor.

Discrimination against the Poor Is Against God's Missional Purpose for the Church (2:1-13)

In this chapter's introduction, we saw that in South Africa, there is generally indifference at best and discrimination at worst against the poor. In the previous section, we saw that James wants the poor to boast about their high position in God, while the rich are to boast about their low position because their riches will "'wither away' (1:11) and be destroyed (5:5)."[77]

---

74 Blomberg and Kamell, *James*, 63.

75 Blomberg, "Perfect Law," 175.

76 Moo, *Letter of James*, 68–69.

77 McKnight, "Poverty, Riches," 169.

In this section, James 2:1–13 opposes discrimination against the poor within the community. James uses the term συναγωγή to set the scene for where this discrimination is taking place. Blomberg suggests that the use of συναγωγή means that this discrimination took place in some gathering other than the worship service and suggests a Christian courtroom where believers adjudicated disputes within the community.[78] While there is debate about where the events of chapter 2 are taking place, the bottom line is that there is discrimination against the poor in favor of the rich, which James condemns in the strongest terms (2:1–4). Interestingly, James 2:1 opens with his use of the sibling language, ἀδελφός, which takes us back to our previous discussion of James 1:9–11.[79] The community is discriminating against its own brother in the Lord.

James 2:1 makes it clear that discrimination against the poor in favor of the rich brother is unacceptable in the Christian community. He writes: "Believers in our glorious Lord Jesus Christ must *not show* favoritism" (emphasis added). The word that James uses for favoritism is προσωπολημψία, which literally means "receiving the face"; the idea is that of judging people based on their outward appearances.[80] It communicates inappropriate biases or prejudice based on external appearance. Verses 2–3 make this clear by describing how the rich person is dressed compared to the poor person and how the community responds to these two individuals; the rich person is honored or looked upon with favor, while the poor person "is treated with disdain and even contempt."[81]

In verse 4, James communicates that Christians who discriminate in this way against the poor are making this judgment based on evil thoughts, a flawed pattern of thinking. Kamell captures this well: "Their internal and interpersonal dialogue reveals a fundamentally faulty value system as they accept the self-importance of the wealthy person as accurate, forgetting that the Glory of God chose to identify instead with the impoverished of the world."[82] Their actions indicate the community's failure to be different and unpolluted by the world (cf. 1:27). Discrimination goes against the missional purpose of God's people. His people are supposed to reflect his attributes, and one thing that is clear from Scripture is God's impartiality and his expectation that his people will

---

78 Blomberg, "Perfect Law," 177.
79 McKnight, "Poverty, Riches," 169.
80 Moo, *Letter of James*, 102.
81 Moo, 103.
82 Kamell, "Soteriology of James," 153.

follow suit (Job 34:17–20; Ps 82:2; Mal 2:9; Matt 22:16;[83] Acts 10:34; Rom 2:11; Gal 2:6; Eph 6:9; Col 3:25; 1 Tim 5:21).[84]

James 2:5–13 lists three reasons why discrimination against the poor is at odds with the missional mandate of the Christian community. First, favoritism toward the rich and discrimination against the poor are at odds with God's own attitude; God has a special concern for the poor who love him. In verses 5–6a, James speaks about the phenomenon that has been observed elsewhere in the New Testament, such as 1 Corinthians 1:27 and Ephesians 1:4, where God seems to delight in choosing the poor to be rich in faith.[85] Bauckham has observed that this is not only a New Testament phenomenon: "This paradox brilliantly encapsulates the Jewish tradition of regarding the pious poor as the paradigms of faith."[86] James wants to highlight to the community that their behavior is inconsistent with the heart of God, who is pro-poor, i.e., those "who love Him."[87]

Second, favoritism toward the rich is incongruent with how the rich should act toward those who belong to Jesus (Jas 2:6b–7). While the community favors the rich, they forget that it is the same rich people who oppress and drag them to court. Moo suggests that the rich made their wealth at the expense of the poor (who would have been the majority of James's readers), using the courts to maintain their wealth and dominance.[88] These rich believers blasphemed the noble name of the Lord, probably not by "directly cursing Christ but by the very act of bringing charges against those who already have the deck stacked against them."[89] James warns the rich throughout his epistle of God's judgment (5:5). Rich Christians need to be careful in how they act, especially in how they treat the poor, as their actions might blaspheme the name of God.

Third, discrimination against the poor in favor of the rich is contrary to the royal law of love (2:8–11).[90] Verses 8–9 contrast two ways to live.

---

83 Ironically, in this verse, the Pharisees want to trap Jesus, but they are fully aware that Jesus is not swayed by people's appearance.

84 Cf. McKnight, "Poverty, Riches," 170; see also 1 Clem. 1:3 and Sir 35:14–16.

85 See Moo, *Letter of James*, 105, and Blomberg, "Perfect Law," 178.

86 Bauckham, *James*, 85.

87 Being poor is not synonymous with being part of the people of God who are rich in faith; it is only the poor who are the members of the community of faith, those who believe in Jesus, of which this is true. See Moo, *James*, 105–8; and Blomberg, "Perfect Law," 178.

88 Moo, *Letter of James*, 108–9.

89 Blomberg, "Perfect Law," 178.

90 McKnight, "Poverty, Riches," 170; cf. Blomberg, "Perfect Law," 178.

One is for us to live out our missional mandate, described as the royal law, corresponding to the kingdom motif of 2:5. He says that if we love our neighbors as ourselves, we are fulfilling the royal law, which is how God's people ought to live out their missional mandate, living as people of the kingdom. However, if we are showing favoritism, we are sinning, meaning that we are not living out our missional mandate. Loving and belonging to God are integrally linked to how we love others. Jesus summed up the two greatest commandments as "Love the Lord your God" and "Love your neighbor" (Matt 22:37–40). These two commandments are our ethical code as his people.[91] Favoritism and indifference to the poor have no place among God's people. The rich have their covenantal obligations to love and serve the poor (Gal 5:13–14; Rom 13:8–10).

Conclusion

The church in South Africa must read James in order to recover its missional mandate. It needs to be a place where people love and serve one another. The poor need to be reminded of their high position in God—God has chosen them to be rich in faith—while the rich need to be reminded about the fleeting nature of their life and riches. God has a special place for the poor who love him, and as his people, we also need to emulate his concern for the poor. The church needs to be a welcoming place for the poor, and favoritism should have no place in this community because it is at odds with God's mission and the mission of the church.

Bibliography

Akabike, Gladys N., Peace N. Ngwoke, and Onyekachi G. Chukwuma. "A Critical Analysis of Tithe and Seed Sowing on Contemporary Christianity in Nigeria." *HTS Teologiese Studies/Theological Studies* 77, no. 1 (2021): a6485. https://doi.org/10.4102/hts.v77i1.6485.

Bauckham, Richard. *James: Wisdom of James, Disciple of Jesus the Sage.* New York: Routledge, 1999.

Blomberg, Craig L. *From Pentecost to Patmos: An Introduction to Acts through Revelation.* Nashville: B&H Publishing, 2006.

Blomberg, Craig L. "The Perfect Law of Liberty on Poverty and Wealth: A Precursor to Paul?" *Tyndale Bulletin* 73 (2022): 171–99.

---

91 Moo, *Letter of James*, 111–13.

Blomberg, Craig L., and Mariam J. Kamell. *James*. Zondervan Exegetical Commentary on the New Testament 16. Grand Rapids: Zondervan, 2008.

Dancy, Graham Paul. "A Missional Reading of the Letter of James: Hearing the Voice of James in Mission." PhD diss., University of Gloucestershire, 2021.

Davids, Peter H. *The Epistle of James: A Commentary on the Greek Text*. New International Greek New Testament Commentary. Grand Rapids: Eerdmans, 1982.

Davids, Peter H. "The Test of Wealth." In *The Mission of James, Peter, and Paul: Tensions in Early Christianity*, edited by Bruce D. Chilton and Craig A. Evans, 355–84. Supplements to Novum Testamentum 15. Leiden: Brill, 2005.

DeSilva, David A. *An Introduction to the New Testament: Contexts, Methods and Ministry Formation*. 2nd ed. Downers Grove, IL: InterVarsity Press, 2018.

Dibelius, Martin. *James: A Commentary on the Epistle of James*. Revised by Heinrich Greeven. Translated by Michael A. Williams. Edited by Helmut Koester. 11th ed. Philadelphia: Fortress, 1976.

Edwards, Louise. "Framing the Challenge: Criminalising Poverty in South Africa." In *Poverty Is Not a Crime: Decriminalising Petty By-laws in South Africa*, edited by Clare Ballard, Patrick Burton, Louise Edwards, Abdirahman Maalim Gossar, and Chumile Sali, 1–5. Cape Town: African Policing Civilian Oversight Forum, 2021.

Flemming, Dean. *Recovering the Full Mission of God: A Biblical Perspective on Being, Doing and Telling*. Downers Grove, IL: IVP Academic, 2013.

Henley and Partners. "Africa Wealth Report 2023." Accessed November 28, 2023. https://www.henleyglobal.com/publications/africa-wealth-report-2023.

International Bank for Reconstruction and the World Bank. "Overcoming Poverty and Inequality in South Africa: An Assessment of Drivers, Constraints and Opportunities." The World Bank. March 2018. https://documents1.worldbank.org/curated/en/530481521735906534/pdf/Overcoming-Poverty-and-Inequality-in-South-Africa-An-Assessment-of-Drivers-Constraints-and-Opportunities.pdf.

Kamell, Mariam J. "The Soteriology of James in Light of Earlier Jewish Wisdom Literature and the Gospel of Matthew." PhD diss., University of St Andrews, 2010.

McCartney, Dan G. *James*. Baker Exegetical Commentary on the New Testament. Grand Rapids: Baker Academic, 2009.

McKnight, Scot. "Poverty, Riches, and God's Blessings: James in the Context of the Biblical Story." In *Reading the Epistle of James: A Resource for Students*, by Darian R. Lockett and Eric F. Mason, 161–76. Atlanta: Society of Biblical Literature, 2019.

Moo, Douglas J. *The Letter of James*. Pillar New Testament Commentary. Grand Rapids: Eerdmans, 2000.

Mussner, Franz. *Der Jakobusbrief.* 4th ed. Herders Theologischer Kommentar zum Neuen Testament. Freiburg: Herder, 1981.

Nwaomah, Sampson. "Overview of the Prosperity Gospel." In *Prosperity Gospel: A Biblical-Theological Evaluation*, edited by Daniel K. Bediako, 3–17. Accra, Ghana: Advent, 2020.

Plummer, Robert L. *Paul's Understanding of the Church's Mission: Did the Apostle Paul Expect the Early Christian Communities to Evangelize?* Bletchley: Paternoster, 2006.

Porter, Stanley E. "Cohesion in James." In *The Epistle of James: Linguistic Exegesis of an Early Christian Letter*, edited by James D. Dvorak and Zachary K. Dawson, 45–68. Eugene, OR: Pickwick, 2019.

Resane, Kelebogile T. "Demographic Change: Ecological and Polycentric Challenges for White Christianity in Urban South Africa." *HTS Teologiese Studies/Theological Studies* 75, no. 1 (2019).

Sanou, Boubakar. "The Prosperity Gospel and the Church in Africa: A Missiological Assessment in the Light of the Great Commission." *Asia-Africa Journal of Mission and Ministry* 23 (2021): 18–46.

South African Embassy in The Netherlands, "Religions." Accessed November 25, 2023. https://zuidafrika.nl/arts-culture/religions/.

United Nations Development Programme. "Human Development Report 2020: The Next Frontier: Human Development and the Anthropocene." United Nations Development Programme. December 15, 2020. https://hdr.undp.org/content/human-development-report-2020.

U.S. Department of State. "2022 Report on International Religious Freedom: South Africa." U.S. Department of State. Accessed November 20, 2023. https://www.state.gov/reports/2022-report-on-international-religious-freedom/south-africa/.

Vlachos, Chris A. *James*. Exegetical Guide to the Greek New Testament. Nashville: B&H Academic, 2013.

Westfall, Cynthia Long. "Mapping the Text: How Discourse Analysis Helps Reveal the Way through James." In *Epistle of James: Linguistic Exegesis of an Early Christian Letter*, edited by James D. Dvorak and Zachary K. Dawson, 11–44. Eugene, OR: Pickwick, 2019.

Wright, Christopher J. H. *The Mission of God: Unlocking the Bible's Grand Narrative*. Nottingham: Inter-Varsity Press, 2006.

Chapter 10

The Word of God and Christian Mission in James 1:22-25

James E. Morrison

This chapter probes the question of the missionary message implicit in the epistle of James by examining the motif of "doers of the word" with reference to James 1:22–25.[1] A key teaching of the epistle is located in 1:22, where James implores his hearers to be active agents in applying the word of God to their lives and not passive receptors. As Wiard Popkes suggests, "James is interested mainly in the practical behavior of the Christians and their relation to the 'world.'"[2] Solomon Andria succinctly summarizes: "Without action, good doctrine is useless."[3] Though the parenetical nature of James's teachings is well established, the question of how this relates to a missiological reading needs further attention. In answering this, this chapter will briefly locate the epistle in the overarching *missio Dei* narrative of the Scriptures, provide a short exposition of James 1:22–25, examine the "doers of the word" in the epistle, and then turn to James himself as a "doer of the word" to explore what may be a significant missional message. An application to Bible translation will also be made.

It is the position of this chapter that James is the brother of Jesus (Matt 13:55; Mark 3:21; 6:3; John 7:5), traditionally known as James the Just.[4] Further, James is the apostle to whom Paul refers (Gal 1:19; 2:9; 1 Cor 15:7)—the leader of the church in Jerusalem (Acts 12:17; 21:18) and a decisive voice in the Jerusalem Council (Acts 15:13). While James initially wrote to Jewish believers in the diaspora outside of Jerusalem, he was equally writing to all believers wherever they could be found.[5] Though the polysemic terms "mission," "missional," "*missio Dei*" and "mission of God" can have different meanings, here they will be used interchangeably. These terms are taken as referring to God's intentional plan and desire that all people everywhere be brought back into a right relationship with him, to honor and glorify him.

---

1 Unless otherwise noted, all Scripture quotations are from the ESV.

2 Popkes, "Mission of James," 92.

3 Andria, "James," 1537.

4 Chilton and Neusner, *Brother of Jesus*.

5 Popkes, "Mission of James," 89.

Situating the Text in the *Missio Dei*

James's address of his audience as the twelve tribes in the diaspora is an example of the outworking of the Abrahamic covenant. Christ-following Jews are now scattered among the nations to be a blessing to others and to be a beacon for God. Once, the nations came to Israel to see the glory of God and experience his blessing (Zech 8:22; Isa 2:2–3; 60:3; 66:18). Now, post-Pentecost, that movement has transitioned "from one place (Israel) to the ends of the earth, and from one nation (Israel) to all nations."[6] James's opening address demonstrates the progression of the biblical narrative "from the one to the many, from Abraham to the nations, from Jesus to every creature in heaven, on earth, and under the earth."[7] Though some of the diaspora James is addressing had been living away from Israel for a considerable period (including exiles who never returned from Babylon), the epistle is located in that significant period when the gospel was moving beyond the regional borders of Israel.[8] Some of James's audience may have been present at Pentecost and others could have been those among the first dispersion of Jewish believers to Antioch (Acts 11:19). In any case, a wide scattering of God's people had been underway with the expansion of the church moving "from the center to the periphery, from Jerusalem to the ends of the earth."[9]

Theme and Genre

Commentators have suggested there is no coherent set of themes or structure to James, and Luther famously labeled the epistle "chaos"[10] and a "book of straw."[11] However, both in content and form, the sapiential nature of the epistle has been well noted, giving rise to scholars classifying the book as "wisdom literature."[12] James prefers terse, pithy sentences and his call for action is seen in his many imperatives (fifty-four in 108 verses) and moral exhortations. Luke Timothy Johnson notes, "James's sentences resemble most those written by ancient moralists. He favors the imperative mode and the kind of brevity often associated with the crafters of moral exhortation."[13]

---

6   Goheen, "History and Introduction," 20.

7   Bauckham, "Mission as Hermeneutic," 27.

8   Adamson, *James*, 18.

9   Bauckham, "Mission as Hermeneutic," 27.

10 Adamson, *James*, 4, 40.

11 Foord, "Epistle of Straw," 291–98.

12 Wendland, *Finding and Translating*, 74.

13 Johnson, *Brother of Jesus*, 25.

It is this proverbial nature of James that may have attracted interest from the Majority World, where proverbs, aphorisms, and pithy sayings typically have high cognitive resonance and wide aesthetic appeal.[14] Philip Jenkins has noted that in the African continent James appears to be "the most-cited work in sermons, perhaps because in both form and content, it so much resembled familiar wisdom literature with all its 'aphorisms, epigrams and similes.'"[15] Though clearly belonging to the broad sapiential genre, James also fits into the genre of protreptic discourse: a style that calls for people to live up to the ideals for which they purport to stand. Johnson continues:

> The rhetorical genre of the Hellenistic world that James most resembles, however, is the protreptic discourse, which sought to exhort those holding a profession to behavior consonant with their ideal. In James, this is expressed in terms of practicing the profession of faith, or, putting it in James's own language, not only hearing the word but doing it.[16]

A Look at James 1:22-25

It may be best to read James not primarily in light of Paul, though there is no necessary tension with the apostle's teaching, but rather in light of the teachings of Jesus, which are clearly the primary source of James's epistle.[17] Douglas J. Moo, among others, has noted that James draws more directly from the teachings of Jesus than any other New Testament author.[18] In 1:22–25, James appears to rely heavily on the Sermon on the Mount (Matt 7:24–27; Luke 6:46–49), where active obedience to Jesus's words is the foundation of wisdom. However, James may also have had in mind other words of Jesus, such as "My mother and my brothers are those who hear the word of God and do it" (Luke 8:21), or "Blessed rather are those who hear the word of God and keep it!" (Luke 11:28), or "If you know these things, blessed are you if you do them" (John 13:17), or "You are my friends if you do what I command you" (John 15:14). Regardless, James has put his own stamp on the words of Jesus:

---

14 For example, see Moon, *African Proverbs Reveal Christianity*.

15 Jenkins, *New Faces of Christianity*, 61.

16 Johnson, *Brother of Jesus*, 26.

17 Bauckham, "James and Jesus," 100; Green, "Reading James Missionally," 118–28.

18 Moo, *Letter of James*, 7; Green, "Reading James Missionally," 122.

> But be doers of the word, and not hearers only, deceiving yourselves. For if anyone is a hearer of the word and not a doer, he is like a man who looks intently at his natural face in a mirror. For he looks at himself and goes away and at once forgets what he was like. But the one who looks into the perfect law, the law of liberty, and perseveres, being no hearer who forgets but a doer who acts, he will be blessed in his doing. (1:22–25)

While in 1:19 listening is preferred over speaking, in 1:22 only listening to God's word is simply not enough. Listening intently without rushing to speak is one thing, but hearing without acting is quite another and amounts to sheer self-deluding folly for James. The "word of truth" (1:18) and the "implanted word" (1:21) cannot be passively entertained through listening alone; it demands that action be taken. James likens non-doers to fools who intently look in a mirror and immediately forget what they look like. Wise people do not forget their appearance or what they have heard but become doers who act (1:25). In echoing the Sermon on the Mount, James shows the foolishness of merely listening to God's word and not obeying it. James also gives a promise of blessing. His use of *makarios* (1:25) may provide a link to the *makarios* frame at the beginning of Jesus's sermon in Matthew 5.[19] James emphasizes the blessings that await the wise ones who look intently into the "law of liberty" and who, through perseverance, act upon it— "he will be blessed in his doing" (1:25).

Central to this passage is what James means by "word" (*logos*). Though James does not explicitly use the term "gospel," it would seem that in his use of the *hapax* "implanted word" he has the gospel, the saving grace of Christ that is able to "save one's soul," firmly in mind.[20] He appears to reference salvation through faith in Christ alone. There may also be an allusion to the word as Christ the Word Incarnate.[21] His "word of truth" (1:18) suggests the oracles of God more explicitly expressed in the message of the good news of Jesus Christ. James also equates the word with the law (*nomos*) of God, which further becomes the perfect "law of liberty" (1:25; 2:12), the "royal law" (2:8), and thus by extension "the Prophets and the Writings."[22] The modern reader may understand the word as referring to the whole canon of Scripture.

---

19 Boyce, "Mirror of Identity," 218.

20 Perhaps in "implanted word" there are echoes of Deut 30:14, "But the word is very near you. It is in your mouth and in your heart, so that you can do it," and Jer 31:33, "I will put my law within them, and I will write it on their hearts."

21 Boyce, "Mirror of Identity," 216.

22 Andria, "James," 1536.

Examples of Doers of the Word

James was a man of action and called others to action. He provides examples of doers of the word, which can comfortably be read from a missional hermeneutic. In 5:10 he references the prophets, who spoke in the name of the Lord, as examples of those who patiently endured in the midst of suffering (5:10) and yet were also considered blessed (5:11)—one of the outcomes of being a doer of the word. More specifically, James's doers of the word are Abraham (2:21–23), Rahab (2:24–26), Job (5:10–11), and Elijah (5:16–18).

Abraham is a doer who acted upon the covenantal promises of God—promises that were always intended to be a blessing to all nations—by offering Isaac on the altar. By such an act of trust and faithfulness, he was pointing forward to the One who would become the ultimate sacrifice for all humanity.[23] Abraham was blessed by being declared righteous through faith and by becoming "a friend of God" (2:23), thereby heralding the path of salvation available to all by faith. Rahab was a doer in welcoming the spies, who were not of her kind, and thereby acted in a missional way of hospitality (2:25). She reached out to "outsiders" and welcomed them. It was through her welcome of strangers (indeed a "friendly welcome") that she was saved and did not perish (Heb 11:31). Along with her entire family, she was blessed with deliverance. Rahab was further blessed by becoming a bearer of the messianic lineage through the tribe of Judah (Matt 1:5). A missional hermeneutic of hospitality appears to be evident.[24]

Job, the archetypal sufferer, was a doer who remained steadfast throughout his ordeal. He became a universal bastion of hope for all sufferers with his cry, "Though he slay me, I will hope in him" (Job 13:15). His recognition of the Savior of all—"I know my Redeemer lives, and at the last he will stand upon the earth" (Job 19:25)—gives further hope to the redemption of all people, regardless of race or geography. He, too, was ultimately blessed as a doer of the word (Jas 5:11).

Elijah (5:17–18) was a doer of earnest, powerful prayer. Joining with Elijah in powerful prayer is available to all, whether Jews or gentiles, who

---

23 Johnson maintains that implicit in the "works" of Abraham is hospitality to strangers and the needy. Though not made explicit in the text of James, Johnson suggests hospitality was indeed a significant work of Abraham's and that this understanding was a traditional reading of the text. *Brother of Jesus*, 178–79.

24 For more on hospitality and mission, see Udall, "Lives That Welcome," 20–34; and Smither, *Mission as Hospitality*.

enjoy right-standing with God through "faith in our Lord Jesus Christ" (2:1). Elijah is an example of one who asked "in faith, with no doubting" (1:6). The blessing of the doer is also seen in the result of Elijah's actions as "the earth bore its fruit" (5:18). James appears to have chosen his examples of doers of the word carefully as he built his theme of active response to hearing the word, showing that true faith is evidenced by concrete actions, each accompanied with resultant blessing (1:25).

James as a Doer of the Word

In uncovering the missional message of James in the motif of "doers of the word" much in the life of "James the doer" warrants attention. James appears to be the kind of person who wants his actions to do most of the talking. He is a decisive man of action whose "yes" meant yes and "no" meant no (5:12). Though James's own example as a doer of the word is left somewhat implicit, it is of considerable missiological significance. Given that the primary genre of James is protreptic, it is reasonable to ask the question: In what ways was James a doer of the word, and what is the missiological significance of this? James himself appears to invite scrutiny and in 2:18 wants to show his faith in action. He openly rails against hypocrisy. It is teachers, among whom James includes himself ("we who teach," 3:1), who are held to higher account. Therefore, it is a fitting appropriation of the protreptic genre that we examine how the author James was a doer of the word in the larger context of the *missio Dei*.

First, James presents himself as a slave of God and Christ (1:1). James could have established his authority with a more apostolic positioning. Indeed, he had more credentials in terms of proximity to Christ and relational longevity than anyone else, yet he chose not to rest on this. James is first and foremost a *doulos* of Christ. Once he may have had doubts about who his brother claimed to be (Mark 3:21), but he was later transformed to the point that only the status of slave could appropriately designate someone who had demonstrated active faith "in our Lord Jesus Christ." This might appear to be the starting point for the doer of the word—to humbly come to the feet of Christ as his willing *doulos*. Offering oneself as a servant of Christ is fundamental to the mission imperative.[25] It is this incarnational posture, universal in its appeal, that James is modeling. The cross-cultural servant does not come to exert power or show partiality to those in privileged positions of power (Jas 2:1–10).

---

25 See, for example, Elmer, *Cross-Cultural Servanthood*.

James presents himself as a servant of God and Christ as he seeks to serve the Christian Jews of the diaspora. James's authoritative voice is shaped by submission to a greater authority, namely Christ.

Second, perhaps the most significant missional action that James the doer undertook was his authoritative and decisive role in the Jerusalem Council of Acts 15. With the emergence of Antiochian believers from non-Jewish backgrounds (Acts 11:19), the tension between Torah-following Jewish believers and pagan-background gentile converts needed a solution. The Jewish believers could not tolerate the unclean pagan practices of the gentile believers. Traditionally, gentiles who wanted to enter Judaism and become part of Israel needed to abandon previous religious practices and take on new Jewish ones, including circumcision, baptism, dietary laws, and a range of cultic rituals. Andrew F. Walls calls this approach the "proselyte model," where the new proselyte had to forsake the old and embrace a new set of rules and requirements.[26] The question for the Jerusalem Council was this: Do gentile believers need to follow the proselyte model, or is a new approach now possible?

We know that James, in weighing the words of Peter, Barnabas, and Paul, was a leading voice in the decision to move beyond the proselyte model. As both a listener and doer of the word, James showed himself to be well aware of what the Scriptures taught about the gentiles. Though in agreement with Peter (Acts 15:14), James adds authoritative scriptural support for the inclusion of the gentiles into God's redeeming plan for all humanity by quoting Amos. Indeed, such plans of God for the salvation of all had been "known from of old" (Acts 15:18). The quotation from Amos further highlights the global nature of the *mission Dei*: "all the Gentiles who are called by my name" (Acts 15:17). James, basing his decision firmly on the *missio Dei* of Scripture, wastes no time in reaching his judgment. He graciously concedes that the church "should not trouble those of the Gentiles who turn to God" (Acts 15:19–20) while only laying down four requirements of abstinence—things polluted by idols, sexual immorality, what has been strangled, and blood. James also advocated sending out a letter to all the diaspora communities to inform them of the decision that would make table fellowship between believing Jews and gentiles possible (Acts 15:22). As James B. Adamson suggests, "James is able to sympathize with the problems of the Gentiles, does not insist on their circumcision,

---

26 Walls, "Old Athens and New Jerusalem," 147.

and appears in every way anxious to cooperate with Paul in his efforts to evangelize them."[27] Timothy C. Tennent further notes the significance of this event, which then allowed Jews and gentiles to "live out their common faith with a new identity, which, remarkably, is linked to neither the law (the Judean proposal) nor pagan religious practices (the Gentiles' experience) but to a new identity in Jesus Christ."[28]

From Proselyte to Convert

This Jerusalem Council decision was a revolutionary move, a break with past proselyte traditions and the dawn of a new era for Christianity. Walls states, "It is hardly possible to exaggerate the importance of this early controversy and its outcome; it is a pivot on which Christian history turns."[29] This declaration of James now allowed for Christianity to take on local expression in new contexts without the troubling yoke of Jewish laws. Maintaining the proselyte model would have required all believers, regardless of ethnicity, to embrace Jewish religious and cultural norms. However, the Jerusalem Council, under the direction of James the doer, abandoned the proselyte model and set in motion "the future cultural diversity of Christianity."[30] Walls labels this new model the "convert model," which allowed for redirecting what was already extant in a culture "turning it in the direction of Christ."[31] Walls further speaks of a refiguration stage where what was part of the "pre-Christian heritage" was now fashioned and shaped for the glorification of God.[32]

This is not to suggest that after the Jerusalem Council everything went smoothly or that the convert model was universally embraced. As we know, many tensions and struggles ensued. Though Christianity did take on local expression in new cultural contexts, the proselyte model—demanding conformity to cultural traditions—often became the default mode, particularly with the institutionalization of the church. It remains a danger for modern missionary endeavors even today, where the proselyte model may often unconsciously prevail. Michel Kenmogne, in building upon Walls's model, has highlighted the ongoing necessity of the refiguration or reorientation of "pre-Christian cultural norms to allow for a true appropriation

---

27 Adamson, *James*, 21.

28 Tennent, *Theology in the Context*, 204.

29 Walls, "Old Athens and New Jerusalem," 148.

30 Walls, 148.

31 Walls, 148.

32 Walls, 149.

of Christianity."[33] This is no simple task. As Lamin Sanneh points out, such indigenization has clear parameters, which ultimately "still leaves culture subordinate to God's truth."[34] He further elaborates: "The ambiguous relation of Christianity to culture hinges on the necessity for the message to assume the specific terms of its context and the equal necessity for the message to inveigh against cultural idolatry."[35] One could imagine James being in agreement. The need for continued reorientation of the gospel in new contexts requires ongoing attention.

From James's example, we can see that his approach to "doing the word" was for it to become a "true appropriation" in the lives of those who heard it and in the new cultural contexts where it spread. James's actions set in motion a major impetus for the indigenization of the gospel and thus the spread of Christianity throughout the world. His actions as a doer of the word, from a missional perspective, cannot be understated.

The Word as Foundational to Mission

It is clear James places a high value on Scripture. The logic then is straightforward. To be a doer of God's word, access to it is required so that the hearing and the doing can take place. Bible translation then becomes a crucial component of the missionary endeavor, a foundation for "all the Gentiles who are called by my name" to hear and act. Sanneh has observed that it is the "translatability" of the Scriptures, particularly into the vernacular languages, which has been the impetus behind what he calls "World Christianity."[36] He further claimed that Bible translation "commits to the bold, radical step that the receiving culture is the decisive destination of God's salvific promise" and that the *missio Dei* was inextricably linked to the "extraordinary tapestry of mother-tongue idioms and cultures upon which God's favor rests."[37] Sanneh has noted how Bible translation "endowed the vernacular with a consecrated value by investing it with a scriptural tradition"[38] and guaranteed "popular lay access … with restrictions and prohibitions deemed unwarranted."[39] In tracing the legacy of Sanneh's

---

33 Kenmogne, "At Home in All Languages," 136.

34 Sanneh, *Translating the Message*, 60.

35 Sanneh, 60.

36 Sanneh, *Translating the Message*; Sanneh, *Whose Religion Is Christianity?*

37 Sanneh, *Translating the Message*, 36, 98.

38 Sanneh, "They Stooped to Conquer," 97.

39 Sanneh, *Translating the Message*, 98.

missiological research, Wanjiru M. Gitau summarizes his conclusion that "vernacular translation is the primary, critical, leavening, or catalytic action in the spread of the Christian faith."[40]

The centrality of Bible translation in mission has been noted by others.[41] Kenmogne states that Bible translation "preserves the essence of Christianity as a religion without a fixed language, culture, or location. It empowers and yet relativises all languages and cultures, thereby furthering an equality in dignity among the speakers of all the languages of the world."[42] Goheen has suggested, "The Bible is the vehicle by which God's kingdom comes into the world."[43] Regarding the task of Bible translation Walls claims that "no other specific activity more clearly represents the mission of the Church," largely because Bible translation represented "Christianity translated, not only into local languages but into the local cultural settings."[44] The centrality James placed on obedience to the word of God allows for this missional reading of the enduring value of Bible translation.

Proselyte and Convert in Bible Translation

In tracing the cultural impact of Bible translation, Stephen Watters has likened Walls's proselyte and convert models to two main types of Bible translation.[45] He parallels the proselyte model to formal equivalence (often referred to as "word-for-word" translation), where the form of the Scriptures is preserved in the receptor language as much as possible, and the audience is expected to "come to the text." The convert model is likened to functional equivalence (so-called "thought-for-thought" translation), where the communicative needs of the receptor language allow for a more contextual approach, or where the text is more intentionally taken to the audience. While both styles may have their place depending on the context, in the modern era the functional equivalence approach has gained precedence, particularly in vernacular language translations.[46] Perhaps there are elements of this convert model of translation in the epistle of James.

------

40 Gitau, "Legacy of Lamin Sanneh."

41 For example, see Robert, *Christian Mission*.

42 Kenmogne, "At Home in All Languages," 112.

43 Goheen, "History and Introduction," 23.

44 Walls, *Missionary Movement*, 33, 40.

45 Watters, "Quality in Translation," 19–21.

46 Nida, *Toward a Science*; Nida and Taber, *Theory and Practice*; de Waard and Nida, *From One Language*.

As noted earlier, James's epistle reflects the words of Jesus more than any other New Testament book. Yet James was not simply mimicking the words of his Lord and Savior but rather making them his own for his specific audience. He could have quoted the words of Jesus directly, but he chose to do otherwise. He not only alluded to the words of his brother but made them his own by reconfiguring them to have local expression. James appears to be comfortable doing this and is perhaps through his actions showing us another example of his indigenizing message. As Richard Bauckham observes,

> As a disciple of Jesus, James was deeply informed by the teaching of his master and made it his own, but, as a wisdom teacher in his own right, he re-expressed it and developed it as his own teaching, both profoundly and broadly indebted to Jesus' teaching and also at the same time characteristically his own.[47]

Conclusion

In tracing the motif of "doers of the word," we have seen that James was a man of action who called his readers and listeners to put into practice the words of God that they heard. James provides examples of doers of the word who can be understood from a universal missional perspective beyond the borders of Jerusalem and Torah-following Jews. These examples also illustrate the promise that doers will receive blessing. Though James implores his audience to be doers of the word by improving their ethical conduct in caring for the marginalized, controlling their tongues, treating all people fairly, and persevering in suffering, he also, by his actions, reveals a significant missional message. In his example as a doer of the word, through his humble servant posture, James has provided a missional imperative for the indigenization of the Christian message. His decisive leadership in moving beyond the Jewish proselyte model to the new conversion and reconfiguration model for all gentiles was a pivotal moment in the spread of the gospel. Indeed, it is an imperative that changed the landscape of the early church and set in motion a grand unfolding of God's kingdom for all *ethne* of the whole world.

The centrality of God's word in James's epistle also gives missional impetus to the Bible translation movement. James's approach of reconfiguring and reorienting the gospel message for specific contextual usage may suggest a more functional equivalent "convert" approach to translation. His

---

47 Bauckham, "James and Jesus," 101. See also Green, "Reading James Missionally," 122.

implicit missional message is that of Christ finding local expression in new, emerging, and ever-changing contexts, free from unnecessarily burdensome constraints. We may need to be reminded of this message time and again, and its appropriation appears to be evidence of being a doer of the word.

———————

Bibliography

Adamson, James B. *James: The Man and His Message*. Grand Rapids: Eerdmans, 1989.

Andria, Solomon. "James." In *Africa Bible Commentary: A One-Volume Commentary Written by 70 African Scholars*, edited by Tokunboh Adeyemo, 1535–42. Grand Rapids: Zondervan, 2006.

Bauckham, Richard. "James and Jesus." In *The Brother of Jesus: James the Just and His Mission*, edited by Bruce Chilton and Jacob Neusner, 100–37. Louisville: Westminster John Knox, 2001.

Bauckham, Richard. "Mission as Hermeneutic for Scriptural Interpretation." In *Reading the Bible Missionally*, edited by Michael W. Goheen, 26–35. Grand Rapids: Eerdmans, 2016.

Boyce, James L. "A Mirror of Identity: Implanted Word and Pure Religion in James 1:17–27." *Word & World* 35, no. 3 (2015): 213–21.

Chilton, Bruce, and Jacob Neusner, eds. *The Brother of Jesus: James the Just and His Mission*. Louisville: Westminster John Knox, 2001.

Elmer, Duane. *Cross-Cultural Servanthood: Serving the World in Christlike Humility*. Downers Grove, IL: InterVarsity Press, 2006.

Foord, Martin. "The 'Epistle of Straw': Reflections on Luther and the Epistle of James." *Themelios* 45, no. 2 (2020): 291–98.

Gitau, Wanjiru M. "The Legacy of Lamin Sanneh: Colonial Missionary Impact, World Christianity, and Muslim-Christian Dialogue." *Lausanne Global Analysis* 9, no. 3 (2020). https://lausanne.org/content/lga/2020-05/the-legacy-of-lamin-sanneh.

Goheen, Michael W. "A History and Introduction to a Missional Reading of the Bible." In *Reading the Bible Missionally*, edited by Michael W. Goheen, 3–27. Grand Rapids: Eerdmans, 2016.

Goheen, Michael W., ed. *Reading the Bible Missionally*. Grand Rapids: Eerdmans, 2016.

Green, Joel B. "Reading James Missionally." In *Reading the Bible Missionally*, edited by Michael W. Goheen, 118–28. Grand Rapids: Eerdmans, 2016.

Jenkins, Philip. *The New Faces of Christianity: Believing the Bible in the Global South*. Oxford: Oxford University Press, 2006.

Johnson, Luke Timothy. *Brother of Jesus, Friend of God: Studies in the Letter of James*. Grand Rapids: Eerdmans, 2004.

Kenmogne, Michel. "At Home in All Languages and Cultures: Bible Translation and World Christianity in the Twenty-First Century." *Journal of Translation* 18, no. 1 (2022): 111–39.

Moo, Douglas J. *The Letter of James*. Pillar New Testament Commentary. Grand Rapids: Eerdmans, 2000.

Moon, W. Jay. *African Proverbs Reveal Christianity in Culture: A Narrative Portrayal of Builsa Proverbs Contextualizing Christianity in Ghana*. American Society of Missiology Monograph Series 5. Eugene, OR: Wipf & Stock, 2009.

Nida, Eugene A. *Toward a Science of Translating: With Special Reference to Principles and Procedures Involved in Bible Translating*. Leiden: Brill, 1964.

Nida, Eugene A., and Charles R. Taber. *The Theory and Practice of Translation*. Helps for Translators 8. Leiden: Brill, 1974.

Popkes, Wiard. "The Mission of James in His Time." In *The Brother of Jesus: James the Just and His Mission*, edited by Bruce Chilton and Jacob Neusner, 88–99. Louisville: Westminster John Knox, 2001.

Robert, Dana L. *Christian Mission: How Christianity Became a World Religion*. Newark: John Wiley & Sons, 2009.

Sanneh, Lamin. "'They Stooped to Conquer': Vernacular Translation and the Socio-Cultural Factor." *Research in African Literatures* 23, no. 1 (1992): 95–106.

Sanneh, Lamin. *Translating the Message: The Missionary Impact on Culture*. 2nd ed. Maryknoll, NY: Orbis Books, 2009.

Sanneh, Lamin. *Whose Religion Is Christianity? The Gospel beyond the West*. Grand Rapids: Eerdmans, 2003.

Smither, Edward L. *Mission as Hospitality: Imitating the Hospitable God in Mission*. Eugene, OR: Wipf & Stock, 2021.

Tennent, Timothy C. *Theology in the Context of World Christianity: How the Global Church Is Influencing the Way We Think About and Discuss Theology*. Grand Rapids: Zondervan Academic, 2009.

Udall, Jessica A. "Lives That Welcome: How a Non-Western Understanding of Hospitality Can Revitalize the American Church's Fellowship and Outreach." *Journal of the Evangelical Missiological Society* 3, no. 1 (2023): 20–34.

de Waard, Jan, and Eugene A. Nida. *From One Language to Another: Functional Equivalence in Bible Translating*. Nashville: Nelson, 1986.

Walls, Andrew F. *Missionary Movement in Christian History: Studies in the Transmission of Faith*. Maryknoll, NY: Orbis Books, 1996.

Walls, Andrew F. "Old Athens and New Jerusalem: Some Signposts for Christian Scholarship in the Early History of Mission Studies." *International Bulletin of Mission Research* 21, no. 4 (1997): 146–53.

Watters, Stephen. "Quality in Translation: The Warp and Weft of Subjective and Objective Threads." In *Quality in Translation: A Multi-Threaded Fabric*, edited by Stephen Watters and Reinier de Blois, 1–25. Pike Center for Integrative Scholarship. Dallas: SIL International, 2023.

Wendland, Ernst R. *Finding and Translating the Oral-Aural Elements in Written Language: The Case of the New Testament Epistles*. Lewiston: Edwin Mellen, 2008.

Chapter 11

Theology of Mission and Prosperity in James

Leita Ngoy

This chapter aims first to discuss the nuanced interplay between the concepts of mission and prosperity as presented in James,[1] a text deeply rooted in practical theology and concerned with the ethical conduct of believers. James was attributed to Jacob, Jesus's brother. Written between AD 48 and 62, it offers a unique perspective on Christianity and was addressed to Jewish Christians living outside Palestine. James combines traditional letter writing with wisdom teachings and emphasizes practical living, faith, love, and community unity.

This chapter then explores the motif of mission in James and links its key themes to modern missionary work, highlighting its focus on active faith, purity of heart, and care for the marginalized. It discusses the changing nature of missions in the contemporary world, as reflected in the teachings of Harvey C. Kwiyani and David J. Bosch, two Majority World missiologists. The contrast between modern and biblical perspectives of prosperity is also examined. This chapter argues that James presents a holistic view of prosperity, emphasizing spiritual growth and ethical living over material wealth. Also, this chapter addresses the relationship between mission and prosperity in James, critiquing the prosperity gospel and underscoring the significance of using prosperity as a resource for mission, in line with James's teachings. This chapter concludes by emphasizing the integration of mission and prosperity in James, focusing on spiritual maturity and community well-being.

African Mission and Prosperity

In the context of African missions and prosperity, James is connected to the prosperity gospel, which has gained significant influence in various African religious settings.[2] Prosperity gospel, a prominent feature of charismatic Christianity, focuses on the idea that God grants physical healing, wealth, and success. This belief is similar to traditional African views in which success is seen as a sign of divine blessing. David T. Adamo, in "The African Background of the Prosperity Gospel," argues that in African Traditional

---

1 All Scripture quotations are from the NIV unless otherwise noted.

2 Adewuya, *African Commentary on the Letter of James*, 14–19.

Religions, God is central and everything in life has a spiritual cause. This belief system includes a Supreme Being, spirits, ancestors, and magic.[3]

From this point of view, prosperity has a holistic effect; it covers health, money, power, and overall well-being, mixing traditional African beliefs with Christian teachings. James indirectly reflects this holistic view, particularly in how it connects the ideas of mission and prosperity. Hence, this chapter examines how James deals with mission and prosperity in this setting.

Mission in James

Majority World Missiologists and James

Allen L. Yeh suggests that Majority World missiologists engage in mission by emphasizing the importance of incorporating contributions from theological disciplines and leaders from Africa, Asia, Latin America, and other Majority World contexts. Their approach recognizes the need for global reciprocity in producing theological knowledge and wisdom and for theological education that prepares mission students for global witness.[4]

In this chapter, I shall engage with a few Majority World missiologists. For example, my working definition of mission in this chapter is drawn from David J. Bosch. He redefined the concept of mission, shifting it from the traditional view of spreading Christianity or expanding the church expansion to a focus on the mission of God, with God as the sender. He posited that "mission is not primarily an activity of the church, but an attribute of God. God is a missionary God."[5] This means mission is the participation of Christians in the liberating mission of Jesus, expecting a future that may not be immediately evident.

Bosch sees the church as a key participant in worldwide missions, guided by the concept of *missio Dei*, which suggests that the church's primary role is to engage in God's mission. This view aligns with the idea that participating in missionary work is a way of sharing in God's love.[6] Bosch views the church and mission as intrinsically linked. He sees the church as essentially missionary, meaning its existence is defined by being sent out to engage in mission. Bosch argues that the mission of the church is not secondary but central to its being. He believes that ecclesiology does not

---

3 Adamo, "African Background of the Prosperity Gospel," 1–15.

4 See Yeh, *Majority World Theologies*.

5 Bosch, *Transforming Mission*, 10–11.

6 Bosch, 399–401.

precede missiology; instead, they are deeply interconnected. The church is missionary and missionizing, meaning its missionary nature is expressed in its sent-out activities and internal life and structure.[7] Therefore, a missionary church is a worshiping community that welcomes outsiders and does not focus only on its members. It equips its members for their societal roles, is adaptable and innovative, and does not only defend the privileges of a select few. Additionally, a missionary church engages directly in society, moving beyond its walls to focus on evangelism, justice, and peace.

Although James does not directly say this, the importance of mission is implied in its focus on showing faith through acts of kindness. Being involved in God's mission means acting as his representative on earth and actively sharing his love with others. This missionary work is more than just talking about faith; it is about showing it in action. This is similarly expressed in John 3:16, where God's love is demonstrated through his actions—namely, the sacrifice of his son. In this light, the accurate measure of our relationship with God is what we say and do. Our actions should match our words when expressing God's love.

Therefore, living out our faith through actions of love is essential to God's mission. Faith is not just something we believe about God or Jesus Christ; it is not just a solid assurance of the invisible things (Heb 11:1–6). Rather, it is something we put into action. This is in line with James's teachings, which stress the importance of combining our faith in Christ with acts of love. It emphasizes that faith should lead to meaningful actions that reflect God's love. Bosch's perspective on mission has been further developed more recently by Majority World missiologists like Jehu Hanciles, Wonsuk Ma, Lamin Sanneh, Harvey C. Kwiyani, and many others.[8] In the following section, I will engage with Kwiyani's *Sent Forth: African Missionary Work in the West* and James as I explore the mission motifs in this epistle.

The Motif of Mission in James

James offers a unique perspective on mission within the context of the Christian faith. Though not traditionally considered a missionary book in the same way as the Gospel of Matthew or the Acts of the Apostles, for example, James provides profound insights into the underlying principles that should drive every Christian's engagement in mission. James emphasizes the

---

7 Bosch, 401.

8 Hanciles, *Beyond Christendom*; Hanciles, *Euthanasia of a Mission*; Ma and Ma, *Mission in the Spirit*; Sanneh, *Disciples of All Nations*; Kwiyani, *Sent Forth*.

importance of living out one's faith and being a living witness of the gospel. He encourages believers to be humble, patient, and forgiving and to serve those in need. He also stresses the importance of having a pure heart and being motivated by love rather than selfish ambition. The following are a few motifs of mission as presented in James.

First, James underscores the importance of active faith, the primary motif of mission. This implies that mission should be motivated by love rather than selfish ambition; mission should be about helping others rather than gaining recognition or building personality cults. For example, James 2:14–17 says, "What good is it, my brothers and sisters, if someone claims to have faith but has no deeds? Can such faith save them? … Faith by itself, if it is not accompanied by action, is dead." This passage makes it abundantly clear that faith without corresponding actions is inadequate. The mission of a Christian is not merely to believe but to act upon that belief. Therefore, the prime motif of mission is to manifest one's faith through practical, tangible expressions of love, compassion, and righteousness.

Second, James emphasizes a call to purity of heart. In James 1:27, he writes, "Religion that God our Father accepts as pure and faultless is this: to look after orphans and widows in their distress and to keep oneself from being polluted by the world." Here, the mission motif is not only about outward actions but also about the inner transformation of the believer. A pure heart, untainted by the values and desires of the world, is a prerequisite for a compelling Christian mission. This motif calls Christians to self-examination and personal holiness as they engage in mission work, recognizing that the task is not only about changing the lives of others but also about allowing God to transform their hearts. According to James, mission needs to be both about spiritual faith and about that faith expressed through actions. It is all about expressing faith through actions. For example, many African missionaries in the West are characterized by their spiritual orientation toward all of life (in contrast to a more Enlightenment-influenced Western orientation).[9] This is not enough, however; they need to share their love and their actions of compassion with the community around them. James 1:27 highlights the importance of caring for orphans and widows, who are among the most vulnerable in society.

____

9 Adogame, *African Christian Diaspora*, 87–88; Kwiyani, *Multicultural Kingdom*, 56–57.

The third motif of mission in James is commitment to caring for the marginalized and vulnerable. For example, James 2:15–17 says,

> Suppose a brother or a sister is without clothes and daily food. If one of you says to them, "Go in peace; keep warm and well fed," but does nothing about their physical needs, what good is it? In the same way, faith by itself, if not accompanied by action, is dead.

This implies that this motif of mission, as presented in James, is rooted in the idea of promoting justice and compassion for those often marginalized and oppressed in society. It calls Christians to advocate for the rights and dignity of the less fortunate, reflecting God's heart for the marginalized. James 2:15–17 in particular emphasizes the necessity of action accompanying faith, especially in addressing the physical needs of others. Another vivid example of this motif is missionaries in the West from the Global South, many of whom are planting Black-majority churches or migrant communities based on their social needs. They are mainly engaged in sharing and caring for each other's needs. These churches are there to support other migrants who are struggling to integrate into foreign lands.[10]

James provides mission motifs within the context of the Christian faith, especially for migrants engaging in missions in the diaspora. These motifs can effectively model the polycentric mission of the twenty-first century. Therefore, Christians should move beyond mere words and rituals and engage in a mission with genuine and transformative action. Ultimately, James 1:27 and 2:1–17 remind us that mission is not just a task to be accomplished but a reflection of our faith, a purification of our hearts, and a demonstration of our commitment to justice and compassion.

The motifs mentioned above align with how Kwiyani views *missio Dei.* It is God's sending of the church to spread the Christian faith to the rest of the world. In James, the Christian religion must be expressed through actions. I agree with Kwiyani that mission in the twenty-first century will take another form; I think that mission in the twenty-first century is more of *missio praxis.* It implies a missiological shift from the Great Commission of Matthew 28:19–20 to Luke 4:18. Mission in the perspective of James is not only about making converts but also about addressing their daily challenges in an ongoing process of discipleship.

---

10 Währisch-Oblau, "Material Salvation," 66–67.

Kwiyani's insights in *Sent Forth* about the evolving nature of mission work in the twenty-first century can be related to the teachings in James in several ways.[11] First, James 2:14–26 emphasizes the importance of living out one's faith through actions, which aligns with Kwiyani's discussion of the changing landscape of mission. He argues that in the twenty-first century, mission work is not just about spreading religious doctrine but also about engaging in practical, meaningful ways with different cultures.

Second, in James 1:27, the author speaks powerfully about caring for the marginalized and disadvantaged; this is reflected in Kwiyani's focus on African missionaries in the West, challenging the traditional, often colonial, dynamics of mission work. He highlights the shift from a predominantly Western-centric approach to a more diverse, globally inclusive mission field, where voices from previously marginalized communities (like African missionaries) are now playing a pivotal role. This reflects James's teachings on social justice and care for the less fortunate (2:5).[12]

Third, James often challenges the status quo and power structures within the early Christian community (e.g., 2:1–9, where he criticizes favoritism toward the wealthy). Similarly, Kwiyani's work challenges the traditional notions of mission work, primarily influenced by Western power structures. He proposes an egalitarian and reciprocal approach to mission, where all cultures can contribute and learn from each other, breaking down traditional power dynamics.[13]

Fourth, both James's stress on the importance of a genuine, authentic expression of faith (3:17–18) and Kwiyani's call for a reinterpretation of mission and missionary work through postcolonial and post-Christendom lenses seek to remove the various influences that may have distorted the authentic expression of Christian mission. This aligns with James's focus on an unpretentious, sincere practice of faith.

In *Sent Forth*, Kwiyani's explorations of the evolving mission work resonate with the themes in James, particularly regarding practical faith, social justice, challenging traditional structures, and authentic faith expression. Both Kwiyani and James advocate for a more inclusive, action-oriented, and authentic approach to living out Christian principles.

---

11 Kwiyani, *Sent Forth*, 69.

12 Kwiyani, 76–80.

13 Kwiyani, 152–59.

Prosperity in James

Prosperity in the Perspective of James

The Bible offers a rich and multifaceted understanding of prosperity as well-being and success. For example, in the New Testament, the Greek word translated as "prosper" is εὐοδόω.[14] It means to "have things turn out well, *prosper, succeed.*"[15] For example, in 3 John 1:2, the apostle John writes, "Beloved, I pray that you may prosper in all things and be in health, just as your soul prospers" (NKJV). This verse reflects the holistic nature of prosperity. It encompasses more than material success and includes overall well-being, health, and the successful undertaking of one's endeavors. In James, this aligns with the idea of trials and perseverance leading to spiritual maturity. James 1:2–4 says, "Consider it pure joy, my brothers and sisters, whenever you face trials of many kinds, because you know that the testing of your faith produces perseverance. Let perseverance finish its work so you may be mature and complete, not lacking anything." Drawing from these passages, true prosperity starts with inner or spiritual growth and the ability to live out one's faith in practical ways rather than accumulating wealth.

In the Old Testament, the Hebrew word for *shalom* (שלום) is a common word for prosperity, meaning peace.[16] Shalom also means completeness, wholeness, or well-being. Another relevant Hebrew term is צָלַח meaning "advance, prosper."[17] An example is Psalm 1:3, describing a blessed person, which says, "He is like a tree planted by streams of water that yields its fruit in season, and its leaf does not wither" (ESV)—whatever they do *prospers*. Hebrew prosperity is not just about wealth but includes personal, communal, and spiritual well-being. James cautions against favoritism (2:1–4) and misuse of wealth (5:1–6), and he advocates for prosperity that prioritizes ethical behavior, community welfare, and humility, consistent with the Hebrew concept of prosperity as holistic, community-focused well-being. The Hebrew concept of *shalom*, encompassing communal peace and welfare, also reflects James's concerns about community dynamics, such as treating the rich and poor equally and responsibly using wealth to benefit others.

---

14 Thayer, "εὐοδόω," 260–70.

15 Danker, Bauer, Arndt, and Gingrich, *Greek-English Lexicon*, 410, emphasis in original.

16 Brown, Driver, and Briggs, "שלום,"

17 Brown, Driver, and Briggs, "צָלַח," 852–

Contemporary and Biblical Perspectives of Prosperity

While both the biblical and contemporary understandings of prosperity include success and well-being, the biblical perspective is broader, encompassing spiritual, communal, and ethical dimensions, unlike the more materially focused contemporary view. First, the modern view of prosperity is heavily centered on material and financial success: "The desire to obtain more wealth is not to support others who are in need but to fatten oneself with God's blessings. The mantra is not 'bless me so that I can bless others' but 'bless me so that I can be blessed,'"[18] while the biblical perspective offers a more holistic view.

Second, the modern view often focuses on individual success and personal achievement. In contrast, the biblical view encompasses, especially in Hebrew, a communal aspect of prosperity—the well-being of the community and relationships. For example, the Hebrew concept of *shalom* reflects James's concerns about community dynamics, such as equal treatment of the rich and poor and responsible use of wealth to benefit others.

Third, biblical understanding of prosperity includes a significant spiritual dimension, often linking prosperity to divine favor and moral living. In contrast, the contemporary view is more secular and tends to separate material success from spiritual beliefs.

Fourth, biblical prosperity, particularly in the Hebrew context, involves ethical living and righteousness, implying that how wealth is obtained and used is as important as the wealth itself. The modern view of prosperity does not always highlight the ethical aspect of acquiring or using wealth. Still, James emphasizes that prosperity should be coupled with spiritual growth and ethical behavior, which resonates with the Greek and Hebrew understandings, where prosperity includes righteousness and aligns with God's will.

The Motif of Prosperity in James

James offers a distinct perspective on prosperity, focusing on spiritual growth rather than material wealth. In this book, prosperity is linked to enduring life's challenges and developing faith (1:2–4). Prosperity is about becoming spiritually mature, not just accumulating wealth. Therefore, James cautions against pursuing prosperity solely for material gain (4:3; 5:1–6). He emphasizes the danger of letting the pursuit of wealth lead to moral compromise and instead suggests that true prosperity aligns with God's purpose (1:12).

---

18 Urga, "Possessions, Greed and the Christian Community," 134.

The concept of prosperity as linked to spiritual maturity, not just material wealth, is described in 1:2–4 and can be explored from different perspectives. For example, in the Evangelical Lutheran Church in Tanzania the Eastern and Coastal Diocese (ELCT-ECD), prosperity is understood within the framework of charismatic Christianity.

Within this Swahili-speaking community in Tanzania, the teachings on prosperity, which they call the *mafanikio* gospel, are seen as motivation to trust in God, work hard, live a transformed life, and become good stewards of God's blessings.[19] This interpretation of prosperity was shaped by Max Weber's *The Protestant Ethic* and their own contextual meaning of prosperity. They believe prosperity or wealth accumulation results from hard work and spiritual growth.

Tamie Davis defines *mafanikio*, or prosperity, from a female Tanzanian perspective as "a process of taking steps to move to the next level which can be applied in the economic, spiritual, social, physical and intellectual spheres as well as experiences of inner peace."[20] In this view, prosperity starts with an inner transformation, leading to spiritual and social change. This approach aligns with the teachings of James, which prioritizes spiritual wealth and ethical living over material accumulation. Thus, the ELCT-ECD's understanding of prosperity emphasizes the importance of hard work, trust in God, and personal transformation as critical elements of a prosperous life. That material or spiritual wealth is meant for communal, not individual, use. Prosperity in the perspective of both James and the Lutherans in Tanzania is shaped by the motif "bless me so I can be a blessing to others" rather than "bless me so I can be rich and wealthy."

Spiritual and Ethical Dimensions of Prosperity in James

What is meant by a holistic sense of prosperity, which goes beyond financial or material success? It encompasses various aspects of a person's life, including physical health and access to healthcare. It means having mental and emotional well-being, reflecting a state of mental balance and emotional resilience. This includes happiness, satisfaction, and psychological health. It refers to social connections, that is, having relationships and a sense of belonging within a community. Holistic prosperity involves a sense of purpose, meaning, and spiritual fulfillment. In the East African context, as well as in many other African cultures, the phrase "God bless you" has a

---

19　Ngoy, "Missional, Contextual, and Transcultural," 146.

20　Davis, "She Sees That Her Trading," 88.

pneumatological meaning and effect on the person upon whom it is said.[21] "God bless you" (*Mungu akubariki* in Swahili of Tanzania) means "May God fight all your spiritual battles and be your provider." This is what people expect to hear after contributing to the church to show their engagement in God's mission or to display their gratitude for God's mercy. They want their spiritual leader to pronounce such a blessing upon them.

Holistic prosperity can also include educational and intellectual growth. For example, learning opportunities are also essential features of a prosperous life. Moreover, having a sense of environmental well-being, that is, living in a healthy, sustainable environment, can be considered part of holistic prosperity. Finally, it includes the well-known meaning of prosperity—financial stability. While not its sole focus, part of prosperity is usually having sufficient financial resources to meet one's needs and some levels of comfort.

Protestant Work Ethic and Prosperity

Max Weber's "Protestant work ethic" is a significant sociological theory that examines the relationship between religion and economic behavior. This ethic emphasizes hard work, discipline, and frugality to achieve economic success and spiritual salvation.[22] Weber primarily focused on how certain philosophies, like Calvinism, influenced the development of capitalism. He argued that the Calvinist emphasis on predestination led to anxiety about one's salvation. To alleviate this anxiety, individuals engaged in intense worldly work, viewing success in their vocations as a sign of God's favor.[23] This attitude fostered a spirit of hard work and economic rationality, contributing to the growth of capitalism.

Weber's theory of the Protestant work ethic relates to prosperity in several ways. It positions hard work as a path to prosperity, moral duty, and worldly success. This ethic valorizes the pursuit of one's professional career as a form of religious devotion.[24] It encourages the accumulation of wealth through hard work and emphasizes the ethical use of wealth. This means that wealth should be used responsibly for the benefit of society, aligning with the broader Christian doctrine of stewardship.

Weber's Protestant work ethic reveals how specific Protestant values have significantly influenced attitudes toward hard work and economic

---

21 Kwiyani, "Holy Spirit in African Theology," 73–85.

22 Weber, *Protestant Ethic*, 8.

23 Weber, 8.

24 Ngoy, "Missional, Contextual, and Transcultural," 148–51.

success. This ethic connects hard work and discipline with prosperity, viewing financial success as a sign of God's favor while promoting wealth's responsible and ethical use. This perspective also aligns with the motif of prosperity. In James 5:1–6, the author provides a stark warning to the wealthy about misusing their riches, urging them to use their prosperity in line with God's mission.

From the perspective of Weber's theory, prosperity emphasizes a transformation that is both spiritual and social. It guides individuals to become good stewards of God's blessings, whether material or spiritual. Its central idea is to desire blessings not just for oneself but also to be a blessing to others.

Mission and Prosperity in James

This section explores the relationship between mission and prosperity from the perspective of James. For example, James 1:22–25 and 2:14–18 are about living out one's faith, and James 1:9–11; 2:5; 4:13–16; and 5:1–6 are about prosperity, especially attitudes toward wealth. These verses highlight the relationship between mission and prosperity in James. They emphasize the importance of doing God's mission by living out one's faith, maintaining a humble and ethical perspective on wealth, and aligning with spiritual values over material prosperity. Throughout his five chapters, James gives practical advice on how Christians must live out their faith. He highlights how spreading the Christian faith through actions (mission in praxis) and having wealth or success (prosperity) are related. Usually, people consider these two concepts as separate. For most, mission is about sharing the gospel with others, while prosperity is about having money and doing well. But James shows that these two ideas can work together and complement each other in the Christian life. James supports the idea that true prosperity is advancing to a certain level in life to share wealth with others (1:2–4; 2:1–17). We need a certain level of relative prosperity to express our faith through actions. This can help us realize that prosperity could be a missional tool.

As discussed in the previous sections, the holistic sense of prosperity includes physical health, mental and emotional well-being, social connections, spiritual fulfillment, educational and intellectual growth, environmental well-being, and financial stability. It is about thriving in all life areas, not just economically. However, aligning prosperity with mission can be challenging, especially in Africa, where missionaries often face hardships. For example, in the Lutheran Church in Tanzania, when a pastor is appointed to a parish in an isolated district, region, or village unreached by the gospel, he is said to be sent on a mission. In Swahili, *usharika wa missioni* means "mission parish." Pastors sent to remote areas expect spiritual, social, and economic challenges. Despite this hardship, James's letter shows how prosperity, in its holistic sense, is crucial in doing a mission in practice. Prosperity and mission complement each other in James's view; it is about using various kinds of tangible and intangible resources to spread the gospel with love and compassion.

Human and material resources are necessary to send gospel messengers into the mission field. Prosperity, in its holistic sense, thus becomes an essential tool for a mission to be carried out through faith and actions. Teaching prosperity equips Christians to achieve *mafanikio* or prosper to support God's mission with their material wealth, spiritual gifts, or skills. For example, in James 2:14–17, if mission is to be expressed through faith in action and caring for the marginalized and poor, this requires money. Thus, James indirectly implies that the mission needs a prosperity message to be preached to motivate people to work hard, accumulate wealth, be good stewards of divine blessings, and share with others in need, rather than for individual gain.

Mafanikio theology offers several lessons that would benefit any Christian: prosperity is for sharing, not hoarding; the spiritual and physical must be integrated; wealth must be obtained in good, godly ways; closeness with Jesus powers life; God (not myself) is the source of prosperity; and the pursuit of prosperity can be good and holy. It would be worthwhile for Christians from other cultures to engage with *mafanikio* theology as a conversation partner on these topics.[25]

Bishop Charles S. Salalah of the Africa Inland Church in Tanzania (AICT) shared a thought-provoking message during my ordination. He asked us to imagine who we would first thank in heaven after our earthly ministry. The choices were God the Father, Jesus, our pastor, or the person whose financial support helped spread the gospel. The answers varied: some said God the Father, others Jesus, and a few, their pastor. But Bishop Salalah offered a different perspective. He said he would first thank the donor who made it possible for him to hear the salvation message. Next, he would thank his pastor for selflessly sharing the gospel, followed by Jesus for sacrificing his life for us, and finally, God the Father for his ultimate gift of eternal life through his Son.

---

25 Ngoy, 174.

Bishop Salalah's words highlight the importance of teamwork in fulfilling the Christian mission, as described in James. He emphasized that prosperity is not just about wealth but a vital resource for enabling mission work. This story underscores the power of collective effort and financial support in spreading the gospel, reflecting a living faith through acts of love and compassion. This perspective underlines the collaborative effort needed for mission work, aligning with James's view that faith must be accompanied by action. James 2:14–17 reiterates this, stating that faith without works is dead, emphasizing the necessity of active love and compassion in faith.

Conclusion

The exploration of mission and prosperity in James offers a deep understanding of how Christians are to be actively involved in mission today. This letter, believed to be written by Jacob, the brother of Jesus, not only addresses the immediate concerns of Jewish Christians living far from home but also shares timeless advice on living a life full of faith. It stresses the importance of an active faith shown through actions, the need for a pure heart, caring for the less fortunate, and not taking advantage of them, as do modern prosperity preachers.

While James does not explicitly focus on mission and prosperity, its teachings about living out faith through action and warnings against favoring the wealthy show key aspects of practical mission work. Engaging in God's mission is more than just making disciples and baptizing them (Jas 2:14–15, 17; Matt 28:18–19); it also addresses their everyday needs (Jas 2:15–17; Luke 4:18). This is how we demonstrate that we serve a living God.

James presents a unique view of prosperity or wealth. This chapter points out that James does not oppose wealth or prosperity; instead, he is concerned with how people use their wealth. James advises using wealth to help those in need (1:9–11; 2:5; 4:13–16; 5:1–6). In this light, being prosperous becomes a crucial tool for practical mission work. The church benefits from prosperous Christians—those who are spiritually mature, have overcome trials, and are filled with the Holy Spirit, as described in Galatians 5:22–23—who are expected to share these spiritual fruits with others as they participate in God's mission. In James's view, mission and prosperity are two sides of the same coin, if prosperity is regarded in its holistic sense. Prosperity is not accumulating wealth for selfish reasons but a way to put faith into action. Therefore, the main motif of mission and prosperity is to be fully equipped (prosperous in its holistic sense) to engage in mission through faith and actions.

Bibliography

Adamo, David T. "The African Background of the Prosperity Gospel." *Theologia Viatorum* 45, no. 1 (2020): 1–15. https://doi.org/https://doi.org/10.4102/tv.v45i1.71.

Adewuya, J. Ayodeji. *An African Commentary on the Letter of James.* Global Readings 1. Eugene, OR: Cascade, 2023.

Adogame, Afe. *The African Christian Diaspora: New Currents and Emerging Trends in World Christianity.* New York: Bloomsbury Academic, 2013.

Blomberg, Craig L., and Mariam J. Kamell. *James.* Zondervan Exegetical Commentary on the New Testament 16. Grand Rapids: Zondervan, 2008.

Bosch, David J. *Transforming Mission: Paradigm Shifts in Theology of Mission.* American Society of Missiology Series 16. Maryknoll, NY: Orbis Books, 1991.

Brown, F., S. Driver, and C. Briggs, eds. "שׁלוֹם." In *The Brown-Driver-Briggs Hebrew and English Lexicon: Code with Strong's Concordance Numbers.* Peabody, MA: Hendrickson, 2018.

Brown, F., S. Driver, and C. Briggs, eds. "צָלֵחַ." In *The Brown-Driver-Briggs Hebrew and English Lexicon: Code with Strong's Concordance Numbers.* Peabody, MA: Hendrickson, 2018.

Danker, Frederick W., Walter Bauer, William F. Arndt, and F. Wilbur Gingrich. *A Greek-English Lexicon of the New Testament and Other Early Christian Literature.* 3rd ed. Chicago: University of Chicago Press, 2000.

Davis, Tamie. "'She Sees That Her Trading Is Profitable' (Prov 31:18): A Theology of Prosperity According to Tafes Women." PhD diss., Sydney Missionary and Bible College, 2023.

Hanciles, Jehu J. *Beyond Christendom: Globalization, African Migration, and the Transformation of the West.* Maryknoll, NY: Orbis Books, 2008.

Hanciles, Jehu. *Euthanasia of a Mission: African Church Autonomy in a Colonial Context.* Westport, CT: Praeger, 2002.

Kwiyani, Harvey C. "The Holy Spirit in African Theology." *Transformed* 1, no. 1 (2001): 73–85.

Kwiyani, Harvey C. *Sent Forth: African Missionary Work in the West.* American Society of Missiology Series. Maryknoll, NY: Orbis Books, 2014.

Kwiyani, Harvey. *Multicultural Kingdom: Ethnic Diversity, Mission and the Church.* London: SCM, 2020.

Ma, Julie C., and Wonsuk Ma. *Mission in the Spirit: Towards a Pentecostal/Charismatic Missiology.* Oxford: Regnum, 2010.

Moo, Douglas J. *The Letter of James.* Pillar New Testament Commentary. 2nd ed. Grand Rapids: Eerdmans, 2021.

Ngoy, Leita. "Missional, Contextual, and Transcultural: Prosperity Gospel and the Charismatisation of the Lutheran Church in Dar Es Salaam." DTh diss., Ruhr University Bochum, 2023.

Sanneh, Lamin. *Disciples of All Nations: Pillars of World Christianity.* Oxford Studies in World Christianity. New York: Oxford University Press, 2008.

Thayer, Joseph H. *Thayer's Greek-English Lexicon of the New Testament: Coded with Strong's Concordance Numbers.* 4th ed. Edinburgh: T&T Clark, 1896. Repr., Peabody, MA: Hendrickson, 2015.

Urga, Abeneazer G. "Possessions, Greed and the Christian Community: Interrogating the Prosperity Gospel in Africa in Light of Hebrews 13:1–6." In *Healthy and Wealthy? A Biblical-Theological Response to the Prosperity Gospel*, edited by Robert L. Plummer, 133–45. Faith & Work. Dallas: Fontes, 2022.

Währisch-Oblau, Claudia. "Material Salvation: Healing, Deliverance, and 'Breakthrough' in African Migrant Churches in Germany." In *Global Pentecostal and Charismatic Healing*, edited by Candy Gunther Brown, 61–80. Oxford: Oxford University Press, 2011.

Weber, Max. *The Protestant Ethic and the Spirit of Capitalism.* London: Unwin University, 1968.

Yeh, Allen L., and Tite Tiénou, eds. *Majority World Theologies: Theologizing from Africa, Asia, Latin America, and the Ends of the Earth.* Evangelical Missiological Society Series 26. Littleton, CO: William Carey Publishing, 2018.

Part 3

The Missionary Methods of James

Chapter 12

Mercy as Mission in James

Practicing Gospel Care toward Those in Need

John D. Harvey

Scholars who have studied James have long noted its echoes of Jesus's teaching in the Sermon on the Mount.[1] Within Jesus's sermon is the "mercy" beatitude of Matthew 5:7 (cf. Luke 6:36): "God blesses those who are merciful, for they will be shown mercy."[2] Scholars are nearly unanimous in seeing an echo of that beatitude in James 2:13: "If you have been merciful, God will be merciful when he judges you."

Beyond Matthew 5, mercy/compassion is a theme that appears throughout the Synoptic Gospels in connection with Jesus's deeds and his words. It also forms a significant but neglected missional connection between Jesus's ministry and James's letter. For James, a critical part of mission is showing mercy to your neighbor who is in need. In order to understand what James has to say about mercy as mission, it is necessary, first, to survey the theme of mercy in Jesus's deeds and words.

Mercy in Jesus's Deeds and Words

The primary Greek nouns and cognate verbs in the New Testament that refer to the concept of mercy are ἔλεος/ἐλεέω and σπλάγχνον/σπλαγχνίζομαι.[3] English versions translate the nouns variously as "mercy," "pity," or "compassion." The cognate verbs denote the actions of showing kindness or concern or of feeling compassion toward someone in need. In the New Testament, "mercy" is best understood as "the emotion roused by contact with an affliction which comes undeservedly on someone else."[4] Just under half of the occurrences of ἔλεος and ἐλεέω and all of the occurrences of σπλαγχνίζομαι in the New Testament relate to Jesus and his ministry. These occurrences are divided fairly evenly into three basic groups:

---

1 For a helpful summary, see Foster, "Q and James," 3–34.

2 All Scripture quotations are from the NLT unless otherwise noted.

3 The third Greek combination is οἰκτιρμός/οἰκτίρω, occuring most frequently in Paul's letters (Rom 9:15; 12:1; 2 Cor 1:3; Phil 2:1; Col 3:12) as well as in Hebrews 10:28. Of interest to this study, the adjective οἰκτίρμων occurs in Luke's version of the "mercy" beatitude (Luke 6:36) and in James 5:11.

4 Bultmann, "ἔλεος, ἐλεέω," 477.

(1) instances when others appealed to Jesus for mercy, (2) instances when Jesus felt compassion for individuals or a group, and (3) instances when Jesus spoke about mercy in his teaching. The first two groups highlight the fact that mercy characterized Jesus and his ministry.

Mercy Characterized Jesus and His Ministry

When people in need appealed to Jesus, they asked for mercy. In each instance, their need was desperate, including blindness, demon possession, and leprosy. Interestingly, Jesus always took time to talk with the individuals who asked for mercy before responding to their needs with healing, exorcism, and cleansing as was appropriate. Table 1 records the request in each incident.

Table 1. Appeals to Jesus for Mercy

Appeals to Jesus for Mercy	
Blind men in Galilee (Matt 9:27–31)	"Son of David, have mercy on us!"
Mother of demon-possessed daughter (Matt 15:21–28)	"Have mercy on me, O Lord, Son of David!"
Father of demon-possessed son (Matt 17:14–18)	"Lord, have mercy on my son!"
Lepers on the way to Jerusalem (Luke 17:11–19)	"Jesus, Master, have mercy on us!"
Blind men outside Jericho (Matt 20:29–34)	"Lord, Son of David, have mercy on us!"

When Jesus encountered individuals or groups in need, he felt compassion for them. Six incidents recorded in the Synoptic Gospels reveal the needs to which Jesus responded, including hunger, lack of leadership, and death. Table 2 records his responses.

Table 2. Jesus's Merciful Responses

Jesus's Merciful Responses	
Healing a leper in Galilee (Mark 1:40–42)	Moved with compassion, Jesus reached out and touched him.
Raising the widow of Nain's son (Luke 7:11–17)	When the Lord saw her, his heart overflowed with compassion.
Seeing the downcast crowds (Matt 9:35–38)	When he saw the crowds, he had compassion on them.
Feeding the five thousand (Matt 14:13–21)	Jesus saw the huge crowd … and he had compassion on them.
Feeding the four thousand (Matt 15:32–39)	Jesus called his disciples and told them, "I feel sorry for these people."
Healing blind men outside Jericho (Matt 20:29–34)	And Jesus felt sorry for them and touched their eyes.

The leper was desperate since leprosy was considered to be incurable. Jesus responded to his need not only with the emotion of compassion but also with the action of cleansing. Jesus's act of touching the leper highlighted his compassion, since leprosy was highly contagious (Mark 1:40–42). There are no more desperate circumstances than the death of a family member. The need of the widow of Nain who had lost both her husband and her son prompted Jesus to show mercy to her by restoring her son to life (Luke 7:11–17).

As a result of his ministry, large crowds followed Jesus, and the sight of those multitudes moved him to compassion for them (Matt 9:35–38). Interestingly, the need that moved Jesus to compassion in this situation was not physical but spiritual. The people were "distressed and downcast like sheep without a shepherd" (NASB), that is, they lacked spiritual leadership and care. Jesus's response was to commission his disciples to extend his ministry of preaching, healing, cleansing, and exorcising (Matt 10:7–8), highlighting the truth that showing mercy applies to the whole person.

Matthew and Mark both record additional examples of Jesus's compassion on the multitudes. When the crowds followed him to a desert place in Jewish territory after the beheading of John the Baptist, Jesus felt compassion for them and healed their sick. He subsequently fed the multitude of more than five thousand using five loaves and two fish, but the narrative notes his compassion on their need for healing (Matt 14:13–21; Mark 6:32–44). In a similar situation in gentile territory, the narrative notes Jesus's compassion for the multitude's hunger (Matt 15:32–39; Mark 8:1–10). In both incidents, the needs of others prompted the emotion of compassion in Jesus, which in turn was outwardly expressed in his actions to meet those needs—first in healing the sick, then in providing food.

The sixth incident falls into the category of an appeal for mercy and appears in all three Synoptic Gospels (Matt 20:29–34; Mark 10:46–52; Luke 18:35–43). As Jesus, his disciples, and a great multitude were on their way to Jerusalem, two blind men heard that Jesus was passing by and appealed to him for mercy. When the crowds told the men to be quiet, they repeated their appeal. After asking the two men to clarify their need, Jesus was moved with compassion and responded by restoring their sight. This passage illustrates what appears to be a normative sequence. First, the individual articulates his or her need through an appeal. Second, the appeal moves the hearer to inward compassion. Third, the inner emotion of compassion prompts the hearer to respond to the need with an outward act of mercy.

Mercy Was a Quality Jesus Encouraged in His Followers
Jesus's teaching about mercy involved two key ideas. First, God desires mercy of his people, and second, Jesus encourages mercy in his disciples. Jesus highlighted God's desire for mercy in his people when he quoted Hosea 6:6 twice:

> But go and learn what this means, "I desire *mercy* and not sacrifice."
> For I did not come to call the righteous, but sinners. (Matt 9:13, NKJV, emphasis added)
> But if you had known what this means, "I desire *mercy* and not sacrifice," you would not have condemned the guiltless. (Matt 12:7, NKJV, emphasis added)

In both instances, Jesus was addressing the Pharisees, who were complaining about perceived breaches of the Mosaic law. Later, he rebuked the same group for their neglect of mercy:

> Woe to you, scribes and Pharisees, hypocrites! For you tithe mint and dill and cumin, and have neglected the weightier provisions of the Law: justice and *mercy* and faithfulness; but these are the things you should have done without neglecting the others. (Matt 23:23, NASB, emphasis added)

For Jesus, mercy is clearly a quality that is important in God's eyes. The Old Testament teaches that mercy is more significant in his Father's sight than offering sacrifices and giving tithes. It is one of the "weightier provisions of the Law" and, therefore, should hold a key place in the attitudes and actions of Jesus's followers.

Two additional passages make it clear that Jesus encouraged mercy in his disciples. When Jesus declined the Gadarene demoniac's request to accompany him, he commissioned the man, "Go home to your people and report to them what great things the Lord has done for you, and how he had *mercy* on you" (Mark 5:19; cf. Luke 8:39, NASB, emphasis added). Jesus encouraged the demoniac to recognize that his deliverance was an act of God's mercy and to proclaim his experience of that mercy to those around him. Further, in the Sermon on the Mount, Jesus taught that the disciples who show mercy to others will, in turn, receive mercy from God (Matt 5:7).[5] Jesus encouraged his disciples to show mercy, therefore, by promising them God's blessing if they would do so.

Table 3. Jesus's Didactic Instruction on Mercy

Jesus's Didactic Instruction on Mercy	
Rebuke of the Pharisees (Matt 9:13; 12:7)	God desires mercy more than sacrifice.
Woe to the Pharisees (Matt 23:23)	Neglecting mercy neglects one of the weightier provisions of God's law.
Commission to the demoniac (Mark 5:19)	Recipients of God's mercy should tell others about it.
Fifth beatitude (Matt 5:7)	God will show mercy to those who show mercy.

Jesus also illustrated the mercy he encouraged in his followers through three parables, shown in table 4.[6] The least explicit encouragement is in one of his most familiar parables, the parable of the lost son (Luke 15:11–32). The parable of the lost son is the third in a series that Jesus spoke in response to the scribes' and Pharisees' grumbling because he received and ate with tax gatherers and sinners (15:1–2). His point is most clearly articulated at the end of the first parable, which describes a shepherd's joy over recovering

---

5 The context of the Beatitudes points to "blessed" (μακάριοι) as a statement of God's objective assessment of disciples who act as indicated and supports understanding the form ἐλεηθήσονται as a divine passive.

6 The parable of the sheep and goats in Matthew 25:31–46 also speaks directly to the importance of showing mercy to those in need, although it includes none of the key New Testament words related to compassion and mercy.

a single lost sheep: "I tell you that in the same way, there will be more joy in heaven over one sinner who repents than over ninety-nine righteous people who have no need of repentance" (15:7, NASB). The parable of the lost coin (15:8–10) and the parable of the lost son both continue the emphasis on joy at the recovery of what has been lost. The lost son decided to return home and "while he was still a long way off, his father saw him and felt compassion, and ran and embraced him and kissed him" (15:20, ESV). The sight of his son in obvious need moved the father to compassion and prompted him to throw a party so lavish that it distressed his elder son (15:28–30). Jesus encouraged his followers to replace Pharisaical resentment over his compassionate response to those in spiritual need with joy over their openness to the gospel.

The parable of the unforgiving servant connects mercy directly with forgiveness (Matt 18:22–35). When Peter asked whether he should forgive someone who has sinned against him up to seven times, Jesus answered "I do not say to you, up to seven times, but up to seventy-seven times" (18:22, NASB).[7] He then told a parable that illustrates the unlimited forgiveness that characterizes the kingdom of heaven. In the parable, a master felt compassion for his servant who owed a substantial amount and forgave the debt. When this first servant failed to forgive a second servant who owed a much smaller amount, he incurred his master's judgment for failing to show mercy: "You wicked slave, I forgave you all that debt because you pleaded with me. Should you not also have had mercy on your fellow slave, in the same way that I had mercy on you?" (18:32–33, NASB). At the end of the parable, when the master punished a servant who failed to forgive one of his fellow servants, Jesus's concluding comment made his point: "My heavenly Father will also do the same to you, if each of you does not forgive his brother from your heart" (18:35, NASB). In other words, *not* forgiving others is a sin that God judges. Jesus encouraged his followers to understand that one way of showing mercy is by forgiving others compassionately, regardless of the scope of the offense.

The parable of the Samaritan is one of Jesus's best-known parables, and it connects mercy to the commandment to love your neighbor as yourself (Luke 10:25–37; cf. Lev 19:18). The context of the parable was Jesus's conversation with an expert in the Jewish law who tested him by asking

---

7 See Carson, "Matthew," 405, for a succinct discussion of whether Peter suggests forgiving 70 + 7 (77) times or 70 x 7 (490) times.

what he should do to inherit eternal life (10:25). Jesus turned the tables on the lawyer and asked him what the Old Testament law said. In response, the lawyer quoted Deuteronomy 6:5 and Leviticus 19:18. Jesus commended him for his answer, but because the lawyer wanted to justify himself, he asked, "And who is my neighbor?" (10:29).

Jesus responded to his question with the parable of the Samaritan. The parable tells the story of a man traveling from Jerusalem to Jericho who was attacked by robbers, stripped, beaten, and left for dead. After both a priest and a Levite passed the man without helping him, a Samaritan saw the man, felt compassion for him, and cared for him. When Jesus asked the lawyer which of the three individuals was a neighbor to the man who had been attacked, he answered, "The one who showed him mercy" (10:37). The central point of the parable, therefore, might be stated in this way: Love for our neighbor is like the actions of the Samaritan because it shows mercy to those in need.

Table 4. Jesus's Parabolic Illustrations of Mercy

Jesus's Parabolic Illustrations of Mercy	
Parable of the lost son (Luke 15:11–32)	Mercy welcomes and celebrates the return of those who have been lost.
Parable of the unforgiving servant (Matt 18:32–33)	Mercy forgives others regardless of the scope of the offense.
Parable of the Samaritan (Luke 10:25–37)	Mercy fulfills the commandment to love your neighbor who is in need.

In summary, Jesus encouraged mercy in his followers by teaching them that mercy is a weighty provision in God's law, that they are to proclaim their experience of God's mercy to those around them, that God promises his blessing on those who show mercy to others, that compassionate joy is the appropriate response to those in spiritual need who are open to the gospel, that they are to show mercy by forgiving others compassionately regardless of the scope of the offense against them, and that they fulfill the royal commandment when they show mercy to others who are in need.

Mercy Was Part of the Commission Jesus Gave to His Apostles

As a result of his ministry activity, large crowds followed Jesus, and the sight of those multitudes moved him to compassion for them (Matt 9:35–38). In response, he commissioned his disciples to extend his ministry (10:1–42).

That commission included the following activities: "Go and announce to them that the Kingdom of Heaven is near. Heal the sick, raise the dead, cleanse those with leprosy, and cast out demons" (10:7–8). The two halves of the commission may be summarized as *proclaim gospel truth* and *practice gospel care*. Unsurprisingly, each of the four activities in the second half of the commission has a parallel in Jesus's own ministry, specifically in incidents where individuals requested mercy from Jesus or where Jesus responded to individuals with compassion.

Table 5. Comparing the Apostles' Commission with Jesus's Ministry

Apostles' Commission	Jesus's Ministry
Heal the sick	Blind men in Galilee (Matt 9:27–31) Multitudes in a lonely place (Matt 14:13–21) Blind men outside Jericho (Matt 20:29–34)
Raise the dead	Widow of Nain's son (Luke 7:11–17)
Cleanse those with leprosy	Leper in Galilee (Mark 1:40–42) Lepers on the way to Jericho (Luke 17:11–19)
Cast out demons	Demon-possessed daughter (Matt 15:21–29) Demon-possessed son (Matt 17:14–18)

Table 5 sets out the parallels and clearly shows that the practice of gospel care is as much a part of extending Jesus's mission as the proclamation of gospel truth. It is that gospel care aspect of mission—encapsulated in the theme of mercy—on which James focuses in his letter to Christian brothers and sisters who are scattered abroad.

Mercy as Mission in the Letter from James

In his dissertation on a missional reading of James, Graham Paul Dancy suggests that one aspect of a missional hermeneutic is considering the way in which an author seeks to form his readers to participate in God's mission.[8] In his letter, James does this by laying a theological foundation and identifying areas for practical application. In particular, he focuses on the practice of gospel care as central to the mission for which he is forming his readers.

---

8 Dancy identifies four "streams" of a missional hermeneutic: "how the text fits within and speaks into the overarching narrative of Scripture … the way the text seeks to form God's people to participate in God's mission … how the social location of the interpreter affects a missional reading … the way the biblical author uses scriptural tradition" ("Missional Reading," 53).

The Theological Foundation for Mission

James uses words denoting "mercy" and "compassion" five times in his letter, which establish five important theological truths that God's people must understand as they participate in his mission. The words occur in three passages: 2:8–13; 3:13–18; 5:7–12. It will be helpful to look at each occurrence in its immediate context.

Mercy fulfills divine law and prompts divine mercy in return. Chapter 2 is divided into two major sections (vv. 1–13, 14–26). Each section follows a four-part sequence: topic sentence (vv. 1, 14), specific example (vv. 2–4, 15–17), logical argument (vv. 5–7, 18–20), and biblical support (vv. 8–13, 21–26).[9] The first biblical support section begins and ends with theological truths that contribute to James's goal of forming his readers for their mission of practicing gospel care.

James begins 2:8–13 by telling his readers, "It is good when you obey the royal law as found in the Scriptures: 'Love your neighbor as yourself'" (v. 8). Although Moses originally articulated that injunction in Leviticus 19:18, Jesus also quoted it in his response to the lawyer who asked about inheriting eternal life (Matt 22:34–40; Mark 12:28–31). Luke sets the encounter in a different context and adds the parable of the Samaritan as Jesus's response to a second question, "Who is my neighbor?" (Luke 10:25–37). The central point of the parable is that showing mercy to the person who is in need fulfills the commandment to love your neighbor as yourself.[10] So, although James 2:8 does not explicitly include the word "mercy," James's first theological foundation stone for mission echoes Jesus's teaching and shows that mercy fulfills divine law.

James concludes the paragraph with two proverbs that stand in antithetical parallelism: "There will be no mercy for those who have not shown mercy to others. But if you have been merciful, God will be merciful when he judges you" (2:13).[11] This verse is the first explicit mention of "mercy" in the letter. Most scholars agree that the first line is a negative framing of the fifth beatitude in Jesus's Sermon on the Mount: "Blessed are the merciful, for they shall receive mercy" (Matt 5:7, ESV). It is also similar to Proverbs

---

9　Davids has a similar analysis (*Epistle of James*, 27).

10　See the discussion above in connection with Jesus's parabolic illustrations of mercy.

11　The NLT rendering of the second line of the saying strays quite a bit from a more literal rendering. The ESV, for example, translates the line as "Mercy triumphs over judgment." Arthur James comments, "The mercy of God is higher than judgment and *triumphs* over it. Thus, believers are to extend mercy and accept all their brothers and sisters with courtesy and compassion" ("James," 1735).

21:13: "Whoever closes his ear to the cry of the poor will himself call out and not be answered" (ESV).

The combination of mercy and judgment also echoes Jesus's parable of the sheep and goats in Matthew 25:31–46. In the parable, the Son of Man separates the sheep from the goats, and he judges each group based on how they have responded to the hungry, the thirsty, the stranger, the naked, the sick, and the imprisoned. The sheep who cared for those in need inherit the Father's kingdom, but the goats who ignored those in need join the devil and his fallen angels in eternal fire. The central point of this parable is identical to James's double parable: Showing mercy prompts divine mercy, while failing to show mercy prompts divine judgment. James's second theological foundation stone for mission also echoes Jesus's teaching and shows that God rewards human mercy with divine mercy.

Mercy comes from a divine source. Chapter 3 also divides into two major sections as James returns to two topics from his thematic introduction. First, he addresses speech (3:1–12; cf. 1:19–21). Then, he addresses wisdom as one of the good and perfect gifts that come down from the Father (3:13–18; cf. 1:5–8, 16–18). James ends each section with a maxim that reflects his preference for proverbial sayings (e.g., 2:13, 26; 4:10, 17) as well as his familiarity with early Jesus traditions. The saying about fresh/bitter water and figs/olives (3:11–12) echoes Matthew 7:16–18, while the saying about peace/righteousness (3:18) echoes Matthew 5:9 (cf. Isa 32:17; Rom 14:19; Heb 12:11).

James 3:13–18 includes a vice list (vv. 14–16) and a virtue list (v. 17) similar to those that appear in both early Christian and Hellenistic writings. Perhaps the best-known lists in the New Testament appear in 1 Corinthians 13:4–7 and Galatians 5:19–26.[12] The virtues in each list have divine sources—in 1 Corinthians, the source is love; in Galatians, the source is the Holy Spirit; in James, the source is wisdom from above.[13] Along with purity, peacefulness, gentleness, reasonableness, impartiality, and sincerity, divine wisdom is "full of mercy and the fruit of good deeds." The phrase includes the second explicit mention of "mercy" in the letter and combines James's interest in good works with his active concern for those in need. It serves as a reminder that the mercy he views as central to mission comes from a divine source rather than from earthly motives, human insight, or demonic inspiration.

---

12 Similar lists occur in Eph 4:25–32; Col 3:1–17; Phil 4:8–9; 2 Pet 1:5–7.

13 See the comment by Davids, *Epistle of James*, 154.

Mercy reflects God's divine nature and encourages endurance in testing. In 4:1–5:12, James returns to the topic of testing (cf. 1:2–4, 12–15).[14] First, he sets out three sources of testing—inner desires (4:1–3), friendship with the world (4:4–6), and the devil (4:7–10)—and closes with a maxim in 4:10. Then, he identifies three wrong responses to testing: criticizing the neighbor (4:11–12), boasting in plans (4:13–17), and trusting in riches (5:1–6).[15] He closes the section with the proper response to testing (5:7–12), which is the subsection where the final explicit mentions of "mercy" and "compassion" occur.

Although most commentators take 5:12 as a free-standing exhortation, it is best to understand 5:7–12 as a single paragraph with two parts (5:7–9, 10–12). Prohibitions that help readers avoid judgment close each part (5:9, 12). The key words that unify the paragraph are "patience" (5:7 [twice], 8, 10) and "endurance" (5:11 [twice]; cf. 1:3–4, 12). Together, they highlight James's point that the proper response to testing is patient endurance. The two truths ("for") that sustain Jesus's followers as they face testing are the coming of the Lord (5:8) and the mercy of the Lord (5:11).

In particular, Job's experience serves as a reminder that "the Lord is full of tenderness and mercy." The words James uses are the less common πολύσπλαγχνος and οἰκτίρμων.[16] The first echoes Jesus's compassionate response when he encountered individuals or groups in need (cf. Matt 9:36; 14:14; 15:32; 20:34; Mark 1:41; Luke 7:13). The second echoes Jesus's "mercy" beatitude in Luke 6:36 and Paul's description of God's mercy (cf. Rom 9:15; 12:1; 2 Cor 1:3). With his reminder, James explicitly highlights the fact that mercy reflects God's divine nature. If his readers show mercy to those who are facing testing, they will reflect the character of their heavenly Father. Implicitly, he challenges them to view their own acts of mercy as the means by which they can encourage others to endure testing. The truths that mercy reflects God's divine nature and encourages endurance in testing are James's fourth and fifth theological foundation stones for mission, as he seeks to form his readers for the mission of practicing gospel care toward those in need.

---

14 Many commentators include 5:7–12 in the closing section of the letter, with verse 12 as a free-standing exhortation. For example, Burdick labels 5:7–20 as "Miscellaneous Exhortations" ("James," 166). Although Davids takes a similar approach, he accurately notes that "one cannot read 5:7–11 separately from 5:1–6" (*Epistle of James*, 181).

15 James 5:1–6 echoes Jesus's teaching in Matthew 6:20; Luke 11:13–21; 16:19–31.

16 James 5:11 is, in fact, the only occurrence of πολύσπλαγχνος in the New Testament.

Table 6. James's Theological Foundation for Mission

James's Theological Foundation for Mission	
James 2:8–13	Mercy fulfills divine law.
	Mercy prompts divine mercy in return.
James 3:13–18	Mercy comes from a divine source.
James 5:7–12	Mercy reflects God's divine nature.
	Mercy encourages endurance in testing.

The Practical Application of Mission

As Andrew Chester and Ralph P. Martin note, "Although the specific terms are not used, it is the showing of love and mercy that James demands in other sections."[17] There are five sections in James's letter in which he provides practical examples of how his readers can fulfill the royal law to love their neighbors as themselves by showing mercy to those in need.

Care for those who are in distress. James 1:26–27 concludes the letter's thematic introduction (1:2–27). The introduction highlights five themes that James will develop at greater length in the body: testing (1:2–4, 12–15; cf. 4:1–12), wisdom (1:5–8; cf. 3:13–18), wealth (1:9–11; cf. 4:13–5:6), speech (1:19–21; cf. 3:1–12), and works (1:22–25; cf. 2:1–26). In his summary, James returns to three of those themes: control of the tongue as a measure of a person's spirituality (1:26), care for those in distress as a sign of true religion (1:27a), and remaining pure while enduring testing (1:27b).

In his second summary statement, James writes, "Pure and genuine religion in the sight of God means caring for orphans and widows in their distress" (1:27). It should come as no surprise that James singles out orphans and widows, since mistreatment and neglect of those two groups—along with strangers and the poor—are repeated concerns in Deuteronomy and the Prophets.[18] Cheating widows was one of the Pharisaical practices that Jesus denounced (Mark 12:40; Luke 20:47), while Luke holds up widows as positive examples of piety and objects of God's special care (Luke 4:25–26; 18:1–8; 21:1–4; Acts 9:39, 41). The first internal problem the Jerusalem church faced was neglect of Greek-speaking widows in the daily distribution of food

---

17 Chester and Martin, *James, Peter, and Jude*, 34.

18 Deut 10:18; 14:29; 16:11, 14; 24:19–21; 26:12–13; 27:19; Isa 1:23; 9:17; 10:2; Jer 7:6; 22:3; 49:11; Ezek 22:7; Zech 7:10; Mal 3:5.

(Acts 6:1–7), and Paul included detailed instructions regarding the care of widows in his first letter to Timothy (1 Tim 5:3–16).

The first example James provides, therefore, of the practical application of mission is practicing gospel care toward those who are in distress. Although James 1:26–27 specifically singles out the distress of widows and orphans, it is logical to view those groups as representative and to extend the application to any individuals who find themselves in difficult circumstances.

Help those who are destitute. James 2:1–4 and 14–17 are part of James's discussion of faith and works (2:1–26). They bookend the double theological truths in 2:8–13 and offer negative examples of what it means to love your neighbor as yourself. In the first example, James denounces partiality when individuals who wear fine clothes impress members of the assembly (2:1–4). In the second example, he denounces inaction when members of that same assembly encounter individuals who lack the necessities of life (2:14–17).[19] Together, these examples form the second practical application of mission in the letter. Both describe actions that are the opposite of mercy that fulfills the royal law and prompts God to extend his own mercy.

This compound application of practicing gospel care connects naturally to the echo of Jesus's Sermon on the Mount in James 2:13. It also echoes Jesus's parable of the sheep and the goats, where he includes the poor and naked among those to whom he expects his disciples to show compassion. Elsewhere in Scripture, Job identifies the mistreatment of those who are poorly clothed and fed as particularly wicked (Job 22:5–8; 24:1–10; 31:16–21), and Isaiah declares that care for the naked and hungry are actions of proper piety (Isa 58:6–7). The naked and hungry are among those for whom God cares (Ps 109:9), among those whom God delivers (Ps 116:7–9), and among those whose fortunes God will ultimately reverse (Luke 6:24–26). As discussed above, Jesus taught that the treatment of the hungry, thirsty, stranger, naked, sick, and imprisoned will be a factor in the final judgment (Matt 25:31–46).

Telling a person who is poorly clothed "You can stand over there, or else sit on the floor" (2:3) or saying to a person without food or clothing "Good-bye and have a good day; stay warm and eat well" (2:16), without helping that person, is the antithesis of the royal law and demonstrates a lack of mercy that will result in divine judgment. James further forms his readers for

---

19 Davids notes that the phrase James uses in 2:16 (τὰ ἐπιτήδεια τοῦ σώματος) "is broad enough to include both food and other bodily needs" (*Epistle of James*, 122).

mission by making it clear that they fail in their missional responsibilities if they show favor toward those who are well off or choose not to assist those who are destitute.

Hear the cries of those who are oppressed. James 5:1–6 is the last of three wrong responses to testing in 4:11–5:6. The primary focus of this paragraph is the judgment that will come upon those who trust in riches—their wealth will rot; moths will eat their clothes; their silver and gold will corrode; their treasure will testify against them. They have lived in luxury, have satisfied their every desire, and have condemned innocent people to death. As a result, the flames of the lake of fire will eat their flesh. The language of ruined riches echoes Jesus's teaching in the Sermon on the Mount (cf. Matt 6:20). The language of living in luxury while ignoring those in need echoes his parable of the rich man and Lazarus (cf. Luke 16:19–31). The language of the eternal fire of judgment echoes his teaching in the Olivet Discourse (cf. Matt 25:41).

Given the paragraph's focus on judgment, it is not surprising that there is no mention of mercy. Chester and Martin, however, note, "It is precisely [mercy] that the rich and oppressors … fail to show."[20] The rich have ignored the cries of those who work their fields and have cheated those workers of their pay. They have condemned and killed innocent individuals who have not resisted them. In all that they have done, they have failed to fulfill the royal commandment because they have not shown mercy to their neighbors who were in need. The cries of those neighbors have reached God's ear.[21] As Jesus's followers consider the mission he has given them, those same cries should also reach their ears, and they should respond by extending gospel care to the oppressed.

Pray for those who are sick. James 5:13–18 makes it clear that the mission of practicing gospel care extends beyond addressing material and social needs to addressing physical needs as well. The paragraph follows a four-part sequence: topic sentence (v. 13), specific example (vv. 14–15), logical summary (v. 16), and biblical support (vv. 17–18). The argumentation in this paragraph is similar to that in 2:1–13 and 14–26, although it is considerably more condensed.

---

20 Chester and Martin, *James, Peter, and Jude*, 34.

21 The sins against workers are clear violations of the Old Testament law (cf. Lev 19:13; Deut 24:14–15). The imagery of God hearing the cries of the oppressed also echoes the Old Testament (cf. Exod 22:23–24; Deut 15:9; 24:15).

The topic sentence reminds James's readers that they should be praying in every circumstance, whether they are suffering or cheerful. The example identifies suffering from serious illness as the specific need for prayer (5:14a). Those who are seriously ill need gospel care, and the proper response is for the elders of the assembly to visit them, pray over them, and anoint them with oil in the name of the Lord Jesus (5:14b). The elders' work of mercy will result in both physical healing and spiritual restoration (5:15). They can be confident in the effectiveness of prayer because of the way in which God answered Elijah's prayer (5:16–18).[22]

Prayer, of course, held a major place in Jesus's life (cf. Mark 1:35–38; 6:46; Luke 6:12–19; 22:39–46; John 17:1–26) and teaching (cf. Matt 6:5–15; Luke 11:1–4; 18:1–8). His commission for his followers included addressing physical needs as part of their work of extending his mission through gospel care (cf. Matt 10:8). Prayer was an integral part of early church life (cf. Acts 1:14, 24; 2:42; 4:24–31; 6:4, 6; 9:40; 10:9, 31; 11:5; 13:3), and Peter turned to God in prayer when he arrived in Joppa after hearing about Dorcas's death. It should be natural for Jesus's followers to extend gospel care to those who are sick by praying for them.

Bring back those who are wandering. James 5:19–20 adds individuals in spiritual need to the list of "neighbors" toward whom those on mission should practice gospel care. As Solomon Andria writes, "The community takes care of the needy, such as orphans, widows and those who are sick. It should also care for anyone who may wander from the truth."[23] James's instruction in these verses follows the same sequence as 5:14–15. The specific need for assistance is, again, serious—a Christian brother or sister has wandered from the truth (5:19a). The proper response is to bring back that person (5:19b–20a). The readers' act of mercy will result in both salvation from death and forgiveness of many sins (5:20b).

The idea of "wandering" (πλανάω/πλάνη) describes the act of straying from a specific way. The closest connections to Jesus's teaching are in the first half of his Ecclesial Discourse in Matthew 18. The idea of turning from sin occurs in 18:3. The act of seeking an individual who has wandered is central to the parable of the lost sheep in 18:12–14. Jesus outlines the process

---

22 The natural reading of James's specific instruction on prayer addresses serious illness within the assembly of Jesus's followers. It is not necessary, however, to limit the principle of praying for those who are sick only to those within the assembly, nor is it necessary to limit the principle only to prayer by the elders of the assembly.

23 Andria, "James," 1542.

for restoring the wanderer in 18:15–20. Previously, James highlighted the importance of showing mercy to others in the context of judgment (cf. 2:12–13), and saving a person from death that leads to final judgment is both James's most significant practical application of mercy as mission and an appropriate way to close his letter.

Table 7. James's Practical Application of Mission

James's Practical Application of Mission	
James 1:26–27	Care for those who are in distress.
James 2:1–4, 14–17	Help those who are destitute.
James 5:1–6	Hear the cries of those who are oppressed.
James 5:13–18	Pray for those who are sick.
James 5:19–20	Bring back those who are wandering.

Mercy as Mission in James

Mercy was a significant theme in Jesus's ministry and teaching, and the practice of gospel care was part of the commission that he gave to his followers. For James, "pure and undefiled religion" expresses itself through faith that works and fulfills the royal law of loving neighbor as self. Jesus's parabolic illustration of the royal law made it clear that love for neighbor shows mercy to those who are in need. For James, the practice of gospel care through acts of mercy is a significant aspect of the mission to which Jesus calls his followers. Consequently, he forms his readers for mission in two ways.

First, he sets out five truths about mercy that establish the theological foundation for mission: Our acts of mercy fulfill divine law (2:8), prompt divine mercy in return (2:13), come from a divine source (3:17), reflect God's divine nature (5:11), and encourage endurance in testing (5:11). Second, he sets out five practical applications of mercy: Mercy cares for those in distress (1:26–27), helps the destitute (2:1–4, 14–17), hears the cries of the oppressed (5:1–6), prays for the sick (5:13–18), and brings back the wandering (5:19–20). Along with his original audience, James's twenty-first-century readers should recognize the important place mercy holds in missional theology and should actively apply their theology by practicing mercy toward those around them who are in material, social, physical, and spiritual need.

Bibliography

Andria, Solomon. "James." In *Africa Bible Commentary: A One-Volume Commentary Written by 70 African Scholars*, edited by Tokunboh Adeyemo, 1535–42. Grand Rapids: Zondervan, 2010.

Bultmann, Rudolf. "ἔλεος, ἐλεέω." In *Theological Dictionary of the New Testament*, volume 2, edited by Gerhard Kittel, translated by Geoffrey Bromiley, 477–87. Grand Rapids: Eerdmans, 1986.

Burdick, Donald. "James." In *Ephesians through Philemon*. Vol. 12 of *The Expositor's Bible Commentary*, edited by Frank Gaebelein, 161–205. Grand Rapids: Zondervan, 1981.

Carson, Donald. "Matthew." In *Matthew, Mark, Luke*. Vol. 8 of *The Expositor's Bible Commentary*, edited by Frank Gaebelein, 3–599. Grand Rapids: Zondervan, 1984.

Chester, Andrew, and Ralph P. Martin. *The Theology of the Letters of James, Peter, and Jude.* Cambridge: Cambridge University Press, 1994.

Dancy, Graham Paul. "A Missional Reading of the Letter of James: Hearing the Voice of James in Mission." PhD diss., University of Gloucestershire, 2021.

Davids, Peter H. *The Epistle of James: A Commentary on the Greek Text.* New International Greek New Testament Commentary. Grand Rapids: Eerdmans, 1982.

Foster, Paul. "Q and James: A Source Critical Conundrum." In *James, 1 & 2 Peter, and Early Jesus Traditions*, edited by Alicia J. Batten and John S. Kloppenborg, 3–34. Library of New Testament Studies. New York: T&T Clark, 2016.

James, Arthur. "James." In *South Asia Biblical Commentary: A One-Volume Commentary on the Whole Bible*, edited by Brian Hintle, 1733–38. Grand Rapids: Zondervan, 2015.

Chapter 13

The Poor, the Rich, and God's Mission in James

Joseph K. Pak

Mission begins with the triune God's purpose to restore the creation and redeem a people from all nations affected by the fallen world and the corruption of sin.[1] The Father sent his Son for this mission, and the church is sent by the Son to continue his mission through the power of the Holy Spirit, whom the Son sent to the church. Thus, mission is built into the identity of God's people.[2] Mission is also central to the main storyline of the Bible. God's people are to embody God's creational design and intention, to look forward to the coming kingdom, the restored world and humanity, and to look outward to the sinful world to bring it back to God and his purposes. Through his word, God first works in his people according to his missional purposes and then through his people for the sake of the nations.[3] The church should carry out its "God-given, Jesus-shaped, Spirit-driven missionary task."[4]

In James, we can see God continuing to seek to gather and renew his people. In this early stage of the new covenant community, James's congregation is still almost exclusively Jewish, and incorporating the gentiles into the kingdom of God is not in James's purview yet. In order for the church to be empowered to live holy lives and function as a priestly nation, it must realize its missional vocation. In James, the poor/pious among the readers are given this missional call to reach out to the rich/ungodly by loving their oppressors into the kingdom. If the church is to fulfill its call to be a light to the nations, it must first be a light to the ungodly among them, such as their rich oppressors. Before it is sent to the ends of the earth (Matt 28:19–20), it must first be sent to its own people. Jesus commanded his disciples first to go to the lost sheep of the house of Israel before going among the gentiles (Matt 10:5–6). When Paul went on his missionary journeys, it was his practice to go to the synagogues first and try to reach the Jews (Rom 1:16; Acts 13:5, 14; 14:1; 17:1, 10; 18:4; 19:8).

---

1 Goheen, "History and Introduction," 21.

2 Goheen, 21–25.

3 Goheen, 21–25.

4 Wright, "Reading the New Testament Missionally," 145.

Paul earnestly longed for the salvation of his Jewish kinsmen, who often sought his death, even if it meant his own damnation for their sake (Rom 9:3), and he did everything he could to win them to Christ (1 Cor 9:20, 22). In the same spirit, James asks the poor who were being oppressed, dragged into court (2:6), defrauded, condemned, and maybe even murdered (5:4–6) by the rich Jewish kinsmen not to retaliate (2:13; 4:11–12; 5:9) but to love them into the kingdom (5:19–20). This way, the church can shine the countercultural Christian distinctiveness of enemy love to the surrounding world and attract them to the kingdom and thus fulfill its worldwide mission. In the case of James's readers, the enemies were not only the unbelieving oppressors who rejected Christ but also those who professed his name and yet lived contrary to their professed faith by abusing and oppressing their poor brothers. The only way for the poor to bring the Jewish nominal believers in their midst to salvation was by refusing to condemn them or take vengeance on them and by bringing them back to the truth and covering a multitude of their sins (4:11–12; 5:9, 19–20). This is how they could fulfill their God-given, Jesus-shaped, and Spirit-empowered mission of loving the enemies sacrificially and without condemnation. This mission manifests a new kind of justice and power in stark contrast to the power-hungry way of this world.[5]

Thus, one of the key messages of James is a call for repentance to the rich and for perseverance to the poor. James calls rich false believers who are only hearers of the word to repent so they may be saved from the eschatological judgment, and he is calling the poor believers not to condemn the oppressive rich believers but instead pray for them and turn them from their apostasy. I will first provide the historical and literary contexts of the letter and then discuss James's calls to the rich and to the poor in turn.

Contextual Discussion

Historical Context

Joel B. Green sees the narrative of James's letter as creation (1:16–18; 3:9; cf. Gen 1:26–27), advent of Jesus (2:1), present exilic life (1:1–3; 4:4), and new creation (1:12; 2:5).[6] Even after Jesus's coming inaugurated the kingdom, Christians in this world presently experience a life of exile and suffering. The mission of James's readers is to live out the royal law (2:8) in a hostile world, refusing to judge others and loving their enemies into the kingdom through the cross-shaped power of the gospel.

---

5 Wright, 151.

6 Green, "Reading James Missionally," 159.

In James's times, injustice and oppression of helpless people, whose only economic asset was their labor, was widespread in Syria-Palestine in the period immediately preceding the Roman War of AD 66–70.[7] "Large landowners who managed estates *in absentia* manipulated the judicial system, forced smaller land owners to borrow at exorbitant interest rates, foreclosed on land, and added estate to estate."[8] Those who worked the land were slaves, hired laborers, tenants, or small land owners living in poverty, never more than a step from financial ruin. Such oppression resulted in financial ruin for some; to a considerable degree, desperation accounts for the brigandage and outbreaks of violence that characterized the period.[9] Defrauding workers was vigorously condemned in Jewish literature.[10] In Malachi 3:5, God says that he will be a swift witness against those who oppress the hired worker in his wages (see also Lev 19:13; Deut 24:14; Jer 22:13; Tob 4:14). In a striking image, James declares that the withheld wages cry out with the harvesters to the Lord of hosts (5:4).

James sees the pursuit of luxury, wealth, and status as greed, envy, and a thirsty desire for acquisition that results in violence and oppression (4:1–2).[11] The wealthy landowners are guilty of living in luxury (5:2–3, 5), storing up treasures and wealth for their own consumption (5:3), exploiting, withholding just payment from those laboring in their fields (5:4), and oppressing the righteous (5:6).[12] The believers James addresses were not exempt from the economic dynamics between the rich and the poor. Thus, it is a lofty calling to the poor among his readers (which is most of them) to pray for their rich oppressors for their healing and salvation (5:14–20).

Literary Context

This chapter assumes the traditional authorship of the letter by James, Jesus's brother, as well as its dating to the 40s–50s, and its Jewish Christian audience. James is a letter that is often considered wisdom literature, containing disparate injunctions similar to the Proverbs. However, in recent years scholars have found a coherent structure in James.[13] The letter seems to

---

7   Warden, "Rich and Poor in James," 251.

8   Warden, 251.

9   Warden, 251.

10 Omanson, "Certainty of Judgment," 427. Cf. Sir 34:21–22; Isa 13:6; 15:3; Amos 8:4–6.

11 Jipp, *Saved by Faith and Hospitality*, 171.

12 Jipp, 171.

13 For the scholars who argue for coherent structure in James, see Varner, "Main Theme and Structure," 115–29; Taylor and Guthrie, "Structure of James," 681–705; and Lockett, "'Two Ways' Motif," 269–86.

owe a great debt to the tradition of Jewish wisdom writing—a tradition that richly incorporated the "two ways" motif.[14] The "two ways" is a common element in moral instruction that contrasts positive and negative ways of living in order to illustrate to young students the way of righteousness.[15] The final destination of the way of the fool, or the covenant breaker, is death, but the end of the way of the wise, or the righteous, is life (Deut 30:15).[16] In Jewish tradition this motif finds its origins in the covenantal blessing and curse material of the Pentateuch (Lev 26:1–39; Deut 28; 30:15–20) and in Hebrew wisdom literature.[17]

Within numerous contrasting ethical commands in James, two clear and simple options are presented so that the audience is challenged to make a clear choice between them.[18] The final destination or ultimate end of the two ways of living is either "death" (1:15; 5:20) or "life" (1:12, 18). James builds his letter around the blatant opposition of two lifestyles: one led in friendship with God, the other in friendship with the world (4:4). This contrast is repeated in different ways throughout the letter: doers vs. hearers only; the poor vs. the rich; wisdom from above vs. earthly, demonic wisdom; faith with works vs. faith without works; helping the poor vs. oppressing the poor; single-minded devotion to God vs. double-mindedness; etc. Not only does James contrast two different ways that end in either death or life, but he also contrasts the guides along the way—"desire" leads the unrighteous on the "way" to death, while the "word/law/wisdom" combination leads the righteous to life.[19]

It is well known that James has drawn much from Jesus's teachings. Jesus also ends his Sermon on the Mount by contrasting the two ways (Matt 7:13–27): narrow gate vs. wide gate (vv. 13–14); bad fruit vs. good fruit (vv. 15–20); workers of lawlessness vs. doers of the will of God (vv. 21–23); and hearers only vs. doers of the words of Jesus (vv. 24–27). Both Jesus and James employ the two ways tradition familiar to their Jewish audience.[20] The contrast between the poor and the rich is also a prominent feature in James. Terms for "poor" almost always carry the idea of oppression as part of their meaning, and it is assumed that the wicked rich are the ones who oppress them. Many biblical scholars recognize that the classifications poor

---

14 Lockett, "'Two Ways' Motif," 274–75.

15 Lockett, 274–75.

16 Lockett, 274–75.

17 Lockett, 274–75.

18 Lockett, 282–83; van de Sandt, "James 4,1–4 in the Light," 38.

19 Lockett, "'Two Ways' Motif," 282.

20 Barton, "Money Matters," 44–45. See also Rhee, *Loving the Poor*, 172.

and rich in the Bible are more about sociopolitical oppression and spiritual disposition and less about monetary possessions.[21]

Another significant feature of James's structure is his use of Leviticus 19:12–18 as the backbone of his epistle.[22] This passage gives several commandments, including commands not to oppress one's neighbor or keep his wages overnight (v. 13), not to be partial to the poor and thereby pervert justice (v. 15), not to hate your neighbor (v. 17), and to love your neighbor as yourself (v. 18). Verse 18 also commands the people of God not to bear a grudge against a brother, as does James 5:9. James seems to understand that God's church can successfully fulfill its mission only by living out the royal law (2:8).

Call to the Rich False Believers to Repent

The Rich Addressed in James Are False Believers

James is not addressing all rich believers, but rather the rich and self-deceived false, or nominal, believers in his audience. He issues a strong warning against their oppression of their poor brothers. There are many indicators of this within the letter, as I have argued elsewhere.[23] To highlight a couple, first, James rebukes two different classes of people among the audience: the self-sufficient merchants who make business plans with no regard to God's will (4:13–17) and the rich landowners who are abusing the poor (5:1–6).[24] Second, James issues strong warnings to those whose deeds and words show that they are self-deceived about their religion (1:22–27). As Helen Rhee observes, orthopraxis and orthodoxy were always part and parcel of salvation, especially in the face of the constantly lurking double threats of apostasy and heresy, which were judged not only by belief (theology) but also by behavior (ethics).[25] James 1:22 states, "But be doers of the word, and

---

21 Scacewater, "Dynamic and Righteous Use of Wealth," 228.

22 Scacewater, 228.

23 Pak, "Case for James's Condemnation," 721–37.

24 The soliloquy of the merchants in James 4:13 seems to echo the soliloquy of the rich man who makes plans to enjoy his life without regard to God and to the poor in the parable of the rich fool (Luke 12:17–19).

25 Rhee, *Loving the Poor*, 74–75; Kamell, "Economics of Humility," 169–70. Those who are on the way of life, the humble, do not blame God for their own failures in the face of temptation (1:13–16), do not judge others by their looks (2:1, 4), remember God's imminence, and as a result, avoid complaining and slandering (5:9). In contrast, those who are on the way of death, the selfish and arrogant, are threatened by their imminent downfall (1:10–11) and with judgment (2:12), warned of possessing a demonic wisdom (3:14–16), charged with being adulterers in their relationship to God (4:4), warned of the Judge's ability to "destroy" them (4:12), reminded of their own transience (4:14), and informed of their coming doom in the "day of slaughter" (5:1–6).

not hearers only, deceiving yourselves."[26] Brosend argues that this is a thesis statement of James, which is explored and applied throughout the remainder of the letter.[27] Hiebert similarly holds that *"tests of living faith* is indeed the unifying theme of the epistle and … provides ready access to its contents."[28]

The call to guard against self-deception in James relates to those who believe that they can receive the redemptive word without obeying it—to pretend that one has received the word but not to obey it serves only to reveal the pretense (cf. 1:22).[29] This includes the rich who refuse to love their poor neighbors and instead abuse and oppress them. In 5:19, as James concludes the letter, he mentions a person who wanders from the truth. This is not one who has accidentally or unconsciously departed from the truth; rather the term implies that the person is guilty of apostasy. Behind the term are the ideas of idolatry and ethical dualism (Jer 23:17; Ezek 33:19; Prov 14:8; Wis 5:6–7; 12:24).[30] Titus 1:13–16 describes those who turn away from the truth as unbelieving and denying God by their works though they profess to know him.[31] In sum, the rich James is addressing in his letter are rich nominal believers who are oppressing the poor. They are the mission field, along with the rest of the nominal believers and unbelieving Jews, that God's church should seek to reach.

The Rich Are Warned about the Eschatological Judgment

In James 5:1–6, the sociopolitical aspect seems to be the dominant concern because the rich have the power to defraud the wages of the poor workers, who presumably have no realistic social or legal recourse due to their lack of wealth, status, and prestige.[32] "You have condemned" in 5:6 may be looking back to 2:6b ("Are not the rich the ones who oppress you, and the ones who drag you into court?"), indicating that these rich Jews controlled their Jewish courts or used their influence with pagan judges to secure an adverse verdict against the poor.[33] "You have condemned and murdered" in 5:6 indicates that the condemnation secured has resulted in the death of the innocent or at least deprivation of their living.[34] Ecclesiasticus 34:22 states, "As one that slays his

---

26 All Scripture quotations are from the ESV unless otherwise noted.

27 Brosend, *James and Jude*, 51; see also Hiebert, "Unifying Theme," 223.

28 Hiebert, "Unifying Theme," 224, emphasis original.

29 Kamell, "Implications of Grace," 282.

30 Martin, *James*, 218.

31 Cf. Martin, 218–19.

32 Scacewater, "Dynamic and Righteous Use," 230–31.

33 Hiebert, *Epistle of James*, 293.

34 Hiebert, 293.

neighbor is he that takes away his living; and as a shedder of blood is he that deprives a hireling of his hire" (WEB). In either case, for the poor to reach these people, nothing short of a literal fulfillment of Jesus's command to love their enemies was required. Integral to successful mission is radical self-sacrifice.

The church fathers held the rich's refusal to help the poor as a serious sin. For Cyprian, the rich who preserve their worldly wealth while neglecting the poor sin gravely with their covetousness and can only expect eternal loss and punishment like the rich fool in the Lukan Gospel.[35] Clement of Alexandria stated: "A Christian who lives in luxury (which itself is an oxymoron) commits not only a 'sin of commission' (avarice, vanity, self-love, and attachment to the world), but also a 'sin of omission' by neglecting the commandment of loving one's neighbor."[36] Christian authors characterized the problem of avarice (love of money) essentially as an idolatry problem and thus as something intrinsically antithetical to Christian identity.[37]

The rich who refuse to help the poor and, worse, oppress and abuse them are warned that their eschatological judgment is imminent (5:1–6). Their judgment day will be a rude awakening, revealing a great reversal of fortune, just like in the parable of the rich man and Lazarus. James may be still thinking about these oppressive rich when he mentions those who are wandering from the truth, or apostatizing (5:19).[38] Unless someone turns them back from their apostasy, their souls are headed toward death and will be punished for a multitude of sins (5:20).[39] The mission of the church begins by reaching those nominal believers who are within the church but are headed to death.

How the Rich Can Escape the Impending Judgment

Some commentators believe that the rich whom James addresses are irreversibly under God's wrath. However, God's prophetic judgments in the Hebrew Bible were often conditional. As with Nineveh, if the wicked repent and turn to God, he may relent from the warned punishment. So, here too, the rich have the opportunity to repent and avoid the coming miseries.[40]

---

35 Rhee, *Loving the Poor*, 101.

36 Rhee, 170, citing Clement, *Paed.* 3.6.34–36; 2.13.120.

37 Rhee, 168.

38 Davids, *Epistle of James*, 198.

39 Davids, 199–201. Covering a multitude of sins refers to gaining forgiveness and is a benefit parallel to the saving from death. To cover sin (5:20) is normally to procure forgiveness (Pss 32:1; 85:2; Dan 4:24; Sir 5:6; Tob 4:10; Rom 4:7). See also Stulac, *James*, 188.

40 Scacewater, "Dynamic and Righteous Use," 231; Painter and DeSilva, *James and Jude*, 153; Pak, "Case for James's Condemnation," 732.

God's mission is to call all sinners to repentance and rescue them from the coming judgment (cf. 2 Pet 3:9). If the rich respond in repentance and faith, they too can avoid God's judgment as God takes no pleasure in the death of the wicked (Ezek 18:23, 32; 33:11).

Rhee avers, "If renunciation of avarice and luxury constituted a negative boundary marker for Christian identity, almsgiving and sharing constituted Christians' positive boundary marker."[41] This is because caring for and sharing possessions with the less fortunate is what distinguishes the genuine and "orthodox" Christians from the false and "heretical" Christians.[42] James cannot be said to argue that the rich cannot be saved, for he uses Abraham as the prime exemplar of faith (2:21–24), and Abraham's wealth is repeatedly announced in Genesis.[43] On the flip side, poverty has no intrinsic value apart from the attendant poverty of the soul, which is available for the rich as well as for the poor.[44] Thus, in contrast to the popular view that the rich in James are irreversibly subject to God's judgment, God issues a mission call to the poor to save the rich from death.

The command in James 4:10 ("Humble yourselves before the Lord, and he will exalt you") is issued to the entire audience, thereby indicating that anyone can, *and should*, be among the humble whom God will raise up.[45] How can the rich humble themselves before the Lord and be saved? According to the church fathers, one way is by loving God and loving one's neighbor through almsgiving.[46] Peter of Alexandria, who was the bishop of Alexandria in the late third century, assumed the rich in general to be the "wicked, merciless rich" unless they were specified as the "merciful and loving." He also points out that a poor man can leave his financial poverty

---

41 Rhee, *Loving the Poor*, 171–72.

42 Rhee, 173.

43 Kamell, "Economics of Humility," 173.

44 Rhee, *Loving the Poor*, 80.

45 Kamell, "Economics of Humility," 169, emphasis original. In James 4:10 the first verb ταπεινώθητε has the same root for humility/humiliation as the adjective and noun in 1:9–10. Likewise, the verb ὑψώσει in 4:10 has the same root for the promised elevation as the noun in 1:9.

46 Rhee, *Loving the Poor*, 81–82. Clement uses transaction and exchange language to express that the rich can buy an eternal abode in heaven by giving the perishing things of the world. For Clement, almsgiving is a quintessential, positive demonstration of loving God and neighbor as well as of using one's wealth properly. Without the love for God, no one can gain salvation. "Because God receives and forgives everyone who turns to him in genuine repentance, almsgiving is an effective means of repentance and rooting out of the soul the postbaptismal sins leading to death" (Rhee, 82, citing Clement, *Quis div.* 39). For Tertullian also, "Almsgiving, a visible act, fulfills both doing justice and loving mercy in Micah 6:8 and the 'one thing' required by Christ for salvation (*Adversus Marcionem* 4.36.7; cf. 4.27.6–9)" (Rhee, 93).

for another poverty that is seven times more evil, such as idleness, arrogance, and stealing. Thus, Peter of Alexandria deconstructs the wicked rich and the pious poor tradition without any attempt to spiritualize wealth and poverty.[47] Both the rich and the poor are God's mission field.

Early Christian leaders and texts connected almsgiving to the salvation of the giver, and an important point to keep in mind is that almsgiving is not so much a human work as it is an index of one's underlying faith.[48] In Paul's words, it is faith working through love (Gal 5:6). How about the poor? How can they demonstrate their faith? James exhorts them not to condemn the rich but instead to pray for them and bring them back from their apostasy. It is to this topic we now turn.

Call to the Poor Believers to Love and Not to Condemn the Rich

Judging Others Is a Serious Sin

The command for God's people to cease from speaking evil against others of the congregation has well-established precedents (Lev 19:16; Prov 18:8; 26:22; Wis 1:11), and evil speech was a problem for the early church (Rom 1:30; 2 Cor 12:20; 1 Pet 2:1; 2 Pet 2:12; 3:16; 1 Clem 30.1–3; 35.5; Barn 20.2).[49] According to Douglas J. Moo, criticism and condemnation of others amount to pronouncing one's own verdict over their spirituality and destiny.[50] Moo thinks that James's concern in 4:11–12 is with jealous, censorious speech by which one judges others as being wrong in the sight of God.[51] It is this sort of judging that Paul rebuked among the Roman Christians, who were apparently questioning the reality of one another's faith because of differing views on the applicability of some ritual laws (Rom 14:1–13).[52] A similar situation was probably responsible for the problems that James addresses.[53]

When James says, "Do not speak evil against one another, brothers" in 4:11, the verb καταλαλέω here means speaking against someone in harsh criticism, accusation, or condemnation (Num 12:8 LXX; 21:7 LXX; Ps 77:19 LXX; 2 Cor 12:20; 1 Pet 2:12; 3:16).[54] To set oneself over against another is

---

47 Rhee, 88.

48 Rhee, 102.

49 Martin, *James*, 163.

50 Moo, *James*, 152.

51 Moo, 152.

52 Moo, 152–53.

53 Moo, 153.

54 Laws, *Epistle of James*, 186.

to break the law of love, and this, in turn, must be seen as implicitly taking up a critical attitude toward the law itself, for failure to keep the law is to judge it invalid or unnecessary.[55] The transgressor thus puts himself into the position of a judge of the law.[56] It is an infringement of the prerogative of God. Judgment belongs to God alone since only he can save and destroy (Deut 32:39; 1 Sam 2:6; 2 Kg 5:7; Ps 68:20; Matt 10:28); only a reckless person deliberately infringes upon the prerogatives of God.[57] When judging a brother or sister with evil intention, one is violating the law of love (Lev 19:18; Matt 22:39; Rom 13:8–10; Gal 5:14), opposing it, criticizing it, and implying that it is not good and should be abrogated.[58]

Most importantly, when we judge and denounce others, we abrogate our God-given mission of bringing the lost into the kingdom of God. It undermines the missional work of God's church in embodying Christ's forgiveness and redemption. Only when we embrace them as Jesus did in a cross-shaped enemy love can we fulfill our mission purpose as a church. And it is only possible through Spirit-empowered forgiveness and reconciliation. This may be why Titus 3:10–11 instructs that a person who stirs up division should be shunned after a couple of warnings.

Those Who Judge Their Neighbors Will Also Be Judged

The poor will inherit the kingdom. But not just any poor—the poor who have genuine faith. Jipp argues that by judging others (whether it be the rich or the poor), one shows oneself to be unfit for the kingdom.[59] The poor who will inherit the kingdom are the ones who rejoice under trial and patiently endure the oppression, leaving God the role of the judge who can both destroy and save.[60] James insists that there is a divine lawgiver and judge who will hold all people accountable—especially those who profess faith yet fail to obey the royal law of love in their attitudes toward their brothers and sisters.[61] Judgment will be severe for those who do not show mercy, for "mercy triumphs over judgment" (Jas 2:13). As mentioned above, Leviticus 19:18 is a key verse in James, and it is set in a context that sternly

---

55 Laws, 187.

56 Laws, 187.

57 Barclay, *Letters of James and Peter*, 112.

58 Hiebert, *Epistle of James*, 268.

59 Jipp, *Saved by Faith and Hospitality*, 170; cf. van de Sandt, "James 4,1–4 in the Light," 57–58.

60 Jipp, *Saved by Faith and Hospitality*, 170.

61 Jipp, 5.

opposes slander, vengeance, and grudges against a neighbor (19:15–18).[62] The command to "love your neighbor as yourself" in 19:18 is "the law" referred to in James 4:11–12, where James says that anyone who speaks against a brother speaks against the law. James suggests that anyone who speaks disdainfully of a sister or a brother is, in fact, breaking this "royal law" (cf. 2:8). Nystrom argues that because this command had the central place in the ethical teaching of Jesus, to ignore this command is, in effect, to repudiate Christ and to render the self-description "Christian" a falsehood.[63]

According to James, when we judge others, we invite and pronounce judgment on ourselves. The sin of harsh criticism, that is, condemnation and accusation (καταλαλέω in 4:11) is condemned all through the Bible. It is the psalmist's charge against the wicked man (Ps 50:20), and God will destroy the one who slanders his neighbor secretly (Ps 101:5).[64] Paul lists it among the sins that are characteristic of the unredeemed evil of the pagan world (Rom 1:30), and it is one of the sins which he fears he might find in the church of Corinth (2 Cor 12:20).[65] Peter denounces it along with malice, envy, hypocrisy, and deceit (1 Pet 2:1). Barclay maintains that there are few sins that the Bible so unsparingly condemns as the sin of irresponsible and malicious gossip.[66] A judgmental attitude destroys the church's unity and its ability to carry out its mission.

The Poor Should Pray for Their Brothers and Turn Them from Apostasy
In 5:13–18, James exhorts his readers to pray. Prayer is offered as the alternative to complaining (5:9) and swearing (5:12). Stulac argues that oaths and prayers represent the verbal expressions of underlying stances of unbelief and faith, respectively.[67] All along, James urges his readers to resist the temptation to compromise righteousness in their trials; instead, they should use the power of prayer, for which they need righteousness.[68] If they commit themselves to do what is right without compromise, they may rely on God in prayer for all their needs.[69] The prayer of genuine faith is

---

62 Martin, *James*, 164.

63 Nystrom, *James*, 249. This "speaking ill" of sisters and brothers is closely allied to the ill-treatment of them in James 2:1–7, and the flagrant refusal to follow the royal law recalls 2:8–13.

64 Barclay, *Letters of James and Peter*, 111.

65 Barclay, 111.

66 Barclay, 111.

67 Stulac, *James*, 179.

68 Stulac, 185.

69 Stulac, 185.

powerful and effective (5:16). Unbelief will cause one to seek protection by unrighteous means in the midst of trials, but confident belief in God's grace will make one strong to act righteously in trials.[70] The miracles in 1 Kings 17–18 were undeniably beyond Elijah's human power—they were divine answers to prayer.[71] James emphasizes that Elijah was a man just like them to encourage his readers to trust God to answer their prayers.

James implies that some of their sickness is caused by sin when he says in 5:15, "And the prayer of faith will save the one who is sick, and the Lord will raise him up. And if he has committed sins, he will be forgiven." The prayer of the righteous believers will bring about healing and forgiveness of the sins that caused the sickness (v. 16). Confession of sins (which must include the sin of oppression by the rich) and prayers by the righteous for such sins will hopefully result in repentance from those sins (v. 19). This seems to be James's solution to the problems of oppression, strife, jealousy, and division in the church: the righteous should not condemn the unrighteous but instead patiently endure and pray for them—for their healing if they are sick, the forgiveness of their sins, and their salvation. If so, James is echoing Jesus's teaching on enemy love and issuing a charge to faithfully carry out the church's mission in a hostile world.

When James mentions a member wandering from the truth (ἀλήθεια) in 5:19, who does he have in mind? Fearghus O. Fearghail's statements are helpful:

> The presence of ἀλήθεια in the concluding exhortation of the letter suggests that its sense should be seen in the broader context of the letter. In this context those who stray from the truth or who are on "the way of error" are those whose faith is not steadfast in the face of trial (1:2–4), whose prayer is not with faith (1:6), who attribute their faults to God (1:13–18), or who fail to put into action the law or word of God (1:19–27), notably the law of charity (2:1–13); they are those who do not put their faith into action (2:14–26) or do not bridle the tongue (3:1–12), those whose wisdom is not from above (3:13–18), whose friendship is with the world instead of with God (4:1–10); they are those who judge a brother (4:11–12), who are not mindful of God (4:13–17), who are unjust towards the poor (5:1–6); they are those who grumble against one another (5:9), who have not patience (5:7–11); they are those whose word is not their bond (5:12).[72]

---

70 Stulac, 185.

71 Stulac, 185. Jesus himself drew attention to Elijah's powerful prayer over the rain when his miracles were hindered by people's unbelief in Nazareth (Luke 4:25; Mark 6:4–6).

72 Fearghail, "On the Conclusion," 90.

In short, James is referring to all in his audience, including the rich and the poor, who are not on the path to life but on the path to death, that is, the nominal believers in the community—those who profess faith but in their deeds show themselves as not having been "brought forth" (ἀπεκύησεν), or regenerated, by the word of truth (1:18).[73] James exhorts the genuine believers to fulfill their mission and love these nominal believers enough to turn them back from their apostasy and save their souls (5:20).

Conclusion

The epistle of James shows the heart of God and his mission to seek and save the lost—including those who persecute God's people. Jesus's incarnation, suffering, and death showed the distance he was willing to travel and the price he was willing to pay for those who mocked him and clamored for his crucifixion. Through his church, Jesus continues his mission of seeking and saving the lost. In James, they are the rich who are persecuting the poor. They profess the name of Jesus, but their judgment is imminent. The way they treat their poor brothers shows their faith to be like that of demons— without works and dead.

For James, those who have genuine faith and thus will receive the crown of life are those who have stood the test of faith with endurance (1:12). The test comes in the form of trials (1:2–3). In James, these trials are persecution by the rich and powerful. Genuine believers respond to the trials with joy and steadfastness and without grumbling (1:2–3; 5:9). The rich are warned because, unless they repent of their evil oppression of their poor brothers, they will face God's eternal judgment (5:1–6); the poor are also warned because unless they respond to their trials with endurance, they too will face God's judgment (5:9; cf. 4:11–12). "Judgment is without mercy to the one who has shown no mercy" (2:13).[74]

James asks the poor not to condemn the rich but instead to endure their hardships caused by the rich's oppression and deprivation of their rightful wages, knowing that the Lord is near to bringing his judgment to the wicked

---

73 In James 1:15 and 18 is seen another contrast of the two ways motif: sin, when fully grown, brings forth (ἀποκύει) death (1:15), whereas God's will and the word of truth bring forth (ἀπεκύησεν) firstfruits of his creatures (1:18).

74 For James, grumbling against the rich oppressors means failing to be patient and proving the superficiality of one's faith. In 5:7–8, James uses the word "be patient" (μακροθυμέω) three times to emphasize the necessity of patience in the midst of trials in order to be prepared to meet the soon-coming Judge (5:8). Grumbling is a sign that one failed to respond to trials with patience.

and his reward to the righteous.[75] The poor along with the rest of the genuine believers ("doers of the word") should pray for God's intervention and for the salvation of the rich along with the rest of the nominal believers ("hearers only"). In James, there are numerous calls to those who are walking the path toward death to repent, as well as calls to those on the path of life to love, pray for, and guide those on the path to death toward repentance unto life, thereby fulfilling their God-given mission.

South African missiologist David J. Bosch rightly describes mission as "the common witness of the whole Church, bringing the whole Gospel to the whole world."[76] Bosch's words about mission in the world apply particularly well to the missiological work that James calls his readers to do: "Mission takes place where the Church, in her total involvement with the world and the comprehensiveness of her message, bears her testimony in word and deed in the form of a servant, with reference to salvation, healing, liberation, reconciliation and righteousness."[77] This testimony is to take place in James's readers' community through their forgiveness and intercession for those who persecute them. They are to follow the footsteps of Jesus in the mission of God by the power of the Holy Spirit.

---

75 Judging the neighbor may have involved evaluating whether they could ever be saved. James says God is able to save and destroy (4:12), so the readers should not call anyone irredeemable. Rather, when they see an apostate, they should bring them back to the truth and save their souls (5:19–20). God is able to save the lost, including the false believers such as the evil rich oppressors. So do not judge them or decide that they are so evil that they are irredeemable. Let God be the ultimate judge of merchants who live and plan as if they are in control of their lives (4:13–17) and rich landowners who withhold wages from their poor tenant brothers and condemn and murder innocent people (5:1–6). God is the judge and his judgment is imminent (5:9). Genuine believers do not resist their evil deeds (5:6); instead, they are exhorted to be patient and establish their hearts (5:7–8) and not grumble against them as God will deal with them himself shortly (5:9). Instead, they should imitate the prophets and Job, who patiently endured their suffering (5:10–11). The prophets suffered at the hands of their own people, not by some outsiders. So too James exhorts his readers to endure their suffering at the hands of the rich in their own community. They should pray for healing and forgiveness for those who are sick (5:13–18) because their prayer can be effective even in bringing apostates such as the rich oppressors back to truth and saving their souls (5:19–20).

76 Bosch, *Witness to the World*, 17.

77 Bosch, 18.

Bibliography

Barclay, William. *The Letters of James and Peter*. Rev. ed. Daily Study Bible Series. Philadelphia: Westminster, 1976.

Barton, Stephen C. "Money Matters: Economic Relations and the Transformation of Value in Early Christianity." In *Engaging Economics: New Testament Scenarios and Early Christian Reception*, edited by Bruce W. Longenecker and Kelly D. Liebengood, 37–59. Grand Rapids: Eerdmans, 2009.

Bosch, David J. *Witness to the World: The Christian Mission in Theological Perspective*. London: Marshall, Morgan & Scott, 1980.

Brosend, William F., II. *James and Jude*. New Cambridge Bible Commentary. Cambridge: Cambridge University Press, 2004.

Davids, Peter H. *The Epistle of James: A Commentary on the Greek Text*. New International Greek Testament Commentary. Grand Rapids: Eerdmans, 1982.

Fearghail, Fearghus O. "On the Conclusion of the Letter of James." *Proceedings of the Irish Biblical Association* 35 (2012): 74–93.

Goheen, Michael W. "A History and Introduction to a Missional Reading of the Bible." In *Reading the Bible Missionally*, edited by Michael W. Goheen, 3–27. Grand Rapids: Eerdmans, 2016.

Green, Joel B. "Reading James Missionally." In *Reading the Bible Missionally*, edited by Michael W. Goheen, 194–212. Grand Rapids: Eerdmans, 2016.

Hiebert, D. Edmond. *The Epistle of James: Tests of a Living Faith*. Chicago: Moody, 1979.

Hiebert, D. Edmond. "The Unifying Theme of the Epistle of James." *Bibliotheca Sacra* 135, no. 539 (1978): 221–31.

Jipp, Joshua W. *Saved by Faith and Hospitality*. Grand Rapids: Eerdmans, 2017.

Kamell, Mariam. "The Economics of Humility: The Rich and the Humble in James." In *Engaging Economics: New Testament Scenarios and Early Christian Reception*, edited by Bruce W. Longenecker and Kelly D. Liebengood, 157–75. Grand Rapids: Eerdmans, 2009.

Kamell, Mariam. "The Implications of Grace for the Ethics of James." *Biblica* 92, no. 2 (2011): 274–87.

Laws, Sophie. *The Epistle of James*. Black's New Testament Commentary. Peabody, MA: Hendrickson, 1980.

Lockett, Darian R. "The 'Two Ways' Motif in James' Theological Instruction." *Neotestimenica* 42, no. 2 (2008): 269–87.

Longenecker, Bruce W, and Kelly D. Liebengood, eds. *Engaging Economics: New Testament Scenarios and Early Christian Reception*. Grand Rapids: Eerdmans, 2009.

Martin, Ralph P. *James*. Word Biblical Commentary 48. Waco, TX: Word, 1988.

Moo, Douglas J. *James*. Tyndale New Testament Commentaries. Grand Rapids: Eerdmans, 1985.

Nystrom, David P. *James*. NIV Application Commentary. Grand Rapids: Zondervan, 1997.

Omanson, Roger L. "The Certainty of Judgment and the Power of Prayer: James 5." *Review and Expositor* 83, no. 3 (1986): 427–38.

Painter, John, and David A. DeSilva. *James and Jude*. Paideia. Grand Rapids: Baker Academic, 2012.

Pak, Joseph K. "A Case for James's Condemnation of the Rich in James 5:1–6 as Addressing False Believers within the Believing Community." *Journal of Evangelical Theological Society* 63, no. 4 (2020): 721–37.

Rhee, Helen. *Loving the Poor, Saving the Rich: Wealth, Poverty, and Early Christian Formation*. Grand Rapids: Baker Academic, 2012.

van de Sandt, Huub. "James 4,1–4 in the Light of the Jewish Two Ways Tradition 3,1–6." *Biblica* 88, no. 1 (2007): 38–63.

Scacewater, Todd. "The Dynamic and Righteous Use of Wealth in James 5:1–6." *Journal of Markets and Morality* 20, no. 2 (2017): 227–42.

Stulac, George M. *James*. IVP New Testament Commentary Series. Downers Grove, IL: InterVarsity Press, 1993.

Taylor, Mark E., and George H. Guthrie. "The Structure of James." *Catholic Biblical Quarterly* 68, no. 4 (2006): 681–705.

Varner, William C. "The Main Theme and Structure of James." *Master's Seminary Journal* 22, no. 1 (2011): 115–29.

Warden, Duane. "The Rich and Poor in James: Implications for Institutionalized Partiality." *Journal of the Evangelical Theological Society* 43, no. 2 (2000): 247–57.

Wright, N. T. "Reading the New Testament Missionally." In *Reading the Bible Missionally*, edited by Michael W. Goheen, 175–93. Grand Rapids: Eerdmans, 2016.

Chapter 14

Wisdom from James for Managerial Missions

Sarah Lunsford

A common debate in modern missiology regards a methodological approach often disparagingly referred to as "managerial" missions.[1] We missionaries often rely so heavily on the scientific method in our efforts to produce an abundant spiritual harvest among the nations that we can sometimes fail to acknowledge the Lord of the harvest. We count the numbers of unreached peoples, chart their languages, evaluate their worldviews, test evangelistic methods, measure their results, and then export effective mission methods to be reproduced in another region. It is as if we believe that there are mathematical laws to the universe, even down to the religious commitments of a people group, and that if we can find the correct formula in our approach, presentation, and discipleship methods, then we can convince the world to follow Christ. While this approach has been numerically productive, some missiologists have decried the problems with this managerial approach to missions, exhorting missionaries to remember the roles of the Holy Spirit and prayer in their efforts. Others argue that if God has given us a task to reach the lost and dying among the nations, then should we not work to be as fruitful as possible? Surely, we should not return to the missionary methods of the past now that we better understand effective methods in intercultural communication, contextualization, and church planting, right? How, then, are we to find a wise and appropriate balance between our managerial methods (our works) and our dependence on God (our faith)?

James addresses this topic in his epistle, teaching that faith without works is dead and that our works are the proof and evidence of our faith (2:17–18). On the surface, this seems to be an easy proof text to use in favor of the managerial missions approach. However, James also says that we are wrong to set forth our plans and goals to produce a future profit unless we say, "If the Lord wills" (4:13–15).[2] In fact, James says that all our planning is

---

1 In this chapter, the term "managerial" refers to all attempts to systematically and scientifically plan and strategize to reach the nations for Christ. One side of the debate decries that our methods are reductionistically pragmatic and have lost their theological moorings, while the other side counters that proper stewardship of our mission implies that we must use means to accomplish the mission God set before us. For a summary of the issue and analysis of the "managerial" approach to missions, see Lunsford, *Missiological Triage*, 1–29.

2 All Scripture quotations are from the ESV.

boasting, and he surprises the reader by calling it "evil" (4:16). If managing and planning for a spiritual harvest among the nations has the potential to be evil, then we clearly have some thinking to do.

James writes his epistle to describe how works demonstrate faith. As such, James does not spend much time elucidating the foundations of faith like many other New Testament epistles. Instead, this can be inferred from what he has to say about good works that properly align with and represent right faith. In this chapter, we will focus primarily on what James 4:13–17 has to say about managerial missions and how we can move away from a double-minded, self-reliant approach to missions and toward the wisdom that comes from prayerfully depending on God's singular integrity in the goodness of his nature and mission.

Overview of the Managerial Missions Debate

In 1912, Roland Allen inspired a significant shift in missiological methods when he argued that although the New Testament message is normative, there is no normative method for evangelization.[3] Allen urged missionaries to move away from a legalistic application of Paul's exact methods and rather to imitate Paul's faith and dependence on the Holy Spirit while employing a more scientific approach in the development contextualized missions strategies and methods. To this day, Allen's argument can be seen as the voice behind such oft-repeated comments that "the Bible is not a handbook for methodology."[4]

This advice played into the Enlightenment-inspired philosophical approaches already at large with their positivistic, deterministic, and mechanistic paradigms. Thus, even in missions, the spiritual aspects (prayer, reliance on the Spirit, theology) began to be segregated from the pragmatic aspects (research, quantitative growth, method analysis, measuring, and testing). This scientific approach was most pronounced through the influence of the church growth movement in the second half of the twentieth century. According to Wilbert Shenk, "One cannot read missions literature of the past fifty years without sensing the determinism of the mechanical paradigm at work."[5] This dichotomy between faith and methods has grown into a significant schism in missiological methods.[6]

---

3 Allen, *Missionary Methods*, 6, 119, 197. See also Dayton and Fraser, *Planning Strategies*, 195.

4 Crawley, *Biblical Light*, 10–13.

5 Shenk, "Role of Theory," 40.

6 For an exploration of this division between science-driven methods and mission theology, see Lunsford, *Missiological Triage*, 1–29.

Samuel Escobar pointedly argues against a missiological emphasis on statistical data: size of congregations, numerical growth curves, number of hours spent in prayer, numerical size of missionary force, etc. He claims that by emphasizing only the quantitative aspect of missions, and only some of them, we have not created tools appropriate to our object of study. This produces an inner contradiction that has not been solved and makes it unacceptable to missionaries and missiologists who want to be consistent and faithful to God's word in their theology and practice.[7]

James F. Engel and William A. Dyrness argue that "managerial reductionism short-circuits the theological cornerstone that the Holy Spirit alone is responsible for conviction, regeneration and sanctification."[8] They go on to say that this reductionism has led missions to an uncritical adoption of strategic planning, a preoccupation with numerical success, and an unhealthy relationship between numerical success and fundraising.[9] Charles R. Taber reveals a problematic underlying assumption that, once missiology learns enough, the missions task ought to be able to operate like an engineering project.[10] Paul G. Hiebert agrees that the uncritical adoption of the social sciences at the point of deterministic materialism has led to managerial and pragmatic ends, far removed from any theological foundation.[11]

The underlying assumption behind managerial missions seems to be that numerical growth validates the methodology.[12] However, Edward R. Dayton and David A. Fraser insist that missionaries "cannot simply adopt a method because it is effective."[13] George Peters points out that "quantitative growth … can be deceptive" and that "in many ways the expansion of Christendom has come at the expense of the purity of the gospel."[14] James A. Sherer makes a pointed critique when he asks, "Whose effectiveness is being tested, God's or the missionary's?" He warns against "substituting a purely instrumental and humanly determined understanding of mission for the mission of the triune God, Father, Son, and Holy Spirit."[15]

---

7   Escobar, "Has McGavran's Missiology," 351–52. See also Escobar, "Evangelical Theology," 328; and Hesselgrave and Stetzer, *Missionshift*, 263.

8   Engel and Dyrness, *Changing the Mind*, 70.

9   Engel and Dyrness, 67–80.

10 Taber, *To Understand the World*, 119.

11 Hiebert, *Anthropological Insights*, 40.

12 Crawley, *Global Mission*, 274. See also Dayton and Fraser, *Planning Strategies*, 131.

13 Dayton and Fraser, *Planning Strategies*, 190.

14 Peters, *Theology of Church Growth*, 23–24.

15 Sherer, "McGavran's Lion," 346–47.

In response to these critiques, many missiologists continue to argue, "If we are in the business of making disciples, then we must measure the number of disciples made."[16] Can we really consider ourselves faithful stewards of our missiological calling if we do not make every effort to approach the task in the most fruitful and effective way possible? Modern methods in missions have had undeniable and phenomenal results in mass movements to Christ and church-planting movements. How do we balance this quantitatively effective managerial approach to missions with the primary spiritual purpose and goal of our mission? Here we turn to James for wisdom on how to balance our faith with our works in our missiological methods.

The Evil of Self-Reliant Planning

> Come now, you who say, "Today or tomorrow we will go into such and such a town and spend a year there and trade and make a profit"—yet you do not know what tomorrow will bring. What is your life? For you are a mist that appears for a little time and then vanishes. Instead you ought to say, "If the Lord wills, we will live and do this or that." As it is, you boast in your arrogance. All such boasting is evil. So whoever knows the right thing to do and fails to do it, for him it is sin. (Jas 4:13–17)

James points to the business manager who makes confident plans for his future efforts and his expected profits as a faulty way to balance our faith and works. We can see a lot in common between the business manager in this passage and the managerial missionary described above, but we find it somewhat shocking to read that making plans and anticipating growth or profit is both foolish (unwise) and arrogant (4:16). Luke L. Cheung and Andrew B. Spurgeon explain, "The schemes are arrogant because the planners are arrogant. They are 'practical atheists'—while not actually denying that God exists, they live as if he does not exist and devote their energy to their own success."[17] Indeed, it is arrogant to believe that life is under our control (cf. Prov 27:1), and it is foolish to focus our efforts on expanding earthly treasures (cf. Luke 12:13–21).

The boasting of the businessman is rooted in earthly wisdom rather than heavenly wisdom (Jas 3:15–17). The foolish boasting that James describes is similar to the way church members were showing partiality to their rich members over their poor (2:1–9). A common assumption at that time was

---

16 Dayton and Fraser, *Planning Strategies*, 204.
17 Cheung and Spurgeon, *James*, 91–93.

that God blesses those who earn his favor. Prosperity was seen as evidence that a man was walking in a manner pleasing to God,[18] while poverty and disease were considered evidence of unrighteousness or sin.[19] Those who assume that prosperity and fruitfulness are a sign of God's pleasure are much more likely to show favoritism and partiality to the wealthy and to boast in the evidence of their own ability to please God. We see a possible correlation here with the assumptions in managerial missions. If we believe that a numerically fruitful ministry (as evidenced by a church-planting movement, for instance) is proof that we are serving God faithfully, then we might be prone to boast in our own methodologies.

The problem with this approach is that Scripture does not correlate earthly blessing with righteousness or God's favor. Rather, as James points out, many are prosperous through exploitation, injustice, and oppression (2:6–7). The fault in this perspective on earthly blessing lies in the underlying belief that we have earned them, that we deserve them, or, God forbid, perhaps even that we have done God a favor. This understanding is entirely contrary to the gospel message (cf. Eph 2:8–10). Nelson R. Morales speaks of the eschatological reversal that James highlights regarding our boasting and arrogance in this life:

> In James 1:9–11, James presents "the correct boast" of both the humble brother and the wealthy. In an eschatological reversal, James calls on the humble to boast in their imminent exaltation (1:9). Conversely, he warns the wealthy about their imminent humiliation. He invites them to boast in their humiliation (1:10–11).[20]

While we cannot boast in our earthly plans or prosperity, there are things that we can correctly boast in, such as Christ's death, our weakness, and God's strength.[21]

---

18 Consider the example of Job's friends who argued that Job's success or tragedy must be directly related to his right standing before God. Consider also Matthew 19:16–30, wherein Jesus told the rich young ruler to donate all of his wealth to the poor, and the amazement of his disciples to hear that the wealthy have great trouble entering the kingdom of heaven. They were flummoxed and asked, "Who then can be saved?" They surmised that the rich were clearly the recipients of God's blessing and favor.

19 We see this hermeneutic of blessing in John 9:1–3 when Jesus's disciples asked whose sin caused a man to be born blind.

20 Morales, "Poor and Rich," 245.

21 Blomberg and Kamell, *James*, 202.

The heavenly wisdom of boasting in our humble status is found in the Hebrew words for poverty, most of which revolve around the dependence of the poor as opposed to the independence of the wealthy.[22] This kind of dependence in relation to other people is unpleasant and humiliating, and it brings a certain level of suffering. However, when we consider poverty in relation to God, we can see how being "poor in spirit" is essential because, along with all of creation, we truly are completely dependent on God (Col 1:16–17).

James directly addresses the boasting in our plans, arguing that we are not in control of our lives. Our human lives are short and insignificant like a mist (Jas 1:10–11; Job 7:7, 9; Pss 37:20; 39:5–6; 68:2; 103:15–16; Prov 27:1; Isa 40:6–7; Hos 13:3). We do not even know what will happen tomorrow. Motyer argues,

> We receive another day neither by natural necessity, nor by mechanical law, nor by right, nor by courtesy of nature, but only by the covenanted mercies of God. The very existence of tomorrow is as much part of our dependence on him as is our life itself and our ability.[23]

Instead of demonstrating a wise and true perspective of our humble dependence on the God of the universe, these managerial plans that James describes reflect a foolish sense of self-reliance and self-glorification. In fact, James refers to self-reliant boasting as evil (4:16) because it reflects the epitome of humanity's fallen sin nature (cf. 1:14–15; Prov 21:24; Hab 2:5; Rom 1:30; 2 Tim 3:2; 1 John 2:16). Indeed, boasting in our methodologies and plans, as if our fruitfulness proves our righteousness, as if our numbers of spiritual decisions, baptisms, disciples, and churches are a deserved blessing, something that we earned by right effort, is evil, reflecting a demonic wisdom rather than a heavenly one. Godly boasting is intended for the glory of God (cf. Jas 1:9; Rom 5:2), but this kind of boasting in plans and methods is idolatry.[24]

---

22 Támez ("Good News for the Poor," 39) breaks down the Hebrew definitions: "In the Old Testament there are a number of Hebrew words that are often translated by 'poor': 1. *'ani* in its most fully developed use describes a situation of inferiority in relation to another. Concretely the *'ani* is one who is dependent. When used in combination with *qal* it describes an economic relationship. The contrary of the *'ani* is the oppressor or user of violence. God is protector of the *'anim* because they are people who have been impoverished through injustice; 2. *dal* is used in two senses: it may refer either to physical weakness or to a lowly, insignificant position in society; 3. *'ebion* often refers to those who are very poor and in a wretched state. Originally it meant someone who asks for alms, a beggar; 4. *rash* is the poor or needy person; its antithesis is the rich person. The social and economic meaning is the prominent one; 5. *misken* means 'dependent', a social inferior."

23 Motyer, *Message of James*, 4:13–17.

24 Motyer, 4:13–17.

Instead of making self-reliant plans and managerial strategies, James tells us to humbly submit to God's control by saying, "If the Lord wills" (4:15), just as Christ taught us to pray (cf. Matt 7:21; 26:42; John 4:34; Acts 18:21; 1 Cor 1:1). Simply saying "Lord willing," however, is not another step to add to a formulaic methodology intended to earn God's favor and blessing. We cannot imagine that if we simply pray more and add the phrase "Lord willing" to our strategies and plans we will have refined the correct formula that God will bless with an abundant spiritual harvest. Such an approach perpetuates the self-reliant evil that James is addressing, and it would reflect the duplicitous and hasty speech that James renounces as a destructive fire rooted in a demonic form of wisdom (3:2–15). Rather, we are to humbly submit to God's control and will (cf. Pss 40:8; 143:10; Isa 46:13; 53:10; Matt 6:10; 26:39; Mark 3:35; Rom 12:2; 15:32; Heb 13:21; 1 Pet 3:17; 4:2).

James does not end with his resounding condemnation of plans and methods as if all works are as meaningless as vapor. Instead, James goes on to use the key word "so" (*oun*) to connect 4:16 with verse 17. "So whoever knows the right thing to do and fails to do it, for him it is sin" (4:17). Our efforts are not meaningless, and we should pursue his kingdom work. The key difference is in doing "the right thing." Sin is not only found in the arrogant boasting that we do but is also found in the good that we fail to do.[25] This can lead to a conundrum for the action-oriented missionary who looks to James for clarity on managerial missions. How can we know which plans and works are good and which are evil (4:16–17)?

God's Nature and His Mission

James repeatedly urges his reader to pray and ask God for wisdom (1:5–6; 5:13–18). He set the stage for this chapter's key passage (4:13–17) by teaching that we are to remain humble, dependent, and prayerful as we keep our eyes set on him (4:5–10). James indirectly points us to the glory of God by reminding us of the insignificance of our lives (4:14; cf. 1:10–11). God is awesome and holy, while we are but a mist or a vapor. We depend on him at every moment, but he does not depend on us to accomplish his missiological task in the world.[26] He is generously loving and gifts us with blessings that we do not earn or deserve. We do not reward or repay him with an abundance

---

25 James, "James," 1737.

26 See also Hiebert's (*Transforming Worldviews*, 276–86) description of the kingdom of God theme set in a robust understanding of the King as a healthy foundation for our missiological hermeneutic.

of converts. He is Judge and Lawgiver (4:12) because he sees the heart, and we are not to judge (4:11) because we look only on the outward signs (2:1–4; 1 Sam 16:7). He is the Father, who includes us in his mission, allowing us to work alongside him, though we cannot possibly comprehend it.[27]

Indeed, as we look at the nature of the God of the mission, we are struck by the absolutely perfect and seamless integrity between his nature and its outworking in his mission.[28] Every step of his interaction with his creation, from beginning to end, reflects his single-mindedness and total unity of identity and purpose, centered in his love and goodness. In contrast, we his people are prone to double-mindedness. We are capable of partially serving the Lord while simultaneously serving our own selfish ambitions. We can say that we are dependent on him while working out of self-reliance (cf. Jas 3:10). We can try to produce a fruitful and self-multiplying harvest among the nations in service to God's kingdom while harboring a belief that he depends on our work. Instead of this duplicity, we can infer from James that we are to reflect God's own integrity and consistency between his character and his mission (coherent faith and works) by depending on him, submitting to him, and drawing near to him (4:6–8).[29]

James explains that true wisdom, built upon the singular and glorious nature of our triune God, is extended as his generous gift to us (1:5–8). We cannot take on his mission in a God-honoring manner unless we reflect a Christlike humility and a creaturely dependence on him, and we cannot share his single-minded mission unless we also share his single-minded *telos*. The singular *missio Dei* is ruled by love, from creation to consummation,

---

27 As Blomberg and Kamell (*James*, 250) summarize, "James teaches us that God dispenses wisdom (1:5) and reward (1:12). He cannot do evil but only good (1:13–18). He chooses those who turn to him as their only hope (2:5). He is one, both in his existence as the only true God and in his unwavering constancy (2:19). God is Creator and Redeemer (1:17–18), Lawgiver and Judge (4:12), compassionate and merciful (5:11). His righteousness requires us to be righteous (1:20), but this can be accomplished only by faith (2:23). He embraces those who humble themselves before him while he resists the proud (4:4–8). He may be viewed as a benefactor (one who gives freely and graciously) but not as a patron (requiring reciprocity). He is Father (3:9), not in any authoritarian sense but as a nurturer of widows and orphans, a caregiver to the most dispossessed (1:27)."

28 See Aymer, *James*, 36. Aymer focuses on the singularity of the one God and how this relates to praxis in the community of faith. I build on this singularity of God, in a missiological hermeneutic, to show the singular unity and integrity between God's own faith and works, the coherence between his nature and his mission.

29 Blomberg and Kamell (*James*, 252–53) write, "Because God never wavers in his character or purposes [his mission], believers should shun all duplicity or vacillation in their allegiance and obedience to Christ and emulate God's trustworthy consistency. In short, they should become people of integrity."

because his nature is love. Augustine taught that God orders the world through love, which leads us to respond with love (the content of our faith). He defines virtue, or goodness, as the active decision to love God, self, and others in the right balance of priorities (the connection to our works).[30]

Thomas Aquinas agrees that the proper ordering of love is the plumbline for human ethics, and he reflects James's position on the source of our double-mindedness (1:13–18; 2:8) when he writes that "every sinful act proceeds from inordinate desire for some temporal good... . Inordinate love of self is the cause of every sin."[31] We are idolatrously double-minded because our fallen nature is distracted by the immediate "good" rather than the eternal good and by "inordinate love of self" rather than correctly balanced love aligned with God's nature.

Our plans can be arrogant and "evil" because our hearts do not pursue properly ordered love, so we do not rightly judge what is truly "good." We assume that large numbers of converts are better than small numbers and that rapid results are better than slow, but the God we serve has a pattern of preferring small gains over large ones and of moving slowly (cf. Judg 7:1–6; Isa 55:8; Rom 11:33; 1 Cor 1:27). James teaches us that in the final days there will be an eschatological reversal that will upend what we thought was good (Jas 1:9–11).[32] We presume that we can manage the mission well with our research, science, and strategic methods, but our plans are aimed at achieving a temporal good. We assume that saving the most people in the fastest way possible is the most loving thing to do, but we fail to realize that treating humans like a science experiment is unloving to others or that God might have big plans for one unseemly person who we would overlook (2:1–5; 1 Sam 16:17; Prov 24:12; Isa 53:1).[33] We presume that God wants us to work hard and fast to harvest the white fields because we secretly believe that he depends on us to accomplish his mission instead of remembering that we depend on him. We distort proper love when we believe that a fruitful ministry reflects God's blessing on our efforts and then go on to boast in our methodologies. We cannot be fully and single-mindedly aligned with his mission unless we humbly look to him as the anchor for properly ordered love so that our works are truly good and virtuous.

---

30 Fitzgerald, *Augustine through the Ages*, 872; Augustine, *City of God* 15.22.

31 Aquinas, *Summa of the Summa*, 497.

32 See Morales, "Poor and Rich," 245; and Blomberg and Kamell, *James*, 202.

33 See Lunsford, *Missiological Triage*, 50–59, 90–95.

James says to "let your 'yes' be yes and your 'no' be no" (5:12). At first glance, this seems to contradict his condemnation of committing to future plans (4:13–16). We find a similar injunction from Paul when he talks about his missionary plans:

> For the Son of God, Jesus Christ ... was not Yes and No, but in him it is always Yes. For all the promises of God find their Yes in him. That is why it is through him that we utter our Amen to God for his glory. (2 Cor 1:19–20)

As James argues, we cannot firmly assert a "yes" or "no" plan about the future because we do not know the future (4:13–16). But as Paul clarifies, we can avoid making double-minded plans (yes *and* no) by committing our steps to his plans rather than our own. God's mission finds its "yes" in Christ because his plan is singularly committed and unwavering in the *missio Dei* trajectory toward the good and loving promises of God. Our plans cannot perfectly and righteously align with the *missio Dei* because (1) our life is a breath and we do not know the future, (2) we are prone to idolatry and double-mindedness that comes from inordinate self-love, and (3) we do not define "good" correctly. James says, "Every good gift and every perfect gift is from above, coming down from the Father of lights, with whom there is no variation or shadow due to change" (1:17). True goodness, and the wisdom to know it, is a generous gift from our immutable God. When we commit our steps to follow his mission, we can trust that our plans and efforts do lead to "yes" in the promises of God.

The danger in asserting our own plans lies in our duplicitous self-love and faulty earthly wisdom to judge good from evil, but James tells us that we sin if we fail to do the good that we know to do (4:17). James puts significant focus on the topic of prayer because of our dependence on God's wisdom to even know the good we ought to do at each step. Herein we see the role of the Spirit in the cohesive and single-minded mission of our trinitarian God. As Roland Allen originally urged, missions involves strategic contextual planning, but we cannot forget our faith-driven dependence on the Holy Spirit. We follow the "yes" in him by trusting his single-minded goodness in his plans for his own mission, by praying constantly in dependence on his good gift of wisdom and his imminent presence and guidance in our lives, and by patiently awaiting the harvest in his perfect timing (5:7–8).

When we hold tightly to our own plans, we are demonstrating a false faith in the goodness of those plans and in God's dependence upon us to accomplish his mission. We show arrogant self-reliance when we ignore witnessing opportunities in front of us because our plan focuses on a different people group, when we are so intent on correcting an obstacle to our plans that we fail to notice the good work the "obstacle" presents, or when we credit a spiritual movement to our methodologies. We can know what good we ought to do today through dependent prayer. We can demonstrate right faith in pursuing that good work because we know that no matter how many changes our own plans require day by day, God's plan does not vacillate. The path he sets before us at every moment is the best plan for his mission.

Hudson Taylor learned this principle in his own missionary work. In his struggle to make right plans to reach the lost and dying masses while remaining fully dependent upon God, Taylor found his peace in full identification with Christ:

> The sweetest part, if one may speak of one part being sweeter than another, is the rest which full identification with Christ brings. I am no longer anxious about anything, as I realize this; for He, I know, is able to carry out His will, and His will is mine. It makes no matter where He places me, or how. That is rather for Him to consider than for me; for in the easiest position He must give me His grace, and in the most difficult His grace is sufficient.... And His resources are mine, for He is mine, and is with me and dwells in me.[34]

Concluding Implications for Managerial Missions

In reading James missiologically, we see the evil of self-reliant methods, rooted in double-minded assumptions that a fruitful harvest reflects an earned blessing. This is further twisted by the belief that we have the wisdom needed to devise good plans and that God's mission depends on our efforts. We see our own earthly wisdom and idolatry in our propensity toward self-love and our preference for the immediate good. We also see the perfect integrity in the way God's loving nature relates to his good mission, and we are awed that through Christ and his Spirit we are united to this singular mission. That said, a bit more direct and practical application to the subject of managerial missions can help to guide us.

---

34 Taylor and Taylor, *Spiritual Secret*, 87.

1. We must perpetually confront our self-reliance. There is no method
    we can discover that will guarantee a harvest. The mission is God's,
    and he sets work for us to do day by day. We should be faithful with
    that work, but we should not run ahead of him in our strategizing
    or grow deaf to his guidance as we dogmatically pursue our own
    agendas.

2. We must remember that we are dependent on his blessings. We do not
    earn a fruitful harvest, and we do not gift God with the blessing of
    additional worshipers. Do we, at any level, portray God as dependent
    on us in missions? Our plans and efforts must reflect genuine
    dependence on the "yes" we have in Christ through his Spirit.

3. We must be faithful and wise stewards of the work he gives us to do.
    We do not apathetically resign to lethargy in the face of our fleeting
    life. Instead, we approach his mission and kingdom with a heart full
    of worship, abiding in him, and in this attitude, we throw ourselves
    into the good work that he gives us to do. We obediently serve his
    kingdom by doing the right thing, and we prayerfully depend on his
    gift of wisdom to discern what that good work is.

4. We approach his work with a "Lord willing" heart that prays without
    ceasing. These action steps are not a methodology that we manage
    in our self-reliance. We remain intimately and constantly connected
    to the Lord, filled with his Spirit and seeking his wisdom. A "Lord
    willing" methodology makes plans and strategies for our best efforts
    but holds those plans in an open palm and remains dependently
    watchful at every moment for diversion between our plans and his.

5. We can accommodate the unpredictable future of our missions work
    by having faith that the mission belongs to a good and invariable God
    and that his plan operates from pure and untainted love and goodness.
    We must acknowledge that our plans will be faulty because we will
    not order love properly or always judge correctly about what is good
    and perfect. However, we can place our faith in the One who is
    faithful.[35]
    In this way, our works will reflect a healthy faith, and our
    missiological strategies and methods will be rightly aligned with the
    missio Dei.

---

35 Taylor and Taylor, 87.

Bibliography

Allen, Roland. *Missionary Methods: St. Paul's or Ours? A Study of the Church in Four Provinces.* London: World Dominion, 1930.

Andria, Solomon. "James." In *Africa Bible Commentary: A One-Volume Commentary Written by 70 African Scholars,* edited by Tokunboh Adeyemo, 1535–42. Grand Rapids: Zondervan, 2006.

Aquinas. *A Summa of the Summa: The Essential Philosophical Passages of St. Thomas Aquinas' Summa Theologica Edited and Explained for Beginners,* edited by Peter Kreeft. San Francisco: Ignatius Press, 1990.

Aymer, Margaret. *James: Diaspora Rhetoric of a Friend of God.* New York: Bloomsbury, 2017.

Bauckham, Richard. *Eerdmans Commentary on the Bible: James.* Grand Rapids: Eerdmans, 2021.

Blomberg, Craig L., and Mariam J. Kamell. *James.* Zondervan Exegetical Commentary on the New Testament 16. Grand Rapids: Zondervan, 2008.

Cheung, Luke L., and Andrew B. Spurgeon. *James: A Pastoral and Contextual Commentary.* Asia Bible Commentary. Carlisle: Langham, 2018.

Crawley, Winston. *Biblical Light for the Global Task: The Bible and Mission Strategy.* Nashville: Convention, 1989.

Crawley, Winston. *Global Mission: A Story to Tell.* Nashville: Broadman, 1985.

Dayton, Edward R., and David A. Fraser. *Planning Strategies for World Evangelization.* Grand Rapids: Eerdmans, 1990.

Engel, James F., and William A. Dyrness. *Changing the Mind of Missions: Where Have We Gone Wrong?* Downers Grove, IL: InterVarsity Press, 2000.

Escobar, Samuel. "Evangelical Theology in Latin America: The Development of a Missiological Christology." *Missiology* 19, no. 3 (1991): 315–32.

Escobar, Samuel. "Has McGavran's Missiology Been Devoured by a Lion?" *Missiology* 17, no. 3 (1989): 349–52.

Fitzgerald, Allan D., ed. *Augustine through the Ages: An Encyclopedia.* Grand Rapids: Eerdmans, 2009.

Hesselgrave, David J., and Ed Stetzer, eds. *Missionshift: Global Mission Issues in the Third Millenium.* Nashville: B&H Academic, 2010.

Hiebert, Paul G. *Anthropological Insights for Missionaries.* Grand Rapids: Baker, 1986.

Hiebert, Paul G. *Transforming Worldviews: An Anthropological Understanding of How People Change.* Grand Rapids: Baker Academic, 2008.

James, Arthur. "James." In *South Asia Bible Commentary,* edited by Brian Wintle, 1732–40. Grand Rapids: Zondervan, 2015.

Köstenberger, Andreas J., and Gregory Goswell. *Biblical Theology: A Canonical, Thematic, and Ethical Approach*. Wheaton: Crossway, 2023.

Lunsford, Sarah. *Missiological Triage: A Framework for Integrating Theology and Social Sciences in Missiological Methods*. Eugene, OR: Wipf & Stock, 2023.

Morales, Nelson R. "Poor and Rich in James: A Relevance Theory Approach to James's Use of the Old Testament." PhD diss., Trinity International University, 2015.

Motyer, J. A. *The Message of James*. Rev. ed. Westmont: InterVarsity Press, 2021.

Osborne, Grant R. *James: Verse by Verse*. Bellingham, WA: Lexham, 2019.

Peters, George. *A Theology of Church Growth*. Grand Rapids: Zondervan, 1981.

Richardson, Kurt A. *James: An Exegetical and Theological Exposition of Holy Scripture*. New American Commentary 36. Nashville: Broadman & Holman, 1997.

Shenk, Wilbert R. "The Role of Theory in Mission Studies." *Missiology* 24, no. 1 (1996): 31–44.

Sherer, James A. "McGavran's Lion: Real or Imaginary?" *Missiology* 17, no. 3 (1989): 344–47.

Taber, Charles R. *To Understand the World, to Save the World: The Interface between Missiology and the Social Sciences*. Harrisburg: Trinity Press International, 2000.

Támez, Elsa. "Good News for the Poor." *Evangelical Review of Theology* 11, no. 3 (1987): 35–41.

Támez, Elsa, and Gloria Kinsler. "James: A Circular Letter for Immigrants." *Review and Expositor* 108, no. 3 (2011): 369–80.

Taylor, Howard, and Geraldine Taylor. *Hudson Taylor's Spiritual Secret*. Chicago: Moody, 2009.

Vanhoozer, Kevin J., ed. *Dictionary for Theological Interpretation of the Bible*. Grand Rapids: Baker Academic, 2005.

Chapter 15

Teaching and Missiological Implications from James 3:1-2

Thomas W. Seckler

People do not like to be discouraged from pursuing a role they aspire to. However, this is what potential teachers encounter in James 3:1–2. James suggests that not many should pursue the role of teaching with the warning that teachers will be judged strictly. These words are found in the center of his letter to followers of Jesus scattered across the nations, providing practical and challenging instructions for the early church.

Most scholars conclude that James was written by James, the brother of Jesus.[1] Luke Timothy Johnson and Peter H. Davids identify the use of speech or "pure speech" as a prominent theme in the letter.[2] Other critical themes include God and ethics, favoritism, and demonstrating faith through action.[3] James's letter is not theoretical. It is practical and intended to address existing problems in the churches.[4] Although James has not been widely used in missiological studies, it can and should inform contemporary mission. This chapter explores the implications of James 3:1–2 for Christian teaching and current mission practice. "Mission" is defined here as "the sending activity of God with the purpose of reconciling to himself and bringing into his kingdom fallen men and women from every people, nation, and tongue."[5] Mission includes God's use of humans to lead individuals into his kingdom and to teach/train them. Its purpose is not simply evangelism but reconciliation, salvation, and the fostering of true disciples of Jesus.

This chapter contains two sections. The first reviews exegetical observations about James 3:1–2. The second focuses on the missiological implications of this passage. Recommendations are provided both for teachers and for mission practice in general. This chapter argues that all Christian teachers, whether originating from the Majority World or Minority World, are to be committed to discipleship, exhibit genuine humility, and teach as if they are being examined by God. Instruction that honors God

---

1 Johnson, *Letter of James*, 93; Moo, *Letter of James*, 22; McKnight, *Letter of James*, 34.

2 Johnson, *Letter of James*, 254; Davids, *Epistle of James*, 135.

3 McKnight, *Letter of James*, 42–43.

4 McCartney, *James*, 37.

5 Ott, Strauss, and Tennent, *Encountering Theology of Mission*, xv–xvi.

uses the tongue wisely to further his global work. Christians are to realize both their frailty and their ability to serve with integrity through God's enabling. James 3:1–2 contains both words of warning and hope for mission engagement.

Exegetical Observations of James 3:1-2

James 3 does not stand alone but instead is sandwiched between other discourses about life and faith. Dan G. McCartney provides an outline that titles the majority of chapter 1 as an "Overview of Life and Faith." Chapter 2 contains the first discourse, "Faith and Behavior." Chapter 3 focuses on "Faith, Wisdom, and Speech Acts." Chapter 4 examines "Strife in the Church as Lack of Faith." After an interjection about warnings for believers, chapter 5 provides a final discourse on "Looking to God."[6]

James 3:1–2 follows exhortations to rein in one's tongue (1:26), avoid favoritism (2:1–9), and demonstrate one's faith with one's deeds (2:14–26). The content of these verses intersects with the material before and after them. Four topics from James 3:1–2 are examined here: (1) few should become teachers, (2) teachers will be judged more strictly, (3) we all stumble, and (4) those who control their tongue can keep their entire body in check.

Few Should Become Teachers

James 3:1 states, "Not many of you should become teachers, my fellow believers, because you know that we who teach will be judged more strictly."[7] What is meant by this statement? Scot McKnight writes that James was not concerned about the number of teachers but rather the impact that teachers have, especially if they are instructing in irresponsible ways.[8] In the early church, the role of a teacher was roughly similar to that of a Jewish rabbi.[9] Teachers had much influence, which could be used positively or negatively. Their instruction could build others up, but their words could also be divisive.

The apostle Paul valued the gift of teaching (1 Cor 12:28). He even encouraged people to desire gifts such as teaching (1 Cor 12:31). In New Testament times, the office of teacher was one of status and prestige.[10]

---

6   McCartney, *James*, vii.

7   Unless otherwise noted, all Scripture quotations are from the NIV.

8   McKnight, *Letter of James*, 268–69.

9   Moo, *Letter of James*, 148.

10 Davids, *Epistle of James*, 136; Moo, *Letter of James*, 149.

Davids explains that many were therefore motivated to achieve this office.[11] In order to bolster their status, unscrupulous individuals may have boastfully promoted themselves while criticizing others.[12] Douglas J. Moo notes that "unfit teachers" contributed to disunity by their arguments and critical words (Jas 3:13–18; 4:1, 11).[13]

Teachers are responsible not only for what they say but for how they live. Their lives are to demonstrate wholeness and integrity.[14] James exhorts believers to pair their faith with appropriate actions. Similarly, teachers are to reveal the fruit of their faith by the way they live.[15] James does not discourage all people from becoming teachers. However, he is quite concerned that the right people are placed in that role.

Teachers Will Be Judged More Strictly
James declares that teachers are subject to more stringent judgment than others. This "greater judgment" is before the eyes of God and not humans.[16] What is meant by stricter judgment? It does not mean a harsher penalty but rather a "greater *danger* of punishment."[17] Teachers use speech to instruct. Because the tongue is the most difficult body part to control, teachers are susceptible to sinning through their words, which can lead those who listen astray.[18] The consequences of stumbling in one's words are greater for those who teach. Thus, they experience an increased risk of judgment.[19] Simply stated, "it is risky to be a teacher."[20] Should these challenges scare all away who aspire to teach? No, but all who teach or desire to teach should do so with an understanding of its weightiness.

We All Stumble
James 3:2 states, "We all stumble in many ways. Anyone who is never at fault in what they say is perfect, able to keep their whole body in check." James includes himself when he speaks of all believers. He states that they stumble in several different ways. The word "stumble" is used in some

---

11 Davids, *Epistle of James*, 136.

12 Wolmarans, "Tongue Guiding the Body," 524.

13 Moo, *Letter of James*, 149.

14 McCartney, *James*, 180.

15 Moo, *Letter of James*, 150.

16 Johnson, *Letter of James*, 265.

17 Moo, *Letter of James*, 149, emphasis original.

18 Moo, 149.

19 McCartney, *James*, 180.

20 McCartney, 176.

New Testament passages to refer to deliberate sin or serious error. Jesus, for example, calls for radical action if one's hand, foot, or eye causes one to "stumble" (Matt 18:8–9). Peter connects stumbling with disobeying the message about Christ (1 Pet 2:8). Most scholars believe that "stumble" in James 3, however, refers to more minor transgressions. Johnson observes that the verb "stumble" refers to a variety of "trippings" but not "moral failure."[21] The meaning here is "a minor or inadvertent sin."[22] McKnight summarizes the verse by explaining that James intends to remind us that all people "trip up in many ways and often."[23] One aspect of this "tripping up" is in the use of one's tongue.

Those Who Control Their Tongue Can Keep Their Entire Body in Check
The second part of James 3:2 addresses various themes: faultlessness in speech, the relationship between speech and one's body, and the ability to control one's body. James states that those who are never at fault in their speech are "perfect." Is he declaring that believers can be faultless in their words? McKnight observes that sinlessness is not possible. However, James focuses here on sins arising from speech. Those who have received the word of truth are able to obey the royal law found in Scripture (1:18). This law is demonstrated in pure speech.[24] McCartney uses the word "maturity" to describe James's intent. Speech is the most difficult action to control. Those who control their speech are not blameless or perfect. However, they have become mature in their faith, acting like adults instead of children who have yet to master themselves.[25]

The tongue affects other parts of the body as well. James 3:3–12 describes the nature and impact of the tongue. The tongue, though small, controls larger aspects of life (vv. 3–4). The tongue can be compared to a fire that corrupts the entire body (vv. 5–6). It cannot be tamed by humans and contains poison (vv. 7–8). One's tongue can be used to both bless God and curse humans. James declares that these contrasting activities should not occur. He illustrates his point by referring to the natural world, where natural springs bring forth only fresh water and fig trees produce only figs (vv. 9–12). These later verses inform the meaning of the preceding ones

---

21 Johnson, *Letter of James*, 256.
22 Moo, *Letter of James*, 150–51.
23 McKnight, *Letter of James*, 274.
24 McKnight, 274.
25 McCartney, *James*, 180.

(vv. 1–2). Just as a large ship is controlled by its small rudder, the tongue affects the entire body. A tongue used for evil can "misdirect" the body. Therefore, it must be controlled.[26] If it is controlled, it can bridle one's entire body. If it is not mastered, severe consequences can result. McCartney writes that because the tongue is susceptible to wickedness, it is to be carefully guarded. Teachers are to be especially diligent as their words have much influence. Others in the church are also to heed these warnings.[27] Johannes L. P. Wolmarans soberly observes, "James contends that only people in control of their tongue are qualified to teach."[28] These verses have valuable implications for teaching and missiological practice.

Missiological Implications

James 3:1–2 applies to a variety of people and groups including ordinary disciples, local churches, teachers, missionaries, and mission organizations. Implications are given for teaching and mission practice.

Implications for Teaching

James provided warnings and encouragement regarding teaching, the use of the tongue, and practical Christian life. How do his words, penned in New Testament times, apply now? Recommendations for applications are presented below.

Teachers are to exhibit mature character. James emphasizes godly character and action throughout his book. He yearns for Jesus's followers to be mature and complete (1:4). He encourages believers not only to listen to God's word but to obey it (1:22–24). He exhorts people to control their tongues (1:26) and observes that covetousness fuels their quarrels and fights (4:1–2). He warns against favoritism and illustrates how it occurs in the church (2:1–11). These instructions about godly character apply to all believers, but they apply especially to teachers and leaders. For example, the dangers of selfish ambition (3:13–16) are given in the context of a discussion about teachers and the use of the tongue.

Reflecting on James 3:1–2, McCartney emphasizes the integrity expected of a teacher, writing, "It is all the more incumbent on teachers that their own lives exhibit the wholeness and integrity that the word they teach is expected

---

26 Davids, *Epistle of James*, 140.

27 McCartney, *James*, 182–83.

28 Wolmarans, "Tongue Guiding the Body," 524.

to engender."[29] Similarly, Moo states that teachers are to personally apply the warning found in verse 1: "When we undertake to guide others in the faith, we must be especially careful to exhibit the fruit of that faith by the way we live."[30] McKnight bluntly writes that teachers are responsible for "both what they teach and how they live."[31] James expects that teachers are men and women of integrity, which is exhibited in their words and lives. Contemporary teachers, whether serving within their own culture or across cultures, are to demonstrate Christian maturity and character.

Teachers are to be disciples who disciple others. Jesus calls his followers to make disciples of all nations. This practice includes baptizing new believers and teaching them to obey all that Jesus instructed (Matt 28:19–20). Years after Jesus uttered those words, James writes about teaching. In order to disciple and teach others about life with Jesus, teachers need to be disciples themselves. Furthermore, teachers are to embrace the goal of discipleship as part of their task. D. A. Carson provides a succinct definition of a disciple: "Disciples are those who hear, understand and obey Jesus' teaching."[32] Contemporary teachers have a responsibility to actively seek God and obey him. Although they are not expected to be perfect, they are to exhibit more maturity than a young believer.

Teacher-disciples are to disciple those they teach. The content of their teaching is to be geared toward developing mature disciples. Reflecting on Matthew 28, Mookgo S. Kgatle observes that this teaching is not limited to cognitive understanding. It extends to practical obedience to Christ and an "adherence" to him as the focus of our belief.[33] Jesus's instructions to teach others to obey indicates a focus not on content to be learned but rather on practically living out his commands.[34] Present-day teaching and discipleship should thus focus not only on material to be understood but also on lived obedience to Jesus. Teachers are to ensure that their lives "are centered in him and his Word."[35] Moreover, they are to anchor their students in Christ and instruct them how to live for him in their daily lives.[36]

---

29 McCartney, *James*, 180.

30 Moo, *Letter of James*, 150.

31 McKnight, *Letter of James*, 271–72.

32 Carson, "Matthew," 596.

33 Kgatle, "Globalisation of Missions," 5.

34 Osborne, *Matthew*, 1082.

35 Osborne, 1085.

36 Osborne, 1084.

Teachers are to teach carefully. James identifies himself as a fellow teacher and writes that "we who teach will be judged more strictly" (3:1). Although James suggests that not many should become teachers, this warning about judgment is not intended to prevent all from teaching. Rather, teachers are to be aware of the weight of their role. They are to approach their task with seriousness, though not necessarily with an ever-present fear of judgment. Teachers are to be humble and avoid selfish ambitions (3:13–16). They are to carry out their task for God's glory.

James does not constrict his advice only to those considered formal teachers. Neither should we. While James's instructions most commonly focus on those who aspire to an official teaching role, his advice is applicable to both formal and informal teachers. Both influence those they teach, and both are observed by students and the wider community. For application to contemporary mission, "teacher" may include a variety of roles ranging from seminary professor to church teacher/trainer to one who is deeply involved in informal instruction and discipling. All are to teach with an awareness of God's presence. Several aspects of "teaching carefully," both within and across cultures, will be explored below.

Samuel Escobar writes from a Latin American perspective, but he has an intimate knowledge of global Christianity. Reflecting on Western theology in contrast to local Majority World theologies, he observes that Western theology does not address certain topics important to those in non-Western contexts. Thus, it is time to read the Scriptures "with new eyes" and have locals examine those topics in the light of Scripture.[37] Escobar points to Kwame Bediako's statement that African students who studied in Western contexts were well aware of the theology of authors like Bultmann and Barth. However, they did not understand the local religious world in their African context.[38] This challenge is not only present in Africa. Writing from the Asian context, Lorenzo Bautista, Hildalgo B. Garcia, and Sze-Kar Wan emphasize that theology is to be grounded in the Scriptures but "must address the concrete problems of Asia today."[39]

Other authors have identified gaps in understanding and effective teaching. In his classic discussion on the "excluded middle," Paul G. Hiebert explains cultural perspectives about the "unseen" and "seen" dimensions and their relationship with what is considered "otherworldly" and "this worldly."

---

37 Escobar, *New Global Mission*, 133–34.

38 Bediako, *Christianity in Africa*, 154–56; referenced in Escobar, *New Global Mission*, 134.

39 Bautista, Garcia, and Wan, "Asian Way of Thinking," 61.

While other cultures may accept that there are unseen realities that are of this world, most Westerners hold to a two-tiered view of reality, where the unseen and otherworldly are associated with religion and the seen and worldly belong to the realm of science. A middle level, describing that which is unseen but is present in this world, is absent.[40] Because of this, Hiebert notes that Western missionaries commonly do not consider or have adequate answers to middle-level topics important to non-Westerners.[41] Themes such as sickness, spirit possession, and curses are not clearly addressed.[42] The local Christian suffers from a lack of sound biblical teaching on these important subjects.

In her research in West Africa, Birgit Meyer notes that the topic of witches was referred to nearly daily.[43] Robert J. Priest conducted research on the topic of witches in both Peru and the Congo.[44] He describes causal ontologies connected to witches in Peru. A reason for misfortune such as sickness is explained by the influence of someone else, such as a witch, in contrast to one's own moral actions.[45] Teachers from other cultures may not understand this reasoning. Priest concludes that Western theological training often fails to consider locally relevant topics such as witches, but it should.[46] Careful and effective teaching biblically addresses real-life topics that are important to students.

Different contexts require different approaches to teaching. Considering James 3, trainers and teachers should utilize the forms and methods easily understood by the learner. There are many avenues to this approach. In certain cultures, storytelling is a powerful tool for communicating. Stories can convey information in a compelling way and "evoke emotion," even causing others to "laugh, cry, or gasp with surprise."[47] Trevor McIlwain developed Chronological Bible Storying materials to communicate biblical truth to cultures with little exposure to Christianity.[48] The use of oral instruction, dialogue, and storying contributes to effective teaching among oral cultures.

Contextualization is a tool that assists teachers in communicating clearly. A. Scott Moreau, Gary R. Corwin, and Gary B. McGee describe contextualization as "taking the gospel to a new context and finding appropriate

---

40 Hiebert, *Anthropological Reflections*, 189–94.

41 Hiebert, 198.

42 Hiebert, 190–91.

43 Meyer, "If You Are a Devil," 118.

44 Priest, "Witch Accusations," 3–6.

45 Priest, 4–5.

46 Priest, 6.

47 Nabi and Green, "Role of a Narrative's Emotional Flow," 138.

48 McIlwain, *Building on Firm Foundations*.

ways to communicate it so that it is understandable to the people in that context. Contextualization refers to more than just theology; it also includes developing church life and ministry that are biblically faithful and culturally appropriate."[49] Jared E. Alcántara writes that "many of today's preachers assume that the behaviors that make sense to them will automatically make sense to those whom they minister, that the language they speak in the pulpit is the same language that people speak everywhere."[50] He cautions against under-contextualization, illustrated in the statement above, and over-contextualization, drawing from Lesslie Newbigin's criticism of "trying to fit the gospel into our culture" instead of allowing it to confront culture.[51] Teachers and preachers are to communicate biblical truth clearly, allowing it to impact lives and cultures.

One way to teach clearly is by using simple and ordinary language. Reflecting on gospel communication in Australia, Robert L. Gallagher highlights the need to be sensitive to Aussie culture to avoid disinterest in the institutional church.[52] He proposes an approach of "mateship evangelism," which includes the use of "ordinary language." This approach fits the local culture and helps foster better communication between those in authority, such as political or church officials, and the common person.[53]

Anthropologist Clifford Geertz delineates between "experience-near" and "experience-distant" language. Experience-near refers to terms people "naturally and effortlessly" use to describe their thoughts or feelings. Experience-distant terms, in contrast, are unfamiliar and are used by specialists who are different from the general population.[54] In his research among the Aguaruna-Jivaro in Peru, Priest discovered that when abstract "experience-distant" terms were used to describe concepts such as morality and sin, the message did not easily connect with the personal lives of the listeners and was not viewed as compelling.[55] However, common terms from within the culture were adequate to describe concepts such as a personal sense of sinfulness.[56] Present-day teachers are encouraged to use natural and ordinary terms to communicate biblical truth.

---

49 Moreau, Corwin, and McGee, *Introducing World Missions*, 16.

50 Alcántara, "Preaching between Scylla and Charybdis," 8.

51 Newbigin, *Word in Season*, 67, quoted in Alcántara, "Preaching between Scylla and Charybdis," 8–9.

52 Gallagher, "Contextualizing the Gospel in Australia," 82–83.

53 Gallagher, 80–82.

54 Geertz, "From the Native's Point of View," 223.

55 Priest, "Experience-Near Theologizing," 189.

56 Priest, "I Discovered My Sin!," 96–97.

Another communication method is to adjust ministry approaches based on the culture of the group being served. Beth Seversen provides a current example of this practice in a Western context, among unchurched emerging adults in the United States. Her research identified five activities of churches that are effectively reaching emerging adults with the gospel. The activities are *initiating* relationships with unchurched people, *inviting* them to church activities, *including* them in the Christian community, *involving* them in service, and *investing* in them through mentoring and training.[57] Seversen's research demonstrates how these approaches were informed by the values and experiences of emerging adults. While her study describes broader activities than just teaching, it provides an example of how teachers and leaders can minister in ways that resonate with the hearts of listeners.

James 3 challenges teachers to be self-aware. The observation that "all stumble" indicates that humans are frail. A description of the powerful influence of the tongue—for good or for evil—calls people to use their words wisely. It is not surprising that teachers, who use the tongue in their role, will be judged more strictly (3:1). The tongue is to be tamed, and controlling it can lead to controlling one's entire being. James points to the vulnerability of teachers. Though they exercise an important role, they do so out of weakness.

Teachers should thus remember two contrasting concepts. First, they are vulnerable as humans. They may be prone to pride, criticism of others, or other weaknesses and sins. Those who step into the role of teaching are to embrace this truth. However, they are to cling to a second truth as well: teachers have much potential influence. They can build up individuals, the local church, and institutions through their actions. They have the privilege to serve God and his people in a unique way. As "jars of clay," teachers can instruct and lead others for God's glory (2 Cor 4:7).

Implications For Mission Practice

James 3:1–2 is not only applicable to teachers. It informs the wider practice of mission. Mission commonly occurs at the intersection of two or more cultures. Cross-cultural workers, mission and church leaders, and those serving within their own culture can benefit from the teachings of James 3. The implications of this passage are expressed as recommendations below.

Cross-cultural workers are to foster personal humility. One's attitudes affect not only one's own actions but also how those actions are perceived by others. Global mission workers are to teach and serve effectively. Humility

---

57 Seversen, *Not Done Yet*, 6–7.

is positively associated with intercultural competence.[58] Being a humble learner is to be applied not only to initial language and culture acquisition; this approach is valuable for interacting with locals and understanding their practices and ministry patterns.

Humility is hindered by ethnocentrism and stereotypes. Although all humans naturally view others through the lens of their own experiences, they can devalue others when they view their own culture as superior and judge others accordingly.[59] In this way, ethnocentrism contributes to unhealthy pride and criticism of others. Craig Ott writes that resisting ethnocentrism does not mean abandoning one's own values or cultural heritage. However, it does require one to "be slow to judge and quick to learn."[60]

Stereotyping also influences attitudes toward those who are different than ourselves. Stella Ting-Toomey and Leeva C. Chung describe a stereotype as "an overgeneralization toward a group of people without any attempt to perceive individual variations."[61] Previous information or experiences— whether accurate or not—are used to assess the actions of others. Little care is given to understanding the individual differences of group members. Stereotyping has profound implications for mission. It can lead to viewing others one-dimensionally and seeing them as less than oneself. Caution is needed for cross-cultural workers as they deliberately engage with those unlike themselves. James emphasizes humility in his letter (3:13; 4:6, 10). Attitudes of genuine humility are needed for contemporary global mission.

Cross-cultural workers are to value local voices. Samuel Escobar expresses frustration that Majority World theological voices are not being heard. While he understands the rich history of Western theology and its influence on mission, he also recognizes that non-Western believers are examining the Scriptures from their perspectives and mining valuable insights. Escobar calls for Westerners to grant Majority World Christians a genuine place at the theological table. He writes, "The time of European and Western monologue is over."[62]

Miriam Adeney communicates the challenges of working with Americans through an illustration. She describes how, from the perspective of some Majority World believers, coordinating ministry with Americans is like mice dancing with elephants. There is much activity, but the mice, representing

---

58 Paine, Jankowski, and Sandage, "Humility as a Predictor," 15.

59 Ott, *Teaching and Learning across Cultures*, 34.

60 Ott, 45.

61 Ting-Toomey and Chung, *Understanding Intercultural Communication*, 165.

62 Escobar, *New Global Mission*, 136–37.

non-Americans, are squashed in the process.[63] Adeney emphasizes the importance of each part of the body of Christ in God's kingdom.[64]

Global workers are to value the voices of God's people, wherever they are found. This is especially important in local ministry. Cross-cultural workers and teachers are to deliberately listen to and learn from national believers, whose insights into the culture are to be affirmed. This demands an attitude of humility and a true appreciation for those around them.

Cross-cultural workers are to adopt approaches that fit local forms and ideas. Teachers are wise to utilize appropriate methods according to the local culture. Adopting local forms has wider implications beyond teaching, however. Understanding and adapting to local patterns can positively influence communication, learning, and relationships with those of the host culture. Cross-cultural workers have, at times, followed approaches that do not resonate with the local culture. These approaches may have proven effective in the worker's original location, but they are not necessarily a good fit in the new context. Escobar expresses concern for what he terms "managerial missiology," a Western approach that narrows mission to a manageable task that can be addressed by using current instruments and tools such as statistics, technology, and active management.[65] Dangers to this approach include identifying mission activity only as a "response to a problem," focusing on evangelism instead of other spiritual and social needs, de-emphasizing the "mystery" of serving others, and depersonalizing people.[66] In his view, these approaches do not contribute to effective ministry in many non-Western contexts. Furthermore, certain aspects of these methods, such as specific approaches to spiritual warfare, do not have solid biblical support.[67]

C. Tim and Ashley E. Chang advise cross-cultural workers to avoid forcing their forms and denominational preferences on locals. They connect these actions with personal pride and encourage workers to sacrifice as Christ did and to "care about what the local people care about."[68] Writing about how Christian traditions were introduced to Australia, Gallagher notes that they were only slightly modified from the practices of other

---

63 Adeney, "Telling Stories," 377.

64 Adeney, 378.

65 Escobar, "Evangelical Missiology," 109; Escobar, *New Global Mission*, 167.

66 Escobar, "Evangelical Missiology," 109–10; Escobar, *New Global Mission*, 167.

67 Escobar, "Evangelical Missiology," 111.

68 Chang and Chang, *Christian Intercultural Communication*, 122.

countries. The result is that the gospel message is viewed as foreign because of its imported packaging, which does not reflect the Australian culture or community.[69] It is not naturally understood or compelling. Describing the contextualization of the gospel message, Dean E. Flemming writes that one needs to communicate the message in such a way that it is both understood by the audience and transformative to the listener.[70] Whether communicating the gospel, teaching, or serving in other ways, cross-cultural workers are to study the local culture and appropriately adopt patterns and forms that contribute to deep understanding and change. This is a wider application of James's instructions about teaching with integrity.

Leaders are to select teachers carefully. God uses leaders and teachers for his kingdom, and James 3 warns of the dangers of the tongue. Thus, it is vital that teachers are selected who will use their tongues wisely to instruct and encourage. While one cannot exhaustively understand the mind and practices of a potential teacher, one can use the content of James as a measuring rod to assess their suitability to teach. Those selecting teachers should heed James's admonition to avoid favoritism (2:1–13). Although James illustrates favoritism as privileging the rich over the poor, his instructions apply to the temptation to select certain teachers, such as close friends or popular individuals, while overlooking other qualified teachers.

Leaders are to value teaching and ensure it is done well. The New Testament contains numerous examples of teaching and instructions to teach (e.g., Matt 4:23; 5:2; Acts 2:42; 18:11; Rom 12:7; Col 1:28; 1 Tim 4:11, 13; Tit 2:1). Paul valued teachers as those whom God has gifted for the church (1 Cor 12:28; Eph 4:11). When Jesus instructed his followers to "go and make disciples of all nations," he further stated that they were to teach the disciples to obey all that he had commanded them (Matt 28:19–20). Reflecting on this passage, Carson writes, "Failure to disciple, baptize, and teach the people of the world is already itself one of the failures of our own discipleship."[71] Teaching is critical for the body of Christ. There are differing opinions about the specific role of teachers, however. David Watson and Paul Watson, describing Church Planting Movements (CPMs) or Disciple-Making Movements (DMMs), note that the disciple-maker "does not do any of the traditional things required by traditional disciple-making. He does

---

69 Gallagher, "Me and God, We'd Be Mates," 127.

70 Flemming, *Contextualization in the New Testament*, 86.

71 Carson, "Matthew," 599.

not preach or teach."[72] Part of the emphasis, rather, is on facilitating the self-discovery of scriptural truth as people study the Bible in groups. This practice is often referred to as Discovery Bible Study (DBS). Outside leaders avoid explaining Scripture but rather allow it to speak for itself. They seek to remove themselves and not usurp God's role in interacting directly with his people.[73]

Matt Rhodes is critical of this approach. He argues that this methodology does not value trained teachers but rather downplays the roles that missionaries and teachers play.[74] When twenty-one pastors associated with a mission organization in East Asia were asked to identify their greatest need, they declared, "Our pastors need training!" They identified weaknesses in the ability of pastors to respond theologically to false teachings and cults.[75] Theological training requires teachers who instruct and equip. Rhodes acknowledges that New Testament teaching methods may not be normative for today and that missionaries can teach in such a way that contributes to unhealthy dependence. He is suspicious, however, of approaches that deemphasize teachers in the church.[76]

The above is just one facet of discussions surrounding ministry, effective learning, and the role of teachers. Deliberate teaching is required for the flourishing of God's kingdom. The book of James recognizes the importance of teachers. Regardless of the specific approach adopted, leaders are to value teachers and the influence they have.

Leaders are to engage in mission in light of wider instructions from James. James gives practical instruction to ordinary disciples and church leaders. It also provides insight into contemporary mission practice. Three concepts from James are applied here. First, all involved in mission are to deliberately practice pure speech (1:26). Unhealthy speech can be related to pride or selfish ambition and may be expressed by criticism toward others (3:14; 4:1, 11). Those involved in all levels of mission, whether teaching, planning, overseeing, or interacting with local leaders, benefit from controlling their tongues. Christ-followers are to speak and act as if they are conscious of God's law (2:12–13). Second, mission is to facilitate believers practically loving one another and avoiding favoritism (2:8–9). James emphasizes

---

72 Watson and Watson, *Contagious Disciple-Making*, 127.

73 Watson and Watson, 149.

74 Rhodes, *No Shortcut to Success*, 84.

75 Massey, "Theological Education and Southern Baptist Missions," 6.

76 Rhodes, *No Shortcut to Success*, 68–69.

the standard of the royal law, which is to "love your neighbor as yourself" (2:8). He contrasts this right action with favoritism, which occurred in that context and can occur in present-day mission activities. Favoritism does not demonstrate true love and is to be avoided in all its forms. James encourages obedience to God's word instead of merely listening to it (1:22). He declares that Abraham's faith and actions were working together (2:20–22). All believers face the danger of focusing on their belief but not completing it by their actions. Mission practitioners are to plan and act to ensure that love is demonstrated, that those commonly discriminated against are valued, and that one's faith is clearly expressed by deeds. Finally, mission is to be carried out justly. James criticizes wealthy believers for not acting justly toward others (5:4–6). Although he is writing about financially taking advantage of those who are less privileged, his instructions about acting justly have implications for what mission activities are chosen and how they are conducted.

Conclusion

James was written to believers and leaders in the early church. Its content is both challenging and practical. James reveals truths about trials and suffering, explains the importance of pairing faith and deeds, exhorts believers to use their tongues wisely, rebukes people for favoritism and dissension, and gently encourages Christ-followers to persevere with patience as they depend on the Lord. The teachings of James are applicable to both New Testament and present-day believers.

This chapter has examined the content of James 3:1–2 and presented recommendations for teachers and mission practice. All Christian teachers, whether from the Majority World or Minority World, are to serve from a foundation of humility and instruct in ways that resonate with the listener. They are to realize both their frailty and their ability to serve with integrity through God's enabling. Mission leaders and practitioners are to value local voices and adopt culturally sensitive approaches in order to teach and serve well. James 3:1–2 provides a sober warning of potential judgment, but it also reveals genuine hope for service and mission.

Bibliography

Adeney, Miriam. "Telling Stories: Contextualization and American Missiology." In *Global Missiology for the 21st Century: The Iguassu Dialogue*, edited by William D. Taylor, 212–45. Globalization of Mission. Grand Rapids: Baker Academic, 2000.

Alcántara, Jared E. "Preaching between Scylla and Charybdis." In *Communication in Mission: Global Opportunities and Challenges*, edited by Marcus Dean, Scott Moreau, Sue Russell, and Rochelle Scheuermann, 3–14. Evangelical Missiological Society Series 30. Littleton, CO: William Carey Publishing, 2022.

Bautista, Lorenzo, Hidalgo B. Garcia, and Sze-Kar Wan. "The Asian Way of Thinking in Theology." *Evangelical Review of Theology* 6, no. 1 (1982): 37–40.

Bediako, Kwame. *Christianity in Africa: The Renewal of a Non-Western Religion.* Edinburgh: Edinburgh University Press, 1995.

Carson, D. A. "Matthew." In *Matthew, Mark, Luke.* Vol. 8 of *The Expositor's Bible Commentary*, edited by Frank E. Gabelein and J. D. Douglas, 3–599. Grand Rapids: Zondervan, 1984.

Chang, C. Tim, and Ashley E. Chang. *Christian Intercultural Communication: Sharing God's Love with People of Other Cultures.* Dubuque, IA: Kendall Hunt, 2021.

Davids, Peter H. *The Epistle of James: A Commentary on the Greek Text.* New International Greek Testament Commentary. Grand Rapids: Eerdmans, 1982.

Escobar, Samuel. "Evangelical Missiology: Peering into the Future at the Turn of the Century." In *Global Missiology for the 21st Century: The Iguassu Dialogue*, edited by William D. Taylor, 101–22. Grand Rapids: Baker Academic, 2000.

Escobar, Samuel. *The New Global Mission: The Gospel from Everywhere to Everyone.* Christian Doctrine in Global Perspective. Downers Grove, IL: InterVarsity Press, 2003.

Flemming, Dean E. *Contextualization in the New Testament: Patterns for Theology and Mission.* Downers Grove, IL: InterVarsity Press, 2005.

Gallagher, Robert L. "Contextualizing the Gospel in Australia." In *Communication in Mission: Global Opportunities and Challenges*, edited by Marcus Dean, Scott Moreau, Sue Russell, and Rochelle Scheuermann, 67–84. Evangelical Missiological Society Series 30. Littleton, CO: William Carey Publishing, 2022.

Gallagher, Robert L. "'Me and God, We'd Be Mates': Toward an Aussie Contextualized Gospel." *International Bulletin of Mission Research* 30, no. 3 (2006): 127–32.

Geertz, Clifford. "'From the Native's Point of View': On the Nature of Anthropological Understanding." In *Meaning in Anthropology*, edited by Keith H. Basso and Henry A. Selby, 221–37. School of American Research Advanced Seminar Series. Albuquerque: University of New Mexico Press, 1976.

Hiebert, Paul G. *Anthropological Reflections on Missiological Issues.* Grand Rapids: Baker, 1994.

Johnson, Luke Timothy. *The Letter of James: A New Translation with Introduction and Commentary*. Anchor Bible 37A. New York: Doubleday, 1995.

Kgatle, Mookgo S. "Globalisation of Missions: An Exegesis on the Great Commission (Mt 28:18–20)." *In die Skriflig* 52, no. 1 (2018): 1–7. doi.org/10.4102/ids.v52i1.2346.

Massey, John D. "Theological Education and Southern Baptist Missions Strategy in the Twenty-First Century." *Southwestern Journal of Theology* 57, no. 1 (2014): 5–16.

McCartney, Dan G. *James*. Baker Exegetical Commentary on the New Testament. Grand Rapids: Baker Academic, 2009.

McIlwain, Trevor. *Building on Firm Foundations*. Sanford: New Tribes Mission, 1987.

McKnight, Scot. *The Letter of James*. The New International Commentary on the New Testament. Grand Rapids: Eerdmans, 2011.

Meyer, Birgit. "'If You Are a Devil, You Are a Witch and, If You Are a Witch, You Are a Devil.' The Integration of 'Pagan' Ideas into the Conceptual Universe of Ewe Christians in Southeastern Ghana." *Journal of Religion in Africa* 22, no. 2 (1992): 98–132.

Moo, Douglas J. *The Letter of James*. Pillar New Testament Commentary. Grand Rapids: Eerdmans, 2000.

Moreau, A. Scott, Gary R. Corwin, and Gary B. McGee. *Introducing World Missions: A Biblical, Historical, and Practical Survey*. 2nd ed. Grand Rapids: Baker Academic, 2015.

Nabi, Robin L., and Melanie C. Green. "The Role of a Narrative's Emotional Flow in Promoting Persuasive Outcomes." *Media Psychology* 18, no. 2 (2015): 137–62.

Newbigin, Lesslie. *A Word in Season: Perspectives on Christian World Missions*. Grand Rapids: Eerdmans, 1994.

Osborne, Grant R. *Matthew*. Zondervan Exegetical Commentary on the New Testament 1. Grand Rapids: Zondervan, 2010.

Ott, Craig. *Teaching and Learning across Cultures: A Guide to Theory and Practice*. Grand Rapids: Baker Academic, 2021.

Ott, Craig, Stephen J. Strauss, and Timothy C. Tennent. *Encountering Theology of Mission Biblical Foundations, Historical Developments, and Contemporary Issues*. Grand Rapids: Baker, 2010.

Paine, David R., Peter J. Jankowski, and Steven J. Sandage. "Humility as a Predictor of Intercultural Competence." *Family Journal* 24, no. 1 (2016): 15.

Priest, Robert J. "'Experience-Near Theologizing' in Diverse Human Contexts." In *Globalizing Theology: Belief and Practice in an Era of World Christianity*, edited by Craig Ott and Harold A. Netland, 180–95. Grand Rapids: Baker Academic, 2006.

Priest, Robert J. "'I Discovered My Sin!' Aguaruna Evangelical Conversion Narratives." In *The Anthropology of Religious Conversion*, edited by Andrew Buckser and Stephen D. Glazier, 95–108. Lanham: Rowman & Littlefield, 2003.

Priest, Robert J. "Putting Witch Accusations on the Missiological Agenda: A Case from Northern Peru." *International Bulletin of Mission Research* 39 (2015): 3–6. https://doi.org/10.1177/2396939315039001102.

Rhodes, Matt. *No Shortcut to Success: A Manifesto for Modern Missions*. Wheaton: Crossway, 2022.

Seversen, Beth. *Not Done Yet: Reaching and Keeping Unchurched Emerging Adults*. Downers Grove, IL: InterVarsity Press, 2020.

Ting-Toomey, Stella, and Leeva C. Chung. *Understanding Intercultural Communication*. 2nd ed. New York: Oxford University Press, 2012.

Watson, David, and Paul Watson. *Contagious Disciple-Making: Leading Others on a Journey of Discovery*. Nashville: Thomas Nelson, 2014.

Wolmarans, Johannes L. P. "The Tongue Guiding the Body: The Anthropological Presuppositions of James 3:1–12." *Neotestamentica* 26, no. 2 (1992): 523–30.

Chapter 16

James and Refugees

A Call to Care for the Vulnerable

Cindy M. Wu

"To the twelve tribes scattered among the nations,"[1] so opens the epistle of James (1:1).[2] With this salutation, the reader is immediately aware, even without details, of a particular context—that of forced migration. As persecution intensified among the early followers of Jesus, they became a church on the move, fulfilling God's mission to take the good news of Jesus Christ to the "ends of the earth" (Acts 1:8). As victims of religious persecution, Jewish Christians of James's day bear similarities to modern-day refugees.[3]

In 2022, forced migration hit a heartbreaking milestone: the number of forcibly displaced persons around the world surpassed 100 million.[4] Among them, more than 30 million people are "refugees"—migrants who have been forcibly displaced outside the borders of their country of origin.[5] That number rose again in 2023, as ongoing conflicts and the eruption of new wars displaced thousands more.

---

1 All Scripture quotations are from the NIV unless otherwise noted.

2 Scholars have debated the meaning of "the twelve tribes" in 1:1. They could be interpreted in a figurative, eschatological sense, or accepting the Jewish Christian origin of James, this text likely addresses the true Israel (Jewish Christians) outside of Palestine (probably in Syria and Asia Minor). See Davids, *Epistle of James*, 64.

3 The United Nations High Commissioner for Refugees (UNHCR) has identified five categories of persecution that produce refugees: race, religion, nationality, political opinion, or membership in a particular social group. The early church was indeed persecuted for its faith and subsequently scattered, but the comparison with modern-day refugees ends with regard to the primary cause of the modern-day refugee crisis—violent war and conflict between people groups and nation-states. See UNHCR, "Who We Protect: Refugees."

4 This figure is monitored by UNHCR.

5 The majority of forcibly displaced persons are still within the borders of their country of origin and are known as internally displaced persons (IDPs). A "refugee" is defined by the United Nations as a forcibly displaced person *outside* of the borders of their country of origin. All types of forcibly displaced migrants deserve protection, but those outside their home countries are especially vulnerable once they lose any rights of nationality. For the purposes of this chapter, we will not make hard distinctions between any legal category of migrant, but some of the practical advice herein will assume third-country migration as experienced by "refugees" in the legal, terminological sense.

A missiological reading of James reveals parallels between James's context and the modern refugee crisis, the greatest humanitarian crisis of our day. This chapter will apply the epistle of James to the ministry of caring for refugees in a holistic and reflective manner, with a focus on the poor and vulnerable. James is rich with practical wisdom on this subject. In fact, no New Testament text compares with James's social conscience.[6] This chapter will furthermore consider the lessons that refugees and the refugee experience can offer the global church, especially from the Global South to the Global North. The author of this chapter resides in North America and has experience mobilizing Christians to welcome refugees from the Global South to North America; hence, this chapter comes from that perspective.

Parallels between James's Context and the Refugee Crisis

To understand the message of James as it relates to refugee ministry today, we must take into account the historical, social, and cultural context of James. Biblical scholars have debated the authorship, form, and purpose of James, asking whether James was truly the half-brother of Jesus, or whether James is *paraenesis* or qualifies as a Jewish diaspora letter, wisdom literature, or both, as we will take it to be.[7]

This chapter does not analyze these features but poses practical questions about what James has to offer the modern reader vis-á-vis the global refugee crisis. The purpose of commenting on the form of James is to underscore that James—with its pithy admonitions and references to Old Testament teachings and sayings of Jesus—embodies timeless, universal wisdom. What does James say about caring for the vulnerable, such as refugees? What social and cultural factors present opportunities or challenges to care? How do we take a holistic approach? The voice of James is calling out in an era when the church in the Global North is losing its hegemony while the church in the Global South is growing—often in proximity to humanitarian crises of many kinds, including an unprecedented global refugee crisis.

---

6 Martin, *James*, lxvii.

7 Dibelius sees no evidence of epistolary remarks or structure. Thus he does not consider James to be a traditional New Testament letter, concluding instead that James is *paraenesis*, a series of general ethical admonitions, strung together without much continuity in thought. Dibelius, *James*, 1. Cheung and Yu, among other scholars, find thematic coherence and propose that James is a diaspora letter to a particular audience and it contains features of wisdom literature. Cheung and Yu, "Genre of James?," 97.

Rich and Poor

In James's day, there was a tiered class system of rich to poor, though this cannot be compared to modern-day concepts of upper, middle, and lower class. The extremes of society were represented by the "rich" (*plousioi*, small, elite group) and the "poor" (*ptōchoi*, small, lowly group). Everyone in between comprised the great majority of society, and this included peasants and artisans who were also "poor" (*penētes*) but could sustain themselves through their vocations. Twenty-first-century readers might consider their lifestyle impoverished or "poor," but in biblical times this was the normal standard of living.[8] Economics determined class, and class was a factor in determining religious belief. Primitive Christianity, with its countercultural message of inclusion and equality, drew the lower classes.[9] Numerous biblical passages refer to the poor as being "poor in spirit" (Matt 5:3; Isa 66:1–2); James's audience was poor in material wealth as well.

The lowest "poor" had endured hardship and oppression and therefore were at the mercy of others for subsistence. Although they often had to resort to begging, selling themselves into slavery, or committing crimes for survival, generally the view toward the poor, understood as victims of unfortunate circumstances or oppression, was one of pity, not contempt for a perceived lack of personal effort. However sympathetic the view toward the "poor" (also *tapeinos*, "lowly," in 1:9 and 4:6), they still lacked social status and honor.

Rich and Poor and Parallel with Refugee Crisis

Most refugees live in poverty or have experienced seasons of intense deprivation of material wealth, relationships, and community. Considering what displacement entails, this is not difficult to imagine. According to the United Nations High Commissioner for Refugees (UNHCR), 76 percent of the world's refugees are currently hosted in low- and middle-income countries, and the least developed countries provide asylum for 20 percent of the total number of refugees.[10] Most refugees live in urban areas, but some live in refugee camps where they might languish in protracted situations for an average of five to thirty years.[11] In any given year, less than one percent of all refugees are resettled (given legal permission to settle) in a third country.

---

8   Bauckham, *James*, 188.

9   Maynard-Reid, *Poverty and Wealth*, 19–20.

10 UNHCR, "Global Trends," 2.

11 This number is gleaned from information provided by UNHCR. The average number of years in exile depends on the particular conflict and the total average changes year to year based on a total number of refugees and geopolitical dynamics.

Refugees who are resettled in wealthy countries can still endure decades of poverty due to language barriers, cultural dissonance, discrimination, and lack of resources and access to quality education.[12] Refugee children are especially vulnerable to poverty.[13]

Patronage and Benefaction

Poor people are susceptible to broken systems that perpetuate or exploit their vulnerability. James's warnings against the rich guests in 2:2 speak against the deeply entrenched system of patronage, a long-term exchange between a wealthy person (patron) and a poor person (client) wherein the client would provide service and honors in exchange for land, food, protection, etc. Patronage was associated with Roman power and politics, a system of relationships between two extreme unequals that could easily lead to abuse, oppression, and even slavery.[14] Benefaction was also present in society and in the body of believers, but it differed from patronage in that it was one-directional, a generous gift from a wealthy person to a needy person that was not expected to be repaid.

James denounces patronage because it undermines the characteristics of a family of God, where bonds are based on love, not wealth, and it places the worldly value of honor on the rich and shame on the poor, which the teachings of Jesus sought to invert.[15] Patronage diminishes faith by promoting self-reliance rather than trust in God as the ultimate benefactor.

Patronage and Benefaction and Parallel with Refugee Crisis

Refugees are easy victims. Out of desperation and a lack of options, they often are duped into employment schemes or exploited for labor and human trafficking, all at the mercy of those who readily exploit them. Refugees attempting to cross borders are often tricked by "coyotes," a slang term used for smugglers of immigrants, especially in a Latin American context. Once in country, even legally, complications around work authorization make it difficult to find lawful, gainful, long-term employment.

Governments, churches, and nonprofits that aid and sponsor refugees often promote models that perpetuate dependency on social services and individuals. Refugees are expected to become "self-sufficient" within a short amount of time such that work competes with language training or cultural

---

12 Constante, "Largest U.S. Refugee Group." Southeast Asians constitute the largest refugee population to be settled in the United States. Burdened by the "model minority myth," their needs are often dismissed.

13 Beltramo et al., "Refugee Children."

14 Batten, *Friendship and Benefaction*, 76, 78.

15 See Luke 6:20; cf. 4:18; Matt 19:23; 25:31–46; Jas 2:5–6.

adjustment. In the long term, this can hinder refugees' personal development. Sponsorship programs provide opportunities for benefaction, but it is often difficult to transition this relationship to mutual friendship when refugees are viewed through the lens of their needs and not their assets. Well-meaning volunteers often view themselves as perpetual benefactors rather than corecipients of God's grace.

Warnings against Favoritism

In the beginning, God created humans in his image and called them "good." Each person is created in the image of God, yet we live in a world where people are often ascribed value based on race, class, gender, or immigration status. Partiality or favoritism is considered an affront to God (Deut 16:19). James writes, "My brothers and sisters, believers in our glorious Lord Jesus Christ must not show favoritism" (2:1). Friendship with the world leads to favoritism, materialism, and judgment; friendship with God leads to charity, faith, and generosity. Embracing one's own lowliness means dependence on God, looking to God to erase our shame and restore our honor. Being wealthy is not inherently sinful, but the love of money that breeds favoritism and oppression is contrary to "the royal law found in Scripture, 'Love your neighbor as yourself'" (2:8).

God showed no partiality in the election of Israel even when they were exiles escaping famine, nor did Jesus in including the poor and uneducated among his disciples or by associating with sinners and outcasts. Our Lord was gentle and *lowly* (Matt 11:29). The poor and lowly serve as the "paradigmatic members" of the kingdom of God, those whom society sees as ignoble, marginal, and poor, but who, like Jesus, in God's plan of reversal will be exalted (Ezek 21:26; 1 Cor 1:28–31).[16]

Favoritism and Parallel with Refugee Crisis

Refugees resettled in the Global North commonly face societal discrimination. They are automatically relegated to a lower social status due to prejudice around their immigration status. Although refugees resettled through the United Nations process obtain a refugee visa and thus are legal immigrants, they are often suspected to be illegal. They are also judged by their appearance, especially if they wear a hijab or ethnic clothing; lack of language proficiency or literacy; differences in diet and cultural mores; and lack of education (though refugees come from a wide range of backgrounds, and many are or have been wealthy and highly educated).

---

16 Bauckham, *James*, 192. See Job 5:11; Prov 29:23; Matt 18:4.

Government policies discriminate too. The United States resettlement program has historically favored Christians.[17] The recent surge of Muslim resettlement was met with opposition, even from high-profile Christian leaders and the president of the United States.[18] Western resettlement programs have favored White, educated refugees over non-White refugees. A recent example is the response to the Ukrainian refugee crisis, which began in 2022. Black refugees trying to escape Ukraine were treated poorly by the military, and racial bias was perceived to be at the root of the disparity.[19] Meanwhile, Ukrainian refugees were processed faster in some Western countries than non-White refugees from other parts of the world.[20] Favoritism has resulted in deleterious treatment of certain refugee populations.

Lessons for the Twenty-First-Century Church

Migration today looks different from biblical times. Modern people may move multiple times in one lifetime, often far from family, driven by environmental, political, or economic reasons, or simply for a sense of adventure. Forced migration also looks different from the era when the global refugee protection regime was established after World War II.[21] In the aftermath of World War II, refugees flowed primarily from Eastern Europe to the Americas. Today, resettlement flows mostly toward the Global North, with refugees coming from every continent.[22]

At first glance, forced migration may be viewed purely negatively, as a phenomenon related to catastrophe or tragedy. Much suffering accompanies forced migration, but the biblical narrative places all types of migration squarely within God's plan for the nations. From Adam and Eve leaving the

---

17 Greenberg, Gelatt, and Holovnia, "As the United States Resettles." See Soerens and Yang, *Welcoming the Stranger*. Chapter 2 is a recommended resource on US historical bias toward Christian (specifically, Protestant) immigration.

18 Reference to Franklin Graham of Samaritan's Purse and Donald Trump. In 2015, both called for a ban on Muslim immigration.

19 Ferris-Rotman, "They Called Ukraine Home."

20 Townsend, "Home Office Accused." For a US perspective, see Marcelo, "In U.S.'s Welcome to Ukrainians."

21 UNHCR was established in 1950 to temporarily and exclusively address the refugee crisis precipitated by World War II.

22 Resettlement does not always cross continents. For example, a refugee from Syria may resettle in a neighboring country, or a refugee from Guatemala in the United States. The United States has historically been the top resettlement country for refugees. Other top resettlement countries include Canada, along with several European nations (Sweden, Germany, and France).

garden of Eden, to Abram and Sarai leaving Ur, to Abraham's descendants sojourning for various reasons, to Jesus and the disciples' itinerant ministry, migration has been a means through which God has spread his fame around the world. Movement through missionary endeavors, often accompanied by humanitarian care to "widows and orphans," is how the church has grown globally (Acts 1:8; Rom 10:14–15).

The forced migration phenomenon carries important lessons for the twenty-first-century church. Let us highlight a few lessons from James as the Global North continues to receive refugees and immigrants from all over the world.[23]

Hearing and Doing, Faith and Works

James views faith and works as two sides of the same coin rather than contradictory. In the same way that hearing should result in doing, so faith should result in works. For James, a lack of action is as incomprehensible as someone looking into a mirror and then immediately forgetting what he looks like (1:23–24). Faith translates into action; lack of action is totally incongruent with our identity as people of a God who acts on behalf of his people. "Holding Jesus' faith (2:1) and fulfilling the Torah (2:10) are synonymous for the author of James. Both find their essence in loving one's neighbor as oneself (2:8)."[24] Faith without works is as useless as a body without a spirit; faith without works is dead (2:17, 26).

"Abraham our father" is named as one whose faith was made complete by his willingness to offer his son Isaac as a sacrifice (2:21–22). This act fulfilled the Scripture that says "Abram believed the LORD, and he credited it to him as righteousness" (Gen 15:6; cf. Heb 11:17–19). In the same passage, Rahab the prostitute is commended as someone whose action of housing the Israelite spies in Jericho justified her faith; though she was a gentile, she became the first recorded convert (Jas 2:25). For James, faith and action are intrinsically inseparable, and only a fool would miss this point (2:20).

Caring for refugees in action and deeds may include welcoming them at the airport, delivering a warm meal, or enrolling children in school. It should also include friendship and relational aspects of welcome. Being aware of the refugee crisis is not enough; the body of Christ is called to get engaged.[25]

---

23 Forced migration impacts every region of the world, but this section will focus on the author's perspective as a North American.

24 Wachob, *Voice of Jesus*, 191.

25 For practical ideas on welcoming refugees, see Wu, *Better Country.*

True Religion: Caring for "Widows and Orphans"

Throughout Scripture, God emphatically calls for justice for the vulnerable. Justice was assumed by Old Testament writers, especially the psalmists: "I know that the LORD secures justice for the poor and upholds the cause of the needy" (Ps 140:12). In the New Testament, perhaps no text conveys the fire of the Old Testament prophets in denouncing mistreatment of the poor and the mercilessness of the rich better than James, and nowhere is language against such oppression more condemning (Isa 5:22–23; Amos 5:11–12; Jas 5:1–6).[26]

God has a special concern for a "quartet of the vulnerable": the poor, the alien (immigrant, foreigner), widows, and orphans.[27] These members are often grouped together, in twos, threes, or fours, as in Zechariah 7:10: "Do not oppress the widow or the fatherless, the foreigner or the poor. Do not plot evil against each other."[28] God even threatened retribution for those who dared to exploit the vulnerable:

> Do not take advantage of the widow or the fatherless. If you do and they cry out to me, I will certainly hear their cry. My anger will be aroused, and I will kill you with the sword; your wives will become widows and your children fatherless. (Exod 22:22–24)

James mentions all four members of this quartet in his letter. Taken together, they symbolize the most vulnerable members of society. God's special concern for the most vulnerable translates into our special mandate to care for them: "Learn to do right; seek justice. Defend the oppressed. Take up the cause of the fatherless; plead the case of the widow" (Isa 1:17). "Doing right" involves meeting physical needs, loving one's neighbor as oneself by not showing favoritism, and combatting wicked worldly systems, like patronage, that oppress and exploit the vulnerable (Matt 25:42–45; Jas 2:1–18). All of these actions regard the vulnerable as dignified, whole persons.

In our world today, abundant opportunities exist to take up the cause of the vulnerable, and refugees are among the world's most vulnerable. Currently, children account for 40 percent of all forcibly displaced persons, many of whom are orphans.[29] Meanwhile, slightly more women than men are forcibly displaced, and many of these women are widows.[30] In biblical

---

26 Maynard-Reid, *Poverty and Wealth*, 97.

27 This phrase was coined by Wolsterstorff in *Justice: Rights and Wrongs*.

28 See also Deut 24:17; 27:19; Ps 146:9; Isa 1:17; 58:6–7.

29 UNHCR, "Global Trends," 3.

30 UNHCR, 3.

times as well as in modern times, being an orphan or widow is virtually a guaranteed path to exploitation and poverty. A high percentage of refugee children are considered poor even if their family falls above the poverty line. In fact, refugee children can be up to three times as likely to be poor than adults.[31] In James's theological imagination, a follower of Christ is defined as standing in solidarity with the poor, and those who care about justice for the vulnerable are the truly righteous who know God (Prov 29:7; Jer 22:16).

Holistic Care

When ministering to hundreds of refugees at once, it is easy to lose sight of refugees' individual agency and humanity; they become a statistic or problem to solve. Paul N. Sydnor with the International Association for Refugees states,

> The first aspect of Christian ministry among refugees is relationship. Christian refugee work is not primarily about meeting needs or even leading others to Christ; it is more than merely a project to be managed. Refugee ministry workers are relational mediators who model their ministry after God's own relationship in the Trinity and in the example of Jesus, who came to reconcile humanity with God.[32]

Relational ministry that builds trust and dignity can provide healing for all parties. Sydnor goes on to write, "[Relational] ministry develops relationships that break the dehumanizing cycle of displacement, along with the rejection and trauma that refugees experience."[33]

Many churches and individuals bifurcate refugee care into humanitarian/practical and faith/spiritual issues. Or they hyper-spiritualize care, such as only praying for physical healing instead of also taking a refugee to the doctor. Or they are so concerned with evangelizing non-Christians that they downplay refugees' physical and psychological needs, leaving those to the government or nonprofit agencies. Christian ministries also tend to shy away from advocacy in the public square—an outlet to empower refugees to develop agency and have a voice—for fear of reprisal from other Christians who want to steer clear of anything political. On that point, Christian Arab Palestinian Yousef K. AlKhour states, "Christians must learn to advocate for displaced people in the public arena and in democratic societies."[34]

---

31 Beltramo et al., "Refugee Children."
32 Sydnor, "Relationship and Scripture," 154.
33 Sydnor, 154.
34 AlKhour, "Refugee Opportunity," 165.

Best practices for refugee ministry should focus on holistic, whole-person care and partnership.[35]

Hospitality

Hospitality is often expressed through a power lens, where a more powerful person hosts a person of lower status, or as a transaction in which some benefit is expected in return. James critiques the type of unjust and ungodly hospitality the community was being tempted to indulge in, that is, showing favoritism to the wealthy who entered their fellowship. The temptation was to offer these guests greater honor and to discriminate against the lowly brother or sister (2:2–4, 15–16). Hospitality was so highly valued in the Jewish tradition that there were Levitical laws protecting sojourners seeking refuge and hospitality: "When a foreigner resides among you in your land, do not mistreat them. The foreigner residing among you must be treated as your native-born. Love them as yourself, for you were foreigners in Egypt. I am the LORD your God" (Lev 19:33–34). These laws did not favor the wealthy; they were applied to all who sought refuge.

It is notable that in the discourse around faith and works, Abraham and Rahab are two biblical characters famous for offering hospitality. Abraham offered hospitality to the visitors under the oaks at Mamre (Gen 18). He was considered righteous by his faith in recognizing these messengers from the Lord (Jas 2:23). Rahab offered hospitality to the Israelite spies whom Joshua had sent to Jericho to scout the land for conquest. She hid the men on her roof and gave them instructions to ensure the success of their mission. Despite her identity as a prostitute, a woman, and a gentile, her acts of hospitality rendered her righteous because they proved her faith (Jas 2:25); she is even mentioned in Matthew's genealogy of Jesus Christ (Matt 1:5).

Modern attitudes toward migrants as threats or burdens do not reflect biblical values of hospitality and communal responsibility found in honor/shame societies. Even among refugees in economic hardship, hospitality is a given. A visit to the home of an Afghan family is sure to turn into an hours-long conversation seated on the floor over bottomless cups of green tea and a snack plate of raisins, cookies, and dried chickpeas. A knock on the door of a Congolese family may turn into a meal of rice and beans, squash, and *fufu* made from cassava flour. The gift of hospitality brings light to the dark hours of suffering and waiting that is so common to the refugee experience. Refugees

---

35 See International Association for Refugees, "Best Practices for Christian Ministry," Core Value #10.

who move to the Global North exemplify how to offer a style of hospitality not contingent upon material wealth but out of abundant cultural values.

When receiving hospitality from a refugee newcomer, it is important not to refuse their gesture out of pity. We strip a host of their dignity when we refuse a gift because we arrogantly determine they cannot afford it. Conversely, when offering hospitality, it is important not to treat refugees as though one is their benefactor, solely in the position to give. Wealthier hosts must resist the tendency to infantilize refugees because of their initial "neediness," social status as a newcomer, and lack of language and cultural fluency. The best-case scenario is to strive for mutuality, where both sides can be hosts and guests, learning, giving, and receiving from one another based on the relationship and not economic situation.

Patience in Suffering

As some of the world's most persecuted and vulnerable people, refugees are tested in suffering and patience on many sides. Refugees bring attention to persecution, and Christian refugees fleeing persecution deserve our particular concern. Scripture commands us to do good to all, but "especially to those who belong to the family of believers" (Gal 6:10). Targeted religious persecution against Christian minorities in places like Myanmar (Burma), Iraq, Eritrea, and Nigeria has led to forced migration and martyrdom.[36] Even Christians living in countries with a strong Christian presence, such as Mexico and Colombia, are under threat when their convictions oppose corrupt governments.[37] The majority of refugees who have come to North America in the past forty years are Christians, many of whom were persecuted for their Christian faith.

James's primary audience was Jewish Christians of lower economic means, and his message instructed and encouraged them in the face of temptations and trials. Mexican liberation theologian and biblical scholar Elsa Támez exhorts readers of James to read the text from the angle of the oppressed poor: "Oppression is one of the principal motives that compelled the author to write the letter."[38] Támez notes that Western scholars tend to consider their personal audiences and focus on what James has to say to the rich. Instead, Támez posits, we should modify our gaze and adopt the perspective of the oppressed, especially because for many in the global

---

36 For more information, see "Church on the Run" by Open Doors, a nonprofit that tracks the persecuted church. The report details instances around the world of intentional religious persecution leading to forced displacement.

37 Open Doors, "Church on the Run."

38 Támez, *Scandalous Message*, 12.

church, oppression and poverty are part of their faith story.[39] "James insists that the vocation of the church, its mission, is the poor, who are rich in faith and the heirs of God's reign (2:5)."[40] Yet for the poor, there is a gap between their eschatological reality and their lived experience, as they are still living in affliction and deprivation.

Chilean biblical scholar Nelson R. Morales observes how James intertwines Old Testament teachings with Jesus's teaching within his discourse, utilizing eschatological language beginning in 1:9–11 to construct his ethics of poverty and wealth, with the poor receiving blessing and the rich judgment.[41] Echoes of Jesus's teaching infuse James's letter:

- The poor are inheritors of the kingdom of God (Jas 2:5; Matt 5:3)
- Mercy is given to the merciful (Jas 2:13; Matt 5:7)
- Caring for the needy (Jas 2:14–17; Matt 6:1–4)
- The fleeting nature of life (Jas 4:13–14; Matt 6:34)
- Loving your neighbor (Jas 2:8; Matt 22:39)
- Judgment upon the rich (Jas 5:1–6; Luke 6:24)

Toward the end of James, the author names two archetypes of faithful men who were known for enduring suffering, Job and Elijah (5:10–11, 17–18). Job lost everything and yet trusted in God. Years later God restored Job with new children and wealth. Elijah lived through a prolonged drought (1 Kgs 17:1), a climate challenge common in areas that produce refugees. He experienced political persecution and had to flee for his life (1 Kgs 19). He also experienced dependency on God's miraculous provision in the form of ravens and an angel, among other miraculous events (1 Kgs 17–19; 2 Kgs 2). Through each trial, Elijah cried out to God for sustenance and succor. James wants his readers to emulate Job and Elijah by developing a militant patience, undergirded by prayer, seeking joy while they suffer, and depending on God for daily sustenance (1:2; 5:7–8).

Mutuality: Engage With, Learn From

The invitation of the gospel is to believe in a Savior who offers salvation not by works but by faith—one who tore down a dividing wall of hostility between humankind (Eph 2:8–22). As equals in God's sight, Christians are designed to learn from one another. This is a mandate especially for the church in the Global North, which for the past millennium has held ecclesial power

---

39 Támez, 21, 25.

40 Támez, 26.

41 Morales, *Poor and Rich*, 236–38.

and has directed missionary endeavors. James's multiple warnings against favoritism, selfish ambition, and envy communicate an equality in human value. In 3:17, he states that godly wisdom must be peace-loving, considerate, and submissive. Submission to God and to one another is key to holy living.

The global church needs a less individualistic and more collectivistic mindset, and with the explosion of Christianity in the Global South, home to predominantly honor/shame cultures that value collective identity, the North and West will be forced to reexamine its methods, values, and power structures. An individualistic mindset tends to view social problems as the result of individual choices; a collectivistic mindset tends to seek solutions together within the community. Jamaican theologian Pedrito U. Maynard-Reid states, "As in Matthew 25:31–46, James reveals that one's social involvement in the present is as important as one's personal religious practices and that, in fact, personal religion is meaningless without social commitment."[42]

One hundred years ago, mission expansion was largely "from the West to the rest." Today, the global church has already moved toward a polycentric model of mission from every nation to every nation, and the catchphrase now is "everyone to everywhere."[43] Malawian mission theologian Harvey Kwiyani challenges missiology to move further toward decolonization. Past missionary methods were unfortunately often coupled with colonial enterprise, and polycentric mission can only be truly celebrated if missionary methods are de-Westernized and informed instead by communities from and in the Majority World.[44] These will include refugee leaders familiar with the experience of migration and cross-cultural adjustment, two dynamics that are so relevant for our day.

Refugees crisscross the globe as they are resettled in lands far from home, especially in North America.[45] Consider the impact Orthodox Iraqis are having in Detroit, Michigan, or Bhutanese Baptists in Harrisburg, Pennsylvania, or Afghan Christians in Houston, Texas. God is raising immigrant churches and leaders in major urban areas where there is potential

---

42 Maynard-Reid, *Poverty and Wealth*, 98.

43 Yeh, "Future of Mission." The concept of polycentric mission is not entirely new. Yeh notes that Israel's location at the crossroads of three continents had missiological implications. For more on polycentric mission, see Yeh's book *Polycentric Missiology*. The motto "Everyone to Everywhere" is used by the Lausanne Movement and others.

44 Kwiyani, "World Christianity and Polycentric Mission."

45 Refugees are temporarily "hosted" primarily in mid- to low-income Global South countries (like Turkey, Iran, Colombia, and Pakistan), but resettlement, which provides a pathway to legal residency, is granted annually to less than one percent of all refugees globally, most of whom are resettled in wealthier Global North countries.

for cross-pollination of discipleship, church planting, and leadership development, leading to mission mobilization back to home countries, to native diaspora, or cross-culturally.

Twenty-first-century Christians must engage with and learn from one another. Within a relational framework of refugee ministry, each person is a "fellow stakeholder in a mutual experience."[46] The Diaspora Network has developed a mutuality framework that seeks to embody the reality of unity and reconciliation within the body of Christ:

> Diaspora Christians can uniquely help the broader Church in North America learn anew how to engage with and stay connected to both a global perspective and to God's mission. Diasporans by their very presence challenge and subvert ethno-centric and paternalistic approaches to mission in the broader North American Church while the broader North American Church can help the immigrant church reach out beyond their cultural and ethnic enclosures.[47]

This is the vision moving forward, and refugees are leading the way in many communities.

Diaspora Identity

James instructs his readers not to be like a man who peers into a mirror and then immediately forgets what he looks like (1:23–24). In the same manner, modern readers should read James like a mirror, regularly reflecting whether we are living into our "diaspora identity" and whether our faith is proven by our works. What is meant by "diaspora identity"? It entails viewing life from the perspective of displacement, whether forced or willing.

Refugees get pushed to the margins of society. While marginality is one of the many costs of displacement, it does not have to be a liability. Being on the margins allows a different experience and perspective. In fact, Jesus our Lord lived a life on the margins as illustrated by his itinerant ministry and his very nature—fully human, fully divine—and his followers lived an alternative lifestyle. Irish biblical scholar David Hutchinson Edgar writes that "the Jesus movement offered an interpretation of social reality within a cosmological framework which gave a positive evaluation of the devalued status of the socially marginal poor."[48] In James, the marginal are affirmed as honorable, most strongly expressed in 2:5: "Has not God chosen those

---

46 Sydnor, "Relationship and Scripture," 155.

47 Diaspora Network, "Framework for Mutuality."

48 Edgar, *Has God Not Chosen*, 110. See Matt 19:30; cf. 20:16; Luke 13:30; Mark 10:31.

who are poor in the eyes of the world to be rich in faith and to inherit the kingdom he promised those who love him?"[49] This eschatological reversal in which the lowly become honorable and the last become first gives value to marginality.

Mission scholars and demographers have documented the "browning" of global Christianity.[50] As the center of gravity of Christianity continues to move south and east to sub-Saharan Africa, the demographic makeup of the church is increasingly reflecting the Global South.[51] These believers tend to be theologically conservative, attuned to the miraculous work of the Holy Spirit, focused on evangelism, and engaged in social justice because of their context. As refugee believers from the Global South come to the Global North, they bring a zealous faith tested by fire to revitalize the church.[52] If majority culture Christians could take a different perspective on migration, they could see the church growing in unexpected but necessary ways.[53] Sierra Leonean missiologist Jehu J. Hanciles writes that "a migrant-outsider experience (or 'otherness')" brings forth the type of faith James espouses.[54] "The migrant experience makes poignantly manifest what may otherwise be muted in the life of the church: *otherness is foundational to outreach.*"[55] It is through boundary-crossing movements of Christianity (through whatever means) that the church has been able to fulfill its mission.

Engaging with refugees from around the world challenges our notions of identity. Many Christians unwittingly embrace a racialized, nationalistic, or ethnic Christian identity rather than a global one. The challenge is to view Christian refugees as sisters and brothers in the same household of faith, and non-Christian refugees as members of the same global human family, and expand our personal identities to a more inclusive, more global identity.[56] This self-understanding should inform the way we view all of humanity.

The sojourner metaphor has deep historical and theological significance for the nation of Israel. Israel's relationship with God, with other nations,

---

49 Edgar, 105–6.

50 Carroll R., *Christians at the Border*, 38–40. See also Jenkins, *Next Christendom*.

51 For more on the shifting demographics within the global church, see Johnson and Wu, *Our Global Families*, ch. 1.

52 George, "Is God Reviving Europe."

53 Carroll R., *Christians at the Border*, 40.

54 Hanciles, *Migration and the Making*, 419.

55 Hanciles, 419, emphasis original.

56 For an exploration of Christian identity vis-à-vis changing demographics and global issues, see Johnson and Wu, *Our Global Families*.

and with eternity is understood within this motif. Our God-given identity is ontological and existential—as a child of God made for eternity, humans are *inherently* sojourners. As sojourners, followers of Jesus have a special mandate to care for refugees. God repeatedly reminds Israel that they, too, are sojourners (Exod 23:9; Lev 25:23; Deut 10:19). All who trust in Christ are sojourners, aliens, itinerants, travelers, and pilgrims on earth (1 Chr 29:15; Ps 39:12; 1 Pet 1:17). As strangers and exiles desiring a better country, we treat this life as temporary, for the best is yet to come—our heavenly home from which we await a Savior, the Lord Jesus Christ (Heb 11:16; Phil 3:20).

Diaspora is a static yet temporary condition for the people of God, for we "live in diaspora until the coming of our Lord."[57] James contains a good word for modern readers: The end of our earthly exile is something we continually long for, when we will receive a better country, a heavenly one. Like refugees, we must persevere through trials and hold our futures loosely. We who receive refugees should not discriminate or show favoritism but rather take on a diaspora identity mindset that remembers that we, too, were once strangers. We can find joy in suffering. God is sovereign over all. These are potent and necessary lessons for the church in the twenty-first century.

Bibliography

AlKhour, Yousef K. "Refugee Opportunity: A Missional Responsibility of the Church." In *Refugee Diaspora: Missions amid the Greatest Humanitarian Crisis of Our Times*, edited by Sam George and Miriam Adeney, 161–66. Littleton, CO: William Carey Publishing, 2018.

Batten, Alicia J. *Friendship and Benefaction in James*. Emory Studies in Early Christianity 15. Blandford Forum, UK: Deo, 2010.

Bauckham, Richard. *James: Wisdom of James, Disciple of Jesus the Sage*. New York: Routledge, 1999.

Beltramo, Theresa, Rossella Calvi, Giacomo De Giorgi, and Ibrahima Sarr. "Refugee Children Are Disproportionately Poor (And Thus More Vulnerable) than Other Household Members and as a Result Require a Larger Share of Social Assistance to Meet Their Basic Needs." UNHCR, The UN Refugee Agency, February 2, 2023. https://www.unhcr.org/blogs/refugee-children-are-disproportionately-poorer-and-thus-more-vulnerable-than-other-household-members/.

---

57 Morales, "James and 1 Peter," 99.

Carroll R., M. Daniel. *Christians at the Border: Immigration, the Church & the Bible*. 2nd ed. Grand Rapids: Brazos, 2013.

Cheung, Luke L., and Kelvin C. L. Yu. "The Genre of James: Diaspora Letter, Wisdom Instruction, or Both?" In *Reading the Epistle of James: A Resource for Students*, edited by Eric F. Mason and Darian R. Lockett, 87–98. Atlanta: Society of Biblical Literature, 2019.

Constante, Agnes. "Largest U.S. Refugee Group Struggling with Poverty 45 Years after Resettlement." *NBC News*, March 4, 2020. https://www.nbcnews.com/news/asian-america/largest-u-s-refugee-group-struggling-poverty-45-years-after-n1150031.

Davids, Peter H. *The Epistle of James: A Commentary on the Greek Text*. Grand Rapids: Eerdmans, 1982.

Diaspora Network. "A Framework for Mutuality: What Mutuality Can Look Like between Immigrant and Non-immigrant Christians." Diaspora Network, August 31, 2023. https://thediasporanetwork.substack.com/p/a-framework-for-mutuality.

Dibelius, Martin. *James: A Commentary on the Epistle of James*. Revised by Heinrich Greeven. Translated by Michael A. Williams. Edited by Helmut Koester. 11th ed. Hermeneia. Philadelphia: Fortress, 1976.

Edgar, David Hutchinson. *Has God Not Chosen the Poor? The Social Setting of the Epistle of James*. Journal for the Study of the New Testament Supplement 206. Sheffield: Sheffield Academic, 2001.

Ferris-Rotman, Amie. "They Called Ukraine Home. But They Faced Violence and Racism When They Tried to Leave." *Time Magazine*, March 1, 2022. https://time.com/6153276/ukraine-refugees-racism/.

George, Sam. "Is God Reviving Europe through Refugees?" Lausanne Global Analysis, April 2017. https://lausanne.org/global-analysis/god-reviving-europe-refugees.

Greenberg, Mark, Julia Gelatt, and Amy Holovnia. "As the United States Resettles Fewer Refugees, Some Countries and Religions Face Bigger Hits than Others." Migration Policy Institute, September 2019. https://www.migrationpolicy.org/news/united-states-refugee-resettlement-some-countries-religions-face-bigger-hits.

Hanciles, Jehu J. *Migration and the Making of Global Christianity*. Grand Rapids: Eerdmans, 2021.

International Association for Refugees. "Best Practices for Christian Ministry among Forcibly Displaced People." International Association for Refugees, November 2015. https://assets-global.website-files.com/5e753e90e64659ba51ecd6ad/5eaad4a74c1f304465df460f_Refugee%20Ministry%20Best%20Practices%202015%20-IAFR.pdf.

Jenkins, Philip. *The Next Christendom: The Coming of Global Christianity*. 3rd ed. Oxford: Oxford University Press, 2011.

Johnson, Todd M., and Cindy M. Wu. *Our Global Families: Embracing Common Identity in a Changing World*. Grand Rapids: Baker Academic, 2015.

Kwiyani, Harvey. "World Christianity and Polycentric Mission." Global Witness, Globally Reimagined, February 2, 2023. https://harveykwiyani.substack. com/p/world-christianity-and-polycentric.

Laws, Sophie. *A Commentary on the Epistle of James*. Black's New Testament Commentary. Peabody, MA: Hendrickson, 1980.

Marcelo, Philip. "In U.S.'s Welcome to Ukrainians, African Refugees See Racial Bias." *PBS News Hour*, April 1, 2022. https://www.pbs.org/newshour/politics/ in-u-s-s-welcome-to-ukrainians-african-refugees-see-racial-bias.

Martin, Ralph P. *James*. Word Biblical Commentary 48. Waco, TX: Word, 1988.

Maynard-Reid, Pedrito U. *Poverty and Wealth in James*. Maryknoll, NY: Orbis Books, 1987.

Morales, Nelson. "James and 1 Peter through the Eyes of a Migrant." In *Global Migration & Christian Faith: Implications for Identity and Mission*, edited by M. Daniel Carroll R. and Vincent E. Bacote, 84–102. Eugene, OR: Wipf & Stock, 2021.

Morales, Nelson R. *Poor and Rich in James: A Relevance Theory Approach to James's Use of the Old Testament*. University Park, PA: Eisenbrauns, 2018.

Open Doors. "The Church on the Run: IDP & Refugee Report 2022." Accessed May 30, 2024. https://www.opendoors.org/en-US/research-reports/idp-persecution/IDP-Refugee-specific-religious-persecution-report-Church-on-the-run-June-2022.pdf.

Soerens, Matthew, and Jenny Yang, *Welcoming the Stranger: Justice, Compassion & Truth in the Immigration Debate*. Downers Grove, IL: InterVarsity Press, 2018.

Sydnor, Paul N. "Relationship and Scripture in Practical Refugee Ministry." In *Refugee Diaspora: Missions amid the Greatest Humanitarian Crisis of Our Times*, edited by Sam George and Miriam Adeney, 153–60. Littleton, CO: William Carey Publishing, 2018.

Támez, Elsa. *The Scandalous Message of James: Faith without Works Is Dead*. Translated by John Eagleson. New York: Crossroad, 1990.

Townsend, Mark. "Home Office Accused of Being 'Unashamedly Racist' Towards Sudanese." *The Guardian*, May 7, 2023. https://www.theguardian.com/ world/2023/may/07/home-office-accused-of-being-unashamedly-racist-towards-sudanese.

UNHCR. "Global Trends: Forced Displacement in 2022." https://www.unhcr.org/ global-trends-report-2022.

UNHCR. "Who We Protect: Refugees." Accessed May 30, 2024. https://www. unhcr.org/us/refugees.

Wachob, Wesley Hiram. *The Voice of Jesus in the Social Rhetoric of James.* Society for New Testament Studies Monograph Series 106. New York: Cambridge University Press, 2000.

Wolsterstorff, Nicholas. *Justice: Rights and Wrongs.* Princeton: Princeton University Press, 2008.

Wu, Cindy M. *A Better Country: Embracing the Refugees in Our Midst.* 2nd ed. Littleton, CO: William Carey Publishing, 2022.

Yeh, Allen. "The Future of Mission Is from Everyone to Everywhere: A Look at Polycentric Missiology." Lausanne Global Analysis, December 2017. https:// lausanne.org/global-analysis/future-mission-everyone-everywhere.

Yeh, Allen. *Polycentric Missiology: 21st-Century Mission from Everyone to Everywhere.* Downers Grove, IL: IVP Academic, 2016.

Chapter 17

Mission to an Unjust World through God's Scattered, Persevering Children

Jeanne Wu

James, a servant of God and of the Lord Jesus Christ,
To the twelve tribes scattered among the nations:

Greetings.

Consider it pure joy, my brothers and sisters, whenever you face trials of many kinds, because you know that the testing of your faith produces perseverance. Let perseverance finish its work so that you may be mature and complete, not lacking anything. (Jas 1:1–4)[1]

We live in a time of crises and turmoil. With the global pandemic barely over, the wars in Ukraine-Russia and the Middle East have cast a shadow on the world. Long before the war, Ukraine had vigorous evangelical churches, while Christianity throughout Europe had been in decline. In 2017, my husband and I worshiped in Kyiv with a good friend and her Ukrainian husband. Sadly, in less than five years, the once beautiful ancient capital has been scarred by war. When Russia invaded Ukraine in 2022, my friend and her family fled Kyiv by car. Their family waited five days and nights in a long queue on the Polish border to clear customs, after which they were resettled in Poland as refugees. Amid that hardship, she shared updates on social media with us: "This time is a test of our faith. Praise God that our faith is tested so it can prove genuine. I am confident God is working through this craziness! We refuse to lose heart." What faith in a time of trials!

My friend is not the only Christian with a testimony of faith during the Ukraine-Russia war. A year after the war, The Gospel Coalition interviewed Ukrainian Christians, reporting, "If you talk to Ukrainian Christians, they'll tell you God hasn't abandoned them."[2] Many churches are growing, and Ukrainian refugees have revived churches in neighboring countries. With the influx of Ukrainian refugees to other countries in Eastern Europe, Ukrainian Christian ministry has extended to Poland, Slovakia, and other European

---

1 All Scripture quotations are from the NIV.
2 Zylstra, "Christians in Ukraine."

countries where evangelical churches were not strong.[3] As my friend said, God has been working in the midst of these difficulties.

The testimonies of my friend and Ukrainian Christians remind us of James 1:1–4. The message of James is an exhortation to Jewish followers of Christ who were scattered outside Palestine in the first century.[4] As the believing community was forced out, it suffered from discrimination, injustice, and persecution as a minority in society. Many of them not only endured suffering and stood firm in their faith, but they also spread the good news of Jesus Christ and expanded the kingdom of God in a miraculous way.

A Letter to Scattered Believers Then and Now

James, whom scholars traditionally believe to be a brother of Jesus and leader of the Jerusalem church, wrote this letter to the believing Jews in diaspora.[5] The word "scattered" in the opening greeting—also occurring in John 7:35 and 1 Peter 1:1—translates the Greek noun *diaspora*, the origin of the English word. It originally referred to an agricultural process of "the fruitful scattering away of seeds," thus carrying the meaning of "to scatter over."[6] One of the earliest biblical usages of this term comes from the third century BC in the Septuagint (LXX), where it refers to the scattered people of God (Deut 28:25, 64 LXX), presenting the idea of diaspora as "a forcible dispersion."[7] In the New Testament, this Greek word repeatedly describes the situation of Jews as a dispersed community in the first century under the rule of the Roman Empire. When John, James, and Peter used the term *diaspora*, they did not modify it with the word "Jews" (*Ioudaioi*), which may imply that diaspora in that era was used particularly for Jews rather than all ethnicities.

In addition, the word also has important resonances with the image of the spreading kingdom of God. The agricultural connotations of the word evoke the image of scattered seeds, a metaphor that Jesus often used in his parables about the growth of his kingdom (Matt 13:3–9, 24–30). In the past two decades, missiologists have introduced the ideas of "diaspora missiology" and "mission through diaspora."[8] In the context of missiological discourse,

---

3 Zylstra, "Christians in Ukraine."

4 Blomberg and Kamell, *James*, 28; Carson and Moo, *Introduction to the New Testament*, 628.

5 Moo, *Letter of James*, 9–22.

6 Tölölyan, "Rethinking Diaspora(s)," 10.

7 Cohen, *Global Diasporas*, 1.

8 Escobar, "Migration: Avenue and Challenge," 19; Wan, "Diaspora Missiology," 3–7.

diaspora includes a wide range of new immigrants, refugees, international students, and migrant workers. The expression "mission through diaspora" refers to migrants (or new immigrants) reaching out to their kin in their country of origin or other countries.[9] The gospel movement in the first century in many ways could be called "mission through diaspora." When we look at church history and study the book of Acts, we see how God used diaspora to expand his kingdom. Just as in the first century, God still uses his scattered children to spread his good news and build his church today.

Mission through Diaspora in Our Time
In 2013, I researched mission activities through diaspora Chinese by surveying the 652 Chinese churches in the United States.[10] The results showed how diaspora Chinese churches planted churches among Chinese students and new immigrants and engaged in mission to their kin in other parts of the world. For example, more than 46 percent of Chinese churches in the United States hold one or more mission conference(s) per year, and more than 61 percent of them organize one or more short-term missions per year.[11]

One example is my home church in Illinois, a medium-sized Chinese church with about three hundred members, three congregations, and one new church plant. They are actively involved in local outreach to Chinese-speaking new immigrants and Chinese students in major universities in Illinois. The church sends out short-term mission teams every year and holds annual mission conferences, and they baptize dozens of new believers each year on Easter and Christmas.

My home church is one of the hundreds of Chinese churches in the United States passionately participating in the *missio Dei*. Soong-Chan Rah reported that Korean churches in the United States do holistic evangelism to reach out to their kin, and he finds "remarkable parallels" among other immigrant communities.[12] It is the power of mission "through—and even beyond"—diaspora.

Mission through Diaspora in Trials
The August 2019 cover story of *National Geographic* is "World on the Move." The story reports massive population movements and refugees uprooted by war, climate change, famine, and other factors in today's world.

---

9   Wan, *Diaspora Missiology*, 138–40.

10 See Wu, *Mission through Diaspora*.

11 Wu, 78, 117.

12 Rah, *Next Evangelicalism*, 177–79.

In this era of globalization and turmoil, God is working mightily among migrants, refugees, and displaced people who come to know the Lord in deeper ways or for the first time through their trials. The aforementioned testimony of Ukrainian Christians is one example. I also had the privilege of witnessing this firsthand in the Middle East. Due to regional conflicts and civil wars, the Lord opened the door for many of his servants to share his truth and love with many afflicted souls.[13]

In a Middle Eastern country where my husband and I served, one of our coworkers served a young man—a long-time refugee. When he shared with this young man about Jesus, he simply refused, saying, "You are a Christian, and I am a Muslim. This will not change." We continued to pray for this young man, and one day, he dreamed that he was bowing down to a man in white and asking for forgiveness for his sins. He told our coworker about the dream, who told him that his dream was about Jesus. Sometime later, he saw a painting of the Samaritan woman in our coworker's home, piquing his curiosity. The young man asked about the meaning of the painting, so our coworker shared the account of John 4, which moved the young man. That same day, he received a notification through the Bible app on his phone—it was a quotation from the same story of the Samaritan woman. He was quite surprised and believed that it was a special message from God to him. He soon accepted Jesus as his Savior. After coming to Christ, this brother preached the gospel among fellow refugees, led a Bible study in his humble home, and later returned to his own country. Many Middle Eastern refugees dream of applying for asylum to emigrate to Western countries, but this brother gave up the opportunity to go to a Western country, instead risking his life to return to his war-torn homeland to spread the gospel.

Love Your Neighbor

James teaches, "If you really keep the royal law found in Scripture, 'Love your neighbor as yourself,' you are doing right" (2:8). James refers here to Leviticus 19:18 and 34, which Jesus himself taught as the second part of the great commandment in Luke 10:25–29 (cf. Matt 22:36–46; Mark 12:28–44). But in Luke's account, there is a twist in the story. The expert in the law responded to Jesus with a key question: "Who is my neighbor?" The subsequent illustration that Jesus gave—the Samaritan who helped the man who had been robbed—is so familiar to us that we forget the reason that Jesus told this story. After finishing the story, Jesus returned to the reason for

---

13 Wu, "Jordan, Home for Refugee," 25–32.

it, asking, "Which of these three do you think was a neighbor to the man who fell into the hands of robbers?" The law expert replied, "The one who had mercy on him." Jesus's response, "Go and do likewise," was another way of saying, "Go show mercy and love your neighbors who are not your people, just as the Samaritan in the story did" (Luke 10:36–37).

As evangelical Christians, we might sometimes ask the same question in our hearts: Who is my neighbor? In our age of globalization and migration, God has brought many least reached people to us from countries to which we may be unable or unwilling to go ourselves. Unfortunately, however, media and political hype often create fear and prejudice against migrants and refugees. During a furlough from serving in the Middle East, when conversing with ministry supporters in the United States, I sometimes heard them express concerns about or resistance to immigrants or refugees. But the Lord teaches us that the church of Christ should not imitate the world (Rom 12:1–2) or follow the values of the media and politicians but should live the gospel by the grace of Christ.

Jesus's illustration for answering the expert of the law was countercultural for his time. From various passages in the New Testament (e.g., John 4), we learn that there were racial and religious tensions between Jews and Samaritans at that time—they discriminated against each other. If we contextualize this parable for a modern context, the parable might translate into something like, "A White evangelical was robbed on a road trip, but a couple of White evangelical ministers passed by him and did not help him. In the end, it was a Black Muslim who helped him and paid the bill for him at the hospital." Why did Jesus tell a lengthy and culturally offensive story to answer the law expert's simple question about who is his neighbor? Is he not trying to say, "Your neighbor is the one who has mercy on you, and it does not matter what ethnic, religious, or political background they are from?" The most important thing is Jesus's instruction to *do likewise*—to show mercy to people from different ethnic, religious, or political backgrounds.

Churches involved in ministries among diaspora peoples find encouragement through experiencing God's mighty work firsthand. Many scholars have shown that diaspora peoples—whether new immigrants, refugees, or international students—are more likely to convert after leaving their home countries.[14] My previous research also shows how vibrant and missional Chinese immigrant churches are. It is evident the Lord has

---

14 Cf. Wu, *Mission through Diaspora*, 52.

been using immigrant churches to expand his kingdom for his glory. If a church is willing to support and send missionaries to a faraway country but does not welcome refugees from that country to enter their own, their understanding of the Great Commission may be inadequate. I sincerely pray that Christian churches around the world will regard migrants and refugees from least reached communities as lost, precious souls—and potential future ambassadors of Christ—brought to their doorstep.

Persevere like Job

James points us toward purpose and meaning in our trials when he tells us to "consider it pure joy, my brothers and sisters, whenever you face trials of many kinds, because you know that the testing of your faith produces perseverance" (1:2–3). More than just passively bracing ourselves until the trials pass, this passage advocates for a more active posture of endurance as we "let perseverance finish its work so that you may be mature and complete, not lacking anything" (1:4). James completes the thought with the promised outcome: "Blessed is the one who perseveres under trial because, having stood the test, that person will receive the crown of life that the Lord has promised to those who love him" (1:12).

Theology of Suffering

The world today is facing the challenges of plague, wars, natural disasters, and their consequences. In a time like this, a sound theology of suffering is essential for God's messengers who engage the world. Likewise, we must prepare ourselves for resistance and persecution in a hostile world. Years ago, the Lord led my husband and me to an underserved, least reached country. As the first of our network to reenter this field after a decade of absence, we had to connect and cooperate with fellow workers from other networks. We visited an elderly couple from another organization with decades of service in the Middle East who had visited that country several years prior when it was still turbulent and dangerous. After a warm greeting, they listened to our stories and experiences. I mentioned my previous experience of serving in a house church in East Asia, during which I had to evacuate the country after a few months due to a police raid. This veteran missionary couple told us in earnest that a sound theology of suffering was necessary to enter a war-torn country like our new field and that my experience of suffering and persecution would help. I believe their wise words are not only valuable to me but also relevant to the kingdom work in our time.

One of the most common questions that people ask regarding a theology of suffering is, Why do good people/Christians suffer? Job presents the classic story of good people suffering, and its message helps us to construct a solid theology of suffering. It is thus no surprise that James encouraged us with Job's perseverance as an example:

> Brothers and sisters, as an example of patience in the face of suffering, take the prophets who spoke in the name of the Lord. As you know, we count as blessed those who have persevered. You have heard of Job's perseverance and have seen what the Lord finally brought about. The Lord is full of compassion and mercy. (5:10–11)

As Christians, our prayers sometimes imply that God will protect devout Christians from evil and troubles. Perhaps due to the difficulty of answering the profound question of why good Christians suffer, we tend to simplify the problem of suffering by assuming that they will be protected from suffering. The same logic leads to another problematic belief: If some Christians suffer, they might not be good Christians. In fact, we are not the first believers who have tried to solve the problem of suffering by applying this logic. This closely resembles the theology of Job's friends, which states that if a person is successful in their life or ministry, they must be "righteous" or "blameless" and thus blessed by God. And if a person suffers calamity, then they must have done something unpleasing to the Lord. This kind of theology is similar to the prosperity gospel, but it has a more subtle outlook and is much more common among Christians. Such theology implies that our good deeds or strong faith are the sources of our blessings, not God himself. Whatever good happens to us, it becomes God's endorsement of us, proving that we are "good Christians." The blessings we have received become a means for us to boast and build up our self-righteousness.

However, James reminds us, "Believers in humble circumstances ought to take pride in their high position. But the rich should take pride in their humiliation—since they will pass away like a wildflower" (1:9–10). Job once enjoyed his wealth, prestige, and high position, but he suffered the tremendous humiliation of losing everything in an instant. At the end of Job, God showed up and rebuked Job's friends, saying, "I am angry with you and your two friends, because you have not spoken the truth about me, as my servant Job has" (Job 42:7). Apparently, God himself made the final judgment that Job's theology was more correct than his friends. John Hartley pointed out that Job's friends had a rigid understanding of the doctrine of God rewarding good and punishing evil. He said, "Because they encourage Job to repent primarily to escape his suffering and to receive God's blessing, they unsuspectingly tempt him to use God for personal gain, the essence of sin."[15]

The Problem of Suffering Christians

None of us wants to be like Job's friends, because none of us wants to be on the side of the "theologically incorrect." However, I have observed that humanity has a tendency to blame the victims, and Christians are not the exception. When missionaries suffer persecution or are killed on the field, voices often question whether the missionaries have done something unwise. A recent example was when our brother John Allen Chau was martyred in 2018. Even some Christians criticized him as unwise, without understanding how much he had prepared himself and followed the calling of the Lord.[16] Sometimes our theology is closer to Job's friends than it is to Job.

James urged, "If any of you lacks wisdom, you should ask God, who gives generously to all without finding fault, and it will be given to you" (1:5). The wisdom literature in the Bible includes Job, Proverbs, and Ecclesiastes. Though Proverbs teaches general principles of traditional wisdom, such as: "No harm overtakes the righteous, but the wicked have their fill of trouble" (12:21), there is no contradiction between Job and Proverbs. They complement each other. In addition, the writings of the prophets and the apostles all point to this truth: The righteous suffer. Many times the Lord has called several servants at the same time to preach the same message and do similar ministries, but the results were different. The prophet Uriah in Jeremiah preached the same prophecy as Jeremiah, but Uriah was killed by King Jehoiakim while Jeremiah's life was spared (Jer 26:20–24). In Acts, James the brother of John and Peter preached the same gospel. As a result, James was killed by King Herod, but Peter was rescued from prison by angels (Acts 12). Can we say that Uriah and James perished because they were unwise or not "good Christians"?

Years ago, on the night we left for a recent country of service, our field director prayed for us at his home: "Lord, we know that it will not be easy to win souls for you on this field... . We will go through many hardships and pains... . But it's all worth it because Jesus is worthy." As we obey the Lord's commandment and carry out his mission in this fallen world, we

---

15 Hartley, *Book of Job*, 48.

16 This led me to write an article to respond to some Christians' criticism: Wu, "They Will Reign," 4–6.

will suffer, but it is worth it for the cause of our Lord. The bottom line is this: If we do not believe good Christians will suffer, we might doubt God's goodness and lose faith when trials come. The foundations of a theology of suffering are twofold. First, good Christians suffer, and second, even if bad things happen to good Christians, God is still good. As James reminds us, "Don't be deceived, my dear brothers and sisters. Every good and perfect gift is from above, coming down from the Father of the heavenly lights, who does not change like shifting shadows" (1:16–17). The life of Job fully illustrates these two truths; Job's perseverance in the face of suffering can be an example to all believers.

Persevere in an Unjust World

One of the main reasons innocent people suffer in this world is because of the reality of injustice. We as messengers of the good news cannot ignore the problem of injustice while seeking to share the truth and righteousness of our Lord. The boldness of James in confronting the unjust deeds of the rich people in his letter is astounding:

> Now listen, you rich people, weep and wail because of the misery that is coming on you. Your wealth has rotted, and moths have eaten your clothes. Your gold and silver are corroded. Their corrosion will testify against you and eat your flesh like fire. You have hoarded wealth in the last days. Look! The wages you failed to pay the workers who mowed your fields are crying out against you. The cries of the harvesters have reached the ears of the Lord Almighty. You have lived on earth in luxury and self-indulgence. You have fattened yourselves in the day of slaughter. You have condemned and murdered the innocent one, who was not opposing you. (5:1–6)

We recently served in a war-torn country. We gained a deeper understanding of injustice through those years living in a country oppressed by tyranny, invaded by world powers, torn apart by bloody civil war, stolen by corrupt government and religious leaders. Criminals and murderers went unpunished, and rights and freedom were violated—the list can go on. Many times after I read the local news, I cried out to the Lord like a psalmist, "Oh Lord, how long must I witness all these injustices?"

In Comparison with Islam

In a world where injustice seems to prevail, Christianity is not alone in teaching "patience in suffering." For example, in Islam "*sabr*" ("endurance," "perseverance") is a highly valued virtue. The Qur'an promises a double reward to those who face trials and yet persevere on the right path (Q Al-Qasas 28:54). The Twelver Shi'a Muslims believe that *Ahl al-Bayt* ("People of the House," referring to the household of the Prophet Muhammad) were all unjustly treated. They believe in the redemptive power of the pain and martyrdom endured by the members of the *Ahl al-Bayt*, particularly Husayn, the grandson of Muhammad.[17] Muslims have a strong longing for justice, and Arab Muslims have a penchant for using the Arabic word *madhlum*, which means "oppressed" or "unjustly treated." Their collective sense of being unjustly treated often comes from colonial history, an example being the British mandates in the Middle East.[18] Yet what sustains them through injustice is the hope of future retaliation or man-made punishment so that justice will be served. In the country in which we served, the local people usually seek justice through their tribes. But since it is easy to get weapons there, the tribal solution often turned into armed tribal fights. At one time, our neighbors' adult sons were nearly killed during a tribal gunfight.

Both Judaism and Islam believe, "An eye for an eye, a tooth for a tooth." Biblical Christianity is the only faith that offers both a hope for final justice and a pathway to reconciliation and forgiveness in an unjust world. When our Lord comes, final justice will be fulfilled. As James encourages us,

> Be patient, then, brothers and sisters, until the Lord's coming. See how the farmer waits for the land to yield its valuable crop, patiently waiting for the autumn and spring rains. You too, be patient and stand firm, because the Lord's coming is near. (5:7–8)

With the assurance of final justice and the forgiveness of our sins by the blood of Jesus, we have the ability to forgive. Furthermore, through Christ, God gave us the ministry of reconciliation with God and with one another (2 Cor 5:18–21). Through the cross, we can put to death our hostility so that we have the hope of reconciliation (Eph 2:14–15).

Persevere with Hope

In our previous host country, the local churches endured dictatorship, foreign invasions, terrorism, and sectarian civil war. After one regime fell, the country was in chaos, and a coalition of foreign troops took control for a period. The local pastor we partnered with told us about a Christian woman

---

17 Campo, "ahl al-bayt," 23.

18 For example, Britain's decision on Mandatory Palestine (1920–1948) resulted in ongoing Palestine-Israel conflicts.

who served at his church more than a decade ago. In that dark time, she chose to stay, though her family had already emigrated to a Western country and as a Christian she could easily seek asylum as well. She was on fire for the Lord and desired to serve his church, and thus she chose to stay in her home country. One day as she was driving on the street and passed through a checkpoint, the Western soldiers shot her with machine guns in the car, perhaps due to a language barrier, fear, discrimination, or all of these factors. She did not have family in the country, so the pastor was the one who went to take her body. He was devastated. What an injustice it was. When we heard this story, we were heartbroken and felt guilty and ashamed.

The longer we lived and served there, the more we recognized the harms and traumas caused by the US invasion. My husband is American by birth. How could we reconcile with the local community and build a trusting relationship with the local church with such baggage? One day we had a ministry meeting with this local pastor, discussing how we could collaborate. In the middle of our meeting, my husband broke down and wept, recognizing the damage that our country has done to this country. With tears, he said he did not know how to love his own country anymore. After a few seconds of silence in the room, the local pastor told us a story.

A few years prior, our local pastor was invited to the United States to speak. One day he was preaching in a church, and after the service the American pastor told him that there were a few wounded American soldiers who fought his country present in his church that day. He told the American pastor that he would like to meet the American soldiers. He saw these wounded soldiers who once fought his country and now sat on wheelchairs, and he had sympathy for them, even though he did not agree with what they had done to his country. After all this, he decided to wash their feet.

We were moved by the humility of the local pastor. We realized he was extending forgiveness to our country and us by telling us this story. In this way, we could reach reconciliation. Since then, we have built a deep, close, and trusting relationship with this local pastor and his church. As we served in that country, we also recognized that, with so much violence, bloodshed, and injustice done there, God has used it to bring many brokenhearted local people to seek him. We witness God's mighty work in this beautiful yet broken country, where people meant it for evil, "but God intended it for good" (Gen 50:20). There is hope in our sufferings and perseverance.

A Final Word

The message of James is relevant in our time. Like the believers in James's day who were scattered in the first-century Roman Empire (1:1), we as God's children are also among the nations as scattered seeds for God's kingdom. While we persevere in trials, we sprout and spread our vines. James provides us with the much-needed exhortation and wisdom to stand firm when we witness conflicts and injustice in the world. As James exhorted us, "The wisdom that comes from heaven is first of all pure; then peace-loving, considerate, submissive, full of mercy and good fruit, impartial and sincere. Peacemakers who sow in peace reap a harvest of righteousness" (3:17–18). May we followers of Jesus be peacemakers instead of sowing fear, prejudice, or hatred in a time of division and polarization. As we seek to spread the True Light in a time of darkness and patiently wait for our Lord's return (5:7), considering trials pure joy (1:2) because we trust the final word and promise of our Lord, "I am with you always" (Matt 28:20) and "I am coming soon" (Rev 22:7).

Bibliography

Blomberg, Craig L., and Mariam J. Kamell. *James.* Zondervan Exegetical Commentary on the New Testament 16. Grand Rapids: Zondervan, 2008.

Campo, Juan Eduardo. "ahl al-bayt." In *Encyclopedia of Islam*, edited by Juan Eduardo Campo, 23. New York: Checkmark Books, 2009.

Carson, D. A., and Douglas Moo. *An Introduction to the New Testament.* 2nd ed. Grand Rapids: Zondervan, 2005.

Cohen, Robin. *Global Diasporas: An Introduction.* Seattle: University of Washington Press, 1997.

Escobar, Samuel. "Migration: Avenue and Challenge to Mission." *Missiology* 31, no. 1 (2003): 17–28.

Hartley, John E. *The Book of Job.* New International Commentary on the Old Testament. Grand Rapids: Eerdmans, 1988.

Moo, Douglas J. *The Letter of James.* Pillar New Testament Commentary. Grand Rapids: Eerdmans, 2000.

Rah, Soong-Chan. *The Next Evangelicalism: Freeing the Church from Western Cultural Captivity.* Downers Grove, IL: InterVarsity Press, 2009.

Tölölyan, Khachig. "Rethinking Diaspora(s): Stateless Power in the Transnational Moment." *Diaspora* 5, no. 1 (1996): 3–36.

Wan, Enoch. "Diaspora Missiology." *Evangelical Missiological Society Occasional Bulletin* 20, no. 2 (2007): 3–7.

Wan, Enoch, ed. *Diaspora Missiology: Theory, Methodology, and Practice.* Portland: Institute of Diaspora Studies, 2011.

Wu, Jeanne. "Jordan, Home for Refugee: Two Challenges." In *Refugee Diaspora: Missions amid the Greatest Humanitarian Crisis of Our Times*, edited by Sam George and Miriam Adeney, 25–32. Pasadena, CA: William Carey Library, 2018.

Wu, Jeanne. *Mission through Diaspora: The Case of the Chinese Church in the USA*. Carlisle: Langham, 2016.

Wu, Jeanne. "'They Will Reign with Him for a Thousand Years': Exploring the Missiology of Persecution." *Evangelical Missions Quarterly* 56, no. 2 (2020): 4–6.

Zylstra, Sarah Eekhoff. "One Year Later, Christians in Ukraine Say, 'We Wouldn't Want to Be Anywhere Else.'" *The Gospel Coalition*, 2023.

Chapter 18

Prayer, Worship, and Holistic Mission in the Letter of James

Grant LeMarquand

This chapter will explore the intersection between the themes of prayer and mission. Even with a limited focus on prayer and mission in James, we immediately encounter two problems. First, concerning prayer. Scholarship on James tends to view the letter as a book about action rather than about contemplation. For example, Scot McKnight's commentary considers the central themes to be God and ethics. The "God" section has two paragraphs; the "ethics" section has eleven.[1] The impression is that James is simply a pragmatic text. Douglas J. Moo's commentary has a section on eight "Theological Emphases of the Letter."[2] He includes a paragraph on prayer (in the section on "The Christian Life"), but clearly he considers "prayer" a secondary theme.[3] The theological summaries of McKnight and Moo are an improvement over the often repeated assertion of Dibelius that the "religiosity [of James] is consistently oriented toward the practical and betrays no definite 'theology.'"[4] It should be acknowledged that James is a thoroughly practical letter but, in the words of Moo, "It will be a sad day for the church when such 'practical divinity' is not considered 'theology.'"[5] Scholars, therefore, acknowledge the relative importance of prayer in James, but few go as far as Sophie Laws, who states that "an interest in prayer, its character and its power, is a marked feature of the epistle."[6] For most, prayer is a subtopic in the midst of a work that emphasizes action. One of the goals of this chapter is to argue that James gives prayer a higher profile than is sometimes acknowledged.

On the subject of "mission" we face a different problem. As is sometimes the case, whether one notices "mission" in a text depends on what one means by the word. Ferdinand Hahn leaves James out of his discussion of mission; Donald Senior gives James two sentences, explaining that a theology of "witness" might be inferred from James but denying that James actually reflects on "the witness value of … good deeds"; Eckhard J. Schnabel's

---

1 McKnight, *Letter of James*, 42–47.

2 Moo, *Letter of James*, 40–55.

3 Moo, 52.

4 Dibelius, *James*, 25.

5 Moo, *Letter of James*, 41.

6 Laws, *Epistle of James*, 56.

Early Christian Mission contains ten references to James in a work of over 1,900 pages, the most significant of which is the mention that James uses the language of "new birth" to describe conversion.[7] These authors (more could be added) conceive of mission in a restricted sense: Mission is primarily verbal witness to the good news of God in Jesus, which leads to conversion. Mission is evangelism.

However, there is a growing consensus among missiologists that the idea of the mission of the church should not be reduced to verbal proclamation but rather should include world-facing action oriented to the kingdom of God. There is little doubt that this shift in missional thinking has occurred largely because of the more holistic focus of non-Western Christianity. The church in the Majority World is not afraid to proclaim the message of the gospel, but most do not believe that the gospel is something that should be only proclaimed verbally. The gospel must be lived. As one African bishop put it while dismissing the congregation, "Go out and preach the gospel—but remember, empty stomachs have no ears."[8] Word and action cannot be separated; evangelism and social justice are not antithetical. If the gospel is about God's kingdom, then God's rule extends to every aspect of life. As Ron Sider asked pointedly, "What If We Defined the Gospel the Way Jesus Did?" Sider answers his own question:

> If the gospel is not just forgiveness of sins, but the Good News of the kingdom of God, we cannot separate a reconciled relationship with God and a reconciled relationship with brothers and sisters… . Reconciled social and economic relationships in the body of Christ are one part of salvation… . Ministering to both the physical and spiritual needs of people is not some optional possibility, but essential to the gospel… . The Christian community … will always challenge what is wrong in the status quo… . Any sharing of the gospel that does not include significant concern for the poor is unbiblical… . There must always be a sharp distinction between the church and the world… . We cannot share the gospel adequately just by preaching… . Words and deeds must go together.[9]

If mission is holistic and not only the verbal proclamation of forgiveness of sins leading to conversion, then the letter of James is thoroughly missional.

---

7 Hahn, *Mission in the New Testament*; Senior and Stuhmueller, *Biblical Foundations for Mission*, 309 [Senior wrote the New Testament]; Schnabel, *Early Christian Mission*, 1565.

8 Archbishop David Gitari, 1997.

9 Sider, "What If We Defined the Gospel," 28–30.

Thankfully some recent interpreters have seen James as missional.[10] One of the earliest biblical scholars to read James from a missional perspective (although she did not use the term "missional") was the Latin American scholar Elsa Támez. For her, the primary concern is the poor. James is not merely concerned for the poor, who seem to be his primary audience, but he is also convinced that people are poor because they are oppressed (2:6). The rich, therefore, are in grave danger of judgment (5:1–2). In the words of Támez, "If the Letter of James were sent to the Christian communities of certain countries that suffer from violence and exploitation, it would very possibly be intercepted by government security agencies. The document would be branded as subversive."[11] Perhaps there is hope that we can spin missional gold from the so-called straw of the letter of James.

In what follows I will attempt to bring together the vertical and the horizontal dimensions of the Christian life as they are found in James: the vertical, God-centered concern (prayer) and horizontal practical concern for those in need (mission).[12]

There are six passages in James that engage the subject of prayer. We will examine these, asking what missiological implications James intends for his readers. Although the structure of James is in dispute, the passages that mention prayer are scattered throughout the letter, implying that James viewed prayer as a key component of every aspect of the Christian life.

Prayer for Wisdom (1:5-8)

James is, first of all, a letter. Whether it is an actual letter, or an essay or sermon published to resemble a letter, it contains formal elements of a Hellenistic letter.[13] For example, James begins with the ubiquitous letter-

---

10 See, e.g., Green, "Reading James Missionally"; Joubert, "*Homo Reciprocus* No More."

11 Támez, *Scandalous Message*, 1.

12 What we might call the missional rehabilitation of James is only beginning to work its way into New Testament scholarship. Surprisingly, many missiologists have not yet reflected on the potential of the letter. Bosch's *Transforming Mission* has no reference to James in the index; Goheen's *Introducing Christian Mission Today* has one reference; Tennent's *Invitation to World Missions* has two references; and Wrongemann's three-volume (nearly 1,500-page) work, *Intercultural Theology*, has two references.

13 Early in the twentieth century Deissmann (*St Paul*) introduced the distinction between "letters" and "epistles." For him Paul's letters were real, written to an actual group of people. Epistles such as James, 1 and 2 Peter and Jude, were not "true" letters, but essays for a general audience. Deissmann was criticized for his implication that "true" letters were "hastily written and relatively formless," but the distinction between specific and general audiences has remained commonplace in New Testament studies (Jervis, *Purpose of Romans*, 12–13).

opening formula: (a) sender, (b) receiver, (c) greetings.[14] According to Richard J. Bauckham, the opening itself is sufficient to designate James as a letter: "The formal prescript or letter opening is sufficient to make it a letter. An ancient letter did not need to have any other generic features specific to a letter in order to make it a letter."[15] The closing is much less epistolary, although 5:12–20, which appears to be part of a concluding exhortation, certainly has similarities to other letters.

For our purposes, the letter's opening is significant because in most Hellenistic letters, a prayer or a "health wish" follows immediately after the prescript. As Stanley Stowers writes, "Often the greeting was followed by a prayer for the recipient, sometimes by a wish for the recipient's health, and occasionally by a statement of thanksgiving to a god or gods."[16] Paul's letters certainly follow this pattern, the opening greeting followed by a prayer section, using words of thanksgiving (εὐχαριστεῶ) or blessing (εὐλογητός in 2 Cor and Eph).

Like Hellenistic letters and Pauline letters, the opening of James focuses on prayer, although with a significant difference. Rather than reporting on what he is praying for his audience, James launches into teaching *about* prayer.

> If any of you is lacking in wisdom, ask God, who gives to all generously and ungrudgingly, and it will be given you. But ask in faith, never doubting, for the one who doubts is like a wave of the sea, driven and tossed by the wind; for the doubter, being double-minded and unstable in every way, must not expect to receive anything from the Lord. (1:5–8)[17]

The reference to "wisdom" in verse 5 modifies our designation of James as a letter. As scholars agree, James is a wisdom writing. Some reject the notion that it is a letter at all, simply calling it an example of "paraenesis," that is, "wisdom instruction," a common form of literature consisting largely of a collection of practical teaching.[18] The structure of James, which moves from topic to topic with loose connections between sections, certainly betrays the work as a wisdom book. Based on its form and content, it might be wise to designate the book as a "wisdom letter."

---

14 All of the New Testament books known as letters follow this pattern, as well as letters contained within other books: Acts 15:23; 23:26; Revelation 1:4.

15 Bauckham, "James and Jesus," 109–10.

16 Stowers, *Letter Writing*, 20. For examples, see the collection by White, *Light from Ancient Letters*.

17 All Scripture quotations are from the NRSV unless otherwise noted.

18 See Dibelius, *James*, 1–11.

The subject of praying for wisdom should remind the attentive reader of another prayer for wisdom, the prayer of Solomon,

> "Give me now wisdom and knowledge to go out and come in before this people, for who can rule this great people of yours?" God answered Solomon, "Because this was in your heart, and you … have asked for wisdom and knowledge for yourself that you may rule my people over whom I have made you king, wisdom and knowledge are granted to you." (2 Chr 1:10–12)

Solomon's request is granted so that he might be faithful in ruling Israel. James begins his instruction by democratizing the royal petition. God's wisdom, says James 1:5, is available to "any of you" (τις ὑμῶν). The basis for James's confidence is the character of God himself: "who gives to all generously and ungrudgingly" (1:5).

There is a qualification, however, because prayer, says 1:6, must be made "in faith" (ἐν πίστει), "never doubting" (μηδὲν διακρινόμενος). Like much of what we read in James, there is an echo of the teaching of Jesus, who was often quick to commend the "faith" (πίστις) of those he healed (e.g., Mark 2:5; 5:34).

The missional implication of this admonition is that the Christian life is not an easy voyage. There are waves and winds (1:6). The disciple will need God's gift of wisdom to negotiate these dangers. Followers of Jesus are in unfriendly waters; they are "in the dispersion" (ἐν τῇ διασπορᾷ, 1:1). They are scattered and, to a degree, homeless. This dispersed people will meet various kinds of trials (1:2). Throughout his epistle James will warn his readers of dangers: Some are from without, like the devil (3:15; 4:7) and the rich who oppress them (2:6), and some are from within, like the temptation to discriminate (2:1–13), the tongue (3:1–12), and cravings (4:1). The antidote to these enemies is wisdom—and wisdom is obtained by *prayer.* Therefore, if one needs wisdom "let him ask" (αἰτείτω, 1:5, 6), knowing that God is a gracious giver (1:5, 17). With trust in God and the wisdom he grants, believers can endeavor to participate in God's mission with confidence. As Graham Paul Dancy writes, "Wisdom is not only a gift from God, it is necessary for the mission of God. James's prioritization of wisdom suggests that the communities he writes to are to be contrast communities that are attractional in nature."[19]

---

19 Dancy, "Missional Reading," 177.

Discrimination in the Worship Assembly (2:1–7)

At first glance, James 2:1–7 does not look like a promising text for exploring either of our topics, prayer or mission. The usual language for prayer does not appear, and the passage seems to deal with an "in-house" problem rather than an outward-facing issue. But another look is instructive. First, concerning prayer, the social context of the problem James is addressing is corporate worship. Second, concerning mission, James expects outsiders to be welcomed into the Christian worship space. The way that both rich and poor are welcomed illuminates the nature of the gospel and the Christian community.

> My brothers and sisters, do you with your acts of favoritism really believe in our glorious Lord Jesus Christ? For if a person with gold rings and in fine clothes comes into your assembly, and if a poor person in dirty clothes also comes in, and if you take notice of the one wearing the fine clothes and say, "Have a seat here, please," while to the one who is poor you say, "Stand there," or, "Sit at my feet," have you not made distinctions among yourselves, and become judges with evil thoughts? Listen, my beloved brothers and sisters. Has not God chosen the poor in the world to be rich in faith and to be heirs of the kingdom that he has promised to those who love him? But you have dishonored the poor. Is it not the rich who oppress you? Is it not they who drag you into court? Is it not they who blaspheme the excellent name that was invoked over you? (2:1–7)

Prayer is not merely a private practice; it is also a corporate activity in which the gathered community engages in praise and intercession. The NRSV, as well as other English translations, sets this passage in the "assembly" (2:2). Although one might have expected James to use the term ἐκκλησία ("church," "assembly"), James uses the word συναγωγὴ ("meeting," "assembly," "synagogue"). The Septuagint uses this term in reference to both "the meeting and the community assembly, the religious fellowship."[20] In the New Testament period, it often designated the Jewish worship space, the building itself. Dibelius has gathered evidence showing that early Christians sometimes used the term for their own worship gatherings: Ignatius of Antioch encourages frequent gatherings (συναγωγαί). The Shepherd of Hermas speaks of the Christian assembly as "a synagogue (συναγωγὴν) of the righteous." Justin Martyr, and Eusebius (quoting Dionysius of Alexandria), use the term similarly.[21] Within the New Testament, Hebrews 10:25 uses the

---

20 Dibelius, *James*, 133.
21 Dibelius, 133.

compound verb (μὴ ἐγκαταλείποντες τὴν ἐπισυναγωγὴν ἑαυτῶν): "Do not neglect the assembling ('synagoguing') of yourselves together."[22] Dibelius reasons that the term fell into disuse because it would conjure up thoughts of Jewish, rather than Christian, assemblies.[23]

A second term in our passage may confirm the corporate worship setting of James 2:1–7. At the end of the paragraph, James appeals to his readers on the basis of a particular act of worship, Christian baptism: "Is it not they [the rich] who blaspheme the excellent name that was invoked over you?" Noting that in the Old Testament "the name" of YHWH was invoked over his people (Deut 28:10; 2 Chr 7:14; Dan 9:19) and that in the New Testament, the name of Jesus is often substituted for the name of YHWH, Bauckham observes that in Acts baptism was performed "in the name of Jesus" (Acts 2:38; 8:16; 10:48; 19:5). Therefore, says Bauckham, "The 'beautiful name' invoked over Christians according to James 2:7 is most likely the name of Jesus invoked in baptism."[24] Bauckham's purpose is to assert that James (although mentioning Jesus only twice in the letter in 1:1 and 2:1) had an implicitly high Christology. Our purpose is more modest: The invocation of the beautiful name of Jesus reinforces the social location of James 2:1–7 as a description of an early Christian worship service.

If we are right in thinking that James 2:1–7 is discussing what should and should not happen in a Christian worship service, a fruitful comparison can be made between this James text and a Pauline text, 1 Corinthians 11:17–34. Both texts raise an ethical concern about the place of the rich and the poor in Christian worship settings, but there are differences. In 1 Corinthians, both groups are members of the Christian community: "There are divisions among you" (11:18). In James, both the rich and the poor are visitors to the assembly: "For if a person with gold rings and in fine clothes comes into your assembly, and if a poor person in dirty clothes also comes in" (2:2). Paul does envision the possibility that visitors may show up to a Christian gathering (1 Cor 14:16, 24–25), but his main concern when discussing the Lord's Supper is the division between rich and poor believers.[25]

Given that the social setting of James 2:1–7 is Christian worship, what is the missiological impact of what James has to say? James is concerned that the public image of the church reflects God's character. James 3:17 states

---

22   My translation.

23   Dibelius, 134.

24   Bauckham, "James and Jesus," 135.

25   Hays, *First Corinthians*, 192–206; Henderson, "If Anyone Hungers."

that "the wisdom from above" (that is, "from God") is "without partiality." If God does not show favoritism, neither should God's people. To give preference to a rich visitor, especially since the rich oppress the poor (2:6–7), dishonors not only the poor but God, who has chosen the poor. Christian worship must reflect God's care for those who are weak and vulnerable. Both the rich and the poor are welcome to Christian "synagogues," but they enter as equal before the creator. The Christian community is called to love God (2:5), just as Israel was (Deut 6:4–5). The Christian community cannot be an attractional witness if the poor are discriminated against. It is significant, therefore, that following James 2:1–7 is a passage concerning loving one's neighbor (2:8–13). Love for God should produce love for others, especially those in need of mercy (2:13).

Blessing and Cursing (3:9-10)

One of James's favorite themes is the regulation of speech. He advises his readers to "be quick to listen, slow to speak" (1:19). To be devout includes keeping a firm rein on the tongue (1:26). Much of chapter 3 is given to the subject of speech, especially the speech of those who teach in the church, since teachers "will be judged with greater strictness" (3:1). He uses imagery to warn about the dangers of the tongue: It is like a bit in a horse's mouth (3:3), like the rudder of a ship, like a spark that can light a forest fire (3:4–5). The tongue is small but can have a great effect, for good or for ill. This includes the tongue at prayer:

> With it [the tongue] we bless the Lord and Father, and with it we curse those who are made in the likeness of God. From the same mouth come blessing and cursing. My brothers and sisters, this ought not to be so. (3:9–10)

Just as James tells his readers that faith must be proved genuine by works (2:14–26), he now instructs them to be genuine with their words: To utter blessings to God but then curse those made in God's image is hypocritical. This aligns well with what James says about "religion." The term that James uses for religion in 1:26–27 is θρησκεία, an "expression of devotion to transcendent beings, esp. as it expresses itself in cultic rites, *worship*."[26] Religion is worthless if the tongue is not controlled (1:26); real devotion to God expresses itself in caring for vulnerable widows and orphans—as well as keeping oneself pure (1:27). In other words, love for God and love for one's neighbor cannot be separated (2:8). In his section on the tongue (3:1–12), James warns that such

---

26 Danker, Bauer, Arndt, and Gingrich, *Greek-English Lexicon*, 459, emphasis original.

hypocrisy leads to judgment (3:1), having its origin in hell (γεέννα) itself (3:6). The inconsistency of blessing God and cursing others "makes moral and logical nonsense from James's theological standpoint."[27] Missiologically, nothing can be more damaging to Christian witness than believers who speak and act in ways that contradict their profession of faith. There is "no sense here that this [prohibition on cursing] is limited to people within the community."[28] Rather, James uses the creation account (Gen 1:26) to assert that *all people*, not just the Christian community, are deserving of respect. For James, gospel witness is damaged when speech directed toward people outside of the faith contradicts speech used in prayer.

Asking Rightly and Drawing Near to God (4:1–3, 7–10)

Writing about community conflict (4:1–10), James twice refers to prayer. First, he suggests that some prayer requests are simply wrong.

> Those conflicts and disputes among you, where do they come from? Do they not come from your cravings that are at war within you? You want something and do not have it; so you commit murder. And you covet something and cannot obtain it; so you engage in disputes and conflicts. You do not have, because you do not ask. You ask and do not receive, because you ask wrongly, in order to spend what you get on your pleasures. (4:1–3)

Conflict originates in "craving." This disposition leads to disobedience of God's law: "you commit murder … you covet." Instead of being models of discipleship, James's interlocutors have neglected prayer ("you do not ask") or else prayed inappropriately ("you ask wrongly"). Prayers that James deems problematic are utterances seeking to fulfill covetous desires: "in order to spend what you get on your pleasures." Luke Timothy Johnson has captured the dynamic well: "The gift-giving God is here manipulated as a kind of vending machine precisely for purposes of self-gratification."[29] This "faulty prayer" is another example of behavior damaging to the community's public witness.[30]

James provides alternative modes of prayer.

> Submit yourselves therefore to God. Resist the devil, and he will flee from you. Draw near to God, and he will draw near to you. Cleanse your

---

27 Davids, *Epistle of James*, 146.

28 Dancy, "Missional Reading," 325–26.

29 Johnson, *Letter of James*, 278.

30 Dancy, "Missional Reading," 196.

> hands, you sinners, and purify your hearts, you double-minded. Lament
> and mourn and weep. Let your laughter be turned into mourning and
> your joy into dejection. Humble yourselves before the Lord, and he will
> exalt you. (4:7–10)

James's audience is encouraged to "submit" to God (4:7), to "humble yourselves before the Lord" (4:10). Between these two synonyms that bracket 4:7–10, James asserts that prayer is required. First, James's readers should "draw near" to God. The wording of 4:8 is cultic language from the worship of Israel—to "draw near" is to come into God's presence (Exod 12:48; 16:9; Lev 9:7; 21:18; Isa 58:2). Not every instance of the term "draw near" in the Old Testament is related to worship, but James links the term together with the phrases "cleanse your hands" and "purify your hearts." Here James echoes the psalmist who, describing the ascent to the temple mount asks, "Who shall ascend the hill of the LORD? And who shall stand in his holy place?" (Ps 24:3). The answer: "Those who have *clean hands* and *pure hearts*" (24:4, emphasis added). The cluster of phrases in James 4:8 ("draw near," "cleanse your hands," "purify your hearts") is Old Testament worship language transferred to the community of Christ-followers.[31] James's addressees are sinful, engaging in self-serving activity—in order to "draw near" they need cleansing. Repentance is needed, and so James requires a particular disposition: they must "lament and mourn and weep" (4:9).

The Christian community in conflict must recognize the need for cleansing. They must humble themselves, submitting to God, and in doing so learn that God is ready to meet them: "He will draw near to you." A corollary of drawing near to God is to "resist the devil … he will flee" (4:7). The story of the temptation narrative is possibly in the background here (Matt 4:1–11; Mark 1:12–13; Luke 4:1–13). James reminds his readers that the Christian life, like the life of Jesus, involves spiritual conflict. A missional implication can be seen here: Just as Jesus began his mission by drawing near to God and resisting the devil, the followers of Jesus prepare for their lives in a sinful world by resisting the evil one and finding communion with God. Prayer, including prayers of repentance and spiritual warfare, is essential for mission.

The Cry of the Poor (5:1-6)

In James 5, the author returns to a theme he stressed near the beginning of his letter: poverty and riches, the rich and the poor (1:9–11; 2:1–13). There is still a chance for the rich, but unless they repent, they are liable to judgment:

---

31 McKnight (*Letter of James,* 350–51) is doubtful that "drawing near" in James 4:8 is cultic, although he recognizes the cultic connections in the language of "cleansing" and "purification" and agrees that Psalm 24:3–4 has played a role in James's language here.

Come now, you rich people, weep and wail for the miseries that are coming to you. Your riches have rotted, and your clothes are motheaten. Your gold and silver have rusted, and their rust will be evidence against you, and it will eat your flesh like fire. You have laid up treasure for the last days. (5:1–3)

In language reminiscent of the Sermon on the Mount (Matt 6:19–21), James proclaims that the goods of this world are passing away and will not help the rich at the judgment.

In 5:4, James turns to the poor who pray for justice: "Listen! The wages of the laborers who mowed your fields, which you kept back by fraud, cry out, and the cries of the harvesters have reached the ears of the Lord of hosts." The poor are not destitute because they are lazy, but because they are oppressed. Being defrauded, they appeal to God. The Scriptures are replete with examples of the desperate calling to God for deliverance and of God responding by coming to judge and to save.[32] Perhaps the most paradigmatic parallel can be found in Exodus 2–3, where we hear of the oppression of God's people under Pharaoh. In the midst of slavery, the people of Israel cried to God for deliverance (2:24). Hearing their cries, God promised to deliver (2:25; 3:7–9).

James 5:1–6 follows this exodus paradigm—the rich (farmers in this case) have oppressed their workers, the workers appeal to God, and God comes down. The prayers of the poor, says James, are not futile; they are effective. The cries of the oppressed have already (note the perfect tense εἰσεληλύθασιν) reached God's ears.

In Exodus, we see God's missional intent. His will is to save—and to make a people for himself in response to pleas for deliverance. The liberation of Israel from oppression is not an end in itself. God has a purpose for his people: They are to witness to God's grace to the whole world, for "the whole earth is mine," says the Lord (Exod 19:5). The rescue of Israel from Egypt prefigures God's deliverance in Christ. This does not mean we can spiritualize the exodus. It is still true that God hears the cry of the poor, as James tells us in 5:1–6. Any mission theology that neglects those in tangible need is truncated. As we saw at the beginning of this chapter, "any sharing of the gospel that does not include significant concern for the poor is unbiblical."[33]

---

32 See Martin, *James*, 179, for parallels.

33 Sider, "What If We Defined the Gospel," 29.

Prayer for Healing and Forgiveness (5:13–18)

Our letter's final instruction (5:12–20) includes an admonition to pray (vv. 13–18), which is in line with other early Christian letters. Almost every New Testament letter closes with some mention of prayer: either prayer requests, a doxology, a benediction, or some combination of these elements. James differs from other letters in that his final mention of prayer is didactic.

> Are any among you suffering? They should pray. Are any cheerful? They should sing songs of praise. Are any among you sick? They should call for the elders of the church and have them pray over them, anointing them with oil in the name of the Lord. The prayer of faith will save the sick, and the Lord will raise them up; and anyone who has committed sins will be forgiven. Therefore confess your sins to one another, and pray for one another, so that you may be healed. The prayer of the righteous is powerful and effective. Elijah was a human being like us, and he prayed fervently that it might not rain, and for three years and six months it did not rain on the earth. Then he prayed again, and the heaven gave rain and the earth yielded its harvest. (5:13–18)

In verse 13, James commends prayer for every situation in the Christian life. Whether the believer is suffering, cheerful, or ill, some form of turning to God is always appropriate. A notable instruction to the cheerful is the imperative ψαλλέτω ("they should sing songs of praise"), which suggests that the book of Psalms was a primary source for the singing in the early church, although a variety of hymns and songs seems to have been used (see Eph 5:19; Col 3:16).

The final condition James mentions, sickness, leads to a description of healing prayer. James implies that a sick person may be in a weakened spiritual state. Therefore, the spiritually wise should be called upon (τοὺς πρεσβυτέρους τῆς ἐκκλησίας) to intercede (5:14). The presence of spiritual leaders does not imply that other believers would be excluded from the time of prayer.

James also commends anointing the sick person in the name of Jesus, literally, "in the name of the Lord" (ἐν τῷ ὀνόματι τοῦ κυρίου), "the Lord" here being the Lord Jesus.[34] Dibelius notes that the oil is "not … a natural medication," but he goes beyond the evidence assuming that the ritual is an exorcism.[35] The Gospel of Mark distinguishes healing (with anointing) from

---

34 Hurtado, *Lord Jesus Christ*, 200n89.

35 Dibelius, *James*, 252.

exorcism: "They cast out many demons, and anointed with oil many who were sick and cured them" (6:13). Likely, the anointing James describes is an act of consecration or spiritual purification.[36] The action is not magical. The oil does not work automatically, and the name of Jesus is not an incantation; rather the act of praying "over" the sick person implies the desire of the intercessors for the healing presence of the Lord himself.[37]

Although not automatic, prayer is effective: The sick person will be "saved" (σῴζω) by "the prayer of faith" (Jas 5:15). Several elements of 5:15 qualify any notion that physical healing is guaranteed. First, the term "saved" is somewhat ambiguous. Although it is often used of physical healing (e.g., Luke 8:50), the word can describe a wide variety of situations from which a person might be rescued. As well, James says that the prayer that saves is the prayer of "faith." In this passage, the faith is that of the gathered community. This excludes any notion that a sick person who is not healed can be blamed for lacking faith. Finally, it is not the community, the oil, or even the prayer that will heal. Rather, the Lord will raise up the prayer recipient (Jas 5:15). Although prayer is commended, healing cannot be attributed to anyone except the Lord himself.

At the end of 5:15, James broadens the notion of healing beyond the physical, asserting that healing prayer may lead also to forgiveness. Although Scripture (and human experience) affirms that some sickness is caused by sin, we must guard against the notion that every sickness is caused by a particular sin. John's Gospel certainly rejects this idea (9:2–3). James 5 teaches that there *may* be cases where the sickness has been caused by sin (cf. Mark 2:5), but it is clear that this is not a universal experience. James uses conditional language: "Anyone who committed sins will be forgiven" could just as easily be translated "*If* the person has committed sins." Having raised the issue of forgiveness, James pivots to the importance of confession (5:16). Just as prayer for healing may lead to forgiveness, so prayers of confession may lead to healing.

Finally, in 5:16–18 James notes the efficacy of faith in prayer, using the example of Elijah. Rather than declaring that Elijah must have been an especially powerful man of God, James asserts the opposite: Elijah was ordinary. He was "a human being like us" (5:17). The Elijah story teaches that *anyone* who prays with trust in God can pray effectively.

---

36 McKnight, *Letter of James*, 439.

37 Cf. Ajibade, "Anointing the Sick," 166–77.

Missiologically, although James is speaking of prayer within the Christian community, we know that healing was an important factor in the growth of the early church. Jesus's ministry was a ministry of both teaching and healing. The early church followed the pattern of Jesus, and the book of Acts suggests that the signs and wonders experienced in mission led to church growth (2:43–47; 5:12–16; 6:7–8).

Conclusion

James's letter describes "religion" as caring for widows and orphans, and keeping unstained from the world (1:27), thereby keeping united things that Christians have sometimes separated: justice and mercy for the poor on the one hand, and personal holiness on the other.[38] James teaches that religious actions (prayer and worship) have holistic missional implications. The worship of the Christian community must reflect God's love for the poor, not giving preferential treatment to the rich (2:1–7). Making requests of God must come from pure motives, not selfish desires, and should result in peaceful interpersonal relationships (1:5–8; 4:2–3, 7–10). Prayers for physical healing are not divorced from issues of forgiveness of sins (5:13–20). Acts of prayer and worship, often seen as purely vertical religious performances between human beings and God, always have horizontal, missional implications, thereby reflecting the great theme of James's letter: "Faith by itself, if it has no works, is dead" (2:17).

Bibliography

Ajibade, Ezekiel A. "Anointing the Sick with Oil: An Exegetical Study of James 5:14–15." *Ogbomosho Journal of Theology* 13, no. 2 (2008): 166–77.

Bauckham, Richard J. "James and Jesus." In *The Brother of Jesus: James the Just and His Mission*, edited by Bruce Chilton and Jacob Neusner, 100–35. Louisville: Westminster John Knox, 2001.

Bosch, David. *Transforming Mission: Paradigm Shifts in Theology of Mission.* American Society of Missiology Series 16. Maryknoll, NY: Orbis Books, 1991.

Dancy, Graham Paul. "A Missional Reading of the Letter of James: Hearing the Voice of James in Mission." PhD diss., University of Gloucestershire, 2021.

---

38 For a helpful exposition of this verse, see Kamell, "James 1:27 and the Church's Call."

Danker, Frederick W., Walter Bauer, William F. Arndt, and F. Wilbur Gingrich. *A Greek-English Lexicon of the New Testament and Other Early Christian Literature*. 3rd ed. Chicago: University of Chicago Press, 2000.

Davids, Peter H. *The Epistle of James: A Commentary on the Greek Text*. New International Greek Testament Commentary. Grand Rapids: Eerdmans, 1982.

Deissmann, G. A. *St Paul: A Study in Social and Religious History*. Translated by L. R. M. Strachan. London: Hodder & Stoughton, 1912.

Dibelius, Martin. *James: A Commentary on the Epistle of James*. Revised by Heinrich Greeven. Translated by Michael A. Williams. Edited by Helmut Koester. Hermeneia. 11th ed. Philadelphia: Fortress, 1975.

Goheen, Michael W. *Introducing Christian Mission Today: Scripture, History and Issues*. Downers Grove, IL: IVP Academic, 2014.

Green, Joel B. "Reading James Missionally." In *Reading the Bible Missionally*, edited by Michael W. Goheen, 194–212. Grand Rapids: Eerdmans, 2016.

Hahn, Ferdinand. *Mission in the New Testament*. Translated by Frank Clarke. Studies in Biblical Theology 47. London: SCM, 1965.

Hays, Richard B. *First Corinthians*. Interpretation. Louisville: Westminster John Knox, 1997.

Henderson, Suzanne Watts. "'If Anyone Hungers …': An Integrated Reading of 1 Cor 11.17–34." *New Testament Studies* 48, no. 2 (2002): 195–208.

Hurtado, Larry W. *Lord Jesus Christ: Devotion to Jesus in Earliest Christianity*. Grand Rapids: Eerdmans, 2003.

Jervis, L. Ann. *The Purpose of Romans: A Comparative Letter Structure Investigation*. Journal for the Study of the New Testament Supplement 55. Sheffield: Sheffield Academic, 1991.

Johnson, Luke Timothy. *The Letter of James: A New Translation with Introduction and Commentary*. Anchor Bible 37A. New York: Doubleday, 1995.

Joubert, Stephan. "*Homo Reciprocus* No More: The 'Missional' Nature of Faith in James." In *Sensitivity towards Outsiders: Exploring the Dynamic Relationship between Mission and Ethics in the New Testament and Early Christianity*, edited by Jacobus Kok, Tobias Nicklas, Dieter T. Roth, and Christopher M. Hays, 382–400. Wissenschaftliche Untersuchungen zum Neuen Testament 2/364. Tübingen: Mohr Siebeck, 2014.

Kamell, Mariam. "James 1:27 and the Church's Call to Mission and Morals." *Crux* 46, no. 4 (2010): 15–23.

Laws, Sophie. *A Commentary on the Epistle of James*. Harper's New Testament Commentary. San Francisco: Harper & Row, 1980.

Martin, Ralph P. *James*. Word Biblical Commentary 48. Waco, TX: Word, 1988.

McKnight, Scot. *The Letter of James.* New International Commentary on the New Testament. Grand Rapids: Eerdmans, 2011.

Moo, Douglas. *The Letter of James.* Tyndale New Testament Commentaries 16. Grand Rapids: Eerdmans, 1985.

Schnabel, Eckhard J. *Early Christian Mission.* 2 vols. Downers Grove, IL: InterVarsity Press, 2004.

Senior, Donald, and Carroll Stuhmueller. *The Biblical Foundations for Mission.* Maryknoll, NY: Orbis Books, 1983.

Sider, Ron. "What If We Defined the Gospel the Way Jesus Did?" In *Holistic Mission: God's Plan for God's People*, edited by Brian Woolnough and Wonsuk Ma, 17–30. Regnum Edinburgh 2010 Series. Eugene, OR: Wipf & Stock, 2010.

Stowers, Stanley K. *Letter Writing in Greco-Roman Antiquity.* Library of Early Christianity 5. Philadelphia: Westminster, 1986.

Támez, Elsa. *The Scandalous Message of James: Faith without Works is Dead.* Rev. ed. New York: Crossroad, 2002.

Tennent, Timothy C. *Invitation to World Missions: A Trinitarian Missiology for the Twenty-First Century*. Invitation to Theological Studies Series. Grand Rapids: Kregel, 2010.

White, John L. *Light from Ancient Letters.* Foundation & Facets. Philadelphia: Fortress, 1986.

Wrongemann, Henning. *Intercultural Theology.* Translated by Karl E. Böhmer. 3 vols. Downers Grove: IVP Academic, 2016–2019.

About the Contributors

Benjamin E. Castaneda (PhD, University of St Andrews) is course organizer and lecturer in Greek and New Testament at Edinburgh Theological Seminary in Edinburgh, Scotland. Raised in the United States, he pastored for six years in the Presbyterian Church in America, taught biblical and theological studies in missionary contexts in Uganda and Serbia, and is now an ordained minister in the Free Church of Scotland.

Nelson R. Morales Fredes (PhD, Trinity International University) teaches New Testament studies and hermeneutics and is provost at Seminario Teológico Centroamericano, Guatemala. He was born in Chile but has lived in Guatemala since 1993. His major publications include *Poor and Rich in James: A Relevance Theory Approach to James's Use of the Old Testament* (Eisenbrauns, 2018) and "2 Corintios," in *Comentario Bíblico Contemporáneo* (Kairós, 2019). He also edited *Buenas Nuevas desde América Latina* (Puma, 2021) / *Good News from Latin America* (Langham, 2024).

John D. Harvey (ThD, University of Toronto) is director of the PhD and DMin programs of Columbia Biblical Seminary in Columbia, South Carolina, USA. He grew up in Pennsylvania and currently lives in South Carolina. He is an ordained teaching elder in the Presbyterian Church in America. Harvey is the author of several books including *A Commentary on Romans* (Kregel, 2019) and *Acts: A Commentary for Biblical Preaching and Teaching* (Kregel, 2023).

Christopher Howles (DIS, Fuller Theological Seminary) serves as director of cross-cultural training at Oak Hill College, London, where he teaches intercultural studies and world Christianity. Born and raised in the UK, he spent twelve years in East Africa as head of theology at Uganda Martyrs Seminary Namugongo (Kampala). He is founder of the online mission resourcing ministry "From Every Nation," and his doctoral research was on the topic of missiological education for Ugandan Anglican leaders.

Jessica Janvier (PhD, Columbia International University) is a writer and academic who focuses on the intersections of African American religious history, church history, and theology. She currently lectures at Meachum School of Haymanot, which focuses on contextualized theological education for Black communities around the nation. She is an associate pastor in the United Methodist Church and has worked as a transition leader for the Global Methodist Church.

Jeffrey S. Krohn (PhD, London School of Theology) is professor of biblical studies at Evangelical Theological College in Addis Ababa, Ethiopia. He and his family served for fourteen years in Peru and five years in Ethiopia before relocating to the United States. Krohn continues to travel to Ethiopia and other countries to teach intensive classes. Krohn is the author of *Mormon Hermeneutics* (Pickwick, 2022).

Grant LeMarquand (ThD, Wycliffe College, University of Toronto) is emeritus professor of biblical studies at Trinity Anglican Seminary (formerly Trinity School for Ministry) in Ambridge, Pennsylvania, USA. He was born and raised in Montreal, Canada, where he studied at McGill University and was ordained as an Anglican priest. He has also taught at St Paul's, Limuru, Kenya, and Wycliffe College, Toronto. From 2012–2018 he was the Anglican Bishop for the Horn of Africa living in Ethiopia. He is married to Wendy, a retired medical doctor. Grant and Wendy now live in Alberta, Canada. He is the author of numerous studies in biblical studies and in mission including *An Issue of Relevance: A Comparative Study of the Story of the Bleeding Woman (Mk 5: 25–34; Mt 9:20–22; Lk 8:43–48) in North Atlantic and African Contexts* (Peter Lang, 2004).

Sarah Lunsford (PhD, Columbia International University) lives with her four children in the Metro Atlanta area and is an instructor of global studies at Liberty University. She previously served as an international church planter in East Asia and has ministered short term in several countries across five continents. She is the author of *Missiological Triage: A Framework for Integrating Theology and Social Sciences in Missiological Methods* (Pickwick, 2023).

James E. Morrison (PhD, Columbia International University) has been involved in cross-cultural ministry for more than three decades, primarily in Bible translation. He is a lead translator and translation consultant in a cluster project in the Himalayas. He is also involved in the development of contextualized Scripture engagement resources, particularly in the digital medium.

Leita Ngoy (DTh, Ruhr University Bochum) is a theologian and missiologist from East Africa. She was born in Tanzania to Congolese parents, grew up in India, studied in Tanzania, and is currently living and working in Germany. She received her Bachelor of Divinity in theology and Master of Missiology from Tumaini University Makumira, Tanzania. Her research expertise focuses on the impact of the charismatization and prosperity gospel on mainline churches. After her doctoral studies, she worked as an education officer for Bread for the World at the OIKOS Institute for Mission and Ecumenism in Evangelische Kirche von Westfalen. She is the author of *Prosperity Gospel Redefined: The Impact of Charismatisation of the Mainline Churches in Tanzania* (Brill, 2024).

Joseph K. Pak (PhD, Dallas Theological Seminary) is professor of biblical studies at Taylor University in Upland, Indiana. He was born and raised in Seoul, Korea, and currently lives in Fishers, Indiana. He is an ordained Southern Baptist pastor and teaches New Testament, theology, and hermeneutics. He is the author of *What the Bible Says about the Dangers of Self-Deception: An Exegetical Approach* (Wipf & Stock, 2025).

James A. Roh (PhD, Midwestern Baptist Theological Seminary) is the director of the leadership institute at McLean Bible Church in Vienna, Virginia, where he is an ordained pastor. His parents immigrated from South Korea, and he was born in New Haven, Connecticut. He earned his BA in economics and sociology at the University of Michigan, MDiv at Trinity Evangelical Divinity School, and ThM in New Testament from Southeastern Baptist Theological Seminary.

Thomas W. Seckler (PhD, Trinity International University) is an assistant professor (adjunct) at Liberty University Rawlings School of Divinity in Lynchburg, Virginia, USA. He is an adjunct professor at Trinity International University. Seckler is a research consultant for the organization New Generations. He was born and raised near Peoria, Illinois. He and his wife served as missionaries with World Team for twenty-three years in Southeast Asia. He is an ordained minister with the Christian Church and editor of *Witness: The Journal of the Academy for Evangelism in Theological Education*. He is the author of *Experiencing the Gospel: An Examination of Muslim Conversion to Christianity in Cambodia* (Pickwick, 2020).

Vuyani Stanley Sindo (PhD, Stellenbosch University) is the vice-principal development and head of biblical studies at George Whitefield College. He is also a research fellow at Stellenbosch University. He is a Pauline scholar and a co-chair of the Pauline Subgroup for the New Testament Society of Southern Africa (NTSSA). He is also an editorial board member for *Neotestamentica* and *Conspectus*. He is the author of *Paul as a Prototype and Entrepreneur of Christian Identity: An Investigation into Leadership and Identity in 1 Corinthians 1–4* (Langham Academic, 2024).

Edward L. Smither (PhD, University of Wales; PhD, University of Pretoria) is dean of the School of Missions and Intercultural Ministry and professor of intercultural studies and history of global Christianity at Columbia International University. Previously, he served for fourteen years in intercultural ministry in North Africa, France, and the USA. His recent works include *Mission as Hospitality: Imitating the Hospitable God in Mission* and *Christian Mission: A Concise Global History*.

Jessica A. Udall (PhD, Columbia International University) is a professor at Evangelical Theological College in Addis Ababa, Ethiopia, an adjunct professor for CIU Global, and a member of SIL Ethiopia/International. She has served in cross-cultural ministry in Ethiopia and among immigrants in the United States. She is the author of *Building Community through Hospitality: Insights from Ethiopia for America's Loneliness Epidemic* (Pickwick, 2024) and co-editor of several books on mission.

Abeneazer G. Urga (PhD, Columbia International University) lectures in biblical studies at Evangelical Theological College in Addis Ababa, Ethiopia, and he is an adjunct professor at Columbia International University and Ethiopian Graduate School of Theology. He is a member of Equip International and SIL Ethiopia/International. He has authored several books and articles. His most recent book is *Intercession of Jesus in Hebrews* (Mohr Siebeck, 2023). He is also the co-editor of and contributor to *Reading Hebrews and 1 Peter from Majority World Perspectives* (T&T Clark, 2024).

Cindy M. Wu (MA, Gordon-Conwell Theological Seminary) is co-director of Mosaic Formation, a spiritual formation ministry that trains leaders serving marginalized and underserved communities. She founded and directs Ride with Refugees, a cycling program raising awareness about resettlement and empowering refugees through mobility. An ordained minister, Cindy is the author of *A Better Country: Embracing the Refugees in our Midst*, 2nd ed. (William Carey Publishing, 2022) and a coauthor (with Todd M. Johnson) of *Our Global Families: Christians Embracing Common Identity in a Changing World* (Baker Academic, 2015).

Jeanne Wu (PhD, Trinity Evangelical Divinity School) currently serves as theological catalyst for the Middle East with Pioneers. She also serves on the board of Gospel Operation International. She was born and raised in Taiwan. Jeanne received her BS and MS at National Central University, Taiwan, and an MA at Western Seminary in Oregon. She has many years of experience serving in the Middle East and in the Chinese diaspora church, and she is active in researching, consulting, writing, and teaching in both English and Chinese. Her publications include *Mission through Diaspora: The Case of the Chinese Church in the USA* (Langham, 2016).

Allen Yeh (DPhil, University of Oxford) is dean and vice president of academic affairs at International Theological Seminary located near Los Angeles. He was formerly professor of intercultural studies and missiology for sixteen years at Biola University. His areas of geographical expertise are Latin America and China, and he is also interested in generational dynamics, particularly ministry to Gen Z. He has been to more than sixty countries on every continent to study, speak at conferences, do missions work, and experience the culture. He is also the author of *Polycentric Missiology: Twenty-First Century Mission from Everyone to Everywhere* (IVP Academic, 2016) and co-editor (with Tite Tiénou) of *Majority World Theologies: Theologizing from Africa, Asia, Latin America, and the Ends of the Earth* (William Carey Publishing, 2018).

Scripture Index

Beyond Poverty
Multiplying Christ-Centered Community Development

Terry Dalrymple

The church is facing a strategic opportunity—85 percent of people living in extreme poverty around the world reside in villages. These villages are also home to the majority of the world's least reached people. Terry Dalrymple calls us to move beyond sustainable projects in a single village to transformational movements that multiply change from village to village. Through multiple case studies based on the actual experiences of more than 900 organizations in 135 different countries, this book tells the story of a large and growing network of ministries around the world using the strategy of Community Health Evangelism to change the life of the poor forever.

Mission in the Way of Daniel
Empowering Believers to Live into God's Plan

Edward L. Smither

Daniel was not a priest or official religious leader—he was a forcibly displaced Israelite, who became a public administrator in the Babylonian and Persian empires. While he may serve as an example of an admirable work ethic—often finding favor and recognition with political leaders—he is also a prime example of a bold and godly individual. Though his boldness resulted in suffering, he consistently experienced and demonstrated God's power in his witness. This same boldness is needed today. Ed Smither illustrates why each of Daniel's qualities and skills is a necessary component of mission today.

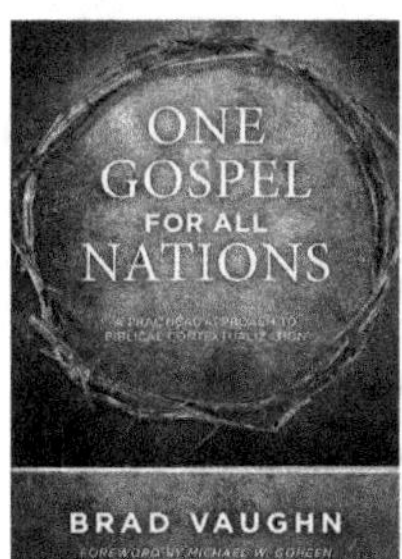

One Gospel for All Nations
A Practical Approach to Biblical Contextualization

Brad Vaughn

The Bible tells us what to believe—the gospel. But did you know it also shows *how* to contextualize the gospel? Brad Vaughn does more than talk about principles. He gets practical. When the biblical writers explain the gospel, they consistently use a pattern that is both firm and flexible. Vaughn builds on this insight to demonstrate a model of contextualization that starts with interpretation and can be applied in any culture. In the process, he explains practically why we must not choose between the Bible and culture. Vaughn highlights various implications for both missionaries and theologians. Contextualization should be practical, not pragmatic; theological, not theoretical.